AF184122

CYBER WARFARE

CYBER WARFARE

Military Cross-Border Computer Network Operations under International Law

Johann-Christoph WOLTAG

intersentia
Cambridge – Antwerp – Portland

Intersentia Publishing Ltd.
Sheraton House | Castle Park
Cambridge | CB3 0AX | United Kingdom
Tel.: +44 1223 370 170 | Email: mail@intersentia.co.uk

Distribution for the UK:
NBN International
Airport Business Centre, 10 Thornbury Road
Plymouth, PL6 7 PP
United Kingdom
Tel.: +44 1752 202 301 | Fax: +44 1752 202 331
Email: orders@nbninternational.com

Distribution for the USA and Canada:
International Specialized Book Services
920 NE 58th Ave. Suite 300
Portland, OR 97213
USA
Tel.: +1 800 944 6190 (toll free)
Email: info@isbs.com

Distribution for Austria:
Neuer Wissenschaftlicher Verlag
Argentinierstraße 42/6
1040 Wien
Austria
Tel.: +43 1 535 61 03 24
Email: office@nwv.at

Distribution for other countries:
Intersentia Publishing nv
Groenstraat 31
2640 Mortsel
Belgium
Tel.: +32 3 680 15 50
Email: mail@intersentia.be

Cyber Warfare. Military Cross-Border Computer Network Operations under International Law
Johann-Christoph Woltag

© 2014 Intersentia
Cambridge – Antwerp – Portland
www.intersentia.com | www.intersentia.co.uk

ISBN 978-1-83970-235-8
D/2014/7849/59
NUR 828

British Library Cataloguing in Publication Data. A catalogue record for this book is available from the British Library.

No part of this book may be reproduced in any form, by print, photoprint, microfilm or any other means, without written permission from the publisher.

To my parents

ACKNOWLEDGEMENTS

This book was largely written during my time as a research fellow at the Max Planck Institute for Comparative Public Law and International Law in Heidelberg and was accepted as a doctoral thesis at the University of Hamburg in 2013. I am especially grateful for the academic supervision of my doctoral supervisor Professor Dr. Dr. h.c. Rüdiger Wolfrum who gave me the necessary freedom in the writing of this book. I would also like to extend my appreciation to Professor Dr. Markus Kotzur, LL.M., who served as my second reader.

Ann-Christin Maak-Scherpe and Rebecca Pound of Intersentia deserve thanks for their guidance and support in the publication process and Professor Dr. Jan Wouters for agreeing to publish the study in the *International Law* series.

I would like to thank everyone at the Max Planck Institute for all of their support, especially my friends and colleagues who, in a variety of different ways, supported me during this time. Deserving of special mention are Dominik Zimmermann, LL.M., Florian Wenk, LL.M., Dr. Clemens Feinäugle, Sigrid Mehring, LL.M., Dr. Daniel Heilmann, LL.M., Dr. Marc Jacob, LL.M., Hans Christian Wilms, Dr. Stephan Schill, LL.M. and Daniela Arrese, LL.M.

I am particularly grateful for the invaluable support of John Henry Dingfelder Stone, LL.M. My personal thanks go to Dr. Isabel Röcker, who read the manuscript and strongly encouraged me throughout the entire writing process.

I dedicate this book to my parents, Dorothee and Helmut Woltag, who accompanied me through the sometimes strenuous undertaking of my doctoral studies in law.

Heidelberg, January 2014 Johann-Christoph Woltag

CONTENTS

ABBREVIATIONS

Banjul Charter	African Charter on Human and Peoples' Rights
ACHR	American Convention on Human Rights
Genocide Convention Case	*Application of the Convention on the Prevention and Punishment of the Crime of Genocide (Bosnia and Herzegovina v Serbia and Montenegro) (Judgment)*
UN Charter	Charter of the United Nations
CNA	Computer Network Attack
CNO	Computer Network Operation
Hague Regulations of 1907	Convention concerning the Laws and Customs of War on Land and its Annex: Regulations Respecting the Laws and Customs of War on Land
Hague Convention V	Convention respecting the Rights and Duties of Neutral Powers and Persons in Case of War on Land
CCDCOE	Cooperative Cyber Defence Centre of Excellence
COE	Council of Europe
ccTLD	Countrycode Top-Level Domain
CIP	Critical Infrastructures Protection
St. Petersburg Declaration	Declaration Renouncing the Use in Time of War of Explosive Projectiles under 400 Grammes Weight
DDoS	Distributed Denial of Service
DNS	Domain Name System
ECHR	European Convention on Human Rights
ECtHR	European Court of Human Rights
ENISA	European Network and Information Security Agency
fn.	Footnote
Geneva Convention III	Geneva Convention relative to the Treatment of Prisoners of War

Manual on Air and Missile Warfare	Humanitarian Policy and Conflict Research Manual on International Law Applicable to Air and Missile Warfare
ILC Articles on State Responsibility	ILC Articles on Responsibility of States for Internationally Wrongful Acts
ICT	Information and Communication Technologies
ICCPR	International Covenant on Civil and Political Rights
ICRC	International Committee of the Red Cross
ICTY	International Criminal Tribunal for the Former Yugoslavia
IEC	International Electrotechnical Commission
ISO	International Organization for Standardization
ITU	International Telecommunication Union
ICANN	Internet Corporation for Assigned Names and Numbers
IP	Internet Protocol
Israeli Wall Advisory Opinion	*Legal Consequences of the Construction of a Wall in the Occupied Palestinian Territory (Advisory Opinion)*
MPEPIL	Max Planck Encyclopedia of Public International Law
Joint Project Agreement	Memorandum of Understanding between the US Department of Commerce and ICANN
Nicaragua Case	*Military and Paramilitary Activities in and against Nicaragua (Nicaragua v United States of America) (Merits)*
NATO	North Atlantic Treaty Organization
Additional Protocol I	Protocol Additional to the Geneva Conventions of 12 August 1949, and relating to the Protection of Victims of International Armed Conflicts
Additional Protocol II	Protocol Additional to the Geneva Conventions of 12 August 1949, and relating to the Protection of Victims of Non-International Armed Conflicts
RIAA	Reports of International Arbitral Awards
RFC	Request for Comment
ICJ Statute	Statute of the International Court of Justice

SCADA Systems	Supervisory Control and Data Acquisition Systems
Tallinn Manual	Tallinn Manual on the International Law Applicable to Cyber Warfare
Outer Space Treaty	Treaty on Principles Governing the Activities of States in the Exploration and Use of Outer Space, Including the Moon and other Celestial Bodies
UN Convention on the Law of the Sea	United Nations Convention on the Law of the Sea
UNGA	United Nations General Assembly
UNSC	United Nations Security Council
Tehran Hostages Case	*United States Diplomatic and Consular Staff in Tehran (United States of America v Iran)*
UDHR	Universal Declaration of Human Rights
WSIS	World Summit on the Information Society

INTRODUCTION

'The mission of the United States Air Force is to fly, fight and win ... in air, space and *cyberspace*'
United States Air Force Mission Statement[1]

1. RESEARCH QUESTION

The last two decades have witnessed the spread of the Internet into manifold fields of daily life, both obvious and unnoticed. On the one hand the growing pervasiveness of networked information and communications technology has been a driving force of global economic growth and as a result Internet access is today seen as an enabling factor for human development. On the other hand the ability of any networked device to receive communications requests has introduced in many fields new vulnerabilities and possibilities for the exploitation of those vulnerabilities.

By adopting methods initially created by individual hackers, militaries now regard the Internet as a new domain of warfare and devices linked therewith as potential military objectives. The ability to also project military strength via the Internet has therefore become a goal for most militaries and led ever more States to establish special units within their armed forces tasked with defensive and offensive computer network operations.

From the outset it is clear that the relevant rules of international law applicable both during armed conflict and in peacetime could not anticipate the emergence of this novel form of operation. This holds true both for the Charter of the United Nations as well as for the most recent noteworthy codifications of humanitarian law – the 1977 Additional Protocols I and II to the Geneva Conventions of 1949. The main question of this study is therefore whether these frameworks also apply to military computer network operations and if so, whether they provide a sufficient basis to regulate and limit these operations in order to safeguard the rules' protective purposes. It might even be the case that there have already been rules on this established under customary international law.

Both the literature and governmental statements or media reports reflect a high level of uncertainty when confronted with a legal appraisal of the novelty of

---

1 Emphasis added by the author; The United States Air Force Mission Statement (as amended on 5 December 2005) is available at <www.af.mil/main/welcome.asp> (date accessed 4 June 2012).

computer network operations. Many share the view that the UN Charter is an outdated instrument unable to cope with this new type of military operation, claiming that these operations take place in a legal vacuum, and thereby calling for a complete ban thereof or at least the drafting of a specific cyber warfare convention.[2] But several States have also proposed the development of a framework or code of conduct for computer network operations.[3] Furthermore

---

2 Davis Brown 'A Proposal for an International Convention to Regulate the Use of Information Systems in Armed Conflict' (2006) 47(1) Harvard International Law Journal pp. 179–221; William Bayles 'The Ethics of Computer Network Attack' (2001) 31 Parameters – US Army War College Quarterly pp. 44 et seq; Scott Shackelford 'From Nuclear War to Net War: Analogizing Cyber Attacks in International Law' (2009) 27 Berkeley Journal of International Law p. 198; Olivier Minkwitz & Georg Schöfbänker 'Information Warfare: Die neue Herausforderung für die Rüstungskontrolle' (2000) 18(2) Sicherheit und Frieden pp. 155–56; Anthony D'Amato 'International Law, Cybernetics, and Cyberspace' in Michael N. Schmitt & Brian T. O'Donnell (eds) *Computer Network Attack and International Law* (Naval War College Newport 2002) p. 68; Abraham D. Sofaer & Seymour E. Goodman 'Proposal for an International Convention on Cyber Crime and Terrorism' (2000) at <http://iis-db.stanford.edu/pubs/11912/sofaergoodman.pdf> (date accessed 27 April 2011); Jason Beckett 'New War, Old Law: Can the Geneva Paradigm Comprehend Computers?' (2000) 13(1) Leiden Journal of International Law p. 51; Ahmad Kamal *The Law of Cyberspace: An Invitation to the Table of Negotiations* (UN Institute of Training and Research Geneva 2005) p. 80; Duncan B. Hollis 'Why States Need an International Law for Information Operations' (2007) 11 Lewis & Clark Law Review pp. 1023–61; Jason Barkham 'Information Warfare and International Law on the Use of Force' (2001) 34(1) New York University Journal of International Law & Politics pp. 112–13; Rex Hughes 'A Treaty for Cyberspace' (2010) 86(2) International Affairs pp. 523–41; Jon P. Jurich 'Cyberwar and Customary International Law: The Potential of a "Bottom-Up" Approach to an International Law of Information Operations' (2008) 9 Chicago Journal of International Law pp. 275–95; Dimitrios Delibasis *The Right to National Self-Defence in Information Warfare Operations* (Arena Books Bury St Edmunds 2007) pp. 325–54; Daniel B. Silver 'Computer Network Attack as a Use of Force under Article 2 (4) of the United Nations Charter' in Michael N. Schmitt & Brian T. O'Donnell (eds) *Computer Network Attack and International Law* (Naval War College Newport 2002) p. 94; World Federation of Scientists Permanent Monitoring Panel on Information Security 'Top Cyber Security Problems that Need Resolution' (2009) at <www.unibw.de/infosecur/documents/published_documents/cyber_security_problems> (date accessed 5 June 2012) p. 2. Arguing for an inclusion of 'acts of cyber aggression' under the definition of the crime of aggression of the Rome Statute by the Assembly of States Parties to the ICC: Jonathan Ophardt 'Cyber Warfare and the Crime of Aggression: The Need for Individual Accountability on Tomorrow's Battlefield' (2010) at <www.law.duke.edu/journals/dltr/articles/pdf/2010dltr003.pdf> (date accessed 20 April 2010) paras. 68–72.

3 As can be seen in the draft UNGA 'Developments in the Field of Information and Telecommunications in the Context of International Security: Russian Federation: Draft Resolution' Letter Dated 23 September 1998 from the Permanent Representative of the Russian Federation to the United Nations Addressed to the Secretary-General (UN Doc A/C.1/53/3 Appendix) considered as the first proposition of a ban of CNOs, but also more recently in Delegation of the Russian Federation 'Statement by Mr S Shestakov, Representative of the Russian Federation, at the Joint Meeting of the OSCE Forum for Security Co-operation and the OSCE Permanent Council' (10 June 2010) Doc FSC-PC.DEL/31/10. Furthermore see also, e.g., the statement of Brazil calling for the 'establishment of a code of conduct for the use of information weapons' in UNGA 'Developments in the Field of Information and Telecommunications in the Context of International Security' (8 July 2009) UN Doc A/65/129 at p. 4. Germany has advocated for the establishment of a code of conduct for State activities in cyberspace noting the necessity of the signature of as many States as possible:

commentators in the media time and again opine along the lines that there are 'few, if any, rules in cyberspace of the kind that govern behaviour, even warfare, in other domains'.[4] In any case the topic has gained attention at the highest levels of the international community, which is for example shown in a statement of UN Secretary-General Ban Ki-Moon, requesting that more attention be given to the issue of 'cyberwarfare' and its impact on international security.[5] Most recently, an international group of experts drafted a manual on cyber warfare at the invitation of the NATO Cooperative Cyber Defence Centre of Excellence.[6]

2. OBJECTIVES OF THE STUDY

The objective of this study is to pursue the question of whether general international law and international humanitarian law in their current form provide a sufficient framework applicable to cross-border computer network operations by States. In this regard it will be shown that neither the utilisation of the Internet, which is often described as borderless or taking place in 'cyberspace', nor the absence of a specific international instrument has led to the emergence of a legal vacuum as has been claimed repeatedly in both literature and media.

The study aims to identify those rules of international law that ensure the sovereign equality of States in regard to sovereign measures taken via the Internet. In order to bring to light whether sovereign computer network operations are imbedded within the system of peaceful settlement of international disputes it will be analysed to what degree the jurisdiction of States is also limited with respect to the Internet. In this regard it will be set out how general international law, as well as those rules pertaining to the ius ad bellum and stemming from the UN Charter, delimit the options legally available to States in their execution of cross-border computer network operations. By having recourse to an analysis of several actual case studies, the attributability of computer network operations to State actors will be scrutinised. In this regard the study establishes an obligation on States to prevent malicious computer network operations emanating from networks within their jurisdiction. Where these are conducted by private individuals, emphasis will be put on the question of whether a State is under an obligation to exercise due diligence in preventing their occurrence.

Bundesministerium des Inneren 'Cyber-Sicherheitsstrategie für Deutschland' (2011) at <www.bmi.bund.de/SharedDocs/Downloads/DE/Themen/OED_Verwaltung/Informations-gesellschaft/cyber.pdf?__blob=publicationFile> (date accessed 7 April 2011) p. 11.

4 *The Economist* of 3–9 July 2010 'Cyberwar' p. 9 is one example of many.

5 UN Secretary-General "Pay More Attention to Cyberwarfare, Verification, Secretary-General Advises in Remarks to Advisory Board on Disarmament Affairs' UN Doc SG/SM/12108' (18 February 2009) at <www.un.org/News/Press/docs//2009/sgsm12108.doc.htm> (date accessed 22 June 2011).

6 Michael N. Schmitt (ed) *Tallinn Manual on the International Law Applicable to Cyber Warfare* (CUP Cambridge 2013).

By depicting military computer network operations as a novel yet simply different means of warfare independent from whether they are qualified as a weapon, it will further be demonstrated how the rules of international humanitarian and neutrality law also regulate their use during international armed conflict in order to protect both civilians and neutral States.

3. RESEARCH SUBJECT

States may utilise computer network operations as a sovereign measure both during and outside of armed conflict. Execution of such operations regularly utilises the Internet, which enables communication between all devices linked thereto, ranging from individual mobile phones up to national infrastructure control systems. By accessing systems in third States these operations necessarily transgress multiple national borders. Yet while the mere access of publicly available information does not normally qualify as an internationally wrongful act, these communications can also be conducted with malicious intent aimed at disrupting or controlling the target system's functions. By taking control of a system that controls infrastructures, for instance, a computer network operation may thereby also have visible effects, ultimately causing physical damage noticeable outside of the system in the 'real' world.

The target of a computer network operation may however also stay within what is commonly referred to as cyberspace, for example when data is being altered that is solely stored in the target system's memory, while at first having no direct physical effect outside thereof. In this regard the terms cyberspace and Internet will be used synonymously throughout the work. Nevertheless the term cyberspace has a wider meaning than that of the Internet, as it utilises the latter to establish a notional environment of communication and rather denotes a social sphere, whereas the Internet refers to the network infrastructure and hence its physical foundation. Yet the terms are generally used synonymously in literature, official statements and the media, rendering futile a distinction that in any case would not make a difference to a legal appraisal.[7]

The study therefore examines both those cross-border computer network operations with the quality of a sovereign measure both below and above the threshold of armed force in the sense of Article 2(4) UN Charter, and the Internet as the global infrastructure on which the operations depend. Domestic computer network operations which are already being used inter alia as a tool of

---

[7] The notion of 'cyberspace' is derived from the works of science-fiction author William Gibson: *Burning Chrome* and *Neuromancer*, first published in 1982 and 1984 respectively. Therein, cyberspace is actually described as an alternative universe. The term was introduced into the Oxford English Dictionary in 1997 where it is defined as 'the space of virtual reality; the notional environment within which electronic communication (esp. via the Internet) occurs'. Etymologically it is derived from the Greek word 'kubernetes', that is steersman.

investigation by police forces are not addressed, however. These do not touch upon the rights of third States and are of interest for international law only from the perspective of human rights. The topic of cybercrime and cyberterrorism will likewise not be considered, unless when of relevance for inferring State responsibility.

4. STRUCTURE OF THE STUDY

Chapter 1 of the study will begin by delineating what is commonly referred to as cyberspace and highlighting its significance for modern societies (section 1). This will serve as a basis for understanding the characteristics of malicious computer network operations, a concise definition of which will be set out together with an overview of their technicalities and usefulness for military purposes in section 2. By having recourse to the most prominent case studies of recent years, section 3 will give an insight into the actual results of computer network operations thus far, as well as their further potential.

Chapter 2 will then look into the general legal regime of cyberspace, especially by setting out the jurisdiction of States therein (section 1), as well as presenting those actors that exercise authority on the Internet (section 2), before analysing a possible development of common cybersecurity standards (section 3).

Having set the stage for an understanding of both the technical and legal regimes of the Internet and computer networks operations, the following principal Part II will provide an assessment of the legality of sovereign computer network operations under international law in general. For this purpose, the traditional classification of military operations under international law will be followed. Firstly, those actions operating below the threshold of armed force in the sense of Article 2(4) UN Charter and taken outside the context of armed conflict will be analysed and reference shall especially be made to general principles of international law. This analysis is embedded within the framework of State responsibility, as the principles shaping and limiting sovereign conduct on the Internet may potentially lead to an operation being qualified as an internationally wrongful act (Chapter 3). Secondly, the justified use of military computer network operations will be scrutinised under the classical ius ad bellum paradigm including the right of self-defence against computer network operations and their utilisation as an enforcement measure of the UN Security Council (Chapter 4). Thirdly, those operations undertaken by one of the belligerent parties during the existence of an international armed conflict will be observed under the applicable framework of international humanitarian law, or ius in bello (Chapter 5). Lastly the applicability of the law of neutrality will be examined (Chapter 6), before coming to the final conclusion.

PART I

THE INTERNET AS A UNIVERSAL YET TERRITORIALISED INFRASTRUCTURE

CHAPTER 1

A SURVEY OF COMPUTER NETWORK OPERATIONS

1. THE MEDIUM OF COMPUTER NETWORK OPERATIONS: THE INTERNET

According to the premise that any application of law requires the knowledge of the circumstances of the case, a short introduction into the technical fundamentals both of the Internet and the methods of computer network operations is necessary as a first step in order to understand the legal challenges connected therewith.

As a second step the relevance of the Internet for post-industrial societies, the State and its armed forces will be identified in order to illustrate the possible objectives of military computer network operations.

1.1. THE INTERNET AS A NETWORK OF NETWORKS: TECHNICAL FUNDAMENTALS

While there exist numerous definitions of the term 'Internet', in the following reference shall be made to a definition stemming from the United States Code which describes it as:

> 'the myriad of computer and telecommunications facilities, including equipment and operating software, which comprise the interconnected world-wide network of networks that employ the Transmission Control Protocol/Internet Protocol, or any predecessor or successor protocols to such protocol, to communicate information of all kinds by wire or radio.'[1]

From this definition becomes apparent one of the fundamental characteristics of the Internet, namely that it is not a physically genuine data network, but an overarching concept of a loose network, the construction of which is based on decentralisation and interconnectedness of smaller networks and singular host

1 As in 15 United States Code §6555 and 21 United States Code §802.

and server computer systems. A unified network architecture with generally accepted protocols enables the individual systems to communicate with each other.[2] This communication is achieved by sending messages over the communication links, thereby using a standard network operating protocol suite – the most important protocols thereof being the Transmission Control Protocol and the Internet Protocol, or TCP/IP – which specifies the data formats and rules of transmission.[3]

The Internet is a so-called packet-switched network, meaning that data to be transmitted via the Internet will be split into several packets – inter alia depending on the size of the data – which contain the actual data to be sent, the destination and source address and other information that supports its reliable transmission.[4] In this regard it differs from circuit-switched networks such as traditional voice telephony which requires a continuous physical link between the source and destination of a message.[5] The technical agreement entitled 'Internet Protocol' manages the transmission of the data that has been split up into packets by the Transmission Control Protocol. Each packet is provided with a so-called IP header that contains the Internet Protocol address of the sender and addressee. IP addresses can hence be compared to regular postal addresses. The packets are transmitted by routers, which connect the multitude of networks with each other that ultimately constitute the Internet, and forwarded to other routers until eventually reaching their destination. These routers determine which route the data packets will take, by considering the packet's destination, its size, the availability of free lines, and other factors. Consequently it is typically not the sender that decides which route the packets will take, but the rules enshrined in the Internet Protocol as applied by relevant routers. As the Internet Protocol also takes dynamic factors into account, such as the availability of free lines and routers, one cannot exactly predict the route the packets will be sent on. When using the Internet to transfer data between two computer systems, the data packets may thus take routes that from a geographical standpoint may seem ineffective, while from a technical standpoint being the most effective.[6]

---

2 Thomas Hoeren & Ulrich Sieber (eds) *Handbuch Multimedia-Recht: Rechtsfragen des elektronischen Geschäftsverkehrs* (Beck München 2008 (19. EL)) Teil 1 para. 42; Howard F. Lipson *Tracking and Tracing Cyber-Attacks: Technical Challenges and Global Policy Issues* (Carnegie Mellon University, Software Engineering Institute Pittsburgh 2002) p. 7; Olivier Pierrot 'Computerviren' in Stefan Ernst (ed) *Hacker, Cracker & Computerviren* (Otto Schmidt Köln 2004) pp. 31–32.

3 Lipson *Tracking and Tracing Cyber-Attacks: Technical Challenges and Global Policy Issues* p. 7.

4 Lipson *Tracking and Tracing Cyber-Attacks: Technical Challenges and Global Policy Issues* p. 7.

5 David Lindsay *International Domain Name Law: ICANN and the UDRP* (Hart Oxford 2007) p. 1.

6 A data packet might for example be transmitted from New York to London via Tokyo and not directly through one of the many transatlantic glass fibrecables. Another packet belonging to the same data set might still be routed through the Atlantic. As the whole transmission process lasts only for milliseconds, the communication partners will (at least for those services not requiring a short latency) not notice the difference.

At least in regard to its underlying technical structure, the Internet may be compared to the traditional postal system, which likewise utilises a message switching system. Any regular piece of post features a recipient and a sender address, enabling it to be sent through the postal network, stopping at several collection points, until reaching the addressee. At each collection point the envelope is examined and sorted manually or automatically, in order to guarantee the most efficient route. The same holds true for data packets sent digitally via the Internet with the major advantage of the transmission being close to instantaneous and able to reroute data around non-functioning parts of the network. These packets not only comprise text messages such as emails but actually any activity that is done 'online', as any form of data exchange via the Internet involves the sending and receiving of data packets. These are then forwarded according to a first come first serve policy, according to which the content of the relevant packet is irrelevant. The networks therefore do not normally distinguish as to the content of the transmitted data, for example whether it comprises an email, a financial transaction or a live video conference.[7]

Similar holds true for the geographical origin and destination of data packets, which are often automatically routed across multiple jurisdictional, administrative and national boundaries. Unlike with telephone systems, these boundaries are not implemented in the protocols on which the Internet is based. It was rather designed to supply connectivity to all computer systems on all the networks that make up the Internet.[8] Therefore, a data packet can be routed from State A to B directly, or also via State C. The packet is also not treated in a different manner when crossing borders, nor does the user notice any of this routing potentially taking place on a worldwide scale.

Even in the nascent period of the Internet, the purpose of this architecture was to make sure it was as unaffected as possible by external influences such as physical attacks or accidents causing damage to its physical infrastructure. If one router fails, the data packet will simply be routed in a different direction to bypass it, causing simply a slowdown of the transmission – which in the most cases will not even be noticed by the user.[9]

While this makes the Internet comparatively immune to external physical interference, the same does not hold true for internal computerised threats. The

---

7 This traditional principle of network neutrality is currently subject of discussions, mainly due to economic interests of the network operators and Internet service providers as shown by Bernd Holznagel 'Netzneutralität als Aufgabe der Vielfaltssicherung' (2010) Kommunikation und Recht pp. 95–100 and see also p. 262 below.

8 Avri Doria & Wolfgang Kleinwächter *Internet Governance Forum (IGF): The First Two Years* at <www.intgovforum.org/cms/hydera/IGFBook_the_first_two_years.pdf> (date accessed 29 April 2012) p. 55.

9 Lipson *Tracking and Tracing Cyber-Attacks: Technical Challenges and Global Policy Issues* p. 13.

architecture did not take into account malicious non-physical behaviour of users within the network via computer network attacks, as the engineers did not bear in mind the general public as potential users of the network, but only anticipated a limited number of individuals from a trustworthy research community.[10] Personal computers and their operating systems are mostly designed in a way that allow users to run any program designed by themselves, the manufacturer, or any other third party, and to make the creation of such software an easy task.[11] The architectural principles of the Internet were designed in a similar way, hence to be open to any computer system that is properly interfaced and configured – a very marginal obstacle – and have essentially remained that way until now.[12] As the Internet was originally a military project[13] and later a scientific yet closed undertaking not intended for public use, it was never designed to track and trace user behaviour and billing was also not considered at first, as the use was free under the initial Advanced Research Projects Agency Network.[14] While this comparatively wide openness of the Internet was at first mainly seen as an advantage, it is increasingly subject to criticism, the more single computer systems and the Internet as a whole are relied upon by applications deemed vital to everyday life.[15] Therefore, some argue that the Internet relies on 'technology designed for a more innocent time',[16] namely a time where an experimental spirit fostered a huge amount of generative growth

---

10 Lipson *Tracking and Tracing Cyber-Attacks: Technical Challenges and Global Policy Issues* p. 14.

11 Jonathan Zittrain 'The Generative Internet' (2006) 119 Harvard Law Review p. 1980.

12 Zittrain 'The Generative Internet' p. 1976; see also Brian Carpenter 'Architectural Principles of the Internet' (June 1996) Request for Comments 1958; The Request for Comments (RFCs) are memoranda published by the (today named) Internet Engineering Task Force to give notice of and open the discourse on, inter alia, new Internet standards. While some RFCs are only for information to the Internet community, in general these comments have had a high impact on the technical functioning of the Internet.

13 The Internet ultimately has a military origin in that it is based on the Advanced Research Projects Agency Network, a project from the 1960s and 1970s developed by the Defense Research Projects Agency of the United States Department of Defense. Its initial goal resulted from the background of the Cold War, namely to create a communications system which could ensure the maintenance of command and control within the armed forces even after a nuclear attack: see Janet Abbate *Inventing the Internet* (MIT Press Cambridge 2000) p. 9 who also provides for an overview of the different research institutions involved in the project (at p. 60). On this see also Jon Bing 'Building Cyberspace: A Brief History of Internet' in Lee A. Bygrave & Jon Bing (eds) *Internet Governance: Infrastructure and Institutions* (OUP Oxford 2009) pp. 8–47.

14 Lipson *Tracking and Tracing Cyber-Attacks: Technical Challenges and Global Policy Issues* p. 13.

15 Zittrain 'The Generative Internet' p. 2040. He therefore fears that if fidelity to the end-to-end network neutrality persists, computer systems and networks may undergo a transformation into what he refers to as gated communities or prisons, thus creating an environment that betrays the very principles of neutrality (at p. 1978).

16 Lipson *Tracking and Tracing Cyber-Attacks: Technical Challenges and Global Policy Issues* p. 15.

driven by large, varied and uncoordinated audiences.[17] Most recently through the introduction of the world wide web service in between 1989 and 1991, which today is commonly used synonymously with the term Internet, the technology began to spread to a wider user group.[18]

1.2. THE SIGNIFICANCE OF THE INTERNET FOR MODERN SOCIETIES

1.2.1. The Information and Knowledge Society

It is a matter of common knowledge that the Internet plays a dominant role in everyday life of developed, but more and more developing countries too, despite the fact that Internet usage is still linked to the level of education and income.[19] Not only is the Internet used actively and voluntarily by individuals, but it also makes an appearance in automatic processes not noticeable to their users.

The manifold possibilities of Internet usage already gave rise in the 1990s to the use of the term 'cyberspace'.[20] But by including the word 'space', cyberspace connotes more than a mere technical infrastructure, namely a medium which is viewed by some to have constituted a social or public sphere of a new kind.[21] In social theory, the Internet is therefore seen as a mixture of a technical network of computer systems and a social subsystem of networked communicative and

---

17 Zittrain 'The Generative Internet' pp. 1980 and 2040.

18 The world wide web was developed at the European Organization for Nuclear Research by Tim Berners-Lee: Isabel Röcker 'European Organization for Nuclear Research (CERN)' in Rüdiger Wolfrum (ed) *MPEPIL* (OUP Oxford Update 2009) para. 19; Johann-Christoph Woltag 'Internet' in Rüdiger Wolfrum (ed) *MPEPIL* (OUP Oxford Update 2010) para. 2.

19 International Telecommunication Union *Measuring the Information Society 2011* at <www.itu.int/net/pressoffice/backgrounders/general/pdf/5.pdf> (date accessed 4 June 2012) pp. 107 et seq. See also the OECD *Information Technology Outlook 2010* (OECD Publishing 2010) which has to its goal the analysis of the growing impact of information technology 'on the economy and society, developments and emerging applications in selected areas of information technology and a review of IT policies and new policy directions' (at p. 3).

20 The US Department of Defense defines cyberspace as 'a global domain within the information environment consisting of the independent network of information technology infrastructures, including the Internet, telecommunications networks, computer systems, and embedded processors and controllers' US Department of Defense 'Joint Publication 1–02: DOD Dictionary of Military and Associated Terms (as amended through 31 October 2009)' (2009) at <www.dtic.mil/doctrine/new_pubs/jp1_02.pdf> (date accessed 8 March 2010) p. 139.

21 Franz Mayer 'Recht und Cyberspace' (1996) Neue Juristische Wochenschrift p. 1783, referring to Habermas' concept of a social sphere laid down in *Faktizität und Geltung* (Suhrkamp Frankfurt 1992) pp. 436 et seq; regarding the Internet as a new 'dynamic techno-social system': Christian Fuchs *Internet and Society: Social Theory in the Information Age* (Routledge New York 2008) pp. 121 et seq; similarly Lawrence Lessig *Code and Other Laws of Cyberspace* (Basic Books New York 1999) who argues that cyberspace is a 'place' where people can be simultaneously to 'real space' (at pp. 190 et seq).

cooperative actions, meaning it qualifies as a techno-social system.[22] These declarations all show the fact that the Internet has long since outgrown its origins as a point-to-point communications infrastructure. Since access and dispersal of information is mostly linked with the Internet as the predominant medium of telecommunication, the notions of network or wired society have additionally been introduced to more clearly emphasise the role of information and communications technology for the information and knowledge society.

The vast number of two billion Internet users, as of 2010, indicates the central role of the Internet for modern societies, meaning activities on the Internet reflect the full range of human motivations and conduct.[23] Internet use by private individuals has therefore become exceedingly varied, ranging from simple communications such as e-mail, chat or Twitter to real-time audio and video communications. More than a mere medium of communication, the Internet also makes access to official information and the press possible, and is used for educational and research purposes, gaming, entertainment, banking, shopping and other commercial transactions. Participatory services such as blogs and wikis allow for easy access to and spread of user-generated content. Especially in recent years, social networking has become a key driving factor for Internet use by children and adolescents, which has helped maintain communications making up the lion's share of private Internet use.[24] Recognising information and communications technology to be a factor enabling development, the International Telecommunication Union ('ITU') has introduced an information and communications technology development index measuring a country's progress in its transformation to an information society.[25] The percentage of persons with personal access to the Internet features as one of the prime indicators.

The high demand for Internet access has led to the flourishing of the information and communications technology sector. It is now no longer only computers and mobile phones that are connected to the Internet, but also entertainment systems and cars, while potentially any electronic device may be equipped with an Internet connection. Ultimately the equipping of all objects with unique identifiers such as radio-frequency identification tags could lead to the establishment of an 'Internet of things', with the prospect of further merging the real with the virtual world.[26] This is flanked by the proclamation of a

---

22 Fuchs *Internet and Society: Social Theory in the Information Age* p. 123.

23 The number of Internet users has doubled over the past five years rising to 29.7% of the world population as of 2010: International Telecommunication Union *Measuring the Information Society 2011* pp. 3–4.

24 International Telecommunication Union *Measuring the Information Society 2011* pp. 121–25 providing detailed country-by-country statistics.

25 International Telecommunication Union *Measuring the Information Society 2011* pp. 7 et seq.

26 On the legal aspects thereof see for example Rolf H. Weber & Romana Weber *Internet of Things: Legal Perspectives* (Springer Heidelberg 2010); the economic benefits and practical

'semantic web' or 'web 3.0', envisioning a new form of web content that is meaningful not only to humans, but also to computers, making these to agents capable of acting independently on the Internet.[27] While not all companies from the information and communication sector earn their revenue solely from direct online activity, this does hold true for a number of companies which are therefore referred to as Internet firms. The international top ten of the latter have earned over US $78 billion and employed more than 107,000 people in 2009.[28] The video games industry has also proved successful with its use of online services, which now generate 30% of the industry's revenue. Similar holds true for the advertising sector, the online revenues of which rose by 23% from 2007 to US $49 billion in 2008.[29]

However, traditional businesses such as the goods-producing sector also benefit from the Internet. This is the case especially for internationally operating companies which can build up via the Internet central databases accessible from any site or can remotely control distant facilities. Studies of broadband Internet usage by the business sector show the technology's positive impact on productivity and growth. In the European Union the adoption of broadband-based processes is estimated to improve labour productivity by 5% in the manufacturing and 10% in the service sector. Broadband-based innovations likewise help to develop new markets thereby driving general economic growth. The latter compensates the loss of jobs due to process optimisation, and has for example lead to a net creation of 105,000 jobs in 2006 in the European Union.[30] The cost-saving aspects of remotely controlled infrastructures such as those underlying gas, electricity, oil and water utilities have led companies to connect the respective industrial control systems to the Internet. Malicious computer network operations therefore especially pose a threat to these businesses and those dependent thereon. Several studies by the World Economic Forum have estimated a 10% probability of a major breakdown of critical information infrastructures in the next ten years. Due to their high level of interconnectedness such a breakdown has been estimated to have a potential global cost of roughly

descriptions are provided in Elgar Fleisch & Friedemann Mattern *Das Internet der Dinge: Ubiquitous Computing und RFID in der Praxis* (Springer Heidelberg 2005).

27 Tim Berners-Lee James Hendler and Ora Lassila 'The Semantic Web' Scientific American May 2001.

28 The Top 10 include such companies as Google, Amazon.com and eBay: OECD *Information Technology Outlook 2010* p. 62. The most revenues in the information and communication technology sector are however made by equipment, electronics and components, and telecommunications firms which make up to 84% thereof as of 2009 (at p. 34).

29 Both data are taken from the OECD *Information Technology Outlook 2010* p. 182.

30 All data taken from Martin Fornefeld, Gilles Delaunay & Dieter Elixmann 'The Impact of Broadband on Growth and Productivity (Study on behalf of the European Commission)' (2008) at <http://ec.europa.eu/information_society/eeurope/i2010/docs/benchmarking/broadband_impact_2008.pdf> (date accessed 22 February 2012) p. 6.

US $250 billion.[31] A 2004 study on the economic impact of 'cyber attacks' prepared for the US Congress shows that businesses targeted by a cyber attack suffered losses of 1–5% of their market value on the stock exchange in the subsequent days.[32] Unsolicited emails, so-called spam, are estimated to amount to about 90% of the worldwide email traffic causing high monetary damages to businesses.[33] The US President cited estimations that 'cyber criminals stole intellectual property from businesses worldwide worth up to [US] $1 trillion' in 2008.[34] While it is highly questionable whether these estimations can be considered accurate, it is clear that monetary damage from cyber attacks today pose a considerable threat to businesses.[35] Consequently insurance companies have already begun to sell special cyber-risk policies, as the effects from cyber attacks are normally excluded from regular insurance coverage.[36]

---

31 Both data taken from the World Economic Forum *Global Risks 2010: A Global Risk Network Report* (World Economic Forum Geneva 2010) p. 32; World Economic Forum *Global Risks 2008: A Global Risk Network Report* (World Economic Forum Geneva 2008) p. 48.

32 Brian Cashell, et al. 'The Economic Impact of Cyber-Attacks' in US Congressional Research Service (ed) *CRS Report for Congress* (2004) pp. 2–6. Some financial institutions even recorded losses of up to 15% following cyber attacks that gained access to confidential customer records (at p. 5). It must be kept in mind though, that such losses are market value losses only, hence shared by all shareholders. Thus, the attacked company does not automatically suffer out-of-pocket losses.

33 The estimates of costs to business caused by spam email vary significantly, e.g. up to the sum of US $100 billion annually as stated by ITU Secretary-General Hamadoun Touré 'Cyber Conflict and Cyber Defence in the Framework of the Global Cybersecurity Agenda' (17 December 2008) at <www.itu.int/osg/sg/speeches/2008/dec17.html> (date accessed 12 August 2010) p. 1.

34 US President Barack Obama 'Remarks by the President on Securing our Nation's Cyber Infrastructure' (2009) at <www.whitehouse.gov/the-press-office/remarks-president-securing-our-nations-cyber-infrastructure> (date accessed 11 March 2011).

35 There are several companies from the computer security sector that provide for similar numbers as to the level of damage caused by cybercrime. McAfee, a major antivirus software company, for example 'conservatively estimates that the global damage from data loss to top one trillion dollars' due to data theft and cybercrime: <www.mcafee.com/us/about/press/corporate/2009/20090129_063500_j.html> (date accessed 16 April 2009). It must be kept in mind however that a high number of cybercrimes is in the genuine interest of these companies. It is therefore questionable how reliable their data are. The problems of loss estimates due to cyber attacks is addressed by G. Stevenson Smith 'Recognizing and Preparing Loss Estimates from Cyber-Attacks' (2004) 12(6) Information Security Journal: A Global Perspective pp. 46 et seq, including an analysis of several standard financial techniques for determining loss valuations from cyber-attacks; Smith likewise warns that press reports estimating financial loss from cyber attacks are mostly inaccurate and should not be relied upon (at p. 56); similarly UNCTAD 'Information Economy Report 2005' UN Doc UNCTAD/SDTE/ECB/2005/1 pp. 229–30; ITU 'Understanding Cybercrime: A Guide for Developing Countries' (2009) at <www.itu.int/ITU-D/cyb/cybersecurity/docs/itu-understanding-cybercrime-guide.pdf> (date accessed 30 August 2011) pp. 60–62.

36 Cashell, et al. 'The Economic Impact of Cyber-Attacks' pp. 23–24. Providing for a damage model for such attacks: Thomas Dübendorfer, Arno Wagner & Bernhard Plattner 'An Economic Damage Model for Large-Scale Internet Attacks' *Proceedings of the 13th IEEE International Workshops on Enabling Technologies: Infrastructure for Collaborative Enterprises* (IEEE Computer Society Washington 2004) pp. 223–28; further on the

1.2.2. State and eGovernment

The Internet has likewise become an asset to States and their public administrations. Just like the business sector, States benefit from an improvement in the productivity of public services and a reduction of administrative costs through a more efficient intra-governmental and government-to-businesses exchange of information.[37] Furthermore so-called eGovernment services are increasingly introduced which will simplify, speed up and improve administrative services provided to citizens.[38] Several States have introduced provisions into their administrative procedural laws, giving electronic communication between government agency and individual via the Internet the same legal quality as the regular written form.[39] This trend will further grow if States adhere to their proclaimed goals inter alia stipulated in a 2009 Ministerial Declaration on eGovernment by EU and EFTA Member States.[40]

States therefore have a demonstrated interest in defending their networks against interferences, as for example shown by a statement of the US President announcing that the United States would 'defend its networks, whether the threat comes from terrorists, cybercriminals, or states and their proxies' and 'respond to hostile acts in cyberspace as we would to any other threat to our country'.[41] As the Internet has grown to play a major role in the provision of

insurability of Internet risks: Torsten Grzebiela 'Internet-Risiken: Versicherungsmöglichkeiten und Grenzen der Versicherbarkeit' in Stefan Ernst (ed) *Hacker, Cracker & Computerviren* (Otto Schmidt Köln 2004) paras. 1017–87.

37 Fornefeld, Delaunay & Elixmann 'The Impact of Broadband on Growth and Productivity (Study on behalf of the European Commission)' pp. 66–72.

38 See inter alia the OECD *E-Government for Better Government* (OECD Publishing 2005) study and the most recent OECD & ITU *M-Government: Mobile Technologies for Responsive Governments and Connected Societies* (OECD Publishing 2011) which elaborates on the benefits of mobile technologies for administrative services especially in areas where the infrastructure for wired Internet access is not readily available, as for example in remote areas and developing countries.

39 See for example Arts. 5(6) and 25(1) Estonian Administrative Procedure Act (passed 6 June 2001) which provide for electronic operations to be equal to written operations in administrative procedure and allowing administrative acts, summonses, notices and other documents to be delivered either by post or electronically (an English translation can be found at <www.legaltext.ee/text/en/X40071K4.htm> (date accessed 22 February 2012)). Comparable provisions can be found in §126(b) German Civil Code and §3(a) German Federal Administrative Procedures Act.

40 The 5th Ministerial eGovernment Conference 'Ministerial Declaration on eGovernment' (18 November 2009) at <www.egov2009.se/wp-content/uploads/Ministerial-Declaration-on-eGovernment.pdf> (date accessed 22 February 2012) has proclaimed the strengthening of eGovernment services of the public administrations by providing for more interaction and user-centric design.

41 The President of the United States of America 'International Strategy for Cyberspace' (May 2011) at <www.whitehouse.gov/sites/default/files/rss_viewer/internationalstrategy_cyberspace.pdf> (date accessed 1 June 2011) pp. 12 and 14.

public services, this defence readiness not only refers to government but all networks within a State's jurisdiction.

1.2.3. *The Military Sector*

Besides the omnipresent importance of the Internet for communications, militaries are becoming increasingly reliant on computerised and networked command-and-control systems. Intelligence, operations and weapons platforms are being increasingly linked together via computer networks in order to provide for swift, knowledgeable and efficient command and control systems. As commanders base their decisions on data provided by such systems the security of this domain is a crucial factor for militaries in their efforts to ensure high reliability of data.[42] In addition, logistical support, real-time provision of intelligence and remote operations rely on networked systems.[43] According to the US Department of Defense it operates over '15,000 networks and seven million computing devices across hundreds of installations in dozens of countries around the globe' and uses cyberspace for the 'command and control of the full spectrum of military operations'.[44] While these military networks may be autonomous to a certain degree, they are nevertheless linked to unclassified networks such as the regular Internet.[45] It has for example been estimated that 98% of US government communications – including intelligence and information reports or military orders – are routed via networks owned and operated by the private sector.[46]

The growing importance of information and network security to the military sector is likewise illustrated by the recent trend of traditional arms-producing firms to acquire security companies from the information technology sector.[47] This emerging market has additionally prompted the creation of companies that provide full-fledged solutions for military and government systems and networks

42 Gen. Keith Alexander (Commander US Cyber Command) 'US Cybersecurity Policy and the Role of US Cybercom' (2010) at <www.nsa.gov/public_info/_files/speeches_testimonies/100603_alexander_transcript.pdf> (date accessed 3 June 2010).

43 William J. Lynn 'Defending a New Domain: The Pentagon's Cyberstrategy' (2010) September/October Foreign Affairs p. 98.

44 US Department of Defense 'Department of Defense Strategy for Operating in Cyberspace' (July 2011) at <www.defense.gov/news/d20110714cyber.pdf> (date accessed 26 July 2011) p. 1.

45 Lynn 'Defending a New Domain: The Pentagon's Cyberstrategy' p. 100.

46 Citing the former US Director of National Intelligence: Eric Talbot Jensen 'Cyber Warfare and Precautions against the Effects of Attacks' (2010) 88 Texas Law Review at pp. 1534 and 1542.

47 Vincent Boulanin 'Major Arms Industry Acquisitions, 2010' in Stockholm International Peace Research Institute (ed) *SIPRI Yearbook 2011: Armaments, Disarmament and International Security* (OUP Oxford 2011) pp. 263–64.

including cyberspace intelligence services or even develop and implement nationwide cyber-security strategies.[48]

All this has led cyberspace to be characterised as a technological environment, or as the fifth domain or dimension of warfare, after land, sea, air and space, as referenced in the aforementioned modification of the US Air Force mission statement in 2005 to 'fly, fight and win ... in air, space and cyberspace'.[49] Consequently simulation environments for cyber warfare scenarios are being developed, while cyber defence exercises have already been organised.[50] The latter have even been endorsed by UN General Assembly Resolution 58/199 of 23 December 2004 which sets out the conduct of 'training and exercises to enhance response capabilities and to test continuity and contingency plans in the event of an information infrastructure attack, and encourage stakeholders to engage in similar activities' as an element of protecting critical information infrastructures.[51]

The objectives pursued by some militaries can for example be shown by means of a project of the US Department of the Air Force entitled Dominant Cyber Offensive Engagement and Supporting Technology for which scientific studies were solicited in 2008.[52] Its objective was to establish:

> 'high risk, high payoff capabilities for gaining access to any remotely located open or closed computer information systems; these systems enabling full control of a network for the purposes of information gathering and effects based operations.'

48 See for example the areas of business of AGT International, a public safety and security solutions company with 2,000 employees worldwide, at <www.agtinternational.com> (date accessed 25 February 2012).

49 UK Cabinet Office 'Cyber Security Strategy of the United Kingdom: Safety, Security and Resilience in Cyber Space (Command Papers 7642 [2009])' (June 2009) at <www.cabinetoffice.gov.uk/media/216620/css0906.pdf> (date accessed 10 August 2010) p. 12; *The Economist* of 3–9 July 2010 'Cyberwar' p. 9; Ulrich Ladurner & Khue Pham 'Iran im Krieg 2.0' in *Die Zeit* of 30 September 2010; Wolff Heintschel von Heinegg 'Automatisierung des Krieges' in *Süddeutsche Zeitung* of 10 February 2011 p. 13. The US Air Force mission statement is available at <www.af.mil/main/welcome.asp> (date accessed 25 February 2012).

50 See for example in the US, the CERT Exercise Network (XNET) programme: Carnegie Mellon University *CERT Research Annual Report* at <www.cert.org/research/2008research-report.pdf> (date accessed 17 March 2010) p. 84; and the Defense Advanced Research Projects Agency's 'National Cyber Range' which is currently under development. Further Kenneth Geers 'Live Fire Exercise: Preparing for Cyber War' (2010) 7(1) Journal of Homeland Security and Emergency Management pp. 1–14. On the early 1997 'Eligible Receiver' exercise of the US army, considered as a wake-up call as it demonstrated the lack of preparation in defending against CNOs, see Steven A. Hildreth 'Cyberwarfare' in US Congressional Research Service (ed) *CRS Report for Congress* (2001) p. 4.

51 UNGA Res 58/199 'Creation of a Global Culture of Cybersecurity and the Protection of Critical Information Infrastructures' (23 December 2004).

52 United States Air Force 'Dominant Cyber Offensive Engagement and Supporting Technology: Solicitation Number BAA-08-04-RIKA' (2008) at <https://www.fbo.gov/index?tab=core&s=opportunity&mode=form&id=b34f1f48d3ed2ce781f85d28f700a870> (date accessed 1 April 2010).

Of interest were thus:

> 'any and all techniques to enable user and/or root level access to both fixed (PC) or mobile computing platforms. Robust methodologies to enable access to any and all operating systems, patch levels, applications and hardware are of interest ... technology to provide the capability to maintain an active presence within the adversaries' information infrastructure completely undetected ... all techniques to enable stealth and persistence capabilities on an adversaries infrastructure... capability to stealthily exfiltrate information from any remotely-located open or closed computer information systems with the possibility to discover information with previously unknown existence.'

In short, the goal of this project is to establish the possibility of clandestinely gaining full remote access to and control of any type of computer system and infrastructure, thereby inter alia allowing the exfiltration of any information stored thereon. Ultimately this means taking over full control of the target computer system.

2. THE CHARACTERISTICS OF COMPUTER NETWORK OPERATIONS

2.1. DEFINING AND DIFFERENTIATING COMPUTER NETWORK OPERATIONS

The usage of terms relating to military computer network operations ('CNOs') is inconsistent both throughout the literature and official military documents. This is partly due to the lack of codification in this field and the immensely diverse possibilities the new technology provides. The lack of agreement on terminology has however complicated the discourse surrounding CNOs to a certain degree and is counterproductive to a rational analysis of the subject. It is thus beneficial to initially depart into the realm of semantics in order to define the different terms used in this work and to distinguish them from related concepts.[53]

From the outset a differentiation between military operations and warfare must be kept in mind. At least from an international law perspective the notion of warfare is only to be applied in situations of armed conflict. Military operations is an umbrella term of which warfare is only one aspect, albeit the most destructive. In contrast, there exist manifold military operations which happen outside of armed conflict and do not amount to armed force in the sense

53 A good overview can also be found in Falko Dittmar *Angriffe auf Computernetzwerke: Ius ad bellum und ius in bello* (Duncker & Humblot Berlin 2005) pp. 32–34.

of Article 2(4) UN Charter, or which happen during armed conflict but do not qualify as an attack in the sense of international humanitarian law.

In legal and sociological literature as well as in military doctrine, the 1990s marked the starting point of the development of the notion of 'cyber warfare'. At first, various conceptions of the use of computer systems both as a weapon and target delayed the development of a coherent definition and usable distinctions.[54] Likewise, variations in the definitions of key terms and a proliferation of those that were newly introduced led to an unnecessary complexity of concepts. Fuelled inter alia by apparently insufficient knowledge of the underlying technical foundations or a deliberate exaggeration of the threats of cyber warfare, this has led to several technically incorrect characterisations of CNOs. Statements such as the 'sending of a destructive stream of electrons into an enemy's computer system'[55] do not reflect the technical realities of CNOs.[56]

2.1.1. In Military Doctrine

The following will make reference mostly to United States military doctrine, for the sole reason of it being the most widely publicly available doctrine which explicitly makes reference to CNOs.[57] This does not mean that customary international law in this regard will only be shaped by US practice, especially as the relevant documents mostly do not include a legal appraisal.[58] Nevertheless they provide an important indicator, which can already be seen by the fact that the Manual on Air and Missile Warfare, which occasionally includes references to computer network attacks as a means of warfare, took

54 See the overview of different concepts blurring the differences between information and cyber warfare given by Fuchs *Internet and Society: Social Theory in the Information Age* pp. 256–57.

55 Jensen 'Cyber Warfare and Precautions against the Effects of Attacks' p. 1554.

56 It is not the electrons that are destructive in themselves but the execution of code on the target system, hence the performance of malicious CNOs. There is not a 'stream of electrons' that is comparable to a laser beam or bullets. CNOs cause damage via an intermediary, namely the target system, or on the target system itself, via the execution of code that is malicious to the system's designated functions.

57 As for example demonstrated by the US Air Force 'Cyberspace Operations: Air Force Doctrine Document 3-12' (15 July 2010) at <www.e-publishing.af.mil/shared/media/epubs/AFDD3-12.pdf> (date accessed 27 October 2010). CNOs are also referred to in the NATO 'Allied Joint Doctrine for Information Operations AJP-3.10' (November 2009) at <http://cyberwar.nl/d/AJP-3.10%20nov%202009.pdf> (date accessed 26 February 2012) and UK Ministry of Defence 'Information Operations: Joint Warfare Publication 3-80' (2002) at <http://ics-www.leeds.ac.uk/papers/pmt/exhibits/2270/jwp3_80.pdf> (date accessed 26 February 2012). The corresponding German document 'Teilkonzeption Informationsoperationen der Bundeswehr' is restricted.

58 While State practice establishing customary international law does not necessarily need to be universal, the practice of a singular State is in any case not sufficient as it must at least be of a general extensive practice; Tullio Treves 'Customary International Law' in Rüdiger Wolfrum (ed) *MPEPIL* (OUP Oxford Update 2006) paras. 35–40; Stephan Hobe *Einführung in das Völkerrecht* (Francke Tübingen 2008) p. 193.

over the definition from US military doctrine.[59] NATO itself, in a study on information operations documents of its Member States, acknowledged that many States used those of the US as blueprints, which ultimately also holds true for NATO documents.[60]

'Information operations' is the umbrella term for any operation that uses information as a means to achieve a particular goal. Under US military doctrine, information operations are defined as:

> '[t]he integrated employment of the core capabilities of electronic warfare, computer network operations, psychological operations, military deception and operations security, in concert with specified supporting and related capabilities, to influence, disrupt, corrupt or usurp adversarial human and automated decision making while protecting our own.'[61]

Thus, information operations under this definition also encompass activities such as influencing foreign audiences favourably to the originator's objectives, for example through media manipulation, but not necessarily via computer network operations. The latter, together with cyber operations as they are sometimes also called, are defined as:

> 'the employment of cyber capabilities where the primary purpose is to achieve objectives in or through cyberspace. Such operations include computer network attack, computer network defense, and related computer network exploitation enabling operations and activities to operate and defend the Global Information Grid.'[62]

---

59 Program on Humanitarian Policy and Conflict Research (ed) *Commentary on the HPCR Manual on International Law Applicable to Air and Missile Warfare* (HPCR Harvard University Cambridge 2010) p. 34.

60 NATO Research & Technology Organisation 'Overview of InfoOps Documents Doc. RTO-TR-SAS-057-WP1' (2006) at <http://ftp.rta.nato.int/public//PubFullText/RTO/TR/RTO-TR-SAS-057///TR-SAS-057-WP-1.pdf> (date accessed 19 November 2009) at WP 1–10; NATO 'NATO Glossary of Terms and Definitions of Military Significance for Use in NATO' (2011) at <http://nsa.nato.int/nsa/zPublic/ap/aap6/AAP-6.pdf> (date accessed 26 February 2012).

61 US Department of Defense 'Joint Publication 1–02: DOD Dictionary of Military and Associated Terms (as amended through 31 October 2009)'.

62 US Department of Defense 'Joint Publication 1–02: DOD Dictionary of Military and Associated Terms (as amended through 31 October 2009)' pp. 111 and 139. The Global Information Grid is understood as the information network reserved for US military use, namely the 'globally interconnected, end-to-end set of information capabilities, associated processes and personnel for collecting, processing, storing, disseminating, and managing information on demand to warfighters, policy makers, and support personnel. The Global Information Grid includes owned and leased communications and computing systems and services, software (including applications), data, security services, other associated services and National Security Systems' (at p. 227).

The umbrella term CNOs therefore encompasses both defensive and offensive, as well as espionage, measures which operate in or through cyberspace. Espionage measures, namely computer network exploitation, are defined as:

> 'enabling operations and intelligence collection capabilities conducted through the use of computer networks to gather data from target or adversary automated information systems or networks.'[63]

Most commonly mentioned in connection with the topic of cyber warfare are, however, computer network attacks, which even by their name indicate their offensive quality as:

> 'actions taken through the use of computer networks to disrupt, deny, degrade, or destroy information resident in computers and computer networks, or the computers and networks themselves.'[64]

CNOs in United States military doctrine are thus not used as a synonym for information operations but form a part thereof.

2.1.2. In Legal Scholarship

In the period prior to the issuing of the relevant military documents scholars were more or less dependent on developing their own concepts. In addition, there was a high level of uncertainty and imaginativeness at that time as to the potential of this new technology. Libicki's seminal paper from 1995 must therefore be read in the light of this background when determining seven distinct forms of what he qualifies as 'information warfare': command-and-control warfare, intelligence-based warfare, electronic warfare, psychological warfare, hacker warfare, economic information warfare and cyber warfare.[65] Cyber warfare itself is further split into information terrorism (aimed not at disrupting computer systems but rather exploiting them to attack individuals, for example by 'attacking' their personal data files), semantic attack (causing targeted systems to generate answers at variance with reality, but perceived to be operating correctly), simula-warfare and so-called Gibson-warfare.[66] At least the latter two notions both of which depict the idea of a computer-based simulation of combat warfare, namely the replacement of war through a computer-based

63 US Joint Chiefs of Staff 'Joint Publication 3-13: Information Operations (13 February 2006)' (2006) at <www.dtic.mil/doctrine/new_pubs/jp3_13.pdf> (date accessed 21 April 2010) Chapter II-5.

64 US Joint Chiefs of Staff 'Joint Publication 3-13: Information Operations (13 February 2006)' Chapter II-5.

65 Martin Libicki *What is Information Warfare?* (National Defense University Washington 1995).

66 Libicki *What is Information Warfare?* pp. 75–83.

war game have not come into effect, which will also remain unlikely in the future.

Frequently utilised are the terms 'information weapons', 'information attacks' and 'information warfare'.[67] This is problematic insofar as it blurs the distinction between information operations and CNOs. Others again have a more broad understanding of CNOs, for example by defining cyber warfare as 'the use of computers or network-based capabilities by a state, or a group or person whose actions can be attributed to a state, in order to launch an attack on another state'.[68] The benefit of this broad definition is justified by arguing that the target hereby need not be another 'computer, network or information'.[69] However, the benefit of expanding the number of actions potentially qualifying as cyber warfare is unclear. Remotely controlled unmanned aerial vehicles – commonly referred to as drones – would also be encompassed by this broad definition; strictly speaking, through the ubiquitous application of computer systems in the military field, most actions would qualify as cyber warfare, thus diluting rather than forming the term.

2.1.3. Approach of this Study

For the purpose of this study reference will firstly be made solely to computer network operations utilised by State actors, which shall be defined as: 'operations utilising networked devices in order to access or manipulate other such devices.'

From a legal perspective this is necessary as the term 'attack' under international law carries a certain legal connotation which should only be attributed in a second stage when legally evaluating the operation. On the one hand a CNO may be of a merely informatory and not even of cross-border nature. This can for example be the case when CNOs are not used by militaries but by public authorities such as the police or public administration. In this regard the denomination of sovereign measures as attacks is not always appropriate. On the other hand a CNO can target industrial control systems thereby potentially causing a level of destruction qualifying it as an armed attack in the sense of Article 51 UN Charter as will be shown below. Only then may reference be made to a computer network attack. Furthermore, there are cases

---

67 Brown 'A Proposal for an International Convention to Regulate the Use of Information Systems in Armed Conflict' pp. 179–221; Lawrence T. Greenberg, Seymour E. Goodman & Kevin J. Soo Hoo *Information Warfare and International Law* (CCRP Washington 1997); Delibasis *The Right to National Self-Defence in Information Warfare Operations*; Barkham 'Information Warfare and International Law on the Use of Force' pp. 57 et seq; Christopher C. Joyner & Catherine Lotrionte 'Information Warfare as International Coercion: Elements of a Legal Framework' (2001) 12(5) European Journal of International Law pp. 825 et seq.

68 Jenny Döge 'Cyber Warfare: Challenges for the Applicability of the Traditional Laws of War Regime' (2010) 48 Archiv des Völkerrechts p. 489.

69 Döge 'Cyber Warfare: Challenges for the Applicability of the Traditional Laws of War Regime' p. 489.

where an international armed conflict already exists and a particular CNO qualifies as an attack in the sense of humanitarian law.[70]

In this respect CNOs are seen as forming their own class of operations and not merely as being part of information operations. This is due to the fact that CNOs provide for a greater spectrum of possibilities than information operations. As the latter merely target the adversary's decision-making capabilities, computer network operations have the potential to cause physical damage not associated with the goal of gaining information superiority, but purely for the sake of destroying military objectives. This activity is however not encompassed under the concept of information operations.

This study is not concerned with propaganda. While the Internet constitutes an important medium for propaganda purposes, it generally does not cause the need to re-evaluate of the rules applicable thereto.[71] Propaganda is primarily a content-based means as it necessitates a certain perception by the target audience. While it could be imagined that malicious CNOs might be utilised for this purpose, for example by altering the content of government websites of the adversary, novel legal problems only arise in connection to the use of CNOs but not to the content of propaganda as such. Cybercrime and cyberterrorism will likewise not be analysed. While both utilise CNOs, these are undertaken independently from State actors. A different question is whether such actions may be attributed to a State, possibly resulting in the international responsibility of the latter.[72]

2.2. THE TECHNICALITIES OF COMPUTER NETWORK OPERATIONS

What actually constitutes a computer network operation or cyber attack is controversial both in jurisprudence and computer sciences. In both disciplines there are different approaches to a taxonomy which do not necessarily conform to each other; for example, the technicalities of an operation are not as relevant for jurisprudence, which instead focuses on the intended or actual results of that operation. Nevertheless the definition given by computer science, which qualifies

---

70 Computer network attacks as a special form of computer network operations are more closely dealt with in connection to humanitarian law in Chapter 5 below.

71 Propaganda for war is for example prohibited by Art. 20(1) ICCPR; on this see generally Michael G. Kearney 'Propaganda for War, Prohibition' in Rüdiger Wolfrum (ed) *MPEPIL* (OUP Oxford Update 2009) and Eric de Brabandere 'Propaganda' in Rüdiger Wolfrum (ed) *MPEPIL* (OUP Oxford Update 2010).

72 The problems pertaining to the attribution of CNOs by non-State actors are shown at pp. 87 et seq below. An analysis of cyberterrorism can be found in Council of Europe (ed) *Cyberterrorism – The Use of the Internet for Terrorist Purposes* (Council of Europe Publishing Strasbourg 2007); Yonah Alexander & Michael S. Swetnam (eds) *Cyber Terrorism and Information Warfare* (Oceana Dobbs Ferry 1999).

a 'network attack' as 'a set of malicious activities to disrupt, deny, degrade or destroy information and service resident in computer networks',[73] is very similar to those referred to above. Yet while in computer science the sending of 'annoying email directed at an individual'[74] is by some also conceived of as an attack, it is obvious that a legal analysis must depart from this understanding.

There is potentially a vast number of different types of CNOs, which ultimately are however all variants of several basic types of operations which will be presented in what follows, together with the technical challenges of identifying their source.

2.2.1. The Main Types of Malicious Computer Network Operations

2.2.1.1. Distributed Denial of Service Attacks

The most widely used form of malicious CNOs that allow the targeting of a particular computer system are so-called distributed denial of service ('DDoS') attacks. These are operations where as many communication requests as possible are sent to the targeted resource, thereby making it either so slow that it will effectively be rendered unavailable to regular communication requests by other computer systems or ultimately causing it to automatically shut down.[75] The goal of such an operation is to deny the use of the computer resource to legitimate users.[76] For example, the information transmission capacity of systems linking military sites with the headquarters can be diminished or disrupted, thus delaying the response time of command and control systems, which is advantageous as a preparatory or supportive measure to a conventional attack. As a singular computer system, for reasons of performance and bandwidth limitations, is not able to exhaust the performance of the target system, the DDoS operation is distributed to many different systems, leading to an exponentiation of its strength.[77] A further benefit of distribution is the blurring of the operation's actual source. While distribution can be reached by a coordinated operation of several persons, in practice this is done by clandestinely and remotely controlling numerous systems belonging to unknowing third

---

73 Ali A. Ghorbani, Wei Lu & Mahbod Tavallaee *Network Intrusion Detection and Prevention: Concepts and Techniques* (Springer New York 2010) p. 1.

74 Ghorbani, Lu & Tavallaee *Network Intrusion Detection and Prevention: Concepts and Techniques* p. 1.

75 Pierrot 'Computerviren' para. 128; Matthias Bossardt, Thomas Dübendorfer & Bernhard Plattner 'Enhanced Internet Security by a Distributed Traffic Control Service Based on Traffic Ownership' (2007) 30(3) Journal of Network and Computer Applications p. 843.

76 ICANN 'Plan for Enhancing Internet Security, Stability, and Resiliency' (16 May 2009) at <www.icann.org/en/topics/ssr/ssr-draft-plan-16may09-en.pdf> (date accessed 23 July 2010) p. 49.

77 On the evolution of DDoS attacks see also generally: Jose Nazario 'DDoS Attack Evolution' (2008)(7) Network Security pp. 7–10.

persons.[78] Although it is possible for network operators to defend against such operations, this becomes more and more complicated due to the many forms in which DDoS attacks occur today and ultimately leads to the disruption of service to regular users.[79]

The comparative simplicity and ready availability of software for initiating DDoS attacks has also made them a prime tool for individuals.[80] This may be done as part of a criminal activity such as extorting companies by threatening to use DDoS attacks against their servers. In several cases in recent years the websites of international corporations were targeted by DDoS attacks. In many of these cases, loosely or non-organised groups, the members of which are not publicly known, had called for such actions, sometimes even providing the relevant tools to do so. The justification of these actions by the perpetrators as 'online demonstrations' has led to the question of whether these actions could fall under the freedom of assembly. A German court in 2006 acquitted the defendant in a case concerning his initiation of a DDoS against the website of the German air carrier Lufthansa by repealing the judgment of a lower court.[81] Similar DDoS attacks were inflicted in 2010 on the websites of major credit card and other companies in a reaction to pressure put on the Wikileaks platform concerning the publication of US diplomatic cables.[82]

2.2.1.2. Trojan Horses, Computer Viruses and Worms

While DDoS attacks are rather simple operations with the sole objective of disrupting the target's functioning, there also exist more sophisticated CNOs which have as their goal gaining control of the target system. In a reference to Greek mythology surrounding the Trojan War, programs that are active on a computer system without the owner's knowledge and able to execute disruptive functions are colloquially referred to as Trojan horses. These programs mostly infiltrate the target system in a camouflaged manner, by appearing to be normal,

---

78 Pierrot 'Computerviren' paras. 131–134; Lipson *Tracking and Tracing Cyber-Attacks: Technical Challenges and Global Policy Issues* p. 15.

79 Nazario 'DDoS Attack Evolution' p. 7; Bossardt, Dübendorfer & Plattner 'Enhanced Internet Security by a Distributed Traffic Control Service Based on Traffic Ownership' p. 843; for prevention and response techniques available against DDoS attacks see Ghorbani, Lu & Tavallaee *Network Intrusion Detection and Prevention: Concepts and Techniques* pp. 13–16.

80 As will be shown in the case studies on Estonia and Georgia at pp. 42 et seq below.

81 Oberlandesgericht Frankfurt/Main 'Strafbarkeit einer "Online-Demo"' (22 May 2006), reprinted in (2006) Multimedia und Recht 547–53 with a comment by *Gercke*. The reasons for this were however not based on the freedom of assembly but on the lack of culpability for such an action under the German penal code. The relevant provision in the code has been amended later on in order to implement an EU Framework Decision, thereby making DDoS attacks a punishable criminal offence. This should be the case in all EU Member States that have implemented the decision.

82 Jan-Keno Janssen 'Ionenkanonen gegen Wikileaks-Gegner: DDoS-Attacken: Ziviler Ungehorsam oder Straftatbestand?' (2011)(1) C't Magazin für Computertechnik p. 50.

seemingly harmless programs, websites or updates. They may then be utilised to remotely control the infected system and access data stored thereon, which has made their use widespread.[83]

Computer viruses similarly infiltrate a target system clandestinely in order to perform predefined malicious actions on the host systems mostly without the user's knowledge. Computer worms as a sub-category thereof additionally replicate themselves from one system to another.[84] In contrast to Trojan horses, viruses and worms do not permit remote control of the target systems. Further, their dispersion on particular systems generally cannot be controlled once they are put into circulation. They do however allow for the targeting of particular software products, thereby only infecting those systems running the relevant software.[85]

While the examples above all feature the utilisation of software that has been especially programmed for the relevant malicious operation, many other types of CNOs exist which merely use known vulnerabilities of existing software products or pre-established backdoors therein.[86] Further measures such as probing or mapping, meaning the gathering of information or search for vulnerabilities of target systems, are done in preparation or support of further or future operations.[87]

As most operations are useful only for a limited number of goals, a sophisticated military CNO tends to use a variety of subsequent operations or software combining several techniques. Evidence for this is given by the case study of Stuxnet considered below. The analysis of the software programmed for this specific operation, which is often cited as the 'first military cyberattack', sets a clear example that standardised software or attack methods are not well suited to make CNOs a reliable method of military operations. In general only programmes tailored for the specific target system and desired outcome are conceived of as being able to achieve this goal.[88]

2.2.2. Tracing Computer Network Operations back to their Source

Of major importance both from a technical and legal standpoint is the attribution of an operation to a specific source. To begin with, exposing the origin may help the computer and network security personnel to decide which

83 Pierrot 'Hacker' paras. 64–68.

84 Pierrot 'Computerviren' paras. 81–141. In contrast to computer viruses which are attached to an infected host file, worms exist as independent entities: Ghorbani, Lu & Tavallaee *Network Intrusion Detection and Prevention: Concepts and Techniques* p. 16.

85 Pierrot 'Computerviren' paras. 100–103.

86 For various examples see Pierrot 'Hacker' paras. 51–77.

87 Ghorbani, Lu & Tavallaee *Network Intrusion Detection and Prevention: Concepts and Techniques* p. 4; Pierrot 'Hacker' paras. 55–61.

88 On Stuxnet see pp. 47–50 below.

defence measures to initialise. In any case, the source is needed if the decision is made to launch counter-operations against the source system. Ultimately, such attribution is required from a legal perspective in order to establish proof in a criminal case, or State responsibility for a particular operation.

In order to find the actor responsible for a CNO, one must at first locate the device from which the operation was launched. Theoretically, this is an easy task as every computer system connected to the Internet is assigned a unique address – the IP address – by the relevant Internet service provider. Finding out that IP address is fairly simple, as it is inherent in any data packet sent via the Internet. Although this assigned IP address may change under certain circumstances, depending on the type of service used, Internet service providers will be able to identify their contractual partner via the allocated IP address.[89] This is achieved by temporarily storing the respective IP address assignment to the contractual partner, whether for billing reasons or legal requirements.[90] By obliging the Internet service provider concerned to disclose the relevant data, governmental knowledge of an IP address may thus be achieved in order to enable authorities to at least reveal the identity of the subscriber under which the connection was established. In the simplest case, that person will be the perpetrator of the operation. However, even without cooperation of the respective Internet service providers, the geographical source of an operation can be identified via analysis of the IP address through the techniques of geolocation and zoning, at least to the country and possibly also city level.[91]

The task is more complicated, however, if the perpetrator decides to conceal his true identity.[92] There exist several techniques to render it nearly impossible to trace the origin of a data packet and thereby establish the operation's source. Firstly, it is possible to modify the source IP address of the data packets, so-called spoofing.[93] Secondly, one can use several intermediary hosts arranged in series – computer systems of third persons – as stepping stones in order to deceive the

89 Lipson *Tracking and Tracing Cyber-Attacks: Technical Challenges and Global Policy Issues* p. 19.

90 In the EU, Directive 2006/24/EC on the Retention of Data Generated or Processed in Connection with the Provision of Publicly Available Electronic Communications Services or of Public Communications Networks and amending Directive 2002/58/EC (15 March 2006) [2006] OJ L 105/54 (so-called Data Retention Directive) provides for a duty of communications providers to store certain communications data for a period of up to two years.

91 Thomas Hoeren 'Zoning und Geolocation – Technische Ansätze zur Reterritorialisierung des Internet' (2007) Multimedia und Recht pp. 5–6.

92 For an overview of several different attribution techniques see David Wheeler & Gregory Larsen 'Techniques for Cyber Attack Attribution' (2003) at <www.dtic.mil/cgi-bin/GetTRDoc?AD=ADA468859&Location=U2&doc=GetTRDoc.pdf> (date accessed 23 March 2010); Alexander Geschonneck *Computer-Forensik* (Dpunkt Heidelberg 2008) pp. 279–96; Sandro Gaycken *Cyberwar: Das Internet als Kriegsschauplatz* (Open Source Press München 2011) pp. 81–84.

93 Claudia Eckert *IT-Sicherheit: Konzepte – Verfahren – Protokolle* (Oldenbourg München 2009) pp. 106–08; Pierrot 'Hacker' paras. 76–77.

target into believing that the operation originates from the last stepping stone, so-called packet laundering.[94] In case of a spoofed source the still relatively basic tracing technique of hop-by-hop traceback can be utilised.[95] It is however only suitable for large and continuous packet flows that are still in progress when the traceback is initiated.[96] By using this method, the Internet service provider inspects the routers under its control until the origin system of the operation is found. This is possible if the source system is within the Internet service provider's network. Since there are numerous such providers worldwide, this will remain the exception. In practice the operation will originate from a computer system connected to a network that the Internet service provider of the target system has no control over. In this case the provider is merely able to identify in which other network the source system is located and notify the provider concerned. Only the latter provider has access to its routers and logfiles, essential to a successful traceback. Depending on the route of the packets, a successful traceback may therefore require the cooperation of many different providers. If all parties are willing and technically able to cooperate, the computer system from which the operation originated can be identified, making the linkage between system and contractual partner possible as the essential element of a legal attribution. In this case, spoofing of the original source address will not prevent a successful traceback.[97]

Alongside these technical difficulties, there are also legal obstacles in place once the operation is of a cross-border nature. As the traceback of an operation mainly relies on the cooperation of all involved Internet service providers, which in this case are subject to different jurisdictions, the relevant national laws will need to oblige or at least not forbid the Internet service providers to disclose the data of their logfiles and ultimately the identity of the subscriber the connection of which was utilised by the source system. But even if there were respective international agreements in place for this form of cooperation, it is unrealistic for these to also envisage the disclosure of CNOs undertaken by public authorities. These problems have led many to conclude that the location of origin of a CNO is a systemic impossibility making a legal attribution likewise unestablishable.[98]

---

94 Lipson *Tracking and Tracing Cyber-Attacks: Technical Challenges and Global Policy Issues* p. 14.

95 As outlined by Lipson *Tracking and Tracing Cyber-Attacks: Technical Challenges and Global Policy Issues* pp. 29–30. Each transmission from one router to another is referred to as a 'hop'.

96 Lipson *Tracking and Tracing Cyber-Attacks: Technical Challenges and Global Policy Issues* p. 29.

97 Lipson *Tracking and Tracing Cyber-Attacks: Technical Challenges and Global Policy Issues* p. 29.

98 Sandro Gaycken 'The Necessity of (Some) Certainty – A Critical Remark concerning Matthew Sklerov's Concept of "Active Defense"' (2010) 12(2) Journal of Military and Strategic Studies pp. 1–6; Sandro Gaycken & Michael Karger 'Entnetzung statt Vernetzung: Paradigmenwechsel in der IT-Sicherheit' (2011) 14 Multimedia und Recht p. 4; and see

2.3. TARGET SCENARIOS OF COMPUTER NETWORK OPERATIONS

2.3.1. *Military Targets*

A major difference between computer network operations and means of regular warfare is simultaneously also their greatest advantage: there is no real frontline needed to be reached in order to attack the adversary as geographic distance does not play a major role to CNOs. While intercontinental ballistic missiles offer similar advantages, CNOs have the potential to reach the desired outcome within milliseconds. While information and telecommunications technology has been used in the planning and support of military operations since the technologies advent, today the very same technology may both be seen as a military target and a weapon alike. Seemingly endless different strategic scenarios have already been mapped out for the military use of computer network operations.[99] As the technical aspects of this new method of warfare are still rather new and constantly in flux – dependent both on general technological development and that of the adversary – the future will provide even more possibilities. Therefore it is not possible to draw up a concluding list of all available options. Some of them shall be highlighted here in order to make the military benefits of the new instrument more concrete.

Command and control of military operations is today to a large extent achieved with the help of networked computer systems. The interception of commands to military units transmitted via the Internet or an adversary's network is therefore already possible and offers a clear military advantage. Data intercepted in this way could first provide the belligerent with valuable information regarding troop movements, position, strength and targets. A similar thing was already achieved during World War II, albeit on a different scale, when the Allies successfully managed to decode German communications

generally Duncan B. Hollis 'An e-SOS for Cyberspace' (2011) 52 Harvard International Law Journal pp. 397 et seq.

99 For examples see in general: Sandro Gaycken 'Die Zukunft des Krieges – Strategische Konzepte und strukturelle Probleme des Cyberwarfare' (2009) at <http://events.ccc.de/sigint/2009/Fahrplan/attachments/1285_Die%20Zukunft%20des%20Krieges.pdf> (date accessed 2 March 2012); Wolff Heintschel von Heinegg 'Informationskrieg und Völkerrecht' in Volker Epping & Knut Ipsen (eds) *Brücken bauen und begehen: Festschrift für Knut Ipsen zum 65. Geburtstag* (Beck München 2000) pp. 136–37; Michael N. Schmitt 'Computer Network Attack and the Use of Force in International Law: Thoughts on a Normative Framework' (1999) 37(3) Columbia Journal of Transnational Law pp. 892–93; Henning Wegener 'Der unsichtbare Feind: Die neuen Gefahrenlagen im digitalen Raum' (2009) 09–10 Internationale Politik pp. 50–55; Christian Stelter *Gewaltanwendung unter und neben der UN-Charta* (Duncker & Humblot Berlin 2007) pp. 30–32; Dittmar *Angriffe auf Computernetzwerke: Ius ad bellum und ius in bello* pp. 40–42 and 103–09.

that were encoded using the so-called Enigma machines.[100] Next the intercepted data could be altered during transmission for example in order to manipulate target positions, for example causing enemy units to engage accidentally in friendly fire.[101]

Another possibility that has emerged from the computerisation of military command and control is to not only interception, but already penetration and manipulation of data stored in an adversary's computer system. Military decision-makers rely heavily on data which is today nearly wholly provided in electronic form. Thus, the modification of data providing the basis for strategic and tactical decisions may corrupt the process of decision-making as a whole, providing for extensive military advantages. Modifying targeting databases – those that store coordinates of important military targets of the adversary – would be of great military advantage, as the information stored therein could be altered in such a way as to cause the adversary to fire on futile targets, friendly targets or even – albeit illegally – civilian targets.[102]

These threats which malicious CNOs pose to an adversary and the vulnerabilities that facilitate them are common knowledge and openly recognised by militaries. The US Department of Defense for instance, in its Strategy for Operating in Cyberspace, acknowledged both the intention of foreign nations and non-State actors to exploit the department's networks, as well as its vulnerabilities and the lack of knowledge whether undetected malicious activities on its networks are already under way.[103] In addition, in preparation for the operations against Libya in March 2011, the United States reportedly debated utilising CNOs against Libyan air-defence systems but ultimately abstained from doing so for fear of setting an unwanted precedent.[104]

While the physical destruction of information infrastructure, computer systems and data storage units will always remain a military option, utilising a CNO might prove the better alternative. In contrast to tangible military objects,

---

100 Johann-Christoph Woltag 'Coded Communications (Encryption)' in Rüdiger Wolfrum (ed) *MPEPIL* (OUP Oxford Update 2009) para. 2.

101 This describes a variation of the in computer sciences so-called 'man in the middle attack' commonly utilized in connection with online-banking fraud; see Pierrot 'Hacker' paras. 71–73.

102 Katharina Ziolkowski 'Computernetzwerkoperationen und die Zusatzprotokolle zu den Genfer Abkommen – Zum "virtuellen Raum" des Internet und dem Schutzstandard der vor 30 Jahren in Kraft getretenen Protokolle' (2008) 21 Humanitäres Völkerrecht p. 203; William Church 'Information Warfare' (2000) 82 International Review of the Red Cross pp. 205 et seq. The latter option would obviously be contrary to international humanitarian law, but favored by some in order to sway public opinion and the international community against the adversary.

103 US Department of Defense 'Department of Defense Strategy for Operating in Cyberspace' p. 1. The usage of more and more commercial-off-the-shelf products for the hard- and software of militaries for example transfers the well-known security vulnerabilities into their networks and applications.

104 Eric Schmitt & Thom Shanker 'U.S. Debated Cyberwarfare in Attack Plan on Libya' in *The New York Times* of 17 October 2011.

data can easily be recovered through the usage of system redundancies and other security measures making it not as easily destructible by kinetic attacks. Utilising CNOs on the other hand provides the possibility to corrupt said data without the adversary's knowledge so that they may not even be aware of the necessity of counter-measures.

Whether CNOs tend to be especially used in cases of so-called asymmetric warfare is disputed. Some see CNOs as particularly attractive for small militaries or terrorists,[105] while others only consider advanced militaries to have the possibility to conduct sophisticated CNOs.[106] From a legal standpoint this is not of particular concern, however. While asymmetric warfare is currently of a high practical importance, it is not a new legal concept providing a specific framework.[107] The discussion of to what degree CNOs will be used by poorer States or terrorist groups is thus of no special legal significance.

2.3.2. *The Public Infrastructure as a Target*

Regardless of the question of legality of attacks on civilian objects – a topic to be considered further below – CNOs have already targeted systems belonging to the civilian infrastructure and will surely continue to do so in the future.[108] This especially holds true in those cases where the public infrastructure is a dual-use target vital not only for the population but also for the government and the armed forces. This is the case especially for those infrastructures labelled as critical, which for example the EU in Directive 2008/114/EC has defined as:

> 'an asset, system or part thereof located in Member States which is essential for the maintenance of vital societal functions, health, safety, security, economic or social

105 Arguing in this sense with further references: Dittmar *Angriffe auf Computernetzwerke: Ius ad bellum und ius in bello* pp. 47–49; Döge 'Cyber Warfare: Challenges for the Applicability of the Traditional Laws of War Regime' pp. 487 and 500; Lynn 'Defending a New Domain: The Pentagon's Cyberstrategy' pp. 98–99; Hughes 'A Treaty for Cyberspace' p. 541.

106 Gaycken 'Die Zukunft des Krieges – Strategische Konzepte und strukturelle Probleme des Cyberwarfare' who regards the resources and thus the high costs of truly effective CNOs as too high for terrorist organisations (at p. 12). This is correct insofar as the comparatively cheaply available botnets (a botnet comprised of 21,000 computer systems was allegedly available for a few thousand dollars: Aviram Jenik 'Cyberwar in Estonia and the Middle East' (2009) 4 Network Security p. 5) can only be utilised for DDoS attacks which are not sufficient for complex military goals.

107 Asymmetric warfare, by no means a legal term of art, can be defined as 'armed hostilities in which one actor/party endeavours to compensate its military, economic or other deficiencies by resorting to the use of methods or means of warfare that is not in accordance with the law of armed conflict (or of other rules of public international law)':Wolff Heintschel von Heinegg 'Asymmetric Warfare' in Rüdiger Wolfrum (ed) *MPEPIL* (OUP Oxford Update 2010) para. 4.

108 An example of such CNOs directed against the civilian infrastructure could be seen in Estonia in 2007, see p. 42 below; further Eneken Tikk, et al. 'Cyber Attacks Against Georgia: Legal Lessons Identified' (2008) at <www.carlisle.army.mil/DIME/documents/Georgia%20 1%200.pdf> (date accessed 11 May 2011) p. 11.

> well-being of people, and the disruption or destruction of which would have a significant impact in a Member State as a result of the failure to maintain those functions.'[109]

These include inter alia transportation, traffic, energy, telecommunications and information technology, as well as the financial and insurance sector.[110] But also the Internet as a whole has by some been qualified as a critical infrastructure.[111] Ultimately it remains within the authority of each State to declare an infrastructure to be critical and many have done so differently.[112] This may serve to provide the infrastructure with a special legal protection under domestic law, for example by a higher penalisation of offences directed against it. As long as there is no internationally agreed definition or comprehensive regime, the domestic classification of a critical infrastructure does not however have any impact under international law. If however such an infrastructure is dual-use, it may become a military objective subject to attacks under humanitarian law.[113]

Three factors significant to most infrastructures have been identified as their greatest vulnerabilities: the lack of redundancies; the close interconnection between different infrastructures; and their unintelligibility due to complexity.[114] In some cases, infrastructures may have redundancies for certain sub-processes, but the more advanced and complex the structures, the higher the probability of a lack of a complete redundant structure as backup. The close interconnection and interdependence of infrastructures therefore poses a subsequent problem, as it may lead to cascading failures once one infrastructure breaks down. The electricity network is surely the most prominent example of this, as nearly all other infrastructures are dependent on it, and there is also no substitute for it.

---

109 Art. 2(a) Council Directive 2008/114/EC of 8 December 2008 on the identification and designation of European critical infrastructures and the assessment of the Need to improve their protection [2008] OJ L 345/75; see also Bundesamt für Sicherheit in der Informationstechnik 'Analysis of Critical Infrastructures – The ACIS Methodology' (2004) at <https://www.bsi.bund.de/SharedDocs/Downloads/EN/BSI/Kritis/acis_paper_en_pdf.pdf?__blob=publicationFile> (date accessed 27 April 2011) p. 1; Myriam Dunn Cavelty 'Critical Information Infrastructure: Vulnerabilities, Threats and Responses' (2007) 3 Disarmament Forum p. 16.

110 Bundesamt für Sicherheit in der Informationstechnik 'Analysis of Critical Infrastructures – The ACIS Methodology' p. 1; see also UNGA Res 58/199 'Creation of a Global Culture of Cybersecurity and the Protection of Critical Information Infrastructures' (23 December 2004).

111 French Government *Défense et Sécurité Nationale: Le Livre Blanc* at <http://lesrapports.ladocumentationfrancaise.fr/BRP/084000341/0000.pdf> (date accessed 31 March 2010) pp. 182–83.

112 An overview is given by the UN WSIS Thematic Meeting on Cybersecurity 'A Comparative Analysis of Cybersecurity Initiatives Worldwide' (2005) at <www.itu.int/osg/spu/cybersecurity/docs/Background_Paper_Comparative_Analysis_Cybersecurity_Initiatives_Worldwide.pdf> (date accessed 4 November 2009) p. 14.

113 See pp. 228 et seq. below.

114 Gaycken 'Die Zukunft des Krieges – Strategische Konzepte und strukturelle Probleme des Cyberwarfare' p. 2.

The outage of large parts of the electricity network over a long period of time will therefore ultimately lead to the breakdown of most vital infrastructures.[115] The same applies to the interdependence of civil and military computer network systems.[116]

A related phenomenon is the unintelligibility of infrastructures. The more complex each structure becomes and the more the interconnectivity expands, the more factors need to be taken into account when assessing the consequences of a singular malfunction of one system or the infrastructure as a whole.[117] This is of special concern when assessing, under humanitarian law, whether or not a computer network attack would be considered indiscriminate.[118]

Almost all of these critical infrastructures today rely on software-based control systems. These are, inter alia, so-called supervisory control and data acquisition ('SCADA') and distributed control systems, inter alia used for sewage, fresh water, electricity or rail systems.[119] These systems that exist since the installation of the respective infrastructure have increasingly been adapted to meet the demands of modern economies, offering remote scalability, control and supervision. For these purposes, the systems were equipped with devices to allow direct or indirect network connections to the global Internet. These add-ons have been criticised as making the SCADA systems particularly vulnerable to

115 The example of the so-called Northeast Blackout of 2003 in the US has shown that only a small outage in the electricity grid may cause large-scale power outages. The blackout that affected over 50 million people in the US and Canada was found to have been caused, inter alia, by the failure to adequately manage tree growth that ultimately led to the cutting of several electricity transmission lines; on this see the U.S.-Canada Power System Outage Task Force 'Final Report on the August 14, 2003 Blackout in the United States and Canada: Causes and Recommendations' (April 2004) at <https://reports.energy.gov/BlackoutFinal-Web.pdf> (date accessed 3 September 2009) p. 18. The investigation into the causes of the blackout included the question of whether a 'malicious cyber event' directly caused or contributed to the power outage, which was answered in the negative however (at pp. 131–32). Due to the mainly non-physical damage inflicted by the blackout, which was estimated to amount to US $6–10 billion, it nevertheless is regarded to provide an outlook for the estimation of costs of a computer network attack, as purported by Cashell, et al. 'The Economic Impact of Cyber-Attacks' p. 32.

116 Heintschel von Heinegg 'Informationskrieg und Völkerrecht' p. 150; Sean P. Kanuck 'Information Warfare: New Challenges for Public International Law' (1996) 37(1) Harvard International Law Journal p. 284.

117 An example for this can be seen in the so-called 'Year 2000 bug'. In the late 1990s, concerns where voiced that through the representation of years in some software to values of only a two-digit manner, the year 2000 would be interpreted as 1900, with the possible break down of major global computer systems. The feared disaster never became reality however. In the first Gulf War, the use of conventional weapons to target power generation equipment did show the devastating effects of attacks on the power grid to a modern society, as a major health crisis erupted due to a lack of electricity: Bayles 'The Ethics of Computer Network Attack' p. 50.

118 As will be shown at pp. 214–216 below.

119 Brian T. O'Donnell & James C. Kraska 'Humanitarian Law: Developing International Rules for the Digital Battlefield' (2003) 8(1) Journal of Conflict and Security Law p. 157.

malicious computer network operations.[120] This was for example recognised by a 1998 US Presidential Decision Directive on critical infrastructure protection, wherein the FBI was made the lead agency to protect the US computer systems, as critical infrastructures had become increasingly automated and interlinked, thereby creating new vulnerabilities inter alia to 'cyber attacks'.[121] For instance, in Australia in 2000, a hacker was able to penetrate the computer-controlled water supply, through which he gained access both to the drinking water and sewage systems. This allowed him to direct millions of litres of waste water into parks, rivers or private property, causing monetary and environmental damage.[122] An infection with malicious software is even possible in cases where SCADA systems are for security reasons not connected to the public Internet, as demonstrated by the 2010 Stuxnet worm allegedly targeting the Iranian nuclear programme, as will be shown later on.[123] A further complicating factor is posed by those cases where the critical infrastructures are controlled by private entities.[124] In these cases States can mostly only indirectly influence the level of security for these infrastructures, either by legal regulation or public-private partnerships.

2.3.3. *Interference with Financial Assets*

Some authors suggest that CNOs could be utilised to interfere with financial assets – for example of a target State's leadership – as a means of pressure, or by targeting the financial sector as a whole.[125] According to a report by the *New York Times*, the United States in 2003 had plans to 'freeze billions of dollars' in the bank accounts of Saddam Hussein through a CNO in order to disable the

---

120 On the security threat posed to SCADA and distributed control systems and the different models of overall risk assessment thereof, see P.A.S. Ralston, J.H. Graham & J.L. Hieb 'Cyber Security Risk Assessment for SCADA and DCS Networks' (2007) 46(4) ISA Transactions pp. 583–94; National Research Council (ed) *Making the Nation Safer: The Role of Science and Technology in Countering Terrorism* (National Acadamies Press Washington 2002) pp. 141 and 327–28; Henning Wegener 'Harnessing the Perils in Cyberspace: Who is in Charge?' (2007) 3 Disarmament Forum p. 47; Udo Helmbrecht 'Die aktuelle Bedrohungslage durch Ausfall von IT-Infrastrukturen' in Michael Kloepfer (ed) *Schutz kritischer Infrastrukturen: IT und Energie* (Nomos Baden-Baden 2010) p. 42.

121 Presidential Decision Directive 63 of 22 May 1998 'The Clinton Administration's Policy on Critical Infrastructure Protection' (1998) at <www.justice.gov/criminal/cybercrime/white_pr.htm> (date accessed 27 April 2011).

122 Helmbrecht 'Die aktuelle Bedrohungslage durch Ausfall von IT-Infrastrukturen' p. 39.

123 See pp. 47–50 below.

124 In Germany, for example, 80% of the companies operating critical infrastructures or providing for the respective services are privately owned; Wolfgang Schäuble 'Schutz kritischer Infrastrukturen als Aufgabe der Politik' in Michael Kloepfer (ed) *Schutz kritischer Infrastrukturen: IT und Energie* (Nomos Baden-Baden 2010) p. 24.

125 Michael N. Schmitt 'Computer Network Attack: The Normative Software' (2001) 4 Yearbook of International Humanitarian Law p. 70; Dittmar *Angriffe auf Computernetzwerke: Ius ad bellum und ius in bello* p. 104; Joyner & Lotrionte 'Information Warfare as International Coercion: Elements of a Legal Framework' p. 850.

Iraqi government's financial system before the US-led invasion. These plans were not carried out however, as there was the worry that the effects could not be limited to Iraq, but could create a worldwide financial crisis.[126]

While such actions are possible from a technical point of view, it is debateable whether they could be an effective means when taking banking law into consideration. Today, the 'freezing' or restriction of transfer of assets of terrorist suspects is a common measure employed by the UN Security Council.[127] In these cases, the UN Member States carry out the decisions of the UN Security Council through their relevant national laws, by instructing banks within their jurisdiction to proceed with the relevant assets as envisaged by the resolution and bound within the relevant statutory frameworks. CNOs are therefore an option if a resolution cannot be adopted, or if the target State refuses to implement it. If the CNO is however directed only against intangible assets such as credit accounts, this may only forfeit documentary proof of such assets by modifying the databases of the relevant banks, but it does not – at least under most national jurisdictions – invalidate the civil claim of the holder.[128] It is however hardly conceivable that a State and its financial institutions which do not implement the desired measures independently will allow forfeiture of the relevant claims once database discrepancies due to CNOs are discovered.

2.4. CONCLUSION

The above has demonstrated the importance of the Internet to individuals, businesses and society as a whole, in addition to governments and militaries. Furthermore, the comparatively high vulnerability of devices connected to the Internet to threats posed by various actors has been identified. Both of these understandings are reflected in policies at the highest levels of international institutions. The UN General Assembly Resolution entitled 'Creation of a Global Culture of Cybersecurity and Taking Stock of National Efforts to Protect Critical Information Infrastructures' for example recognises the

> 'increasing contribution made by networked information technologies to many of the essential functions of daily life, commerce and the provision of goods and services, research, innovation and entrepreneurship, and to the free flow of information among individuals and organizations, Governments, business and civil society.'[129]

---

126 John Markoff 'Halted '03 Iraq Plan Illustrates US Fear of Cyberwar Risk' in *The New York Times* of 2 August 2009.

127 As can exemplarily be seen in UNSC Res 1333 'Afghanistan' (19 December 2000) SCOR 55th Year 32.

128 Johann-Christoph Woltag 'Cyber Warfare' in Rüdiger Wolfrum (ed) *MPEPIL* (OUP Oxford Update 2010) para. 16.

129 UNGA Res 64/211 (17 March 2010) UN Doc A/RES/64/211.

Likewise, the threats to this critical information structure are seen to be growing both in sophistication and gravity, calling for an international coordinated response in order to effectively confront this threat perceived as transnational in nature. Therefore, Member States are called upon to assess and improve their national efforts in protecting their critical information infrastructures. The same holds true for the OECD Member States which have given the security of information systems and networks top policy priority for governments in connection to information and communications technologies as of 2010.[130]

3. CASE STUDIES

Opinions in the media, legal scholarship and statements or reports from public authorities embrace the full spectrum of possible threats attributed to computer network operations. Some describe these as being able to amount to an 'electronic' or 'digital Pearl Harbor' with effects comparable to those of nuclear weapons.[131] Others in turn only see economic damages or an impairment of infrastructure performance as realistic,[132] with many further opinions in between the two extremes. While the above has shown the abstract potential of computer network operations directed against diverse targets, the following case studies will provide for an analysis of CNOs that have actually taken place in order to assess to what extent such visions are realistic.

---

130 OECD *Information Technology Outlook 2010* p. 261.

131 Wegener 'Der unsichtbare Feind: Die neuen Gefahrenlagen im digitalen Raum' p. 54; Shackelford 'From Nuclear War to Net War: Analogizing Cyber Attacks in International Law' p. 195; Arie J. Schaap 'Cyber Warfare Operations: Development and Use Under International Law' (2009) 64 Air Force Law Review p. 173; countering such scenarios as too difficult to be achieved even by the most sophisticated cyber warfare-capable armies: Bruce Berkowitz *The New Face of War: How War Will be Fought in the 21st Century* (Free Press New York 2003) pp. 135 et seq.

132 VM Antolin-Jenkins 'Defining the Parameters of Cyberwar Operations: Looking for Law in All the Wrong Places?' (2005) 51 Naval Law Review pp. 144–46; James Andrew Lewis 'Cyberwarfare and Its Impact on International Security' (2010) No. 19 UNODA Occasional Papers p. 5; James A. Lewis 'Assessing the Risks of Cyber Terrorism, Cyber War and Other Cyber Threats' (December 2002) at <http://csis.org/files/media/csis/pubs/021101_risks_of_cyberterror.pdf> (date accessed 23 July 2010) stating that the threat of computer network vulnerabilities to national security is overstated, qualifying attacks as mere 'weapons of mass annoyance' (at pp. 2–4); similarly George Smith 'An Electronic Pearl Harbor? Not Likely' (1998) 15 Issues on Science and Technology pp. 68–73. Voicing concern the threat associated with CNOs may have only be instigated by parts of the US military and defense contractors in order to counter budget cuts and propel cyber security into a major growth industry: Seymour M. Hersh 'The Online Threat' in *The New Yorker* of 1 November 2010; similarly Constanze Kurz 'Kybernetische Krieger werden überschätzt' in *Frankfurter Allgemeine Zeitung* of 18 February 2011; predicting a 'true cyberwar' as unlikely to occur: Peter Sommer & Ian Brown *Reducing Systemic Cybersecurity Risk, OECD/IFP Profect on Future Global Shocks Doc IFP/WKP/FGS(2011)3* at <www.oecd.org/dataoecd/57/44/46889922.pdf> (date accessed 4 June 2012) p. 7.

One of the practical problems in assessing the quality of CNOs lies in the fact that they are mostly undertaken covertly. Their effects will therefore often remain unnoticed, or be attributed to a malfunction of either soft- or hardware of the targeted systems. Furthermore, militaries and governments are reluctant to admit and promulgate that they have been the victim of such an operation, especially if it is successful. Moreover, it is far more difficult for the press or civil society to gain knowledge of such operations when compared to 'regular' attacks using traditional kinetic weapons. It is therefore impossible to name an exact figure of how many CNOs have been undertaken so far. The figures named in other publications or in public documents are consequently mostly estimates. In addition, these figures do not show whether a CNO originates from an individual, a terrorist organisation or the military or other public authority of a foreign State. The following examples will for that reason be limited to some incidents that are sufficiently documented and have also received publicity outside the circle of computer security experts.

3.1. COMPUTER NETWORK ESPIONAGE

There exist numerous instances of computer espionage especially in the field of industrial espionage. While most of these remain unnoticed or unreported, occasionally some have become generally known to the public. There are those cases where sensitive data is mined from government systems with the intention of financial gain, making those cases comparable to regular cybercrime. During the Gulf War of 1991 for example, Dutch hackers managed to gain access to information concerning the tactics, positioning and armament of United States forces in the Gulf area. This information was reportedly offered to the Iraqi side for US $1 million; the Iraqis rejected the proposal, however.[133]

In March 1994, the Rome Laboratory, the premier command and control research institute of the US Air Force, became target of several malicious CNOs.[134] These were finally traced back to two hackers, a 16-year-old British student and a 22-year-old Israeli technician. The British hacker was also discovered later on to have targeted several other government and military sites, inter alia the NATO headquarters. Via these operations the hackers managed to copy tactical and artificial intelligence research data resident on the accessed computer systems.[135] In sum, the assessment of the damage inflicted, the

133 Richard W. Aldrich 'How Do You Know You Are at War in the Information Age' (2000) 22 Houston Journal of International Law p. 227; Dittmar *Angriffe auf Computernetzwerke: Ius ad bellum und ius in bello* p. 44.

134 150 intrusions from 100 different points of origin were reported; Hildreth 'Cyberwarfare' pp. 3–4; Delibasis *The Right to National Self-Defence in Information Warfare Operations* pp. 311–13.

135 US General Accounting Office *Information Security: Computer Attacks at Department of Defense Pose Increasing Risks* (US GAO Washington DC 1996) p. 2.

patching of vulnerabilities and the operations to identify the perpetrators and their location are estimated to have cost the US Department of Defense US $500,000.[136] After the final identification of the perpetrators, the British hacker was fined, while the Israeli hacker could not be indicted, as his behaviour at that time did not constitute a crime under Israeli law.

Other cases more closely resemble traditional espionage, such as when in 2008, according to the US Deputy Secretary of Defense, the US Department of Defense suffered the 'most significant breach of US military computers ever', instigated by a foreign intelligence agency.[137] The perpetrators in this case allegedly managed to transfer vast amounts of data concerning blueprints of design and development of the prestigious Joint Strike Fighter project.

Similar cases have been reported on a regular basis by many governments. In 2007 for example, several German ministries fell victim to CNOs which were traced back to China.[138] While the amount and exact type of data that was actually transferred to China remains unknown, the data typically stored on the exploited government computer systems is generally regarded as primarily being only of interest for public authorities, causing the German Federal Office for the Protection of the Constitution to conclude that Chinese authorities were involved in the operations.[139] The number of CNOs directed against German government networks has increased ever since, with 1,511 registered in 2009 and 2,108 in 2010.[140] The German Federal Ministry of the Interior confirmed that the majority of these operations have been attributed to a Chinese origin, while the amount of damage done remains unclear or is not disclosed.[141]

A particularly detailed analysis of computer network exploitation has been made in an investigation from June 2008 to March 2009 of alleged Chinese computer espionage directed mainly against Tibetan and South-East Asian institutions. Two widely recognised technical reports[142] exposed a large

---

136 US General Accounting Office *Information Security: Computer Attacks at Department of Defense Pose Increasing Risks* p. 4. The tracing back of the operation's origin was not possible from within the United States but could only be achieved because one of the perpetrators boasted himself of the deed: Hildreth 'Cyberwarfare' pp. 3–4.

137 Lynn 'Defending a New Domain: The Pentagon's Cyberstrategy' p. 97.

138 Jürgen Dahlkamp, et al. 'Prinzip Sandkorn' in *Der Spiegel* of 35/2007 p. 19.

139 Bundesministerium des Inneren *Verfassungsschutzbericht 2008* (BMI Berlin 2009) p. 335; Bundesministerium des Inneren *Verfassungsschutzbericht 2009* (BMI Berlin 2010) pp. 354–55.

140 Bundesministerium des Inneren *Verfassungsschutzbericht 2010* (BMI Berlin 2011) p. 367. The report also predicts a further increase of these operations in the years to come.

141 'Berlin plant "Cyber-Abwehr-Zentrum"' in *Frankfurter Allgemeine Zeitung* of 27 December 2010.

142 The SecDev Group and Munk Centre for International Studies 'Tracking GhostNet: Investigating a Cyber Espionage Network' (2009) at <www.f-secure.com/weblog/archives/ghostnet.pdf> (date accessed 20 April 2011) and Shishir Nagaraja & Ross Anderson 'The Snooping Dragon: Social-Malware Surveillance of the Tibetan Movement' (2009) 746 University of Cambridge Technical Report; drawing parallels to the operations of Chinese origin directed against German institutions: Bundesministerium des Inneren *Verfassungsschutzbericht 2009* p. 355.

computer espionage network given the title 'GhostNet', which was found to have infected approximately 1,300 computer systems, nearly a third of which are considered to be high value targets – inter alia computers located at ministries of foreign affairs, embassies, international organisations, news media and non-governmental organisations.[143] GhostNet allows its operator to take real-time control of the infected systems, inter alia by searching and downloading specific files but also covertly operating external devices attached to the system, such as microphones or webcams.[144] While investigations did show that the operation originated from systems located in China, the reports disagreed on the question of whether GhostNet was a deliberate intelligence gathering operation by Chinese authorities. Although the explanation that the targets were to be exploited by Chinese authorities is somewhat obvious,[145] it is not inconceivable that the targets connected with GhostNet were just collected by an individual or group, whether for the purpose of profit – as critical data can be sold to States or private entities – or mere curiosity and vandalism. It is even theoretically possible that a third State used China-based computer systems as proxies in order to deliberately mislead observers to assume Chinese authorities as the operators.[146] However, characteristics of GhostNet in fact point to State involvement: the network was directed at the collection of political intelligence and not of financial or personal data, which criminal organisations are typically interested in. Furthermore, the effective analysis of all data gathered required significant resources and linguistic skills, which is not regularly available to criminal organisations.[147] Nevertheless, any attribution of GhostNet to the Chinese State solely rests on the political context of relations between China and its neighbour States.[148]

Another case of computer espionage was discovered in June 2012 in the highly complex malware entitled 'Flame'. The programme has been analysed to be able to record conversations and take screenshots from the infected systems as well as monitoring its network communications. The purpose and aim of the malware can however only be speculated, as no pattern of infected systems has been detected so far. The same holds true for its authors. Many consider States to

---

143 The SecDev Group and Munk Centre for International Studies 'Tracking GhostNet: Investigating a Cyber Espionage Network' p. 40.

144 The SecDev Group and Munk Centre for International Studies 'Tracking GhostNet: Investigating a Cyber Espionage Network' p. 5.

145 Especially when taking into consideration that the IP addresses of the attackers were traced back to the Chinese Hainan Island, home of a major Chinese signals intelligence facility: The SecDev Group and Munk Centre for International Studies 'Tracking GhostNet: Investigating a Cyber Espionage Network' p. 48.

146 The SecDev Group and Munk Centre for International Studies 'Tracking GhostNet: Investigating a Cyber Espionage Network' pp. 48–49.

147 US-China Economic and Security Review Commission (ed) *2009 Report to Congress* (US Government Printing Office Washington 2009) p. 178.

148 Gaycken *Cyberwar: Das Internet als Kriegsschauplatz* p. 90.

be the only possible source due to the vast amount of resources needed for its creation.[149]

The most recent example of CNOs the alleged worldwide espionage activities by the US National Security Agency (NSA) and the British Government Communications Headquarters (GCHQ) disclosed in 2013 by several newspapers on the grounds of material from former NSA employee Edward Snowden.[150] Both services allegedly used several software programs to be able to listen into mobile phone conversations or directly access data stored on servers of major Internet companies. Whether the latter cooperated with the intelligence agencies in this regard remains disputed. Mobile phones of senior foreign government officials and heads of State were allegedly also targeted, possibly even from within US embassies abroad.[151]

By infiltrating computer systems in order to exploit data resident thereon, the examples all feature traditional espionage activities with the difference of utilising the Internet as a new medium. These forms of data collection may however also serve to identify vulnerabilities in the targeted computer systems, in order to exploit these in preparation for future military computer network operations. Consequently there is a close relationship between computer network exploitations and computer network attacks, which is inter alia exemplified in the double function of Keith Alexander, Director of the National Security Agency, an US intelligence agency, who until 2013 was also the Commander of US Cyber Command, an US armed forces sub-unified command.[152]

3.2. ESTONIA 2007

The computer network operations directed against Estonian systems in 2007 are certainly one of the most widely analysed and discussed cases. They have their origin in the relocation of a Soviet-era war memorial and must be seen against the background of a generally tense relationship between Estonia and the Russia Federation. This is also due inter alia to the large Russian minority living in Estonia, a significant proportion of which is not considered to be fully integrated into Estonian society.[153]

---

149 As stated by one of the discoverers of the malware, Eugene Kaspersky, in an interview reprinted in Lukas Grunwald 'Profi-Attacke – Die schleichende Gefahr: Advanced Persistent Threats' (2012)(7) iX – Magazin für professionelle Informationstechnik pp. 50–51.

150 For details see *The Guardian* 'The NSA Files' <www.theguardian.com/world/the-nsa-files> (date accessed 12 December 2013).

151 Mark Landler & David E. Sanger 'Obama May Ban Spying on Heads of Allied States' in *The New York Times* of 28 October 2013.

152 US Department of Defense 'Department of Defense Strategy for Operating in Cyberspace' p. 5.

153 As of 1 January 2007, approximately 25% of the Estonia population were of Russian ethnic origin: Estonian Statistical Database, available in English at <http://pub.stat.ee/px-web.2001/>

The operations started after the beginning of a conflict between Estonia and Russia that originated in the removal of a World War II war memorial alongside several adjoining war graves built by the Soviets in 1947. The memorial – a two-metre high bronze statue of a soldier – had been erected in central Tallinn to commemorate the Soviet Army's lost soldiers and as a symbol of victory over Nazi Germany. Yet Estonians regarded the memorial as a symbol of Soviet occupation. As the gatherings of groups at the memorial commemorating their losses were increasingly often becoming a rallying point for national extremists, the Estonian government decided to relocate the memorial to the Tallinn military cemetery located in the city's outskirts. On 26 April 2007 after the first preparatory works for the relocation had begun, street riots and looting occurred in Tallinn and Johvi, as well as in front of the Estonian embassy in Moscow.[154]

Beginning on 27 April 2007 and lasting approximately three weeks, a large number of DDoS attacks were inflicted on computer systems of the Estonian government, Parliament, hospitals, systems managing emergency call numbers, banks and other targets.[155] The initial operations of the first days can be described as spontaneous reactions to the memorial's relocation – they were relatively simple and uncoordinated DDoS attacks that were easily mitigated.[156] In a second phase, however, the operations appeared to be coordinated and made use of large botnets.[157] As the Estonian government and administration, as well as society, makes a comparatively high use of the Internet, these DDoS attacks proved to be quite effective, obstructing the operations of public authorities and emergency services.[158]

(17 September 2009); on the Estonian case see generally Eneken Tikk, Kadri Kaska & Liis Vihul *International Cyber Incidents: Legal Considerations* (Cooperative Cyber Defence Centre of Excellence Tallinn 2010) pp. 14–35; and Susan W. Brenner *Cyberthreats: The Emerging Fault Lines of the Nation State* (OUP Oxford 2009) pp. 85–94.

154 Shackelford 'From Nuclear War to Net War: Analogizing Cyber Attacks in International Law' pp. 205–06.

155 Ziolkowski 'Computernetzwerkoperationen und die Zusatzprotokolle zu den Genfer Abkommen – Zum "virtuellen Raum" des Internet und dem Schutzstandard der vor 30 Jahren in Kraft getretenen Protokolle' p. 204; Shackelford 'From Nuclear War to Net War: Analogizing Cyber Attacks in International Law' p. 193; Ian Traynor 'Russia Accused of Unleashing Cyberwar to Disable Estonia' in *The Guardian* of 17 May 2007.

156 Tikk, Kaska & Vihul *International Cyber Incidents: Legal Considerations* p. 23.

157 A botnet (in its vicious version) comprises a high number of distributed malicious programs running on a preferably high number of computer systems. The program allows the originator of the botnet to gain a certain level of remote command and control over the compromised computer systems. These systems may then be used to start large-scale DDoS attacks or other types of operations. See also David Barroso 'Botnets – The Silent Threat (ENISA Position Paper No. 3)' (2007) at <www.enisa.europa.eu/act/res/other-areas/botnets/botnets-2013-the-silent-threat/at_download/fullReport> (date accessed 24 February 2011); and ENISA 'Botnets: Detection, Measurement, Disinfection & Defence' (2011) at <www.enisa.europa.eu/act/res/botnets/botnets-measurement-detection-disinfection-and-defence/at_download/fullReport> (date accessed 22 June 2011).

158 At the time of the attacks in 2007, 64%–70% of the Estonian population were Internet users (United Nations Statistics Division 'Millennium Development Goals Database' (data as of

Never before had CNOs been targeted against a whole country on such a massive scale, causing the Estonian incident to be frequently referred to as the first large-scale cyber assault on a State.[159] In an attempt to stop the operations originating from outside of the country, large parts of the national networks were blocked to connections from abroad.[160] In the incident's aftermath only one ethnic Russian living in Estonia was found guilty of targeting the political party website of the Estonian Prime Minister. Although many pointed their fingers at Russia, responsibility for the operations has still not been determined.[161]

Many of the computers used for the attack were actually located in the United States, belonging to individuals completely unaware that they had been remotely hijacked, which is typical for large-scale DDoS attacks using botnets.[162] Software performing predefined attacks on predefined Estonian systems or instructions on how to do so was readily available on Russian-language websites. Thus, any individual, with or without specialist knowledge of information technology, that was willing to do so could participate in the ongoing DDoS attacks. The fact that this rather simple CNO technique was used has led observers to conclude that the attacks were in fact not initiated by the Russian government, but by agitated teenagers or individuals with a Russian nationalistic background.[163]

Ultimately the effects of the DDoS attacks were mainly of an economic and societal nature. Business activities relying on Internet connection were impaired due to the breakdown of email and web servers. Sovereign functions such as the electronic communications between public authorities and citizens and the latter's ability to access public information were disrupted. Furthermore, access to domestic and foreign media distributed on the Internet was obstructed, thereby encroaching upon the free flow of information.[164] However, no physical

---

3 August 2009) <http://data.un.org/Data.aspx?d=MDG&f=seriesRowID:605#MDG> (date accessed 3 September 2009); Estonian Ministry of Defence 'Cyber Security Strategy' (2008) at <www.mod.gov.ee/files/kmin/img/files/Kuberjulgeoleku_strateegia_2008-2013_ENG.pdf> (date accessed 23 July 2010); *The Economist* – Technology Quarterly of 6 December 2008 'Marching Off to Cyberwar' p. 18.

159 Shackelford 'From Nuclear War to Net War: Analogizing Cyber Attacks in International Law' p. 194.

160 Jody Westby 'Stabilität statt Cyberkrieg' (2009) 09–10 Internationale Politik pp. 64–65.

161 Shackelford 'From Nuclear War to Net War: Analogizing Cyber Attacks in International Law' p. 208; Tikk, et al. 'Cyber Attacks Against Georgia: Legal Lessons Identified' p. 12; Brenner *Cyberthreats: The Emerging Fault Lines of the Nation State* p. 6.

162 *The Economist* of 3–9 July 2010 'Cyberwar' p. 9.

163 Michael Lesk 'The New Front Line: Estonia under Cyberassault' (2007) 5(4) IEEE Security and Privacy pp. 76–79; Cavelty 'Critical Information Infrastructure: Vulnerabilities, Threats and Responses' p. 15.
This presumption is underpinned by a statement of Konstantin Goloskokov, a leading figure within the Russian youth organisation 'Nashi', who openly declares the Nashi to have orchestrated the CNOs in a documentary on the incidents: Antoine Vitkine (Dir) *Der Siegeszug der Hacker* (Arte France 7 June 2011) at 3:30–6:00 min running time.

164 Tikk, Kaska & Vihul *International Cyber Incidents: Legal Considerations* pp. 24–25.

damage was reported and estimations regarding the possible monetary damages inflicted are not available.

Nevertheless, in reaction to the attacks, the President of the Republic of Estonia in an address to the UN General Assembly found it necessary to call upon the international community to cooperate in legal matters concerning cyber security and to establish an appropriate international legal framework.[165] The operations directed against Estonian targets were thereby categorised as a threat not only to sophisticated information communications systems but to the community as a whole.

3.3. GEORGIA 2008

The Georgian incidents of 2008 are the only publicly known CNOs so far taking place within the context of traditional military operations, namely during the Russian-Georgian conflict of August 2008. The methods used in this case were likewise DDoS attacks, which started on 8 August 2008, and additionally the defacement of websites.[166] The latter refers to the changing of content and visual appearance of a website; in the Georgian case several official government websites were modified to show pictures of dictators of the 20th century lined up next to then Georgian President Saakashvili's picture with obvious implications. On several publicly available websites software and instructions needed to perform DDoS attacks were readily available for download, like in the Estonian case. Besides the ongoing Russian-Georgian conflict, further other indicators led to the assumption that the attacks had their origin in Russia. An example of this was the Russian-hosted website www.stopgeorgia.ru, which was created explicitly to allow a large number of individuals to perform attacks on Georgian government websites. The website provided software, instructions and target information so that even the technologically untrained were able to undertake CNOs against Georgian targets.

Several commentators have suspected the so-called Russian Business Network of being involved in the operations, a Russian Internet service provider

165 Toomas Hendrik Ilves 'Address by Toomas Hendrik Ilves President of the Republic of Estonia to the 62nd Session of the United Nations General Assembly (25 September 2007)' (2007) at <www.un.org/webcast/ga/62/2007/pdfs/estonia-eng.pdf> (date accessed 6 May 2011) pp. 3–4.

166 On this see generally Tikk, et al. 'Cyber Attacks Against Georgia: Legal Lessons Identified' providing for a chronology of the 'cyber attacks' against Georgia in Annex III; *The Economist* – Technology Quarterly of 6 December 2008 'Marching Off to Cyberwar' p. 18; Tikk, Kaska & Vihul *International Cyber Incidents: Legal Considerations* pp. 69–70 and Lesley Swanson 'The Era of Cyber Warfare: Applying International Humanitarian Law to the 2008 Russian-Georgian Cyber Conflict' (2010) 32 Loyola of Los Angeles International and Comparative Law Review pp. 303 et seq; William C. Ashmore 'Impact of Alleged Russian Cyber Attacks' (2009) 11 Baltic Security & Defence Review pp. 10–11.

based in St Petersburg.[167] However, the level of involvement was never identified and it could also merely have consisted of providing hosting services.[168] Nor was it established that the website containing the links to the malicious software was hosted by or under the direction of a Russian State organ. Most information security analysts characterised the attackers as patriotic hackers and at any rate as non-State actors.[169]

Just as in the Estonian case it is difficult to assess the amount of damage inflicted.[170] Direct physical damage did not occur and was probably also not intended. The effects must therefore be considered as more of a psychological nature. Since major government websites were no longer reachable, the Georgian government had difficulties in informing the national and international public about the military conflict, while at the same time the Georgian people's access to information was obstructed. As winning over the international public opinion is today a major goal of warring parties, preventing one side to the conflict from effectively contributing to the debate may prove a valuable military objective. Furthermore, the National Bank of Georgia instructed all banks to stop their electronic services, an outage that lasted for ten days.[171]

In order to make the websites of Georgian public authorities available, the content was moved to servers located outside of Georgia, for example in the US, Poland and Estonia, including the website of Georgia's President and of the Ministry of Defence. As a result, the DDoS attacks followed the relocation and were directed at the relevant servers now located in the US instead of Georgia.[172]

---

167 Georgian Government 'Russian Cyberwar on Georgia' (10 November 2008) at <http://georgiaupdate.gov.ge> (date accessed 18 August 2011) p. 8; John Markoff 'Before the Gunfire, Cyberattacks' in *The New York Times* of 12 August 2008; Ophardt 'Cyber Warfare and the Crime of Aggression: The Need for Individual Accountability on Tomorrow's Battlefield' paras. 13–14. A technical study by David Bizeuil on the activities of the Russian Business Network can be found at <www.bizeul.org/files/RBN_study.pdf> (date accessed 18 August 2011).

168 Tikk, et al. 'Cyber Attacks Against Georgia: Legal Lessons Identified' p. 12.

169 Joshua E. Kastenberg 'Non-Intervention and Neutrality in Cyberspace: An Emerging Principle in the National Practice of International Law' (2009) 64 United States Air Force Law Review pp. 59–60 with further references.

170 As only 8% of the Georgian population in 2007 were Internet users, the number of potentially negatively affected persons and businesses was at any rate much smaller than in the Estonian case; United Nations Statistics Division 'Millennium Development Goals Database' (data as of 3 August 2009) <http://data.un.org/Data.aspx?d=MDG&f=seriesRowID:605#MDG> (date accessed 3 September 2009).

171 Tikk, et al. 'Cyber Attacks Against Georgia: Legal Lessons Identified' p. 16.

172 Stephen Korns & Joshua Kastenberg 'Georgia's Cyber Left Hook' (2009) 38 Parameters – US Army War College Quarterly p. 67. On the legal implications of this measure in respect to the laws of neutrality see pp. 267 et seq. below.

3.4. STUXNET AND THE IRANIAN NUCLEAR PROGRAMME

In September 2010, a malicious software referred to as 'Stuxnet' attracted wide attention due to its alleged targeting of the Iranian nuclear programme.[173] The software, the existence of which was firstly uncovered in July 2010 by a Belarussian computer security company, clandestinely infiltrated computer systems all around the world. In comparison to the DDoS attacks in Estonia and Georgia, which were simple operations the functions of which are well known and documented, Stuxnet is a computer worm and thus capable of being subjected to digital forensics via analysis of its program code. As Stuxnet dispersed all over the Internet, computer security companies or individual forensic scientists were easily able to obtain an individual copy of Stuxnet for analysis.[174]

The ensuing analysis showed that Stuxnet included a programme specifically designed to manipulate industrial plants running a Siemens S-7 supervisory control and data acquisition ('SCADA') system, which is inter alia used to control temperatures, pressure, rotation speeds and other parameters of centrifuges.[175] These SCADA systems are allegedly frequently used by Iran for its nuclear programmes, inter alia in the control of the newly-built Bushehr nuclear power plant or the Natanz nuclear facility. This soon made analysts believe that the Iranian nuclear programme was the target of Stuxnet, which is supported by the finding of Symantec, a computer security company, that 60% of the systems infected with Stuxnet were located in Iran.[176]

Several incidents in the Iranian nuclear programmes in the recent years also point in that direction. In July 2009 a nuclear accident was reported in Natanz, followed by the resignation of the chief of the Iranian atomic energy agency. Furthermore, the number of actually usable enrichment centrifuges, which are generally controlled via SCADA systems, had dropped significantly in the spring

173 See only: Frank Rieger 'Der digitale Erstschlag ist erfolgt' in *Frankfurter Allgemeine Zeitung* of 22 September 2010; Helmut Martin-Jung & Paul-Anton Krüger 'Gezielte Sabotage: Eine iranische Atomanlage könnte Ziel eines Trojaner-Angriffs gewesen sein' in *Süddeutsche Zeitung* of 23 September 2010; *The Economist* of 2–8 October 2010 'A Worm in the Centrifuge'; John Markoff 'A Silent Attack, but Not a Subtle One' in *The New York Times* of 26 September 2010; Spiegel Online 'Stuxnet-Wurm befällt Rechner in iranischem AKW' (26 September 2010) at <www.spiegel.de/netzwelt/netzpolitik/0,1518,719654,00.html> (date accessed 27 September 2010); Michael Joseph Gross 'A Declaration of Cyber-War' in *Vanity Fair* of April 2011, describing Stuxnet as the 'Hiroshima of cyber-war'.

174 While Stuxnet has been technically analysed by several computer security companies, the study by Symantec is of special significance due to its thoroughness; see Nicolas Falliere, Liam O. Murchu & Eric Chien *W32.Stuxnet Dossier Version 1.4* at <www.symantec.com/content/en/us/enterprise/media/security_response/whitepapers/w32_stuxnet_dossier.pdf> (date accessed 23 March 2011).

175 Rieger 'Der digitale Erstschlag ist erfolgt'.

176 Vikram Thakur 'W32.Stuxnet – Network Information' (23 July 2010) at <www.symantec.com/connect/blogs/w32stuxnet-network-information> (date accessed 28 February 2012).

of 2009.[177] Iranian authorities confirmed that thousands of Iranian computer systems have been infected, including several of the staff of the Bushehr plant. However, the main systems of the plant were allegedly not compromised.[178] Then, in February 2011, Iranian authorities reported severe problems with the Bushehr reactor to atomic inspectors of the IAEA, giving rise to new speculations that Stuxnet was the reason.[179] Siemens itself stated that its customers had reported 24 Stuxnet infections in plants worldwide that operate with the relevant SCADA software, although allegedly none of the operations had been negatively affected.[180]

The original infection of a system with Stuxnet is likely to have been caused via a USB or other removable device, hence it has to be directly connected to the target computer system in order to infect it.[181] From here a self-replication on other USB storage devices attached to the system was possible. Installation and replication of the software on the target system was done clandestinely and automatically, without the user's knowledge. The mere requirement therefore was for someone to connect an infected USB device to a computer system. By choosing this method of distribution, even computer systems that are not connected to the public Internet can be targeted, as long as one of the systems within the internal network is equipped with an USB connection and thereby infected.

Several factors indicate a State-sponsored origin of Stuxnet, in particular its high level of sophistication and accuracy, and the resources needed for development. The analysis uncovered the utilisation of four different zero-day exploits and two stolen digital signatures. Zero-day exploits describe methods that use previously unknown software vulnerabilities. This has the advantage that the vulnerability will mostly not have been closed before the beginning of the operation, as its existence is unknown to the operator of the vulnerable system. The knowledge of such vulnerabilities and the methods of their exploitation are thus of high value. Organised criminals, software vendors, as well as intelligence services, are known to pay large sums for these kinds of exploits, which has actually generated the emergence of a marketplace for security vulnerabilities.[182] For this reason analysts do not believe Stuxnet to

---

177 Rieger 'Der digitale Erstschlag ist erfolgt'.

178 Spiegel Online 'Stuxnet-Wurm befällt Rechner in iranischem AKW'; *Iran Daily* of 27 September 2010 'Bushehr Plant Safe from Stuxnet Worm' p. 1.

179 William J. Broad & David E. Sanger 'Iran Reports a Major Setback at a Nuclear Power Plant' in *The New York Times* of 25 February 2011.

180 Siemens 'SIMATIC WinCC / SIMATIC PCS 7: Information bezüglich Malware / Virus / Trojaner' (2011) at <http://support.automation.siemens.com/WW/view/de/43876783> (date accessed 28 February 2012).

181 Falliere, Murchu & Chien *W32.Stuxnet Dossier Version 1.4* p. 3; Gaycken *Cyberwar: Das Internet als Kriegsschauplatz* p. 177.

182 Uli Ries 'Das Geschäft mit den Bugs: Sicherheitslücken als Handelsware' (2011)(5) C't Magazin für Computertechnik p. 82; Rieger 'Der digitale Erstschlag ist erfolgt'; Frank Rieger 'Angriff ist besser als Verteidigung' in *Frankfurter Allgemeine Zeitung* of 18 January 2011.

have been programmed by regular cybercriminals as these would rather have sold the information necessary to exploit the zero-day vulnerabilities.

Furthermore, the sophistication of Stuxnet indicates both a high level of knowledge about the targeted SCADA system and a high level of resources spent on its development. Some argue that such a high level of knowledge of the targeted SCADA systems and the components they control could only be reached through simulated attacks under realistic conditions on a system identical to the actual target.[183] Complexes coming into consideration are reported to exist both in Israel, where the Dimona complex is widely believed to be the heart of Israel's nuclear arms program, and the United States, with the Idaho National Laboratory hosting a SCADA-testbed which was officially set up for research on the protection of critical infrastructure systems against CNOs.[184] According to media reports, some nuclear enrichment experts, computer scientists and former State officials link the creation and execution of Stuxnet to the United States and Israel.[185]

What also has to be taken into account in evaluating Stuxnet as having a State-sponsored origin is its accuracy. While the programme has ultimately infected thousands of computer systems, it generally remains inactive thereon. Only once the specific target system is identified through extensive tests does it become active.[186] It is furthermore equipped with an 'expiry date' after which it will stop operating.[187] This high level of sophistication and the vast amount of resources needed for its development, paired with the failure to use the exploits to earn money has led most analysts to conclude that Stuxnet could only have been designed by a government or on its request.[188] This is why commentators have already qualified Stuxnet as making history as the first cyberweapon ever to be utilised by a State and amounting to a use of force.[189] However, while an argument can be made that Stuxnet has a State-sponsored origin, there exists no evidence so far that would imply the responsibility of any particular State and

---

183 Rieger 'Angriff ist besser als Verteidigung' p. 27.

184 William J. Broad, John Markoff & David E. Sanger 'Israeli Test on Worm Called Crucial in Iran Nuclear Delay' in *The New York Times* of 15 January 2011.

185 Broad, Markoff & Sanger 'Israeli Test on Worm Called Crucial in Iran Nuclear Delay'.

186 Grunwald 'Profi-Attacke – Die schleichende Gefahr: Advanced Persistent Threats' p. 44.

187 Falliere, Murchu & Chien *W32.Stuxnet Dossier Version 1.4* p. 18; In the version analysed this was 24 June 2012. This date could however be different in an alternate version of the worm.

188 Markoff 'A Silent Attack, but Not a Subtle One'; *The Economist* of 2–8 October 2010 'A Worm in the Centrifuge' p. 56; Gaycken & Karger 'Entnetzung statt Vernetzung: Paradigmenwechsel in der IT-Sicherheit' p. 4.

189 Rieger 'Der digitale Erstschlag ist erfolgt'. The commentary to Rule 10 Tallinn Manual evaluates Stuxnet as a clear case of a cyber operation amounting to a use of force, however without reasoning: Schmitt (ed) *Tallinn Manual on the International Law Applicable to Cyber Warfare* p. 45 para. 9; a minority of the group of experts drafting the Manual even opined it to have amounted to an armed attack: ibid p. 58 para. 13. Contrariwise Stuxnet has also been qualified as a 'legal masterpiece' by not reaching the threshold of illegality as long as no damage of a physical nature has been inflicted: Katharina Ziolkowski 'Stuxnet – Legal Considerations' (2012) 25(3) Humanitäres Völkerrecht p. 147.

the allegations of US and Israeli involvement ultimately rest on their political role as traditional adversaries of Iran. In June 2012 Stuxnet once more became the centre of discussion due to an investigative report alleging US President Obama to have ordered the execution of Stuxnet.[190]

3.5. CONCLUSION

The reported cases so far have shown a comparatively low level of damage inflicted, mostly amounting to indirect damage the quantity of which is difficult to assess, leading some to speak of a 'cyber cold war'.[191] The question of what level of damage may be caused solely by means of computer network operations in order for the 'cyber cold war' to turn hot can therefore not be answered by reference to any particular example but is restricted to a prognosis of the technologically possible.

In any case a rise both in the number of participants in CNOs and in the number of targeted systems can be observed, both of which have increased together with the expansion of the Internet into everyday life. As the number of available targets has grown, so has the incentive and the number of potential actors capable of undertaking malicious CNOs. Over the years, CNOs have become more and more sophisticated, while the technical knowledge of the average user has declined.[192] This is due to the shift of the use of information technologies from a small circle of experts to its current widespread use. The latter is also the cause of CNOs being an option available to most States independent from their level of development. After all, in contrast to, for example, nuclear and biological weapons which require materials that are not easy to come by and entail operations to develop them that are mostly detectable and leave tell-tale by-products, the hard- and software, as well as manpower, needed for CNOs is readily available.[193]

This comparatively high availability of tools needed to undertake malicious CNOs coupled with their simplicity of application has on the one hand led many individuals to utilise these inter alia as a form of expressing (extremist) political views also however manifested through damage, such as in the Georgian and Estonian cases. On the other hand, the level of resources needed for an operation

---

190 David E. Sanger 'Obama Order Sped Up Wave of Cyberattacks Against Iran' in *The New York Times* of 1 June 2012, referring to his detailed report: David E. Sanger *Confront and Conceal: Obama's Secret Wars and Surprising Use of American Power* (Crown New York 2012).

191 McAfee *Virtual Criminology Report 2009* at <www.mcafee.com/uk/local_content/reports/virtual_criminology_report/uk_virtual_criminology_09_report.pdf> (date accessed 15 October 2010) p. 3.

192 Lipson *Tracking and Tracing Cyber-Attacks: Technical Challenges and Global Policy Issues* p. 9.

193 Robert G. Hanseman 'The Realities and Legalities of Information Warfare' (1997) 42 The Air Force Law Review p. 196.

like Stuxnet, which is not put into effect for financial gain, can only be seen as an indicator that CNOs providing such a high level of sophistication require a State actor as initiator. The qualification of Stuxnet as 'one of the first organised, well prepared attacks against major industrial resources'[194] therefore correctly describes the current state of the art of CNOs. And in late 2011 a new variant of Stuxnet labelled 'Duqu' was discovered, allegedly designed by the same programmers as Stuxnet with the goal of gathering intelligence of industrial control system manufacturers in order to be able to more easily conduct further operations against similar targets.[195] Together with the examples shown above, this shows that espionage is also of high relevance on the Internet, here becoming manifest in the form of computer network exploitation.[196]

The cases demonstrate that while the occurrence of malicious CNOs has been studied in detail on a number of occasions, their attribution to a specific actor has proved a major obstacle, in particular in connection with State actors, which has so far never been definitely achieved. Considering the higher resources available to militaries, CNOs utilised as a means of warfare have the potential to achieve graver effects than those observed in the case studies above.

194 ENISA Press Release of 7 October 2010 'EU Agency Analysis of 'Stuxnet' Malware: A Paradigm Shift in Threats and Critical Information Infrastructure Protection' (2010) at <http://enisa.europa.eu> (date accessed 28 April 2011), which argues that the appearance of this new class and dimension of malware has caused a paradigm shift in critical information infrastructure protection. This evaluation is even shared by those who evaluate the presumption of the Iranian nuclear programme as the target of Stuxnet as unrealistic, as stipulated by Gaycken *Cyberwar: Das Internet als Kriegsschauplatz*at pp. 175–80.

195 John Markoff 'New Malicious Program by Creators of Stuxnet is Suspected' in *The New York Times* of 18 October 2011, quoting the report: Symantec *W32.Duqu: The Precursor to the Next Stuxnet* at <www.symantec.com/content/en/us/enterprise/media/security_response/whitepapers/w32_duqu_the_precursor_to_the_next_stuxnet_research.pdf> (date accessed 22 October 2011), which firstly uncovered the new malware.

196 The threat posed by espionage of intellectual property has even been characterised as posing the 'most pervasive cyber threat today' in the US Department of Defense 'Department of Defense Strategy for Operating in Cyberspace' p. 4.

CHAPTER 2
THE LEGAL REGIME OF CYBERSPACE

From the perspective of international law, the starting point in any legal evaluation of military computer network operations is the question of the regime applicable thereto. What all computer network operations have in common is their underlying technology, which in most cases will in one way or another utilise the public Internet, the technical background of which has been outlined above. Based on these findings, the intention is to analyse to what extent a legal regime has been developed that applies to conduct on the Internet.

Such a regime need not necessarily be introduced specifically for the Internet as from the outset it is clear that there is no such thing as an 'International Convention on the Internet'. However, also in the case of the law of the sea or space law, both of which have more or less widely ratified treaty regimes and a considerable amount of established customary international law, the territorial sovereignty of States has even from the outset diminished the geographical scope of the area available for regulation. General international law therefore might already have carved out certain core elements of an Internet regime.

1. JURISDICTION IN CYBERSPACE

In order to be able to qualify the legality of computer network operations by States it must first be analysed in what way the jurisdiction of States is manifested in cyberspace as a fundamental feature of sovereignty. This is of particular concern as until now the question has not been settled comprehensively.

1.1. CYBERSPACE AS A JURISDICTION SUI GENERIS

Especially at the start of the Internet's spread in the 1990s, it was a widespread view that cyberspace constitutes a sphere sui generis, outside both of State authority and legal regulations.[1] This view is exemplified by statements

1 The most widely cited document in this regard is the 'Declaration of the Independence of Cyberspace' of 1996 by John Perry Barlow, founding member of the Electronic Frontier Foundation, a 'digital rights' advocacy group. The Declaration is available at <https://projects.

describing cyberspace as an intangible virtual world or 'an abstract reality of ideas, information, and logic'.[2] 'Netiquette' was widely claimed to be able to provide a high level of self-government for this space by the Internet users themselves.[3] Others put forward propositions aimed at adopting an international framework for cyberspace including the establishment of a corresponding international organisation.[4] This somewhat idealistic understanding of the Internet was nonetheless quickly recognised to be a myth as soon as Internet use spread beyond its beginnings as a military and academic undertaking and into everyday life.[5] However, some still view cyberspace as a notional environment which lies outside the jurisdiction of any single nation.[6] Others argue that the traditional concepts of sovereignty and territoriality do not apply in relation to cyberspace, as they were connected with tangible, divisible media and discrete objects that can be located precisely. This was not the case in cyberspace, however, as both the physical location and ownership of information were too difficult to identify and ascertain since there was no tangible manifestation that could be subject to regulation under international law.[7] Cyberspace would therefore be devoid of the concept of boundaries and rather be described as borderless.[8] As a consequence, cyberspace – in contrast to the classical media of land and airspace – could neither be divided and held as sovereign territory, nor declared common and shared like the high seas or outer space, thereby precluding States from asserting territorial jurisdiction over activities on the Internet.[9] It has therefore been stated that because computer network operations are undertaken in cyberspace, there would be no State territory that could be militarily protected at its boundaries.[10]

---

eff.org/~barlow/Declaration-Final.html> (date accessed 9 May 2011). The Declaration has no legal relevance whatsoever.

2 Shackelford 'From Nuclear War to Net War: Analogizing Cyber Attacks in International Law' p. 213. Therefore some see persons 'entering the cyberspace' to shed ties of citizenship in order to become anonymous or masquerade themselves as another entity while crossing sovereign boundaries without a trace: Stephen Lukasik 'Protecting the Global Information Commons' (2000) 24 Telecommunications Policy p. 525.

3 See p. 67 below.

4 See Mayer 'Recht und Cyberspace' pp. 1789–91.

5 Stephan Wilske & Teresa Schiller 'International Jurisdiction in Cyberspace: Which States May Regulate the Internet?' (1997–1998) 50 Federal Communications Law Journal pp. 120–21.

6 As for example stated in the International Institute of Humanitarian Law (ed) *Rules of Engagement Handbook* (IIHL San Remo 2009) p. 15.

7 Kanuck 'Information Warfare: New Challenges for Public International Law' p. 287.

8 Hughes 'A Treaty for Cyberspace' pp. 539–40. It has been suggested that the challenges brought about by threats in cyberspace may ultimately lie in abandoning the prevalent adherence to territoriality and developing new governance systems: Brenner *Cyberthreats: The Emerging Fault Lines of the Nation State* p. 302.

9 Kanuck 'Information Warfare: New Challenges for Public International Law' p. 286.

10 As stated by Gebhard Geiger *Offensive Informationskriegsführung: Die Joint Doctrine for Information Operations der US-Streitkräfte: Sicherheitspolitische Perspektiven* (SWP Berlin 2002) p. 10.

Still others conclude the exact opposite from the ambiguity surrounding the concept of territoriality in cyberspace. The lack of national boundaries and territory could enable States to consider the global information infrastructure as a whole to rest within their own territory, with the consequence they that could claim jurisdiction over it and take action to defend it against foreign influence.[11]

1.2. CYBERSPACE AS AN INTERNATIONAL COMMONS

A related conception of jurisdiction in cyberspace is given by those who view it as an international commons or common heritage of mankind, with conceptual analogies to the regime of the law of the sea and outer space.[12] One can understand those areas outside national jurisdiction – traditionally outer space, Antarctica, the seabed and the high seas – to fall under the concept of international commons.[13] If cyberspace were understood as an international commons this would have grave consequences for the freedom of action of States in undertaking computer network operations and for the level of their sovereignty in this field in general. It would be a similar case if cyberspace were viewed as part of the common heritage of mankind. This principle creates general legal obligations as to the utilisation of the international commons, which under this principle shall only be exploited for peaceful purposes and for the benefit of whole mankind, while for some – albeit to a lesser degree – such intangible notions as cultural and natural heritage are also covered by the principle.[14]

---

11 A.A. Streltsov 'International Information Security: Description and Legal Aspects' (2007) 3 Disarmament Forum p. 11.

12 Wegener 'Der unsichtbare Feind: Die neuen Gefahrenlagen im digitalen Raum' p. 57; Antonio Segura-Serrano 'Internet Regulation and the Role of International Law' (2006) 10 Max Planck Yearbook of United Nations Law pp. 254–60; Graham H. Todd 'Armed Attack in Cyberspace: Deterring Asymmetric Warfare with an Asymmetric Definition' (2009) 64 Air Force Law Review p. 97; the US National Security Council *Cyberspace Policy Review: Assuring a Trusted and Resilient Information and Communications Infrastructure* at <www.whitehouse.gov/assets/documents/Cyberspace_Policy_Review_final.pdf> (date accessed 17 March 2010) calls for further study of this question (at B-4).

13 On the meaning of the term international commons see Rüdiger Wolfrum *Die Internationalisierung staatsfreier Räume: Die Entwicklung einer internationalen Verwaltung für Antarktis, Weltraum, Hohe See und Meeresboden* (Springer Berlin 1984) pp. 4–9 giving an overview of further (diverging) understandings of the notion.

14 See Arts. 4 and 11(1) Agreement Governing the Activities of States on the Moon and Other Celestial Bodies (adopted 5 December 1979, entered into force 11 July 1984) 1363 UNTS 3 and Art. 136 United Nations Convention on the Law of the Sea (concluded 10 December 1982, entered into force 16 November 1994) 1833 UNTS 396. On the natural and cultural heritage see Rüdiger Wolfrum 'Common Heritage of Mankind' in Rüdiger Wolfrum (ed) *MPEPIL* (OUP Oxford Update 2009) paras. 4–10 and 25; Segura-Serrano 'Internet Regulation and the Role of International Law' pp. 249–54. Whether the common heritage of mankind is a principle, concept or doctrine – on this see Kemal Baslar *The Concept of the Common Heritage*

The common heritage principle – although not precisely defined – is generally considered to encompass five core elements: (i) the absence of a right to appropriation or occupation, (ii) the duty to exploit the resources in the interest and benefit of all mankind, (iii) the duty to explore and exploit only for peaceful reasons, (iv) the duty to pay due regard to scientific interests, and (v) the duty to protect the environment.[15] Put together, these elements establish an obligation of cooperation which can inter alia be put into effect by a common management system.[16]

If it is to be qualified as part of the common heritage of mankind, regulation and utilisation of the Internet would have to adhere to these rules mentioned above, which for its proponents would mean that:[17] (i) the Internet's 'resource', the data it transmits, may not be appropriated, and its governance shall be transferred to an internationally legitimised institution;[18] (ii) it should benefit all mankind: everyone on a non-discriminatory basis should thus be able to connect to the Internet and be eligible to interact on an equal basis; an institution protecting these interests could be set up or the competences of the ICANN expanded, but removed from the oversight of the United States; (iii) the Internet may only be used for peaceful purposes, which could oblige States to refrain from utilising military CNOs. The latter two elements in the previous paragraph – (iv) and (v), the duty to protect the environment and to pay due regard to scientific interests – are not seen as being of great significance in relation to the Internet. For something comparable to environmental protection, one could only envisage the protection of the physical Internet infrastructure as a means of preservation to allow future generations to benefit from it.[19] In summary, the qualification of the Internet as a part of the common heritage of mankind would mean that the care for its well-being – namely the unimpeded functioning of the network infrastructure – would have to be seen as a common concern for all States, thereby establishing an obligation to cooperate in this regard.

Yet this view cannot be supported. Cyberspace is not an area outside of national jurisdiction, hence an international commons, nor does it share the features commonly connected with the principle of a common heritage of

of Mankind in International Law (Nijhoff The Hague 1998) pp. 2 and 3 – shall not be discussed here, as it is of no relevance for cyberspace which will be shown below.

15 Antonio Cassese *International Law* (OUP Oxford 2005) p. 93; Wolfrum 'Common Heritage of Mankind' para. 26.

16 Wolfrum 'Common Heritage of Mankind' para. 26.

17 As listed in Shackelford 'From Nuclear War to Net War: Analogizing Cyber Attacks in International Law' pp. 212–13, and Segura-Serrano 'Internet Regulation and the Role of International Law' pp. 254–60.

18 One proposal put forward is to use the regimes of international waterways or trusteeship systems as a model by limiting sovereignty of the trustee over the entity: Sean Kanuck 'Sovereign Discourse on Cyber Conflict under International Law' (2010) 88 Texas Law Review pp. 1579–80.

19 Segura-Serrano 'Internet Regulation and the Role of International Law' p. 260.

mankind. While the international commons were once seen as being subjectable to purely national interests, this was changed by the upcoming view of a need to take into account the interests of the world community as exemplified through the principle of a common heritage of mankind.[20] A comparable situation does not exist for cyberspace. While the seabed and celestial bodies are physically manifest and measureable, their major difference from land is that they lie outside the territory of States and thus outside of States' primary jurisdiction. Cyberspace on the other hand is a creation of mankind which was from its very beginning subject to national jurisdictions. This is due to the fact that both the computer systems as well as the cables, switches and routers from which the Internet infrastructure is composed of are physically manifest and for the most part located on State territory, thereby falling under some genuine national jurisdiction.[21]

The reasoning behind placing international commons such as the seabed and celestial bodies in outer space under a regime of limited utilisation through the principle of a common heritage of mankind was due to the assumed presence of mineral resources and the inability of the majority of States – especially developing countries – to gain access to those resources. If this assumption of existing resources proves to be correct, only technologically highly developed countries would be able to exploit them. It was therefore in the interest especially of developing countries to declare the seabed beyond the exclusive economic zone to be part of the common heritage.[22] The idea of an international management paired with the prohibition of military installations and weapons on such territory is an implementation of the obligation to preserve the heritage for future generations as part of the concepts of intergenerational equity and sustainable development. By mainly being concerned with securing and distributing resources the common heritage principle is ultimately a resource-oriented approach.[23] Cyberspace on the other hand does not possess a resource

20 Wolfrum *Die Internationalisierung staatsfreier Räume: Die Entwicklung einer internationalen Verwaltung für Antarktis, Weltraum, Hohe See und Meeresboden* p. 707.

21 The sole exception being submarine cables lying on the bed of the high seas and thus outside the exclusive jurisdiction of a State, as there is no rule comparable to that of flag State jurisdiction under Art. 92 UN Convention on the Law of the Sea existing for submarine pipelines or cables. The rules of international law applicable to the latter, which are vital for the functioning of the worldwide Internet, are stipulated in the UN Convention on the Law of the Sea in which they are treated (with few exceptions) in the same manner as submarine pipelines (see generally Rainer Lagoni 'Pipelines' in Rüdiger Wolfrum (ed) *MPEPIL* (OUP Oxford Update 2011) and Sarah Wolf *Unterseeische Rohrleitungen und Meeresumweltschutz: Eine völkerrechtliche Untersuchung am Beispiel der Ostsee* (Springer Heidelberg 2011) pp. 39–41. Nevertheless, States which lay cables (in practice mostly undertaken by the commercial sector) have limited sovereign rights over these stemming from the freedom to lay and operate cables on the bed of the high seas, which can only be given effect if States are then also entitled to a legal regulation and its enforcement (ibid at pp. 126–28).

22 Cassese *International Law* pp. 96–97.

23 Klaus Bosselmann *The Principle of Sustainability: Transforming Law and Governance* (Ashgate Aldershot 2008) p. 164.

comparable to those natural resources so valuable for the whole of mankind. That is why the proposition of treating it as a common resource as in the case of international environmental law, obliging States to an equitable utilisation thereof, is likewise unfounded.[24] The only 'resource' inherent in cyberspace is its underlying infrastructure and the information resident therein and travelling therethrough as data packets, as well as the services the creation of which the Internet has made possible and accessible. Even when viewing these as a resource, the main difference with natural resources lies in their non-exhaustibility, making their preservation superfluous. Not only does this apply to data, but also to the physical infrastructure, which can easily be rebuilt and is already currently subject to constant change due to technological improvements.

Furthermore, the notion of peaceful purposes also encompassed under the common heritage principle has not yet been given a generally accepted definition but is applied only on a case-by-case basis.[25] The seabed for example is not to be seen as a completely demilitarised zone.[26] Likewise there also does not exist a prohibition on the use of space for military means.[27] Only the testing and stationing of nuclear weapons or any other weapons of mass destruction in outer space or on the moon or other celestial bodies is explicitly forbidden by some treaties.[28] Hence even if cyberspace qualifies as a common heritage, this alone could not lead to its demilitarisation.

1.3. THE TERRITORIALISATION OF CYBERSPACE

The fact that cyberspace is lacking the quality of an international commons or a sphere sui generis is further exemplified by the manner in which States assert jurisdiction in Internet-related cases. Through the territoriality and nationality principles jurisdiction of States – to prescribe, adjudicate and enforce – is generally mostly linked to a State's defined territory and permanent population

---

24 As proposed by Torsten Stein & Thilo Marauhn 'Völkerrechtliche Aspekte von Informationsoperationen' (2000) 60(1) Zeitschrift für ausländisches öffentliches Recht und Völkerrecht pp. 21–22.

25 Alexander Proelß 'Peaceful Purposes' in Rüdiger Wolfrum (ed) *MPEPIL* (OUP Oxford Update 2009) para. 22.

26 This can both be seen by the inclusion of Art. 301 UN Convention on the Law of the Sea and the second section of Art. 141 UN Convention on the Law of the Sea: Rüdiger Wolfrum 'Restricting the Use of the Sea to Peaceful Purposes: Demilitarization in Being?' (1981) 24 German Yearbook of International Law p. 226; Proelß 'Peaceful Purposes' para. 19.

27 Shackelford 'From Nuclear War to Net War: Analogizing Cyber Attacks in International Law' p. 220.

28 See the Treaty Banning Nuclear Weapon Tests in the Atmosphere, in Outer Space and under Water (signed 5 August 1963, entered into force 10 October 1963) 480 UNTS 43 and Art. 4 Treaty on Principles Governing the Activities of States in the Exploration and Use of Outer Space Including the Moon and other Celestial Bodies (signed 27 January 1967, entered into force 10 October 1967) 610 UNTS 205.

with the consequence of a State having jurisdiction on the one hand over all persons, property and activity on its territory and on the other hand over its nationals irrespective of their location.[29]

1.3.1. *Jurisdiction to Prescribe*

The geographical scope of territorial jurisdiction which includes the adjacent sea of States and their airspace is therefore well defined. As cyberspace is not a 'space' adjacent to State territory which could be subject to, for example, a delimitation, the territorial jurisdiction in relation to Internet-related cases solely has recourse to the geographical location of the systems connected to the Internet, or constituting its infrastructure. This can for example be seen in the EU Council Framework Decision on Attacks against Information Systems of 2005 which only utilises the territoriality principle as a basis of jurisdiction in cases involving cross-border offences directed against the functioning of the targeted information system.[30] Its Article 10(2) obliges Member States to assert jurisdiction over cases where:

(a) the offender commits the offence when physically present on its territory, whether or not the offence is against an information system on its territory; or
(b) the offence is against an information system on its territory, whether or not the offender commits the offence when physically present on its territory.

Through this system-based approach to jurisdiction concerning Internet activities it is implicitly made clear that States have jurisdiction over all systems whatever their quality, as long as they are physically located on their State territory. This stance is also demonstrated by the large number of States that have enacted specific legislation applicable to so-called cybercrime, which has made obsolete the formerly widespread statement that the Internet was an unregulated 'legal vacuum'.[31]

Some States, such as for example China, which is known for its massive and sophisticated Internet filtering systems, have even attempted to set new technical network standards by requiring a particular technology to be incorporated into certain devices of wireless communication used in that State.[32] This stance is

---

29 Bernard H. Oxman 'Jurisdiction of States' in Rüdiger Wolfrum (ed) *MPEPIL* (OUP Oxford Update 2007) para. 11.

30 EU Council 'Framework Decision 2005/222/JHA of 24 February 2005 on Attacks against Information Systems' [2005] OJ L69/67.

31 For an overview of national cybercrime legislation see Marc D. Goodman & Susan W. Brenner 'The Emerging Consensus on Criminal Conduct in Cyberspace' (2002) 10(2) International Journal of Law and Information Technology pp. 139–223.

32 Jack L. Goldsmith & Tim Wu *Who Controls the Internet? Illusions of a Borderless World* (OUP Oxford 2006) p. 101.

also reiterated by China in international fora by stating that 'each country has the right to manage its own cyberspace in accordance with its domestic legislation'.[33] The emphasis on territorialising cyberspace by the assertion of State sovereignty is part of a general consensus which can inter alia be found in the Declaration of Principles by the UN World Summit on the Information Society, stipulating that '[p]olicy authority for Internet-related public policy issues is the sovereign right of States. They have rights and responsibilities for international Internet-related public policy issues'.[34] The same holds true for the field of international domain name law, where it is a generally accepted principle that the ultimate public policy authority over the country code top-level domains (such as .uk, .de, .fr, etc.) belongs to the relevant government or public authority.[35]

1.3.2. Jurisdiction to Adjudicate

A further example of how States exercise jurisdiction pertaining to Internet activity – in this instance in the form of adjudication – can be seen in their application of the effects principle in relation to content-related cases in particular.[36] Digital content referred to as being stored 'on the Internet' is actually hosted on systems connected to the global networks, thereby making it accessible from almost anywhere in the world. In this respect the problem often arises that a dissemination of the particular content is deemed legal in the country of origin, but illegal in a third country.[37] This can be the case both with

---

33 Chinese Statement of 24 May 2006 in UNGA 'Developments in the Field of Information and Telecommunications in the Context of International Security: Report of the Secretary-General' (18 July 2006) UN Doc A/61/161 at p. 4.

34 Para. 49(a) UN WSIS 'Declaration of Principles: Building the Information Society: A Global Challenge in the New Millennium (12 December 2003)' (2003) at <www.itu.int/wsis/docs/geneva/official/dop.html> (date accessed 17 December 2009); on this see also Robert Uerpmann-Wittzack 'Internetvölkerrecht' (2009) 47 Archiv des Völkerrechts pp. 261–62.

35 As stipulated in paras. 4.1 and 7.1 ICANN Governmental Advisory Committee 'Principles and Guidelines for the Delegation and Administration of Country Code Top Level Domains' (done 5 April 2005) <http://gac.icann.org/system/files/ccTLD_Principles_0.pdf> (date accessed 19 July 2010). The Governmental Advisory Committee consists of members appointed by national governments and is entrusted to consider and provide advice on the activities of ICANN as they relate to concerns of governments, especially where they may affect public policy issues. While it functions solely as an advisory body to ICANN, lacking any decision-making power, in practice ICANN's Board of Directors has apparently always adhered to the recommendations of the Governmental Advisory Committee: Woltag 'Internet' para. 10, referring to Hans-Georg Dederer 'ICANN und die Dominanz der USA: Internet Governance auf dem Weg in die Internationalisierung' (2009) 47 Archiv des Völkerrechts p. 384.

36 Another possibility of a basis of jurisdiction is seen in invoking the protective principle in cases where Internet espionage or sabotage threatens the security of a State: Oxman 'Jurisdiction of States' paras. 27–28 and 32.

37 As was the case, e.g., in *La Ligue Contre Le Racisme et L'Antisemitisme v Yahoo!, Inc.* ([20 November 2000] Tribunal de Grande Instance Paris), concerning the hosting of an offer

content qualified as morally offensive and therefore used in criminal proceedings or infringing other legally protected interests, which in practice mainly concerns intellectual property and anti-trust cases. Ultimately it is this divergence between the globality of the Internet and the differing local values which poses the major obstacle for any coherent content-related regulation of the Internet on the international level. National courts are thus often confronted with cases concerning actions originating from abroad but having effects within their jurisdiction to adjudicate. In this regard the application of the effects principle grants jurisdiction to a State which experiences the effects of an action on its territory, as already recognised in the *Lotus Case*.[38] While most domestic courts in these cases base their jurisdiction on the effects principle, the interpretation of its scope and content varies considerably.[39] Yet despite these divergences, jurisprudence does show a common trend towards limiting the effects principle in Internet-related cases by requiring the element of a deliberate influence in the foreign State as a prerequisite for establishing a genuine link between the offence and its effects on the forum State.[40]

The application of the effects principle consequently depicts States' understanding of cyberspace as neither a coherently regulated area nor regime in such a way as to exclude the application of domestic jurisdiction. By requiring the element of a deliberate influence on the forum State, courts likewise limit the overlapping of jurisdictions to those instances where the originator aims at the forum State thereby excluding the assertion of universal jurisdiction over any Internet activity.

---

of Nazi memorabilia on the US based Yahoo! auction portal, an action constituting a crime under French penal law.

38 *The 'Lotus' (France v Turkey)* PCIJ Series A No 10 p. 23.

39 Stefanie Schmahl 'Zwischenstaatliche Kompetenzabgrenzung im Cyberspace' (2009) 47 Archiv des Völkerrechts pp. 300–09; Menno T. Kamminga 'Extraterritoriality' in Rüdiger Wolfrum (ed) *MPEPIL* (OUP Oxford Update 2008) para. 15.

40 Woltag 'Internet' para. 19; Schmahl 'Zwischenstaatliche Kompetenzabgrenzung im Cyberspace' p. 309 et seq. A recent example of this trend can also be seen in the jurisprudence of the ECJ: In *Peter Pammer v Reederei Karl Schlüter GmbH & Co KG and Hotel Alpenhof GesmbH v Oliver Heller* (ECJ) Joined Cases C-585/08 and C-144/09 (7 December 2010) the ECJ stipulates some minimal requirements which have to be met in order to consider a trader's activity via a publicly accessible Internet website as directed to consumers in other EU Member States, thereby qualifying the activity as one of an international nature; under US law a similar change concerning personal jurisdiction in Internet related cases is taking place from the so-called *Zippo* test introduced by *Zippo Mfg Co v Zippo Dot Com, Inc* (US District Court WD Pennsylvania [16 January 1997] 952 F.Supp. 1119) towards an approach taking into account the intent of the defendant to target a specific forum state; see Holger P. Hestermayer 'Transboundary Harm: Internet Torts' in Rebecca M. Bratspies & Russell A. Miller (eds) *Transboundary Harm in International Law: Lessons from the Trail Smelter Arbitration* (CUP Cambridge 2006) pp. 271–73. Similarly in respect to conflicts of jurisdictions in general: Torsten Stein & Christian von Buttlar *Völkerrecht* (Heymann Köln 2009) p. 220.

2. ACTORS IN CYBERSPACE

Drawing upon the demonstrated legal territorialisation of cyberspace, the second step in the analysis of its regime is concerned with the actors exercising authority on the Internet. As a man-made technical entity, the Internet is to a large degree shaped and administrated by private actors. Such actors do not however have public authority, unless it has been assigned to them by States, which is partially already the case. But States have also themselves begun to create institutions which exercise public authority in a sovereign manner on the Internet. In the following, the major actors on the Internet will be introduced, which mainly consist of those involved with Internet governance and security. Further it will be shown how militaries have begun to establish special units within the armed forces responsible for conducting computer network operations via the Internet.

2.1. INTERNATIONAL INTERNET REGULATION

Unlike with other technologies, regulation has accompanied the development of the Internet since its very beginning, not through an imposition by public authorities, but mostly in the form of self-regulation. The trigger for any such regulation was at first merely the high technical demands posed by the infrastructure and architecture of the Internet.[41] This has led to the situation that there now exist several non-State actors which deal to some extent with the regulation or governance of the Internet.

2.1.1. Internet Governance

The content of the term 'Internet governance' even today remains somewhat vague. It can be understood both from a legal and technical perspective, which do not necessarily coincide.[42]

---

41 Hanno Kube 'Neue Medien – Internet' in Josef Isensee & Paul Kirchhof (eds) *Handbuch des Staatsrechts der Bundesrepublik Deutschland vol. 4: Aufgaben des Staates* (CF Müller Heidelberg 2006) para. 9.

42 The 2005 UN World Summit on the Information Society ('WSIS') Tunis Agenda for the Information Society gave a broad definition of Internet governance, namely: 'the development and application by governments, the private sector and civil society, in their respective roles, of shared principles, norms, rules, decision-making procedures, and programmes that shape the evolution and use of the Internet' para. 34 UN WSIS 'Tunis Agenda for the Information Society (18 November 2005)' (2005) at <www.itu.int/wsis/docs2/tunis/off/6rev1.pdf> (date accessed 27 April 2010). By making reference to practically any activity of any actor that can potentially shape the use of the Internet this definition goes far beyond the mere administration of the Domain Name System, which is traditionally understood as the core of Internet governance. In the following recourse will not be made to this wide definition, as

Traditionally it refers to the administration of the core functions of the Internet's infrastructure which is mostly of a technical nature, and due to the historic origin of the Internet originally rested with the authority of the US government. This was particularly the case for the administration of the Domain Name System ('DNS'). The DNS, which is a hierarchical naming system for computer systems and similar devices, is broadly comparable to that of a telephone book. It provides the technical framework which enables devices capable of connecting to the Internet to communicate with each other. The DNS makes it possible to assign a name to a specific computer resource and translates domain names – which were only introduced in order to be easily understandable and memorisable by humans – into the relevant Internet Protocol addresses.[43] This is important because control over the DNS and the so-called root zone file ultimately confers de facto control over who can allocate domain names to end users and thereby indirectly has an influence on the terms and conditions of registering a domain name.[44] Theoretically the controller of the DNS can therefore render certain websites inaccessible.[45]

Because of the Internet's origins as a project of the United States, the latter originally fulfilled the core elements of administration. In 1998 these core functions – the administration of the DNS – were partly handed over to the Internet Corporation for Assigned Names and Numbers ('ICANN'), as formulated in the Memorandum of Understanding between the US Department of Commerce and ICANN (commonly known as the Joint Project Agreement).[46] According to this, the US Department of Commerce promoted the privatisation of the technical management of the DNS. However, before making a transition to private-sector DNS management, the Department of Commerce required 'assurances that the private sector has the capability and resources to assume the important responsibilities related to the technical management of the DNS'.[47] Therefore, the Department of Commerce and ICANN were to 'jointly design, develop, and test the mechanisms, methods, and procedures that will achieve the transition'.[48]

---

already the legitimacy of governing the core functions is highly disputed, and the WSIS definition too wide to be able to carry content of a legal import.

43 Woltag 'Internet' para. 6; Lindsay *International Domain Name Law: ICANN and the UDRP* pp. 3–8. The functions of the DNS are specified in P. Mockapetris 'Domain Names – Concepts and Facilities' (November 1987) Request for Comments 1034. For example <www.mpil.de> is translated into the Internet Protocol address 149.217.72.46 (on 13 March 2012).

44 Lindsay *International Domain Name Law: ICANN and the UDRP* p. 32.

45 Although limited as to the extent to which name servers accept the root zone file as authoritative, which from a technological standpoint is not necessary: Lindsay *International Domain Name Law: ICANN and the UDRP* p. 32.

46 Memorandum of Understanding between the U.S. Department of Commerce and Internet Corporation for Assigned Names and Numbers (25 November 1998) www.icann.org/en/general/icann-mou-25nov98.htm (date accessed 10 August 2011).

47 Para. II B Joint Project Agreement.

48 Para. II B Joint Project Agreement; Woltag 'Internet' para. 8.

ICANN is itself comprised of mainly private but also public actors and makes binding decisions on both the architecture of the Internet and the policies on the DNS, including the creation and assignment of both generic and country code top-level domains (such as .com, .uk, .de, etc.). It is also responsible for the allocation and delegation of IP addresses, which it manages via the Internet Assigned Numbers Authority.[49] Even though these far-reaching competencies are mostly limited to decisions of a technical nature, the consequences thereof may be of a content- and political-related character,[50] which is the case for example in the creation of top-level domains for territories the independence of which is disputed. The powers are mainly exercised by ICANN's Board of Directors, the members of which are selected by various stakeholders from the Internet community – i.e. the registries, commercial and regular users – thus representing a bottom-up approach excluding direct governmental involvement. It is this structure of ICANN that qualifies Internet governance for many as one of self-regulation.[51]

Article XI(2)(1)(a) ICANN Bylaws does however provide for an institutionalised possibility for governments to voice their concerns regarding ICANN's Board of Directors.[52] This so-called Governmental Advisory Committee shall advise the Board particularly in matters where there is an interaction between ICANN's policies and various laws and international agreements or where they may affect public policy issues. Membership of the Committee is open to all national governments and currently has 109 members. But as it functions solely as an advisory body without any decision-making power, governmental influence on ICANN other than that of the United States technically remains at a very low level. The practice of the Board of Directors demonstrates differently, however, as it has apparently always adhered to the recommendations of the Committee.[53] Nevertheless it must be noted that this level of cooperation is merely of a voluntary nature. Even the Operating Principles of the Governmental Advisory Committee state that both the ICANN Bylaws and Articles of Incorporation prevail over the Committee's Operating Principles in case of a difference in interpretation.[54]

---

49 These are allocated batch-wise to Regional Internet Registries pursuant to the IANA Policy for Allocation of IPv4 Blocks to Regional Internet Registries or the Policy For Allocation of IPv6 Blocks to Regional Internet Registries, respectively, which in turn reallocate them to local internet registries such as Internet service providers. The latter assign IP addresses to end users.

50 Kube 'Neue Medien – Internet' para. 9.

51 See generally Woltag 'Internet' paras. 8 et seq.

52 ICANN 'Bylaws for Internet Corporation for Assigned Names and Numbers' (effective as of 6 November 1998, as amended 24 June 2011) www.icann.org/en/general/bylaws.htm (date accessed 10 August 2011).

53 Dederer 'ICANN und die Dominanz der USA: Internet Governance auf dem Weg in die Internationalisierung' p. 384.

54 Art. XV ICANN Governmental Advisory Committee 'Principles and Guidelines for the Delegation and Administration of Country Code Top Level Domains' (done 5 April 2005).

Due to these far-reaching competencies, the question of legitimacy of ICANN's decisions soon came up and is still heavily questioned today.[55] In a 1998 White Paper the US stated that it would allow the private sector to take leadership for DNS management.[56] In the Internet community, hopes were therefore high that ICANN, as a hybrid between an online community and real-world governance structure, would cause the Internet to be self-regulated by its community.[57] But ICANN remained under contract with the US Department of Commerce despite its establishment as a non-profit organisation under Californian Nonprofit Public-Benefit Corporation Law, causing the corporation to be seen critically from the very start. This is equally due to the involvement of the US government in the corporation's creation, its internal governance structure and it being subject both to the state laws of California and US federal law.[58] Further, in 2005 the United States announced that it will maintain its role as the keeper of the root zone file, and will thus from a technical standpoint be in control of Internet governance.[59] While ICANN can therefore be seen as the most important actor in the field of Internet governance, for some the level of political supervision and control by the US government over ICANN is regarded as so high as to qualify ICANN as a quasi-public authority.[60]

This lack of democratic legitimacy and the dominance of the United States over Internet governance was addressed at the 2003 UN WSIS in Geneva, where most developing countries, China and the G20 proposed a shift in governance from ICANN to an intergovernmental level such as the International Telecommunication Union.[61] As a concession especially to pressure from the

55 Andrew D. Murray *The Regulation of Cyberspace: Control in the Online Environment* (Routledge-Cavendish Abingdon 2007) pp. 114–18.

56 US Department of Commerce 'Management of Internet Names and Addresses' Federal Register (1998).

57 *The Economist* of 8–14 June 2000 'The Consensus Machine'.

58 Woltag 'Internet' para. 8. For a critique see inter alia Jochen von Bernstorff 'Democratic Global Internet Regulation? Governance Networks, International Law and the Shadow of Hegemony' (2003) 9 European Law Journal pp. 511–26, who characterises ICANN's governance structure as an instrument of hegemony; and Matthias Hartwig 'ICANN – Governance by Technical Necessity' in Armin von Bogdandy & Rüdiger Wolfrum (eds) *The Exercise of Public Authority by International Institutions: Advancing International Institutional Law* (Springer Heidelberg 2010) pp. 575–605.

59 The root zone file contains the list of computer systems that have the master lists for registrations in each top level domain. Control over these data allows a considerable de facto control which top-level domains are visible to a majority of Internet users; Michael Froomkin 'Habermas@discourse.net: Toward a Critical Theory of Cyberspace' (2002) 116(3) Harvard Law Review p. 839; Lindsay *International Domain Name Law: ICANN and the UDRP* pp. 20–21.

60 Dederer 'ICANN und die Dominanz der USA: Internet Governance auf dem Weg in die Internationalisierung' pp. 377–79.Others qualify it as a 'hybrid public-private body': Benedict Kingsbury & Megan Donaldson 'Global Administrative Law' in Rüdiger Wolfrum (ed) *MPEPIL* (OUP Oxford Update 2011) para. 39.

61 Sabine von Schorlemer 'Telecommunications, International Regulation' in Rüdiger Wolfrum (ed) *MPEPIL* (OUP Oxford Update 2009) para. 133.

European Union, the Internet Governance Forum ('IGF') was established as a meeting for multi-stakeholder policy dialogue, in order to allow governments to debate Internet policy matters and issue recommendations.[62] However, para. 72(a) and (j) Tunis Agenda for the Information Society merely gives the IGF the mandate to, inter alia, discuss issues relating to critical Internet resources and public policy issues related to key elements of Internet governance in order to foster the security of the Internet but giving the IGF no decision-making powers. Therefore the existing system with ICANN remaining the administrator of core elements of Internet governance has been retained.

This form of governance does not however encompass questions directly relating to military computer network operations. While ICANN itself has stated that it is willing to collaborate with governments in 'combating malicious activity enabled by abuse of the systems to assist in protection of these systems',[63] it is under no legal obligation to do so. First and foremost ICANN has in any case stated that it does not play a role:

(i) in policing the Internet or operationally combating criminal behaviour, or
(ii) in use of Internet related to cyber-espionage and cyber war, or
(iii) in determining what constitutes illicit content on the Internet.[64]

2.1.2. *Technical Regulation*

Other actors which are mainly active in the field of technical regulation include the Internet Society, a non-profit organisation incorporated in Washington DC, which claims to provide leadership in Internet-related standards, education and policy. Further it is the 'organisational home' of the Internet Engineering Task Force, an open international community consisting mainly of IT professionals, which in turn is responsible for Internet protocol standardisation.[65] Also of significance is the World Wide Web Consortium, taking care of the standardisation of computer languages used on the Internet. Although the decisions of the aforementioned bodies are mostly of a technical nature, they often simultaneously entail political or content-based decisions, as for example the definition of industry standards may have major economic impact on competitors. Despite these concerns, most bodies are constituted as private companies, non-profit organisations, or are not constituted at all, lacking any form of formal membership. Their democratic legitimisation is therefore, just as

---

62 Goldsmith & Wu *Who Controls the Internet? Illusions of a Borderless World*p. 171; UN WSIS 'Tunis Agenda for the Information Society (18 November 2005)' paras. 72–73.

63 ICANN 'Plan for Enhancing Internet Security, Stability, and Resiliency' p. 8.

64 ICANN 'Plan for Enhancing Internet Security, Stability, and Resiliency' p. 3.

65 The IETF itself provides for an overview of its activities in an informational RFC: P. Hoffman and S. Harris 'The Tao of IETF: A Novice's Guide to the Internet Engineering Task Force' (September 2006) Request for Comments 4677.

that of ICANN, heavily contested.[66] Nonetheless, many of their decisions have become de facto standards for the technical functioning of the Internet.

2.1.3. *Content Regulation*

On the international level, genuinely content-based regulation lags far behind its technical counterpart. Codes of conduct as introduced by Internet service providers vary even within individual jurisdictions and are, if not embedded within a legally binding framework, hardly able to create a uniform structure.[67] It was in the early days of the Internet that a small and homogenous group of users existed that could easily agree to so-called 'netiquette', a kind of customary code of conduct between Internet users.[68] The often vainly invoked netiquette has not however, at least in terms of legally binding arrangements, managed to create any international consensus. Voices suggesting a genuine 'cyberlaw' applicable to actions via the Internet that conflicts with, or even excludes, sovereign regulation cannot be justified from a legal perspective.[69] Even the DNS managed by ICANN, which in its effects might be considered a transnational legal regime, ultimately remains subject to US jurisdiction and oversight.[70] Therefore there exists no organisation vested with the right of content-based regulation on the international level, apart from the domain name dispute resolution system established by ICANN, which is however mostly of economic importance and does not play a role for issues of security.

2.2. INTERNET SECURITY ORGANISATIONS

While the organisations involved in the technical regulation of the Internet referred to above are involved in promoting security on the Internet via standard-setting, several other organisations have also been established that specifically deal with Internet security.

66 Kube 'Neue Medien – Internet' para. 9.

67 Kube 'Neue Medien – Internet' para. 10.

68 Schmahl 'Zwischenstaatliche Kompetenzabgrenzung im Cyberspace' p. 284. An attempt to establish a netiquette can be seen in the RFC by S. Hambridge 'Netiquette Guidelines' (October 1995) Request for Comments 1855.

69 Arguing that the 'Net can develop its own effective legal institutions': David R. Johnson & David Post 'Law and Borders – The Rise of Law in Cyberspace' (1996) 48(5) Stanford Law Review at p. 1387 et seq; the authors argue that individuals were entitled to create spheres exempt from State authority whereas users joining the sphere would thereby give a tacit approval to accept and comply with the rules created by the founders. Opposing this approach see generally: Jack L. Goldsmith 'Against Cyberanarchy' (1998) 65(4) The University of Chicago Law Review pp. 1199 et seq; Goldsmith & Wu *Who Controls the Internet? Illusions of a Borderless World*; Kube 'Neue Medien – Internet' para. 10.

70 Matthias Herdegen 'International Economic Law' in Rüdiger Wolfrum (ed) *MPEPIL* (OUP Oxford Update 2011) para. 16.

The International Telecommunication Union for example launched the Global Cybersecurity Agenda in 2007, an international framework for cooperation in the field of information society. Under this agenda several documents on cybercrime have been issued which inter alia promote the legal harmonisation of national criminal laws in the field of cybercrime.[71] The International Organization for Standardization as the largest creator of voluntary technical standards has in collaboration with the International Electrotechnical Commission developed a family of standards setting up an information security management system, the ISO/IEC 27000 family of standards. As the standards are rather broad and are thus applicable to all kinds of businesses and processes, the family may possibly achieve such widespread compliance as the well-known ISO 9000 series.[72] On the European level, the European Network and Information Security Agency was established in 2004.[73] Institutionalised as a 'policy agency' in the EU system, it is envisaged to provide expertise in order to assist EU institutions and Member States in ensuring a high and effective level of network and information security within the EU.

While these organisations address the issues of computer security from a preventive side, none of them is vested with law-making powers or can issue decisions of a legally binding nature; they are instead restricted to distributing recommendations or best practices.

The first major computer security incident on the Internet, which is mostly seen in the so-called Morris Worm of November 1988, led to the establishment of a new type of security organisation inter alia assigned with reactive functions: the Computer Emergency Response Team ('CERT').[74] Typical tasks of CERTs include proactive and reactive services. These are typically helping to prepare, protect, and secure constituent systems in anticipation of attacks (proactive), and the provision of incident response and coordination capabilities, collecting forensic evidence and handling vulnerabilities (reactive).[75] The powers of a CERT over its constituencies depend on the relevant statutory framework or company policy and can consequentially not be generalised. A start was made by

---

71 e.g. the ITU 'Toolkit for Cybercrime Legislation', the 'Understanding Cybercrime: A Guide for Developing Countries' and the 'National Cybersecurity/CIIP Self-Assessment Tool', all of 2009. Furthermore, a 'Botnet Mitigation Toolkit' is currently under development.

72 On the ISO in general and the ISO 9000 and 14000 families see Gerald G. Sander 'International Organization for Standardization (ISO)' in Rüdiger Wolfrum (ed) *MPEPIL* (OUP Oxford Update 2006).

73 Regulation (EC) No 460/2004 of the European Parliament and of the Council of 10 March 2004 establishing the European Network and Information Security Agency [2004] OJ L77/1.

74 Lipson *Tracking and Tracing Cyber-Attacks: Technical Challenges and Global Policy Issues* p. 5; the term 'Computer Security and Incident Response Team' (CSIRT) has been developed in order to reflect the growing level of preventive services of CERTs but both terms are generally used synonymously.

75 Moira J. West-Brown, et al. *Handbook for Computer Security Incident Response Teams (CSIRTs)* (2nd edn Carnegie Mellon University Software Engineering Institute 2003) pp. 23–35.

the US Defense Advanced Research Projects Agency which founded the first CERT and the CERT Coordination Center. Its task is to provide a central place for coordinated responses to malicious CNOs.[76] Subsequently different CERTs began to emerge all around the world, comprised of members from the government and commercial and academic sectors. In 1990, the Forum of Incident Response and Security Teams was established as a forum of voluntary cooperation between the different CERTs, of which more than 250 have now been established globally.[77] Some of these are located within public authorities, others are set up and operated privately by businesses in the information and telecommunications sector or larger companies that rely heavily on such technology.

Of heightened relevance in this regard are national CERTs, which are those protecting a government's information infrastructure.[78] In contrast to CERTs operated by companies they are responsible for large-scale operations directed against critical infrastructures and in the most cases are integrated into a State organ. The importance of establishing national CERTs is widely acknowledged in the international community which can for example be seen in the encouragement of the ITU especially for developing countries which so far do not benefit from a large number of CERTs.[79] In addition, the 'Cybersecurity Strategy' of the Organization of American States envisages their establishment and cooperation as a necessary element of cybersecurity, while the EU has already set up a CERT for its institutions in 2011.[80]

International cooperation between these national CERTs is by many seen as the best option to effectively safeguard Internet security.[81] The US International Strategy for Cyberspace of 2011 for example envisages international cooperation

76 Lipson *Tracking and Tracing Cyber-Attacks: Technical Challenges and Global Policy Issues* p. 5.

77 The Forum of Incident Response and Security Teams, according to its Operational Framework 'consists of a network of individual computer security incident response teams that work together voluntarily to deal with computer security problems and their prevention. These teams represent government, law enforcement, academia, the private sector, and other organizations with justifiable interest as determined by the Steering Committee'; FIRST Operational Framework; available at <www.first.org/about/policies/op-framework/> (date accessed 12 August 2011).

78 ITU *Global Cybersecurity Agenda: High-Level Experts Group: Global Strategic Report* at <www.itu.int/osg/csd/cybersecurity/gca/global_strategic_report/global_strategic_report.pdf> (date accessed 30 August 2011) p. 96; see also the IETF best practice document by N. Brownlee and E. Guttman 'Expectations for Computer Security Incident Response' (June 1998) Request for Comments 2350.

79 ITU-T Resolution 58 (2008) 'Encourage the Creation of National Computer Incident Response Teams, Particularly for Developing Countries'.

80 OAS General Assembly Resolution 2004 (XXXIV-O/04) 'A Comprehensive Inter-American Cybersecurity Strategy: A Multidimensional and Multidisciplinary Approach to Creating a Culture of Cybersecurity' (8 June 2004); European Commission 'Cyber Security: EU Prepares to Set Up Computer Emergency Response Team for EU Institutions (10 June 2011)' Press Release IP/11/694.

81 See only Wegener 'Harnessing the Perils in Cyberspace: Who is in Charge?' p. 47.

as the first principle to sustain and promote an open, interoperable, secure and reliable information and communications infrastructure while conceding that incident response cannot be fully addressed by any single nation but requires collaboration and information sharing with the private sector and the international community.[82] This collaboration was even characterised as a duty of every nation and its peoples by the US President in his 2011 International Strategy for Cyberspace.[83] The Convention on Cybercrime may serve as an example of this. Herein, Article 35 obliges Member States to setup a so-called 24/7 Network, meaning a

> 'point of contact available on a twenty-four hour, seven-day-a-week basis, in order to ensure the provision of immediate assistance for the purpose of investigations or proceedings concerning criminal offences related to computer systems and data, or for the collection of evidence in electronic form of a criminal offence.'

The establishment of this network was agreed to be among the most important means provided by the Cybercrime Convention of ensuring an effective response to law enforcement challenges posed by cybercrime.[84] The establishment of the network was expressly based on a similar (informal) network established by the G8 in 1997, with over 50 States currently participating.[85] In addition, Interpol has launched a 24/7 network with Member States designating national central reference points responsible for cybercrimes.[86] In these 24/7 networks it is often national CERTs that are designated as a national point of contact.

Nevertheless, aside from the 24/7 Network institutionalised through the Cybercrime Convention which is applicable only to criminal actions, cooperation between CERTs on an international level is not legally formalised.[87] Because of this solely informal status, the cooperation lacks enforceability and is further complicated by the existence of both public and private CERTs in several States, while many States still do not have such institutions at all.[88] The proliferation of organisations that deal to a certain extent with 'Internet security' witnessed in the last decade may be an important step in assuring security of domestic computer systems; however, from the perspective of international law these organisations to a large degree remain powerless. Aside from the general

82 The President of the United States of America 'International Strategy for Cyberspace' p. 8.
83 The President of the United States of America 'International Strategy for Cyberspace' pp. 9 and 19.
84 COE 'Explanatory Report to the Convention on Cybercrime' para. 298.
85 ITU *Global Cybersecurity Agenda: High-Level Experts Group: Global Strategic Report* p. 54; COE 'Explanatory Report to the Convention on Cybercrime' para. 298.
86 ITU *Global Cybersecurity Agenda: High-Level Experts Group: Global Strategic Report* p. 54.
87 Providing an overview of some forms of CERT cooperation: ENISA 'CERT Cooperation and Its Further Facilitation by Relevant Stakeholders' (2006) at <www.enisa.europa.eu> (date accessed 2 September 2011).
88 Woltag 'Cyber Warfare' para. 20.

rule-making institutions of international law there exists no international organisation specifically vested with the competence of issuing binding security policies pertaining to the Internet.

2.3. THE MILITARISATION OF CYBERSPACE

Once malicious computer network operations were perceived as representing a threat to national security, increased by the fear they could be used supplementary to conventional arms or even as a substitute, States began contemplating the installation of 'cyber units'. Under NATO's 2010 Strategic Concept 'cyber attacks' were for example qualified as able to 'reach a threshold that threatens national and Euro-Atlantic prosperity, security and stability' while 'foreign militaries and intelligence services, organised criminals, terrorist and/or extremist groups can each be the source of such attacks'.[89] NATO has generally become attentive to the issue, as can inter alia be seen by giving full accreditation to the Cooperative Cyber Defence Centre of Excellence established by Estonia in 2008, which shall enhance the alliance's capabilities in cyber defence. Furthermore, a Policy on Cyber Defence was developed (the details of which are classified, however), and in the 2008 Bucharest Summit Declaration, NATO noted that it remained committed to strengthening key alliance information systems against cyber attacks.[90] The past years have therefore witnessed an increased establishment of units specifically tasked with undertaking both defensive and offensive CNOs. These have been established not only within the armed forces, but also as offices integrated into for example ministries of the interior, and provided with the relevant operational doctrines and strategies.

2.3.1. *Within the United States Military*

The United States was and still is the most active nation in this regard. In 1996, the US Field Manual on Information Operations was issued, primarily still

89 NATO 'Strategic Concept for the Defence and Security of the Members of the North Atlantic Treaty Organisation' (19 November 2010) <www.nato.int/cps/en/natolive/official_texts_68580.htm> (date accessed 2 September 2011) at para. 12.

90 The NATO Bucharest Summit Declaration further lays emphasis on the topic in stating: 'We have recently adopted a Policy on Cyber Defence, and are developing the structures and authorities to carry it out. Our Policy on Cyber Defence emphasises the need for NATO and nations to protect key information systems in accordance with their respective responsibilities; share best practices; and provide a capability to assist Allied nations, upon request, to counter a cyber attack. We look forward to continuing the development of NATO's cyber defence capabilities and strengthening the linkages between NATO and national authorities' Heads of State and Government Participating in the Meeting of the North Atlantic Council in Bucharest on 3 April 2008 'Bucharest Summit Declaration' (2008) at <www.nato.int/docu/pr/2008/p08-049e.html> (date accessed 30 June 2012) para. 47.

focusing on command and control warfare through more traditional means such as electronic warfare.[91] The US Air Force issued a Doctrine Document on the matter in 1998.[92] By 2003 the so-called National Strategy to Secure Cyberspace was in place and in the same year the US Department of Defense issued an Informations Operations Roadmap which recommended that a national policy for offensive computer network operations should be developed, with the desired outcome of attaining 'forces trained with well-tested and reliable CNA [i.e. Computer Network Attack] weapons that are aligned with appropriate target sets and integrated with other information operation capabilities and weapons systems'.[93] Having been spread over several joint task forces, this task of 'cyberdefence' has finally been consolidated at the newly created US Cyber Command, established in May 2010. As of 2013 it is led by four-star General Keith Alexander, who is likewise Director of the National Security Agency. Constituted as a sub-unified command subordinate to the US Strategic Command, it oversees the relevant cyber commands of each military branch: the Army Forces Cyber Command, Navy Fleet Cyber Command/10th Fleet, 24th Air Force and Marine Corps Forces Cyberspace Command.[94]

Besides this increase of manpower, automated responses to cyberthreats have also been put into place in the United States. Having assessed the US to not being adequately prepared to counter the challenge of cyber conflict, the US President in 2009 established a Comprehensive National Cybersecurity Initiative, which announced the development and deployment of intrusion detection and prevention systems into government networks.[95] These systems shall have the ability to automatically detect and respond 'appropriately' to cyber threats by conducting real-time packet inspections of incoming and outgoing network traffic. While this can be read as embracing also so-called active defence

---

91 Department of the Army *Field Manual No. 100-6: Information Operations* (Department of the Army Washington DC 1996). The US military defines electronic warfare as military action involving the use of electromagnetic and directed energy to control the electromagnetic spectrum or attack the adversary. In utilising the electromagnetic spectrum, electronic warfare operates in a natural medium, thereby allowing the targeting of both humans and objects which both are susceptible to electromagnetic waves, thereby constituting a major difference to cyber warfare.

92 United States Air Force 'Air Force Doctrine Document 2-5: Information Operations' (1998).

93 US Department of Homeland Security 'The National Strategy to Secure Cyberspace 2003' (2003) at <www.dhs.gov/xlibrary/assets/National_Cyberspace_Strategy.pdf> (date accessed 25 March 2011). See the (due to nondisclosure issues partly blackened) US Department of Defense 'Information Operations Roadmap' (2003) at <www.gwu.edu/~nsarchiv/NSAEBB/NSAEBB177/info_ops_roadmap.pdf> (date accessed 5 June 2012) pp. 49–52.

94 US Air Force 'Cyberspace Operations: Air Force Doctrine Document 3-12' p. 24; Lynn 'Defending a New Domain: The Pentagon's Cyberstrategy' p. 102; US Department of Defense 'Department of Defense Strategy for Operating in Cyberspace' p. 5.

95 Executive Office of the US President 'The Comprehensive National Cybersecurity Initiative' (2009) at <www.whitehouse.gov/cybersecurity/comprehensive-national-cybersecurity-initiative> (date accessed 10 March 2010).

mechanisms,[96] the recent US Department of Defence Strategy for Operating in Cyberspace of July 2011 at least in its unclassified version is more cautious in this regard. Focus is rather placed on passive defensive measures such as strengthening networks' resilience, fostering a stronger culture of 'cyber hygiene', educating and recruiting technically skilled personnel and cooperating with both the private sector and international partners.[97]

2.3.2. *Within Other Militaries*

Like the United States all major States have issued cyberspace security policies. The United Kingdom in its Cyber Security Strategy of 2009 created two bodies: the Office of Cyber Security and the Cyber Security Operations Centre. While the Office of Cyber Security set up at the Cabinet Office is intended to provide 'strategic leadership' for coherence across the government, the Cyber Security Operations Centre has been created at the British Government Communications Headquarters, Britain's signal intelligence unit. By 'actively monitoring the health of cyber space' and coordinating incident response its role is of a more active and operational nature.[98]

While there are no official doctrines or strategies available as to the activities of the Chinese People's Liberation Army, it has reportedly already formed cyber militia units and institutionalised many of its capabilities for computer network operations within elements of the army since the late 1990s.[99] These militia units are allegedly comprised of personnel from the commercial information technology sector and academia, thus forming an operational nexus between the

96 On the legal challenges of active defence mechanisms or automated responses see pp. 159 et seq below.

97 US Department of Defense 'Department of Defense Strategy for Operating in Cyberspace' pp. 5–12. One of the major threats to military networks is actually seen in the members of the armed forces themselves. Imprudent use of information systems, especially the use of the Internet or the connection of personal electronic devices such as USB sticks to computer systems connected to classified or specially-protected networks, facilitate these to be infiltrated by malicious software. The US Department of Defense has estimated that in 2007 at least 60% of all Internet traffic of its computer systems originated from unofficial, hence private use. As consequence, such activity has now been forbidden in order to protect the department's systems: US Department of Defense 'Directive on Protection of DOD Information Systems' (2009) 64 Air Force Law Review pp. 202 et seq; further elaborating on social behaviour of military personnel as a risk for military networks: Joshua E. Kastenberg 'Changing the Paradigm of Internet Access from Government Information Systems: A Solution to the Need for the DOD to Take Time-Sensitive Action of the NIPRNET' (2009) 64 United States Air Force Law Review pp. 175 et seq.

98 UK Cabinet Office 'Cyber Security Strategy of the United Kingdom: Safety, Security and Resilience in Cyber Space (Command Papers 7642 [2009])' p. 5.

99 US-China Economic and Security Review Commission (ed) *2009 Report to Congress* pp. 173; on this issue see also the detailed report by Bryan Krekel 'Capability of the People's Republic of China to Conduct Cyber Warfare and Computer Network Exploitation: Prepared for the US-China Economic and Security Review Commission' (2009).

army and Chinese civilian information technology professionals.[100] For example, when in 2008 such an information warfare militia unit was established in Yongning County, the county government stated that during peacetime, the unit was to extensively collect information from adversary networks and establish databases of adversary network data. During wartime, the unit was to attack adversary systems and resist enemy network attacks.[101]

The German Bundeswehr reportedly likewise established a respective unit with the Abteilung Informations- und Computernetzwerkoperationen (Department of Information and Computer Network Operations).[102] Further, Germany has established the Bundesamt für Sicherheit in der Informationstechnik (Federal Office for Information Security), which inter alia is responsible for defending the security of the federal government's information technology, but also for assisting the German intelligence service.[103] Additionally on 1 April 2011, a national cyber defence centre was established under general management of the Federal Office for Information Security with the mission to optimise the cooperation between all national public authorities.

The Russian Federation, which at first encouraged a ban on any kind of information warfare capabilities, seems to have renounced this course. The Military Doctrine of the Russian Federation of 2010 rather speaks of a rise of the role of 'information confrontation' in modern military conflicts, resulting in the need to develop forces and means for such an 'information confrontation'.[104] Russia has further proclaimed a protectionist approach towards the information and communication technology industry as part of its information security doctrine. While a protectionist approach towards the arms industry is an old means of defence for many States, this is valued as particularly important with regard to information technology which is seen as posing higher security risks than traditional military goods such as 'ordinary' weapons systems running without sophisticated software.[105] As it is technically

---

100 Krekel 'Capability of the People's Republic of China to Conduct Cyber Warfare and Computer Network Exploitation: Prepared for the US-China Economic and Security Review Commission' p. 33.

101 As reported in the US-China Economic and Security Review Commission (ed) *2009 Report to Congress* p. 174; the translation from the original Chinese statement hereby being provided by the Commission's staff.

102 John Goetz, Marcel Rosenbach & Alexander Szandar 'Krieg der Zukunft' in *Der Spiegel* of July 2009 p. 34; Alard von Kittlitz 'Stuxnet und der Krieg, der kommt' in *Frankfurter Allgemeine Zeitung* of 5 December 2010. There is however no official information available as to the mission of this unit.

103 Art. 1(3) Gesetz zur Stärkung der Sicherheit in der Informationstechnik des Bundes (14 August 2009) (2009) BGBl I 2821.

104 See paras. 12(d) and 41(c) Russian Federation 'Военная доктрина Российской Федерации (Military Doctrine of the Russian Federation; no official translation available)' (5 February 2010) at <http://news.kremlin.ru/ref_notes/461> (date accessed 24 June 2010).

105 In the US, as in most countries, the majority of ICT products are developed and manufactured abroad, which according to the US Department of Defense poses challenges in managing risk

possible to purposely implement so-called 'backdoors' into software, which would allow for unauthorised third-party access, the Russian Federation has stipulated that control over the development, use, export and import of information protection tools is a principle of its information security policy. Furthermore, the domestic Russian market is envisaged to be protected by measures against its penetration through 'inferior informatization tools and products', which is expressly qualified as a 'requisite protectionist policy toward informatization and information protection tool producers within Russia'.[106]

Smaller militaries are also attentive to the issue. Australia in 2009 announced that it would 'invest in a major enhancement of Defence's cyber warfare capability' and issued a Cyber Security Strategy.[107] The Swiss Centre des opérations électroniques is assembling a unit for CNOs.[108] The Canadian Forces have established a Network Operation Centre with the mission motto to 'fight the networks'[109] and many other States have issued cyber security strategies.[110] It can therefore be concluded that a militarisation of cyberspace has already taken place and will continue to do so as more and more States assign their armed forces the mission of ensuring cyber security, which is generally seen as also including offensive CNOs.

---

from the point of design to service and disposal: US Department of Defense 'Department of Defense Strategy for Operating in Cyberspace' p. 3.

106 Russian Federation 'Information Security Doctrine of the Russian Federation (approved by President Putin on 9 September 2000)' (2000) at <www.mid.ru/ns-osndoc.nsf/1e5f0de28fe77fdcc32575d900298676/2deaa9ee15ddd24bc32575d9002c442b?OpenDocument> (date accessed 24 June 2010) para. 8.

107 Australian Government Department of Defence *Defending Australia in the Asia Pacific Century: Force 2030 (Defence White Paper 2009)* at <www.defence.gov.au/whitepaper/docs/defence_white_paper_2009.pdf> (date accessed 19 August 2010) p. 83. Australian Government 'Cyber Security Strategy' (2009) at <www.ag.gov.au/www/agd/agd.nsf/Page/CyberSecurity_CyberSecurity> (date accessed 19 August 2010) including the creation of a Cyber Security Operations Centre with the alleged capability to detect and defeat sophisticated cyber threats (at p. 27).

108 Daniel Möckli 'Cyberwar: Konzept, Stand und Grenzen' (2010) 71 CSS Analysen zur Sicherheitspolitik p. 3; Yves Petignat 'La cyber-impuissnace helvétique' in *Le Temps* of 13 April 2010; an expert opinion on the legal foundations of CNOs has been given by the Swiss Ministry of Justice: Schweizer Bundesamt für Justiz und EDA 'Gutachten über Rechtsgrundlagen für Computernetzwerkoperationen durch Dienststellen des VBS' (2009) VPB 3/2009 Verwaltungspraxis der Bundesbehörden pp. 141–77.

109 <www.img-ggi.forces.gc.ca/org/cfi-goi/cfnoc-corfc-eng.asp> (date accessed 15 April 2010).

110 See inter alia the Estonian Ministry of Defence 'Cyber Security Strategy' issued in 2008; the 'Cyber Security Strategy of the Czech Republic for the 2011 – 2015 Period' (2011) at <www.enisa.europa.eu/media/news-items/CZ_Cyber_Security_Strategy_20112015.PDF> (date accessed 8 April 2012); or the French Government *Défense et Sécurité Nationale: Le Livre Blanc* which envisages the establishment of units able to engage in the '*lutte informatique offensive*', i.e. offensive CNOs (at p. 207).

3. THE GRADUAL DEVELOPMENT OF COMMON CYBERSECURITY STANDARDS

In a third step it shall be analysed to what degree State actors might be limited through a cybersecurity regime. In this regard recourse will be had both to international and regional instruments adopted specifically with the aim of providing computer system and network security, while omitting more general treaties or principles of international law, which will be analysed in the next chapter.

3.1. THE INTERNATIONAL LEVEL

For approximately ten years, the UN General Assembly has connected international security with the integrity of information and telecommunications technology.[111] The respective resolutions annually reiterate the stance that it is 'necessary to prevent the use of information resources or technologies for criminal or terrorist purposes'. In UNGA Res 58/199 of 23 December 2004 entitled 'Creation of a Global Culture of Cybersecurity and the Protection of Critical Information Infrastructures' the General Assembly notes that as a result of increasing interconnectivity, critical information infrastructures are now exposed to a growing number and a wider variety of threats and vulnerabilities that raise new security concerns. As a result it has drawn up 'Elements for Protecting Critical Information Infrastructures'[112] including several recommendations to Member States such as to:

> 'Have emergency warning networks regarding cyber-vulnerabilities, threats and incidents;
> Promote partnerships among stakeholders, both public and private, to share and analyze critical infrastructure information in order to prevent, investigate and respond to damage to or attacks on such infrastructures;
> Facilitate the tracing of attacks on critical information infrastructures and, where appropriate, the disclosure of tracing information to other States;
> Have adequate substantive and procedural laws and trained personnel to enable States to investigate and prosecute attacks on critical information infrastructures and to coordinate such investigations with other States, as appropriate;
> Engage in international cooperation, when appropriate, to secure critical information infrastructures, including by developing and coordinating emergency warning

---

111 See the yearly resolutions entitled 'Developments in the Field of Information and Telecommunications in the Context of International Security', namely UNGA Res 53/70 (4 December 1998); 54/49 (1 December 1999); 55/28 (20 November 2000); 56/19 (29 November 2001); 57/53 (22 November 2002); 58/32 (8 December 2003); 59/61 (3 December 2004); 60/45 (8 December 2005); 61/54 (6 December 2006); 62/17 (5 December 2007); 63/37 (2 December 2008); 64/25 (2 December 2009); 65/54 (8 December 2010); 66/24 (2 December 2011).

112 UNGA Res 58/199 (23 December 2004) Annex.

> systems, sharing and analysing information regarding vulnerabilities, threats and incidents and coordinating investigations of attacks on such infrastructures in accordance with domestic laws.'[113]

States have further been called to 'ensure that their laws and practice eliminate safe havens for those who criminally misuse information technologies' and coordinate their law enforcement authorities in investigating and prosecuting the criminal misuse of information technology.[114] The 2003 UN WSIS Plan of Action demands similar by stipulating that governments

> 'should prevent, detect and respond to cyber-crime and misuse of ICTs by ... considering legislation that allows for effective investigation and prosecution of misuse; promoting effective mutual assistance efforts; strengthening institutional support at the international level for preventing, detecting and recovering from such incidents.'[115]

In the follow-up document, the 2005 UN WSIS Tunis Agenda, the ITU is envisaged as facilitator for building confidence and security in the use of information and communication technology. As a result the ITU issued a Global Cybersecurity Agenda in 2007, amongst the declared goals of which is the development of a strategy for the 'establishment of globally accepted minimum security criteria and accreditation schemes for hardware and software applications and systems' as well as the 'creation of a global framework for watch, warning and incident response to ensure cross-border coordination'.[116]

Despite these efforts especially of the UN General Assembly and the UN World Summit on the Information Society, there seems to be little consensus amongst States on how to cooperatively deal with cyberthreats through legally binding instruments on an international level. The respective instruments all remain mere recommendations without any legal import even for the field of cybercrimes, while completely failing to address the issue of State-sponsored CNOs.

3.2. THE REGIONAL LEVEL

This situation is different on the regional level at least as regards the penalisation of cybercrimes. In this respect the Council of Europe Convention on Cybercrime is the most significant legally binding instrument. This is mainly due to the

---

113 *Ibid* paras. 1, 4, 7, 9 and 10 Elements for Protecting Critical Information Infrastructures.

114 Para. 1(a) UNGA Res 55/63 'Combating the Criminal Misuse of Information Technologies' (4 December 2000) and UNGA Res 56/121 'Combating the Criminal Misuse of Information Technologies' (19 December 2001).

115 Para. 12b UN WSIS 'Plan of Action' (12 December 2003) at <www.itu.int/wsis/docs/geneva/official/poa.html> (date accessed 30 August 2011).

116 ITU 'Global Cybersecurity Agenda' at <www.itu.int/osg/csd/cybersecurity/gca/pillars-goals/index.html> (date accessed 9 April 2012).

considerable number of ratifications including also major non-Council of Europe Member States such as the United States.[117] It is further considered to be a role model for other harmonisation initiatives and has been endorsed by the Ministers of Justice of the Americas in their regular meetings which recommend States to 'consider applying the principles of the Council of Europe's Convention on Cyber-Crime, acceding thereto, and adopting the legal and other measures required for its implementation'.[118] Yet the reasons for this noteworthy success of the Cybercrime Convention lie in the fact that it does not deal with State-sponsored cybercrime or cyber warfare. Hence the Convention does not limit States' possible courses of action concerning CNOs by State organs.

The Convention obliges Member States to penalise illegal access and interception, data and system interference and misuse of devices.[119] Most importantly States Parties are obliged to provide mutual assistance in investigations and criminal proceedings to the widest possible extent including the preservation of data and access thereto.[120] Furthermore, an obligation to extradite or prosecute is included for cases where the requested party refuses to extradite on basis of the suspect being its national.[121] By subjecting extradition to the general extradition treaties existing between the States Parties, the exception for political offences which is widely contained in these is also applicable in regard to cybercrimes.[122] In the case of mutual assistance this exception is expressly included in the Convention, together with an ordre public exception.[123]

The European Union has likewise issued a number of documents relating to computer security. The Council of the EU adopted Council Framework Decision 2005/222/JHA of 24 February 2005 on Attacks against Information Systems, likewise solely focusing on cybercrime.[124] This includes the usage of a network of operational points of contact available on a 24-hours-a-day, seven-days-a-week basis, the establishment of which was already recommended in 2001.[125]

---

117 As of 7 January 2014 the COE Cybercrime Convention has been ratified or acceded to by 41 States and signed but not ratified by an additional 11 States.

118 OAS 'Conclusions and Recommendations of REMJA-VII' at <www.oas.org/juridico/english/cybVII_CR.pdf> (date accessed 9 April 2012). Ian Walden 'Crime and Security in Cyberspace' (2005) 18(1) Cambridge Review of International Affairs p. 57; a text similar to the Cybercrime Convention has been drafted as a proposal by scholars: the Stanford Proposal for an International Convention on Cyber Crime and Terrorism: Sofaer & Goodman 'Proposal for an International Convention on Cyber Crime and Terrorism'.

119 Arts. 2–6 Cybercrime Convention.

120 Arts. 25, 29 and 31 Cybercrime Convention.

121 Arts. 22 and 24 Cybercrime Convention.

122 Art. 24(5) Cybercrime Convention.

123 Arts. 27(4), 29(5) and 30(2) Cybercrime Convention.

124 EU Council 'Framework Decision 2005/222/JHA of 24 February 2005 on Attacks against Information Systems' [2005] OJ L69/67.

125 EU Council 'Recommendation of 25 June 2001 on Contact Points Maintaining a 24-Hour Service for Combating High-Tech Crime' [2001] OJ C 187/5.

The European Commission in 2009 identified several deficits in critical information infrastructure protection within the EU. As a consequence, more coordination and cooperation has been called for, mostly to be accomplished through the establishment of CERTs in all Member States and the development of common minimum standards for their operation as well as principles and guidelines for Internet resilience and stability. In addition, practical exercises on Internet security incidents shall be undertaken.[126]

In the 2010 Digital Agenda for Europe the European Commission presented several measures to strengthen Internet security that are envisaged to be adopted in the near future. These include, inter alia:

> 'Legislative initiatives, to combat cyber attacks against information systems by 2010, and related rules on jurisdiction in cyberspace at European and international levels by 2013;
> To establish a European cybercrime platform by 2012;
> Examine the feasibility by 2011 to create a European cybercrime centre;
> Work with global stakeholders notably to strengthen global risk management in the digital and in the physical sphere and conduct internationally coordinated targeted actions against computer-based crime and security attacks;
> Support EU-wide cyber-security preparedness exercises, from 2010.'[127]

Member States were called on to establish 'by 2012 a well-functioning network of CERTs at national level covering all of Europe' and in cooperation with the Commission to 'carry out large scale attack simulation and test mitigation strategies as of 2010'.[128]

4. CONCLUSION: THE TERRITORIALISATION OF A UNIVERSAL INFRASTRUCTURE

The analysis above has shown that cyberspace is neither regulated by a central body nor is it embedded into an international legal regime. There is no central regulative authority that is democratically legitimised and entrusted with the competence to enact legally binding rules applicable to actions or content on the Internet. Regulation instead follows the technical structure of the underlying

126 Communication from the Commission to the European Parliament, the Council, the European Economic and Social Committee and the Committee of the Regions, 'On Critical Information Infrastructure Protection: Protecting Europe from Large Scale Cyber-Attacks and Disruptions: Enhancing Preparedness, Security and Resilience' (30 March 2009) COM(2009) 149 final.

127 Communication From the Commission to the European Parliament, the Council, the European Economic and Social Committee and the Committee of the Regions 'A Digital Agenda for Europe' COM(2010) 245 final/2 p. 18.

128 *Ibid.*

networks which in effect constitute the Internet.[129] These networks or rather the systems they link, are located in the territories of States. Hence they rest within the territorial jurisdiction of the relevant State, which is also the reason why cyberspace does not qualify as an international commons as it does not constitute an area outside of national jurisdictions. It can therefore be concluded that cyberspace was in the first place never able to form a sphere beyond State jurisdiction as the infrastructure fundamental to it rests within the latter's territory.

But even proponents of a jurisdiction sui generis cannot deny the fact that States through their practice have ultimately deprived cyberspace of any such quality by asserting jurisdiction over all forms of Internet activity. This State practice does not only demonstrate a general will of States not only to exercise their jurisdiction to prescribe and adjudicate on the Internet, but also their ability to do so. Considering that under international law territory is not defined by having recourse to private law analogies of real property, but by reference to the extent of government power exercised, or capable of being exercised, with respect to some area and population,[130] it is this governing power of States over 'their part of cyberspace' which at least from a legal standpoint results in the territorial fragmentation of the Internet.[131] This power is also manifested in the growing militarisation of the Internet in the last decade.

The same period has further witnessed a proliferation of instruments both on the international and regional level relating to the field frequently referred to as cybersecurity. What the instruments illustrated above have in common is that they are not legally binding, the exceptions being the Convention on Cybercrime and the European Framework Decision on cybercrime. Nevertheless the instruments do show that a wide consensus exists as to the importance of information and communication systems for States, businesses and individuals. Likewise, both the vulnerabilities of these systems and the resulting necessity of a higher level of security and protection are commonly agreed upon.

The methods envisaged to be able to achieve this protection equally show a remarkable degree of conformity. They can be divided into three categories: technical, organisational and legal measures. Technically, best practices are promoted and the development of new standards in future technology advised. This is inter alia being undertaken through ITU and ISO forums.[132] Organisationally, CERTs and 24/7 national points of contact – which in some

---

129 Johann-Christoph Woltag 'Computer Network Operations Below the Level of Armed Force' in Nico Krisch Lauri Mälksoo & Mario Prost (eds) *ESIL 4th Research Forum Tallinn* 1 ESIL Conference Paper Series No 1 at <http://ssrn.com/abstract=1967593> (date accessed 19 June 2012) p. 16.

130 James Crawford *The Creation of States in International Law* (Clarendon Oxford 1979) p. 42.

131 Similar is held by Rule 1 Tallinn Manual, which states that 'a State may exercise control over cyber infrastructure and activities within its sovereign territory'.

132 As defined in the ISO/IEC 27000 family of standards.

States are identical – have been widely established both at governmental and private levels. On the legal level, international and regional organisations have called for the criminalisation of cybercrimes under national law and a higher level of mutual assistance, supported by toolkits and model laws.[133] If not already accomplished on their own accord, these recommendations have led to a growing consensus among States at least in the field of cybercrime.[134]

This high level of consensus is however not reflected with regard to computer network operations undertaken by States, whether through armed forces as a method of warfare or by law enforcement or other State actors. International instruments instead completely omit the issue. This is due to the fact that a number of States have strongly objected to the idea of regulating the military application of information technology through international instruments. In the forum of the UN General Assembly's First Committee, both the United Kingdom and the United States have voiced the opinion that such is 'completely unnecessary' as the 'law of armed conflict, in particular the principles of necessity and proportionality, governs the use of such technologies'.[135] In their opinion, such an attempt to regulate might only impinge on the free flow of information, considered to be a key principle of the information society. Sweden, on behalf of all EU Member States, in 2001 stated that 'it is first and foremost both the right and the responsibility of every country to protect its own information and information-based systems'.[136] More fundamentally it asserted that the issue of information security should not even be discussed in the forum of the First Committee, as it would mainly not encompass the subjects of disarmament and international security.[137] Others have argued contrariwise that 'now is the time to draw up an international instrument on security of information technology'.[138]

These developments lead to a twofold conclusion. On the one hand the level of harmonisation of national criminal laws relating to cybercrimes has risen

---

133 See also the OECD 'Guidelines for the Security of Information Systems and Networks: Towards a Culture of Security' (25 July 2002) at <www.oecd.org/dataoecd/16/22/15582260.pdf> (date accessed 31 August 2011).

134 See already Goodman & Brenner 'The Emerging Consensus on Criminal Conduct in Cyberspace'.

135 Statement by the UK and US, respectively, in UNGA 'Developments in the Field of Information and Telecommunications in the Context of International Security: Report of the Secretary-General' (23 June 2004 and 28 December 2004) UN Docs A/59/116 and A/59/116/Add.1; most recently by the UK in the current version of said report ([20 July 2010] UN Doc A/65/154) at p. 15.

136 Statement by Sweden on behalf of all EU Member States, in UNGA 'Developments in the Field of Information and Telecommunications in the Context of International Security: Report of the Secretary-General' (3 July 2001) UN Doc A/56/164 para. 5.

137 *Ibid* para. 8.

138 Statement by Burkina Faso, in UNGA 'Developments in the Field of Information and Telecommunications in the Context of International Security: Report of the Secretary-General' (2 July 2007) UN Doc A/62/98.

considerably in the last decade, inter alia through the two European initiatives. The introduction of relevant offences is, however, not only a consequence of international cooperation but is in fact in the original interest of States as cybercrimes need not necessarily be of a cross-border nature but can equally be a domestic threat. Nevertheless these national efforts, but also the Convention on Cybercrime, have established some core standards which reflect a growing consensus in the international community towards a regime directed against cybercrime. While the standards and recommendations given in soft law instruments are not legally binding per se, they could possibly as best practices help to clarify indefinite legal concepts or serve as guidelines in assessing due diligence obligations of States.[139] On the other hand a specific regulation of computer network operations by States does not yet exist in a nascent form as any attempted developments on this issue have so far met with heavy resistance.

139 This is considered at pp. 99 et seq. below.

PART II

THE LEGAL QUALIFICATION OF COMPUTER NETWORK OPERATIONS

CHAPTER 3

COMPUTER NETWORK OPERATIONS OUTSIDE OF ARMED CONFLICT

The legal appraisal of military computer network operations under international law serves several purposes, depending on the relevant regime applicable. When considering military operations a division will naturally be drawn between the regimes applicable during and outside of armed conflict. During armed conflict the legal qualification of military computer network operations is necessary in order to be able to fulfil humanitarian law obligations.[1] Outside of armed conflict, under the ius ad bellum paradigm, the necessity lies in being able to justify the use of force directed against another State as a means of self-defence. More cardinally, the qualification of a computer network operation as an internationally wrongful act of a State invokes its responsibility. The first step in any claim to restitution and reparation or ultimately any justification of countermeasures will thus lie in the legal appraisal of the relevant operation.

In the following, a legal qualification of computer network operations will be undertaken in ascending order, dependent on the level of harm expected to be inflicted. This firstly concerns those operations that are taken outside of armed conflict and which do not reach the quality of armed force in the sense of the UN Charter, followed by those which do transgress this threshold and ultimately those taken during international armed conflict.

As with other forms of military operations, the possibility of computer network operations not amounting to armed force in the sense of the prohibition of Article 2(4) UN Charter is a given. After all, taking into consideration the aforementioned case studies it is conceivable that the lion's share of CNOs lies in this area, and will likely remain so also in the future. This does not mean that such activities will automatically be in conformity with international law. If CNOs for example qualify as coercion but not as armed force, the overall principle of non-intervention, of which the rules on the use of armed force are a specific application, might be affected.[2] But depending on the relevant regimes

1 Due to the general standard of a prohibition of the use of force, some authors have started to speak of ius contra bellum. This does not however lead to a reappraisal of the prohibition, hence the classical term ius ad bellum will be used in the following.

2 Maziar Jamnejad & Michael Wood 'The Principle of Non-Intervention' (2009) 22 Leiden Journal of International Law pp. 348–49.

or bilateral treaties applicable, the conduct of military operations in cyberspace may be identified as an unlawful act from many different angles.[3]

Due to the general prohibition of the use of force and the general rule of a peaceful settlement of disputes, a State is – outside of armed conflict – limited in how it may respond to a wrongful act of another State. With the performance of the wrongful conduct a special regime is established between the injuring and injured State. While this might be an elaborate or even self-contained regime such as the WTO dispute settlement system, only a few of these have been proven to exist. In the absence thereof, recourse is to be made to the more general secondary rules on State responsibility.[4]

There is no treaty law specifically dealing with the issue of State responsibility in general. Hence, the rules on State responsibility for wrongful acts must be derived from customary international law. The 2001 ILC Articles on State Responsibility are of particular relevance in this regard. These have not been formed into a convention but were merely included in an UN General Assembly resolution.[5] Nevertheless, both the ICJ and the ITLOS have de facto treated them as a source of international law and they have been widely cited by most of the other international courts and tribunals.[6] Hence the ILC Articles are generally considered to largely reflect customary international law on the matter.[7] They will be treated accordingly in the following without particular reference to their status.

State responsibility arises from State conduct – either through an action or omission – which is attributable to the State and constitutes a breach of an international obligations of said State.[8] As States are juridical abstractions their

3 Qualifying CNOs that destroy a State's banking system as a prohibited intervention, however without reasoning: Schweizer Bundesamt für Justiz und EDA 'Gutachten über Rechtsgrundlagen für Computernetzwerkoperationen durch Dienststellen des VBS' p. 166.

4 As stated in the lex specialis principle of Art. 55 UN ILC 'Draft Articles on Responsibility of States for Internationally Wrongful Acts' (2001) GAOR 56th Session Supp 10, 43.

5 This approach was actually recommended by the ILC itself and a considerable number of States. The reason for this was the concern that in case of a convention ratified only by a small number of States, acceptance of the Articles would have been lower than by adoption through the UN General Assembly.

6 Georg Dahm, Jost Delbrück & Rüdiger Wolfrum *Völkerrecht vol I/3* (de Gruyter Berlin 2002) p. 866; James Crawford 'State Responsibility' in Rüdiger Wolfrum (ed) *MPEPIL* (OUP Oxford Update 2006) para. 65; *Gabčíkovo-Nagymaros Project (Hungary/Slovakia)* [1997] ICJ Rep 7 at paras 47 et seq. and para. 83; *M/V 'SAIGA' (No 2) (Saint Vincent and the Grenadines v Guinea) (Merits) (Judgment)* ITLOS Case No 2 (1 July 1999) 1999 ITLOS Reports 10. The UNGA 'Compilation of Decisions of International Courts, Tribunals and other Bodies: Report of the Secretary-General' (1 February 2007) UN Doc A/62/62 lists 129 cases of international courts and tribunals containing reference to the Draft Articles and its provisionally adopted precursors.

7 Hobe *Einführung in das Völkerrecht* p. 249.

8 As established in the *Factory at Chorzów (Germany v Poland) (Claim for Indemnity) (Merits)* PCIJ Series A No 17 at p. 47 and now stated in Arts. 1 and 2 UN ILC Articles on State Responsibility; Dahm, Delbrück & Wolfrum *Völkerrecht vol I/3* pp. 864 et seq.; Hobe *Einführung in das Völkerrecht* p. 250; James Crawford & Simon Olleson 'The Nature and

actions can only be taken through their organs and agents, hence ultimately through natural persons. Therefore the attribution of these actions to a State is to be understood as a legal fiction providing the possibility of assigning the conduct of a natural person to a State, but not as a form of causality or fault.[9] For this reason the attribution to a State of the conduct in question must necessarily come as a first step before establishing the wrongfulness of the act.[10] This is of special relevance with respect to computer network operations as even the technical attribution to a source system meets with serious difficulties.[11]

Furthermore, no circumstances precluding wrongfulness may be proven to exist. This however is an assertion which must be proven by the respondent State.[12]

1. RULES OF ATTRIBUTION

Generally a certain conduct can only be attributed to a State if it is undertaken by a State organ or agent. The conduct concerned can be an action or omission, which are equal under Article 2 ILC Articles. But these two are the only existing variants. As a general principle, a State is not responsible for the conduct of private persons or entities.[13] Only under certain circumstances can such conduct be attributed to a State, thus invoking the latter's responsibility. Attention must be paid to the fact that despite the conduct being exercised by a private individual, it always remains the action or omission of a State organ which establishes State responsibility.[14] The ILC Articles provide for three such

Forms of International Responsibility' in Malcolm D. Evans (ed) *International Law* (OUP Oxford 2010) p. 451. Rule 6 Tallinn Manual in this regard rightly stipulates that 'a State bears international legal responsibility for a cyber operation attributable to it and which constitutes a breach of an international obligation'.

9 Dahm, Delbrück & Wolfrum *Völkerrecht vol I/3* p. 895; Knut Ipsen 'Völkerrechtliche Verantwortlichkeit und Völkerstrafrecht' in Knut Ipsen (ed) *Völkerrecht* (Beck München 2004) p. 629.

10 Hobe *Einführung in das Völkerrecht* pp. 250–51; Crawford & Olleson 'The Nature and Forms of International Responsibility' p. 452. This order has also been followed in the phrasing of Art. 2 ILC Articles on State Responsibility.

11 See pp. 28 et seq. above.

12 Crawford & Olleson 'The Nature and Forms of International Responsibility' p. 451.

13 *Corfu Channel (United Kingdom of Great Britain and Northern Ireland v Albania) (Merits)* [1949] ICJ Rep 4 p. 18; *United States Diplomatic and Consular Staff in Tehran (United States of America v Iran)* [1980] ICJ Rep 3 paras 58–61; Alexander Kees 'Responsibility of States for Private Actors' in Rüdiger Wolfrum (ed) *MPEPIL* (OUP Oxford Update 2011) para. 1; Hobe *Einführung in das Völkerrecht* p. 251; Meinhard Schröder 'Verantwortlichkeit, Völkerstrafrecht, Streitbeilegung und Sanktionen' in Wolfgang Vitzthum (ed) *Völkerrecht* (De Gruyter Berlin 2010) p. 594; Dahm, Delbrück & Wolfrum *Völkerrecht vol I/3* p. 906; Olivier De Frouville 'Attribution of Conduct to the State: Private Individuals' in James Crawford Alain Pellet & Simon Olleson (eds) *The Law of International Responsibility* (OUP Oxford 2010) pp. 261 et seq.

14 Ipsen 'Völkerrechtliche Verantwortlichkeit und Völkerstrafrecht' p. 646.

cases: when a person or group of persons 'is in fact acting on the instructions of, or under the direction or control of' a State in carrying out the conduct (Article 8); when these are in fact 'exercising elements of the governmental authority in the absence or default of the official authorities and in circumstances such as to call for the exercise of those elements of authority' (Article 9); or when the State 'acknowledges and adopts the conduct in question as its own' (Article 11). But States can also oblige themselves in a contract for example for supervision of the conduct of private actors, a breach of which may then incur State responsibility for the private actor's misconduct.[15] As a contractual responsibility it is of a voluntary nature and ultimately dependent on the relevant agreement; but no such agreements have been concluded for CNOs.

In any case, whether the conduct concerned is performed by a de iure State organ or by a private individual, the attribution is established either through an action or an omission of a State organ.

1.1. ACTIONS OF STATES

1.1.1. Actions of States through their Organs

Conduct of de iure State organs, whatever their function, position or character as an organ in the internal organisation of that State, is attributable to said State.[16] Likewise it is of no relevance whether the organ is empowered by national law to act as a representative of the State on the international level.[17] The same holds true for persons or entities which are empowered by law to exercise elements of governmental authority.[18] In addition, ultra vires conduct by the acting entity, namely conduct in excess of the entity's authority or contravening instructions, does not preclude attribution.[19] De facto organs are likewise treated as organs of a State. These are composed of individuals or entities that act under complete

---

15 Dahm, Delbrück & Wolfrum *Völkerrecht vol I/3* p. 909 and Rüdiger Wolfrum 'State Responsibility for Private Actors: An Old Problem of Renewed Relevance' in Maurizio Ragazzi (ed) *International Responsibility Today: Essays in Memory of Oscar Schachter* (Nijhoff Leiden 2005) pp. 425–26 giving examples from the field of the law of the sea and the Antarctic treaty system.

16 This rule, as stipulated in Art. 4 Draft Articles on State Responsibility, was held to be of a customary character by the ICJ in the *Difference relating to Immunity from Legal Process of a Special Rapporteur of the Commission on Human Rights (Advisory Opinion)* [1999] ICJ Rep 62 at para. 62; Schröder 'Verantwortlichkeit, Völkerstrafrecht, Streitbeilegung und Sanktionen' p. 593.

17 Dahm, Delbrück & Wolfrum *Völkerrecht vol I/3* p. 891.

18 Arts. 4–5 and 8 ILC Articles on State Responsibility; Hobe *Einführung in das Völkerrecht* p. 251; Kees 'Responsibility of States for Private Actors' para. 2.

19 Art. 7 ILC Articles on State Responsibility. Whether this also holds true in case the contravention of competence was evident for the injured State is disputed: Schröder 'Verantwortlichkeit, Völkerstrafrecht, Streitbeilegung und Sanktionen' pp. 593–94.

dependence on the State, irrespective of their legal characterisation under domestic law.[20]

Hence it is undisputed that CNOs by a State's armed forces, police, intelligence services or any other of its authorities are attributable to it. The same holds true in the other cases in which the ILC Articles on State Responsibility envisage an attribution: the placing of an organ at the disposal of another State, and actions taken in connection with wrongful acts of another State. In all of these cases the attribution of CNOs does not pose different legal questions, as is the case for more traditional conduct.[21]

1.1.2. Actions of States through Non-State Actors

Highly problematic on the other hand is the attribution of conduct by private persons or entities to a State. The topicality of this issue is reflected in the case studies of CNOs outlined above and the discussions surrounding the responsibility for these.

According to Article 8 ILC Articles on State Responsibility:

> '[t]he conduct of a person or group of persons shall be considered an act of a State under international law if the person or group of persons is in fact acting on the instructions of, or under the direction or control of, that State in carrying out the conduct.'

1.1.2.1. The Required Level of Control

Defining the degree of control to be exercised by the State has proven to be a highly contested issue, recently once again through the emergence of international terrorism. Two opposing tests have been applied by international courts and tribunals: on the one hand, the 'effective control' test, on the other hand the 'overall control' test. The effective control test, as developed by the ICJ in the *Nicaragua Case* demands non-State actors to be under complete dependence on the State, and therefore under its instructions, direction or control, in order to consider the act to be one of the State.[22] This specific level of control is required over each and every individual action.[23]

---

20 Paolo Palchetti 'De Facto Organs of a State' in Rüdiger Wolfrum (ed) *MPEPIL* (OUP Oxford Update 2006) para. 1, who sees this rule encompassed by Art. 4(2) ILC Articles on State Responsibility (at para. 10); others view Art. 8 as the corresponding rule, e.g. De Frouville 'Attribution of Conduct to the State: Private Individuals' pp. 268–69.

21 On the specific problems of attribution pertaining to conduct by State organs see only Dahm, Delbrück & Wolfrum *Völkerrecht vol I/3* pp. 890–905.

22 *Military and Paramilitary Activities in and against Nicaragua (Nicaragua v United States of America) (Merits)* [1986] ICJ Rep 14 para. 115; *Application of the Convention on the Prevention and Punishment of the Crime of Genocide (Bosnia and Herzegovina v Serbia and Montenegro) (Judgment)* [2007] ICJ Rep 43 paras. 413–15.

23 Stein & Buttlar *Völkerrecht* p. 405.

In comparison, the overall control test is less strict. Under this test, as utilised by the ICTY Appeals Chamber in the *Tadić Case*, the organisation, coordination and supporting of non-State actors suffices to attribute the group's acts to the supporting State while it is unnecessary to show that specific instructions were given in relation to an individual operation.[24] In its ruling the Court expressly rejected the 'effective control' test of the ICJ in the *Nicaragua Case*.[25] In that case it was however restricted to 'individuals making up an organised and hierarchically structured group, such as a military unit or, in case of war or civil strife armed bands of irregulars or rebels' as these have 'a structure, a chain of command and a set of rules as well as the outward symbols of authority' making individuals conform to the standards prevailing in the group and subject to the authority of the head of the group.[26] The mere equipping and financing is by itself not considered to be sufficient: the State must additionally also organise, coordinate or help in the general planning of the military activity.[27]

The overall control standard has further been used by the ECtHR in the case of violations of human rights by non-State actors over which a State exercised a certain amount of authority. This was done in the *Loizidou Case* in which the general control exercised over a foreign territory was used as a justification to somewhat relax the required standard of control deemed necessary in respect of the individual acts by non-State actors.[28]

Admittedly, the two standards have led to a certain level of ambiguity concerning the attribution of conduct. Yet for some the different thresholds established by the courts and tribunals do not necessarily have to compete with each other but are rather consequence of the different regimes applicable.[29] This was reiterated by the ICJ in the *Genocide Convention Case* where the Court stated that, as the ICTY is in general not called upon to rule on questions of State responsibility, its overall control standard might only be applicable as regards the question of whether or not an armed conflict is of an international nature.[30]

24 *Prosecutor v Tadić (Judgment)* IT-94-1-A (15 July 1999) paras. 98 et seq, especially at para. 145; Susan Lamb 'Tadic Case' in Rüdiger Wolfrum (ed) *MPEPIL* (OUP Oxford Update 2009) para. 23.

25 *Prosecutor v Tadić (Judgment)* IT-94-1-A (15 July 1999) paras. 116 et seq.

26 *Prosecutor v Tadić (Judgment)* IT-94-1-A (15 July 1999) para. 120.

27 *Prosecutor v Tadić (Judgment)* IT-94-1-A (15 July 1999) paras. 131 and 137.

28 *Loizidou v Turkey (Merits)* (ECtHR) Reports 1996-VI 2216 para. 56; Jerzy Kranz 'Die völkerrechtliche Verantwortlichkeit für die Anwendung militärischer Gewalt' (2010) 48 Archiv des Völkerrechts p. 325. Herein the conduct of authorities in northern Cyprus was imputed to Turkey under the question of whether Turkey had jurisdiction over the victim.

29 As stated in the Commentary on Art. 8 of the UN ILC 'Text of the Draft Articles with Commentaries Thereto: Responsibility of States for Internationally Wrongful Acts' (2001) GAOR 56th Session Supp 10, 59 (at para. 5); Kees 'Responsibility of States for Private Actors' para. 15; similarly Kranz 'Die völkerrechtliche Verantwortlichkeit für die Anwendung militärischer Gewalt' p. 336.

30 *Genocide Convention Case* paras. 403–04; similarly *Prosecutor v Dusko Tadić (Judgment) (Separate Opinion of Judge Shahabuddeen)* ICTY-94-1-A (15 July 1999) para. 17; James Crawford 'Military and Paramilitary Activities in and against Nicaragua Case (Nicaragua v

Moreover the Court expressly stated that 'the rules for attributing alleged internationally wrongful conduct to a State do not vary with the nature of the wrongful act in question in the absence of a clearly expressed lex specialis'.[31] In any case, the overall control test was seen to have 'the major drawback of broadening the scope of State responsibility' and was hence unsuitable for this issue 'for it stretches too far, almost to breaking point, the connection which must exist between the conduct of a State's organs and its international responsibility'.[32] So while the ICJ did show a high level of deference to the ICTY in the latter's area of expertise it retained its own interpretation in the field of general international law.[33]

1.1.2.2. The Level of Control over Computer Network Operations

1.1.2.2.1. The Two Standards as Applied to Computer Network Operations

These different concepts have been picked up in the debate concerning computer network operations, although the legal attribution of CNOs has not been scrutinised extensively so far. For *Shackelford*, the application of the overall control standard is the only possibility to be able to reach an attribution in the case of CNOs because of their inherent secretiveness.[34] Otherwise States could evade any responsibility for their operations through the exploitation of the stricter effective control standard.

The problems in identifying the source of CNOs can, however, also be used to argue for the effective control standard, as in the contrasting view of *Roscini*: the effective control standard is said to be the only possibility to be able to ensure that States will not be wrongfully accused of perpetrating CNOs originating from their territory.[35] Furthermore, even when taking into account the jurisprudence of the ICTY, the practice of CNOs so far has not shown any cases of organised and hierarchically structured 'cyber insurgents' in case of which the overall control standard is applicable, making it a purely theoretical possibility.[36]

United States of America)' in Rüdiger Wolfrum (ed) *MPEPIL* (OUP Oxford Update 2006) para. 42.

31 *Genocide Convention Case* para. 401.

32 *Genocide Convention Case* para. 406.

33 William A. Schabas 'Application of the Convention on the Prevention and Punishment of the Crime of Genocide Case (Bosnia and Herzegovina v Serbia and Montenegro)' in Rüdiger Wolfrum (ed) *MPEPIL* (OUP Oxford Update 2008) para. 17.

34 Shackelford 'From Nuclear War to Net War: Analogizing Cyber Attacks in International Law' p. 235; Scott Shackelford 'State Responsibility for Cyber Attacks: Competing Standards for a Growing Problem' in C. Czosseck & K. Podins (eds) *Conference on Cyber Conflict Proceedings 2010* (CCD COE Tallinn 2010) p. 203.

35 Marco Roscini 'World Wide Warfare: Jus ad Bellum and the Use of Cyber Force' (2010) 14 Max Planck Yearbook of United Nations Law p. 100.

36 Roscini 'World Wide Warfare: Jus ad Bellum and the Use of Cyber Force' pp. 100–01.

Both of these views cannot be supported, however, as they attempt to modify the general rules of attribution solely in order to reach a desired outcome for a particular instance of actions, namely computer network operations. While this may admittedly be helpful from a practical point of view, there is so far no State practice that would support even the emergence of such a change of rules. Moreover the latter is also not necessary. Both standards are applicable for the same legal task, namely when establishing the conditions under international law in which a private person may be held to be acting as a de facto State official.[37] Nevertheless the introduction of the overall control test by the ICTY must not be understood as a renunciation of the effective control test in general, but as a supplement. This is due to the fact that the two standards – while applicable as to the same legal task – assess the actions of two different actors: the effective control standard for actions performed by private individuals and groups not organised into military structures, and the overall control standard for actions performed by organised and hierarchically structured armed groups.[38]

These differences in the level of control demanded from States – in summary, the more the non-State actors resemble regular armed forces, the lower the level of control required – are justified when taking into consideration the differences in command and disciplinary structures of the two groups and supported both by State practice and case law.[39] In the case of a group with tight structures and an internal disciplinary system, the standards in the group and the authority of the heads of the group lower the probability of individuals disregarding these in comparison with a loosely organised group without a strict hierarchy. The former are therefore more easily controlled by a State, and by giving support and providing for coordination of such a group the State implicitly also approves of the group's agenda. Therefore a hierarchically structured military group more closely resembles an organ than an unorganised group or individual actors. Hence for the State controlling such a group, it is also both apparent and foreseeable for the group to be conceived of as a de facto organ. Ultra vires acts of individuals which are part of an organised group can therefore be attributable to the State in the same manner as in the case of its regular organs once overall control over the group is established. Furthermore an organised group, in

---

37 *Prosecutor v Tadić (Judgment)* IT-94-1-A (15 July 1999) para. 104; Cassese *International Law* p. 249; Antonio Cassese 'The Nicaragua and Tadic Tests Revisited in Light of the ICJ Judgment on Genocide in Bosnia' (2007) 18 European Journal of International Law pp. 655–56.

38 Cassese 'The Nicaragua and Tadic Tests Revisited in Light of the ICJ Judgment on Genocide in Bosnia' p. 657 making reference to *Prosecutor v Tadić (Judgment)* IT-94-1-A (15 July 1999) paras. 118–19, 132 and 141.

39 Cassese 'The Nicaragua and Tadic Tests Revisited in Light of the ICJ Judgment on Genocide in Bosnia' p. 657; *Prosecutor v Tadić (Judgment)* IT-94-1-A (15 July 1999) paras. 132–36.

contrast to individuals, is mostly engaged in a series of actions.[40] This also makes specific direction of every individual activity unrealistic in practice.

But this also means in return that in order to establish an attribution for individuals or groups not organised into military structures, specific instructions or directives are required in form of an effective control, which was emphasised by the ICTY itself in the *Tadić Case*. This stance is also supported by further case law and State practice.[41]

CNOs can be orchestrated by the same actors and thus the same standards for their attribution to a State also apply. The specific problematic of CNOs, namely the difficulty of ascertaining their origin, cannot be solved by generally using the overall control standard, as opined by *Shackelford*. In order for the overall standard to be applicable it must at any rate first be proven which actor was actually the source of the operation, leading to a reoccurrence of the problem. Only once this can be proven can attribution be reached via the two standards.

1.1.2.2.2. The Level of Control Exercised in the Case Studies

The reported cases of CNOs have so far not provided any evidence of being exercised by organised and hierarchically structured groups. In the Georgian incident, the involvement of the so-called Russian Business Network was never proven.[42] But even assuming this was the case, there are no indications of the 'network' having a hierarchical structure.[43] The Russian Nashi youth movement apparently involved in the Estonian case on the other hand more closely resembles an organised and hierarchically structured group. An argument can also be made that the element of armament – traditionally rather denoting conventional arms – can likewise be fulfilled through the utilisation of computer systems for orchestrating CNOs, as these were used for a destructive effect. To what extent the youth movement is controlled by Russian public authorities remains unclear however.

In the Georgian case of 2008, software was hosted on a publicly accessible server that enabled users to use malicious CNOs against computer systems, provided instructions on how to do so and gave a list of 'exemplary targets'.[44] It

---

40 *Prosecutor v Tadić (Judgment)* IT-94-1-A (15 July 1999) para. 122.

41 *Prosecutor v Tadić (Judgment)* IT-94-1-A (15 July 1999) paras. 132–37; citing the *United States Diplomatic and Consular Staff in Tehran* and *Nicaragua Case* as supportive as well as case law by national courts (at fn. 167).

42 See pp. 45 et seq. above.

43 The same also applies to the group 'Anonymous' which apparently does not have any structure at all as there is no membership, hence allowing anyone to affiliate. The group gained widespread media attention especially in 2010 concerning its operations directed against companies and institutions seen to negatively interfere with the wikileaks platform.

44 See already pp. 45 et seq. above and generally on this case: Tikk, et al. 'Cyber Attacks Against Georgia: Legal Lessons Identified'.

was also possible to predefine target systems in the software, leaving motivated persons with the sole task of executing the program on their system. There were however no indicators of the involvement of public authorities in this case that could have led to an attribution of the CNOs to the Russian State.

However if this were the case – namely the relevant software were uploaded or hosted by or under instruction of some State organ – the result would be different. While the performance of each operation would still qualify as a voluntary act by those individuals who at first had to download the software, an instruction or direction would be difficult to establish in these cases. Without the existence of an organised military group only the effective control standard could be applied for an attribution. In this case it is ultimately the State which equips individuals with the malicious software and plans the operations by predefining targets. What is left to the individual is merely the decision to participate and the actual execution of the CNOs. The individual even lacks the possibility to employ the software in a way not intended by the State. Hence a State has effective control over these CNOs, attributing such conduct via Article 8 ILC Articles. But even if this is not considered sufficient, in any case attribution would be reached via Article 11 ILC Articles: providing a freely available tool the only purpose of which is to target foreign computer systems implies tacit acknowledgment and adoption of the ensuing operations.

Ultimately the emergence of CNOs neither poses a new challenge to the level of control standard, nor does it contribute significantly to the ongoing discussions in relation thereto. As CNOs are merely a new form of operation they can be performed both by organised military groups or, in particular, by individuals. The hitherto existing cases have not however featured such organised groups. Furthermore there has also not been evidence of a State directly instructing individuals to conduct CNOs or of carrying out CNOs by itself through de iure State organs. Naturally, if this becomes a modus operandi, the attribution of CNOs to State organs will follow the established rules.

1.2. OMISSIONS OF STATE ORGANS

Given the limited possibilities of technical attribution, the standard case of a computer network operation being undertaken in a situation outside of armed conflict features an operation whose geographical source might be determined technically, but without legal attribution to a specific State. Furthermore, in particular when taking into account the aforementioned case studies, so-called patriotic hacking has also been identified as an issue of great relevance.[45] The

45 UK Cabinet Office 'Cyber Security Strategy of the United Kingdom: Safety, Security and Resilience in Cyber Space (Command Papers 7642 [2009])' p. 13; US-China Economic and Security Review Commission (ed) *2009 Report to Congress* pp. 174–76; Rain Ottis 'From

notion refers to cases of individuals who, in their private capacity, engage in CNOs against foreign targets. The motivation in these cases has a political element in that the goal is to somehow inflict damage on a State deemed an 'enemy'. This is generally accepted to have been the motivation in the operations against Estonian and Georgian targets.[46] In both cases, in order for the injured State to bring forward a claim or take countermeasures, it is thus significant whether CNOs can be attributed to the State in whose territory the computer systems technically identified as the source are located.

In neither case is it possible to directly attribute the CNOs to State organs, either due to the lack of evidentiary proof or because the operations have in fact been performed by private individuals. Nevertheless, in both cases there remains the possibility of inferring attribution through the omission of an action by a State organ. In the event of a State being under an obligation to prevent a certain outcome from happening, the omission of its organs to do so may establish the attribution. Depending on the relevant obligation, this can include an obligation to intervene in the behaviour of private actors that violates internationally protected rights or positions.[47] In these cases the breach of the obligation lies not in the failure to reach the desired result but in the failure to endeavour to reach the result by taking the necessary actions towards that end, hence to exercise due diligence.[48] In the event of an invocation of State responsibility on the basis of a lack of due diligence, the latter is to be methodically treated as an omission.[49] This method of attribution is also referred to by several authors as the 'indirect responsibility' of States.[50]

However, in order to define the omission of a State organ to act, both the existence and content of an obligation of conduct must at first be established.

Pitchforks to Laptops: Volunteers in Cyber Conflicts' in C. Czosseck & K. Podins (eds) *Conference on Cyber Conflict Proceedings 2010* (CCD COE Tallinn 2010) pp. 97–109.

46 See pp. 42 et seq. above.

47 Dahm, Delbrück & Wolfrum *Völkerrecht vol I/3* p. 910; Wolfrum 'State Responsibility for Private Actors: An Old Problem of Renewed Relevance' p. 425, citing the *Velásquez Rodríguez v Honduras (Judgment)* IACtHR Series C No 4 (29 July 1988).

48 Timo Koivurova 'Due Diligence' in Rüdiger Wolfrum (ed) *MPEPIL* (OUP Oxford Update 2007) para. 3; Kees 'Responsibility of States for Private Actors' para. 3; Joachim Wolf *Die Haftung der Staaten für Privatpersonen nach Völkerrecht* (Duncker & Humblot Berlin 1997) p. 69.

49 Pierre-Marie Dupuy & Cristina Hoss 'Trail Smelter and Terrorism: International Mechanisms to Combat Transboundary Harm' in Rebecca M. Bratspies & Russell A. Miller (eds) *Transboundary Harm in International Law: Lessons from the Trail Smelter Arbitration* (CUP Cambridge 2006) p. 233; Wolf *Die Haftung der Staaten für Privatpersonen nach Völkerrecht* pp. 463–64.

50 See, inter alia, Marja Lehto *Indirect Responsibility for Terrorist Acts: Redefinition of the Concept of Terrorism Beyond Violent Acts* (Martinus Nijhoff Leiden 2009); Vincent-Joel Proulx 'Babysitting Terrorists: Should States be Strictly Liable for Failing to Prevent Transborder Attacks?' (2005) 23(3) Berkeley Journal of International Law pp. 626 et seq.; Matthew Sklerov 'Solving the Dilemma of State Response to Cyberattacks: A Justification for the Use of Active Defenses against States who Neglect Their Duty to Prevent' (2009) 201 Military Law Review pp. 44 et seq.

This is why the relevant obligation – in cases without a special standard, that of due diligence – is similar if not identical to the attribution of the omission.[51] Something similar has been stated in the Commentary to the ILC Articles, which stipulates that:

> '[a]s a normative operation, attribution must be clearly distinguished from the characterization of conduct as internationally wrongful ... a State may be responsible for the effects of the conduct of private parties, if it failed to take necessary measures to prevent those effects. For example, a receiving State is not responsible, as such, for the acts of private individuals in seizing an embassy, but it will be responsible if it fails to take all necessary steps to protect the embassy from seizure, or to regain control over it. In this respect there is often a close link between the basis of attribution and the particular obligation said to have been breached, even though the two elements are analytically distinct.'[52]

1.2.1. The General Criteria of the Duty to Exercise Due Diligence

The obligation to exercise due diligence arises in cases in which a State is afforded discretion as how to fulfil its international obligations. This is why due diligence is an obligation of conduct, hence an obligation 'that require[s] States to endeavour to reach the result set out in the obligation'.[53] Therefore it is already made clear that due diligence is a general juridical standard containing not a specific obligation but differing depending on the relevant situation and applicable primary norms.[54] Despite this dependence several criteria have been developed in the decisions of international courts and tribunals which can be considered as shaping the scope and content of most due diligence obligations.[55]

1.2.1.1. No Justification by Recourse to National Law

The first application of the due diligence obligation is generally considered to be the *Alabama Arbitration* of 1872. Therein it was held that a breach of international law arising from a failure to act with due diligence could not be justified by recourse to domestic law. Rather, the scope and content of the due diligence obligation are defined by international law. From this general rule

---

51 Dupuy & Hoss 'Trail Smelter and Terrorism: International Mechanisms to Combat Transboundary Harm' p. 233.

52 Para. 4 Commentary to Chapter II UN ILC 'Text of the Draft Articles with Commentaries Thereto: Responsibility of States for Internationally Wrongful Acts'.

53 Koivurova 'Due Diligence' para. 8.

54 Dahm, Delbrück & Wolfrum *Völkerrecht vol I/3* pp. 947–48; Koivurova 'Due Diligence' para. 42.

55 See already Astrid Epiney *Die völkerrechtliche Verantwortlichkeit von Staaten für rechtswidriges Verhalten im Zusammenhang mit Aktionen Privater* (Nomos Baden-Baden 1992) pp. 245–55.

follows that States are likewise prevented from claiming to apply diligentia quam in suis, hence diligence as applied by the State in its own affairs, as this standard is ultimately shaped by domestic law.[56]

1.2.1.2. The Element of Disposability of Means

It is generally accepted that due diligence is limited by the condition that a State need only use the means at its disposal.[57] In the *Genocide Convention Case* the ICJ used this criterion in demanding a manifest failure to take all measures within the State's power to prevent the wrongful act, provided these might have contributed to preventing it.[58] The availability of means depends on several factors. This may for example be the geographic location of events which can produce both a higher and lower level of diligence required from the territorial State. For instance in the case of the duty of the State to prevent illegal acts by individuals, a lower standard exists in scarcely populated and isolated regions by taking into account the effectiveness of territorial control. On the other hand a higher standard may be employable where the probability of illegal actions is higher. This can be the case for example in border regions to a country in which there is a state of insurgency.[59]

The parameter of availability makes the required level of diligence vary both from State to State and within the State. Hence the standards required of a territorial sovereign are not absolute, but are inter alia subject to the resources available to it.[60] These include the 'capacity to influence effectively the action of persons' likely to commit a wrongful act.[61] In this regard the international legal

---

56 This was already held in the *Alabama Arbitration* in JB Moore (ed) *History and Digest of the International Arbitrations to which the United States Has Been a Party* vol 1 Chapter XIV (Government Printing Office Washington 1898), where the defense of Britain of a diligentia quam in suis was rejected. Tom Bingham 'Alabama Arbitration' in Rüdiger Wolfrum (ed) *MPEPIL* (OUP Oxford Update 2006) paras. 34–35; Wolf *Die Haftung der Staaten für Privatpersonen nach Völkerrecht* p. 555; Epiney *Die völkerrechtliche Verantwortlichkeit von Staaten für rechtswidriges Verhalten im Zusammenhang mit Aktionen Privater* pp. 245–46 taking recourse to *Neer (USA) v United Mexican States* (1926) 4 RIAA 60 and *Venable (USA) v United Mexican States* (1926) 4 RIAA 219; differently Ian Brownlie *Principles of Public International Law* (OUP Oxford 2008) p. 526. The irrelevance of domestic law in the establishment of State responsibility has been recognised in Arts. 3 and 32 UN ILC Articles on State Responsibility.

57 Epiney *Die völkerrechtliche Verantwortlichkeit von Staaten für rechtswidriges Verhalten im Zusammenhang mit Aktionen Privater* pp. 253–55; *Nicaragua Case* para. 157; *Tehran Hostages Case* para. 68; Koivurova 'Due Diligence' paras. 19 and 40.

58 *Genocide Convention Case* para. 430.

59 Epiney *Die völkerrechtliche Verantwortlichkeit von Staaten für rechtswidriges Verhalten im Zusammenhang mit Aktionen Privater* pp. 246–47 providing for references to arbitral decisions.

60 *Nicaragua Case* para. 157; Dupuy & Hoss 'Trail Smelter and Terrorism: International Mechanisms to Combat Transboundary Harm' p. 233.

61 *Genocide Convention Case* para. 430.

position of the State is also to be taken into account, as due diligence only requires such actions that are permissible under international law, whereas the permissibility under domestic law is irrelevant.[62]

Hence, this criterion makes it possible to take into consideration the differing levels of development of States.[63] In this regard it is similar to the principle of so-called common but differentiated responsibilities which is contained in several declarations concerning international environmental law, but not unique to this body of law.[64] This flexibility in the level of obligations is limited however where international minimum standards exist. These must always be met and enforced in order for a State to act diligently.[65]

1.2.1.3. Prosecution of Individual Perpetrators und National Criminal Laws

Due diligence is not limited to preventive duties but can also entail duties of conduct that arise subsequent to the wrongful act that should have been prevented. In relation to the wrongful acts by private persons against foreigners or a foreign State, Judge Huber in the *Spanish Zone of Morocco* claims opined that State responsibility could arise from a lack of both preventive and repressive measures.[66] States are thus also obliged to prosecute and punish the individual perpetrators under criminal law.[67] This has also been acknowledged in the field of human rights by both the ACtHR and the ECtHR, which in their respective case law have recognised positive State obligations under the notion of due diligence.[68] States are under a duty to take appropriate preventive and repressive measures against human rights violations also through private actors. This includes the organisation of a governmental apparatus in such a way as to judicially ensure the possibility of a free and full enjoyment of human rights.[69] A failure to do so opens the possibility to impute a human rights violation to the State.

---

62 *Genocide Convention Case* para. 430.

63 Epiney *Die völkerrechtliche Verantwortlichkeit von Staaten für rechtswidriges Verhalten im Zusammenhang mit Aktionen Privater* pp. 254–55.

64 Ellen Hey 'Common but Differentiated Responsibilities' in Rüdiger Wolfrum (ed) *MPEPIL* (OUP Oxford Update 2008) paras. 1–2.

65 Dahm, Delbrück & Wolfrum *Völkerrecht vol I/3* p. 948; Koivurova 'Due Diligence' para. 16; Wolf *Die Haftung der Staaten für Privatpersonen nach Völkerrecht* p. 105.

66 Or as in the French original: 'non seulement par un manque de vigilance dans la prevention des actes dommageables, mais aussi par un manque de diligence dans la poursuite pénale des fauteurs, ainsi que dans l'application des sanctions civiles voulues' *Affaire des biens britanniques au Maroc espagnol* (1925) 2 RIAA 615 at p. 645.

67 Schröder 'Verantwortlichkeit, Völkerstrafrecht, Streitbeilegung und Sanktionen' p. 594.

68 Martin Scheinin 'Security, Right to, International Protection' in Rüdiger Wolfrum (ed) *MPEPIL* (OUP Oxford Update 2007) paras. 18–19, citing *Velásquez Rodríguez v Honduras (Judgment)* para. 172; *Güleç v Turkey (Judgment of 27 July 1998)* (ECtHR) Reports 1998-IV 1698 paras. 81–83; *Osman v United Kingdom* (ECtHR) Reports 1998-VIII 3124 paras. 115–16.

69 María Pía Carazo 'Velásquez Rodríguez v Honduras Case' in Rüdiger Wolfrum (ed) *MPEPIL* (OUP Oxford Update 2008) paras. 10 and 23; Koivurova 'Due Diligence' para. 33.

1.2.1.4. The Principle of Proportionality

In application of the general principle of proportionality recognised under international law, the level of harm expected from a failure to fulfil the relevant obligation is to be taken into consideration when assessing the scope of the due diligence obligation.[70] A higher level of diligence can likewise be expected the higher the predictability of private actions, or if a State has actual or potential knowledge.[71]

1.2.2. Due Diligence and Malicious Computer Network Operations

Outside of international environmental law, due diligence mostly has a role to play in cases where illegal conduct of private actors is not directly attributable to the State despite its physical control over the territory from which it originates.[72] The *Alabama Arbitration* as well as the *Tehran Hostages Case* and *Nicaragua Case* are examples of this.

The question thus arises as to whether there exists any international obligation on States to prevent malicious cross-border computer network operations originating from their territory. If this is proven to exist, the failure to exercise due diligence in preventing CNOs could be qualified as an omission which in turn is necessary for the attribution under the rules of State responsibility.

As has been shown, there exists no specific legally binding international regime applicable to CNOs by States. Hence nor is there an explicit obligation for States to prevent malicious cross-border CNOs emanating from territory under their jurisdiction. As a consequence an obligation of prevention can only be proven to exist if it is either established under customary international law or constitutes a general principle of law. If undertaken by a State organ this could in any case be attributed directly to the State. Therefore a duty to prevent will concentrate on acts by non-State actors or on those of which nothing more is known than their geographical origin. This is supported by the incidents analysed up to this point, which have shown the limits of the possibility to directly attribute CNOs to State actors. So far the cases suggest that CNOs are either attributable to non-State actors, or not at all, while a direct attribution to a State has never been accomplished.

---

70 Koivurova 'Due Diligence' para. 35; Dahm, Delbrück & Wolfrum *Völkerrecht vol I/3* p. 948; Epiney *Die völkerrechtliche Verantwortlichkeit von Staaten für rechtswidriges Verhalten im Zusammenhang mit Aktionen Privater* p. 248.

71 Epiney *Die völkerrechtliche Verantwortlichkeit von Staaten für rechtswidriges Verhalten im Zusammenhang mit Aktionen Privater* pp. 250–53 taking, inter alia, recourse to the *Corfu Channel Case* p. 22. Similarly *Tehran Hostages Case* para. 68.

72 Koivurova 'Due Diligence' para. 41; Wolf *Die Haftung der Staaten für Privatpersonen nach Völkerrecht* p. 230.

1.2.2.1. The Thesis of a Specific Obligation

According to one opinion an obligation on States to prevent malicious CNOs originating from territory under their control has already been established as a rule of customary international law. Additionally, this obligation is said to entail several other duties: the duty to pass stringent criminal laws, to conduct vigorous investigations, prosecute the perpetrators and cooperate with the victim States.[73] This thesis is substantiated by several examples of State practice in this field:

(1) Firstly, the heavy reliance on the Internet of the States that have ratified the Convention on Cybercrime gives special weight to their practice under the specially affected States doctrine. According to this, the practice of 'specially affected' States is a prerequisite or even given a higher weight in establishing the State practice relevant for customary international law.[74] In this way the rules of the Cybercrime Convention could be given special weight in establishing State practice.
(2) Secondly, the large number of States that penalise malicious CNOs under their national criminal laws provide additional practice in this regard. Moreover, this practice has also been voiced via UN General Assembly resolutions on the subject, which call upon States to refuse to allow their territory to be used as a safe haven to conduct cyberattacks.[75]
(3) This is further substantiated by reference to judicial opinions on general international law. These recognise the duty not to knowingly allow a State's territory to be used for acts contrary to the rights of other States.[76]

A specific obligation to prevent malicious cross-border computer network operations including a duty to criminalise and prosecute these under national

---

[73] Sklerov 'Solving the Dilemma of State Response to Cyberattacks: A Justification for the Use of Active Defenses against States who Neglect Their Duty to Prevent' p. 62.

[74] *North Sea Continental Shelf Cases (Federal Republic of Germany/Denmark; Federal Republic of Germany/Netherlands)* [1969] ICJ Rep 3 para. 74.

[75] Sklerov 'Solving the Dilemma of State Response to Cyberattacks: A Justification for the Use of Active Defenses against States who Neglect Their Duty to Prevent' pp. 65–69; for the relevant UN General Assembly resolutions see already pp. 76 et seq. above.

[76] Sklerov 'Solving the Dilemma of State Response to Cyberattacks: A Justification for the Use of Active Defenses against States who Neglect Their Duty to Prevent' pp. 69–71, citing the *Lotus Case* and *Corfu Channel Case*. A further argument is given by *Sklerov* in reference to general principles of law: Causation as a principle for establishing individual responsibility is recognised under next to all national criminal laws, which in consequence means that international State responsibility must also be based on causation; hence the omission to penalise malicious CNOs were to establish State responsibility in case of causing the creation of a safe haven for non-State actors undertaking CNOs. This reasoning cannot convince however as it is circular in that it presupposes the obligation to prevent CNOs emanating from its territory which it seeks to substantiate.

law can, however, not be seen to have been established under customary international law.

Firstly, it is already controversial whether the practice by specially affected States is sufficient for the establishment of a customary rule.[77] At any rate it is not possible to qualify which States are specially affected in the case of CNOs. Admittedly it is clear that some States rely on the Internet to a greater degree than others.[78] Nevertheless all States are connected to the Internet, making virtually every State's interests 'specially affected'. It must not be forgotten that the majority of States are not parties to the Cybercrime Convention and the percentage of their population which uses the Internet makes up the majority of total Internet users.[79] In the future this percentage is likely to grow as the number of Internet users in developing countries is growing at a faster rate compared to that in developed States, of which the members of the Cybercrime Convention are mainly composed. Hence one can no longer single out merely developed countries as those specially affected by malicious CNOs conducted via the Internet.

Secondly, it is hardly conceivable that a customary rule has emerged which obliges States to introduce specific national criminal laws and prosecute accordingly. As shown above, it is true that the level of harmonisation in the penalisation of cybercrimes under national laws has been strengthened in the last decade.[80] Without binding UN Security Council resolutions on the issue, State practice in the field of national criminal laws can however not generally impose obligations upon sovereign States to introduce specific offences in their laws. This holds especially true for the field of criminal law, the establishment and enforcement of which is among the core functions of State sovereignty.[81] In the case of 'cyberterrorism' this may be different. In the efforts to contain terrorism, a considerable number of binding instruments have been introduced which indicate the development of an international regime with obligations to cooperate and ensure extradition or prosecution.[82] But while a generally

---

77 Wolfgang Vitzthum 'Begriff, Geschichte und Rechtsquellen des Völkerrechts' in Wolfgang Vitzthum (ed) *Völkerrecht* (De Gruyter Berlin 2010) p. 63; Treves 'Customary International Law' paras. 35–40. The level of State participation is seen by the relevant ILA report as a rather qualitative than quantitative criterion, admitting that the international system as a whole were far from being democratic however in touch with political realities; see the commentary to Sec. 14 (e) of the ILA Committee on Formation of Customary (General) International Law 'Statement of Principles Applicable to the Formation of General Customary International Law' in ILA (ed) *Report of the Sixty-Ninth Conference, London 2000* (ILA 2000).

78 Woltag 'Internet' para. 31.

79 Internet users from the Latin American, Asian and African States in 2012 made up approximately 62% of the total amount of Internet users: <www.internetworldstats.com/stats.htm> (date accessed 7 January 2014).

80 See pp. 76 et seq. above.

81 On this see Isabel Röcker *Die Pflicht zur rahmenbeschlusskonformen Auslegung nationalen Rechts* (Springer Heidelberg 2012) pp. 190–92.

82 Christian Walter 'Terrorism' in Rüdiger Wolfrum (ed) *MPEPIL* (OUP Oxford Update 2011) para. 83.

accepted definition of terrorism is still to be found, there is agreement that it is concerned with actions that amount to a use of force or support of such.[83] Consequently, whatever regime one sees to have been developed as regards terrorist actions, it is not applicable to CNOs that do not amount to a use of force.

Thirdly, the introduction of new cybercrime offences in national laws does not necessarily depict an opinio iuris sive necessitatis of an international obligation to that end on the part of the States. This can for example be shown by the Cybercrime Convention: the principle of aut dedere aut iudicare contained in its Article 24(6) obliges the requested party, if extradition is refused on the basis of nationality, to 'submit the case at the request of the requesting Party to its competent authorities for the purpose of prosecution'. An obligation to prosecute therefore only exists in case of a prior refusal to extradite. This qualifies the Cybercrime Convention as belonging to the field of vicarious administration of justice and not following the principle of universal jurisdiction.[84] Despite States Parties' obligation to penalise certain actions the Convention does not show the similarity to the principle of universal jurisdiction found in several instruments directed against terrorism.[85] This is due to the fact that the Cybercrime Convention does not follow the approach utilised in those instruments by protecting the legal interests of the international community as a whole. Rather, emphasis is put on the protection of computer systems and data, legal interests which mostly lie in the interest of singular States and individuals but not in that of the international community as a whole. It can therefore be concluded that the Cybercrime Convention ensures that States Parties have the legal ability to prosecute the relevant offences but only establishes an obligation to prosecute in a very limited number of cases. If this duty is not fully established even under this specialised instrument, it can hardly be concluded to have formed a customary rule. States thus do not envisage an international obligation towards the penalisation and prosecution of individual malicious CNOs but rather a national interest to do so.

1.2.2.2. A General Obligation to Prevent Malicious Cross-Border Computer Network Operations

There could however be a more general obligation on the host State to prevent CNOs emanating from its territory.[86] This could be derived from the generally

83 As was already stated in the Friendly Relations Declaration: 'every State has the duty to refrain from organizing [etc] ... terrorist acts ... when the acts ... involve a threat or use of force'.

84 Cf. Dahm, Delbrück & Wolfrum *Völkerrecht vol I/3* pp. 1010 et seq.

85 On this see Dahm, Delbrück & Wolfrum *Völkerrecht vol I/3* p. 1119.

86 Rule 5 Tallinn Manual stipulates the following: 'A State shall not knowingly allow the cyber infrastructure located in its territory or under its exclusive governmental control to be used for acts that adversely and unlawfully affect other States'.

recognised international law obligation on States not to allow knowingly their territory to be used for acts contrary to the rights of other States.[87] In the *Corfu Channel Case*, the ICJ laid the foundation for the existence of a general rule to the effect that a State is obliged to use due diligence to prevent harm to other States arising from activities within its territory of which it has knowledge.[88] A similar point was made by *Moore* in his dissenting opinion in the *Lotus Case*.[89] In the *Corfu Channel Case*, Albania's knowledge of the fact that mines had been laid in its territorial waters paired with the minefield's danger led the ICJ to recognise an obligation of Albania to notify users of the Channel of this danger.[90]

From the outset it must be acknowledged that malicious CNOs are harmful activities in the sense of said general international obligation. The numerous national criminal laws and the UN General Assembly resolutions on the subject show that these actions undisputedly qualify as harmful. The absence of a consensus on the legal consequences thereof does not prevent this qualification.

1.2.2.2.1. Knowledge of Harmful Computer Network Operations

First of all, the level of knowledge required from the responsible State must be established. The ICJ went into some detail on this issue. On the one hand it was stated that it 'cannot be concluded from the mere fact of the control exercised by a State over its territory and waters that that State necessarily knew, or ought to have known, of any unlawful act perpetrated therein, nor yet that it necessarily knew, or should have known, the authors'.[91] On the other hand, actual knowledge need not necessarily be proven. In the case at hand the ICJ inferred knowledge of the minelaying both from the possibility of attaining such knowledge from the relevant observation posts operated along the Corfu Channel and the length of time needed to place such mines. Albania's knowledge was thus inferred indirectly. Additionally the general attitude of the Albanian government towards the passage of foreign ships through its territorial waters was taken into account.[92]

---

87 *Corfu Channel Case* p. 22.

88 Malgosia A. Fitzmaurice 'The Corfu Channel Case and the Development of International Law' in Nisuke Ando Edward McWhinney & Rüdiger Wolfrum (eds) *Liber Amicorum Judge Shigeru Oda vol 1* (Kluwer The Hague 2002) pp. 138–39.

89 Herein *Moore* stated that 'a State is bound to use due diligence to prevent the commission within its dominions of criminal acts against another nation or its people'; *The 'Lotus' (France v Turkey) (Dissenting Opinion of Mr Moore)* PCIJ Series A No 10 at p. 88.

90 Michael Waibel 'Corfu Channel Case' in Rüdiger Wolfrum (ed) *MPEPIL* (OUP Oxford Update 2009) para. 10.

91 *Corfu Channel Case* p. 18; Rule 7 Tallinn Manual points in the same direction by stating: 'The mere fact that a cyber operation has been launched or otherwise originates from governmental cyber infrastructure is not sufficient evidence for attributing the operation to that State, but is an indication that the State in question is associated with the operation'.

92 *Corfu Channel Case* pp. 18–23.

It is unclear how to establish the knowledge of a State of cross-border malicious CNOs emanating from its territory. A presumption of knowledge for States the networks of which are repeatedly utilised for malicious cross-border CNOs has been argued for.[93] A similar reasoning has been stipulated if the source of a CNO can be traced back to originating from the territory of a particular State. In this case a rebuttable presumption of attribution of the operation to said State has been proposed.[94] However, as was stated in the *Corfu Channel Case*, knowledge is not already established simply because the action originates from within the State's territory. This holds especially true in the case of CNOs. The complete surveillance of a country's networks is already from a technical standpoint difficult to achieve. Users still have many opportunities to remain anonymous.[95] Even if the most promising method of surveillance – data retention – is utilised, this is only of a retroactive nature and cannot help to technically prevent malicious CNOs. More importantly, such a high level of surveillance would have to be balanced with the relevant international civil and political rights applicable to communications and privacy on the Internet. An indirect inferring of knowledge as in the *Corfu Channel Case* is therefore likewise more difficult in the case of CNOs. However this is dependent on the facts of each individual case and cannot be generalised.[96]

The modality through which the knowledge is obtained, for instance through own intelligence or via the notification of the target State, is irrelevant. Hence the situation is different if the target State informs the source State of CNOs emanating from networks in its territory. If these allegations are sufficiently substantiated the source State has necessarily gained actual knowledge. In essence States have already started these notification procedures which generally take place through national CERTs. Even if there are no specific legal frameworks applicable to this information exchange, States have through the establishment of national CERTs provided for points of contact competent for inter-State communications relating to malicious activity in the networks under their

---

93 Richard Garnett & Paul Clarke 'Cyberterrorism: A New Challenge for International Law' in Andrea Bianchi (ed) *Enforcing International Law Norms against Terrorism* (Hart Oxford 2004) p. 479.

94 Heintschel von Heinegg 'Automatisierung des Krieges' p. 13.

95 Phillip W. Brunst *Anonymität im Internet – rechtliche und tatsächliche Rahmenbedingungen zum Spannungsfeld zwischen einem Recht auf Anonymität bei der elektronischen Kommunikation und den Möglichkeiten zur Identifizierung und Strafverfolgung* (Duncker & Humblot Berlin 2009) pp. 84 et seq.

96 The group of experts drafting the Tallinn Manual could likewise not achieve consensus as to whether the obligation to prevent malicious CNOs emanating from its territory stipulated in Rule 5 Tallinn Manual encompasses cases where the State has only constructive ('should have known') knowledge: Schmitt (ed) *Tallinn Manual on the International Law Applicable to Cyber Warfare* p. 28 para. 11.

supervision. From this follows that the notification of a national CERT presumes knowledge of the host State of the harmful activities.[97]

A further model proposes to treat those CNOs that are directed against critical infrastructure targets as automatically qualifying as an armed attack, thereby devising a strict liability regime. This should allow the attacked State to respond in kind without the need to at first legally attribute the attack to a State.[98] As the State of origin would under this model automatically be liable for such a CNO, knowledge of said State would be irrelevant. However, such an approach is hardly tenable.[99] So far there exist only treaty-based strict liability regimes for States, as in the case of liability for damage caused by space objects.[100] But even under this regime the attribution of an act is not overridden, but merely the element of fault omitted, so that principally no causes of exoneration are admitted.[101] Neither do the ILC Articles on State Responsibility envisage a strict liability regime. The ICJ was likewise clear on this issue: in the *Corfu Channel Case*, responsibility was not founded on the mere existence of a hazard or the knowledge thereof, but on the duty to avert damage emanating from it. Then again, this duty was limited to such actions that were actually open to it.[102] The Court thus implicitly rejected the theories both of strict and semi-strict (i.e. based on knowledge alone) liability for harms originating from its territory.[103]

---

97 The group of experts drafting the Tallinn Manual likewise saw the obtaining of credible information as sufficient for having actual knowledge: Schmitt (ed) *Tallinn Manual on the International Law Applicable to Cyber Warfare* p. 28 para. 10.

98 Sean Condron 'Getting it Right: Protecting American Critical Infrastructure in Cyberspace' (2007) 20 Harvard Journal of Law & Technology pp. 415–16; arguing for the need of international law to evolve into allowing automated active defence measures be employed: Eric Talbot Jensen 'Computer Attacks on Critical National Infrastructure: A Use of Force Invoking the Right of Self-Defense' (2002) 38(2) Stanford Journal of International Law pp. 228–31.

99 A major flaw is already the fact that each State defines its critical infrastructure differently; see p. 34 fn. 112 above.

100 Convention on International Liability for Damage Caused by Space Objects (signed 29 March 1972, entered into force 1 September 1972) 961 UNTS 187; Jutta Brunnée 'Sic utere tuo ut alienum non laedas' in Rüdiger Wolfrum (ed) *MPEPIL* (OUP Oxford Update 2010) para. 12.

101 With the exception of gross negligence or dolus on part of the claimant State; Marco Pedrazzi 'Outer Space, Liability for Damage' in Rüdiger Wolfrum (ed) *MPEPIL* (OUP Oxford Update 2008) para. 9.

102 Fitzmaurice 'The Corfu Channel Case and the Development of International Law' p. 136.

103 Waibel 'Corfu Channel Case' para. 23; Fitzmaurice 'The Corfu Channel Case and the Development of International Law' p. 136; also today there does not exist a rule of strict liability under customary international law: even the strongest risks such as those emanating from extremely hazardous activities not prohibited by international law are addressed merely through obligations of prevention; Alain Pellet 'The Definition of Responsibility in International Law' in James Crawford Alain Pellet & Simon Olleson (eds) *The Law of International Responsibility* (OUP Oxford 2010) p. 10.

1.2.2.2.2. Failure to Prevent Harmful Computer Network Operations

The mere knowledge of a State of its networks being utilised for harmful CNOs can thus not establish responsibility by itself. This is the case only when the State further fails to exercise due diligence in the prevention thereof. It is thus necessary to establish an objective minimum standard which needs to be observed in order for a State to fulfil its due diligence obligation.[104] The generally recognised standards of due diligence have been outlined above.[105] Firstly a State has to provide for a certain level of governmental structure and legal order so as to enable the implementation and enforcement of the relevant measures necessary to prevent malicious CNOs. The utilisation of a highly developed and ubiquitous information and communications technology infrastructure requires a higher level of security measures, whether of a technical or legal nature. On the other end of the spectrum this does not mean that a developing State can evade responsibility by failing to provide the simplest structures of network security. By creating information and communications technology infrastructures, a State is under an obligation to adhere to the prevailing minimum security standards, which are context-specific to the relevant regime.[106] The establishment of a national CERT has developed as the organisational minimum standard in this regard.[107] These institutions have proliferated to a large degree and the same holds true for 24/7 national points of contact which EU Member States are for example already obliged to establish.[108] While the incorporation or legal powers of such a body are at the discretion of the host State, the designation of one national point of contact is necessary in order for States to be able to address network security issues in a timely manner for a third State. Although it is questionable whether CERTs are sufficient to prevent or repress malicious CNOs, minimum standards need not be the most effective means, but those to which a relevant number of States can agree. In any case, States are free to establish more effective measures that exceed the minimum standards.

---

104 Epiney *Die völkerrechtliche Verantwortlichkeit von Staaten für rechtswidriges Verhalten im Zusammenhang mit Aktionen Privater* pp. 220–21.

105 See pp. 96 et seq. above.

106 Koivurova 'Due Diligence' para. 16; analysing due diligence obligations from the perspective of the precautionary principle of international environmental law: Heike Krieger 'Krieg gegen Anonymous: Völkerrechtliche Regelungsmöglichkeiten bei unsicherer Zurechnung im Cyberwar' (2012) 50 Archiv des Völkerrechts pp. 16 et seq.

107 There do not however seem to exist any relevant statements of States that they see themselves under a legal obligation to establish CERTs, so that their establishment cannot be deemed an obligation of customary international law. This does not however hold true for EU Member States, see fn. 108 below.

108 Art. 11 EU Council 'Framework Decision 2005/222/JHA of 24 February 2005 on Attacks against Information Systems' [2005] OJ L69/67 in combination with EU Council 'Recommendation of 25 June 2001 on Contact Points Maintaining a 24-Hour Service for Combating High-Tech Crime' [2001] OJ C 187/5.

1.2.2.2.3. Selective Measures and Proportionality

Besides this more general and organisational duty, the State also has to take selective measures suitable to the specific situation at hand.[109] Due regard must be had to the means at the disposal of the State in the concrete situation.[110] Just as it is impossible for States to control each and every act of private persons on their territory, this also, or rather especially, holds true for the case of CNOs. As long as there are technical ways to completely conceal the origin of CNOs, a State is barred from effectively preventing these. While data retention is considered by some to be the most effective measure to find individual perpetrators and preventively provide for deterrence, it is ultimately at the discretion of States to introduce.

Attention must further be paid to the principle of proportionality. This is due to the fact that most of the malicious cross-border CNOs are taking place on a very low level inflicting the lowest forms of harm if at all, mostly being a mere nuisance or causing marginal monetary damages. These cases are so numerous that they are generally not even reported and need not be analysed here. From the outset it is clear that under the principle of proportionality the source State in these cases is not obliged to take major measures. In the case of operations taking place on a larger scale, such as those observed in the Estonian and Georgian cases, a greater effort is required. This is especially the case when the operations are still ongoing and take place over a longer time period. Here the source State is actually able to suppress the operations. In the case of websites which incite participation in these CNOs or even provide the relevant software to do so – as was the case in the Georgian incident – once the territorial State has gained knowledge of this, it is likewise under an obligation to prevent the further availability of the software, for example by invoking take-down procedures established under copyright law. However it is at the discretion of States as to how to prevent further illegal actions. This is no different in the case of more sophisticated CNOs such as Stuxnet, or Trojan horses in general. While the technical effort needed to identify the originator is much higher in these cases this may be balanced by the greater level of harm to be expected.

1.2.2.2.4. Comparability with Liability Regimes Applicable to Areas Beyond the Limits of National Jurisdiction

A further argument can be made by considering more general principles of due diligence and liability of States for private actors. Principally illegal acts of non-

---

109 Epiney *Die völkerrechtliche Verantwortlichkeit von Staaten für rechtswidriges Verhalten im Zusammenhang mit Aktionen Privater* p. 230.

110 See pp. 96 et seq. above and Epiney *Die völkerrechtliche Verantwortlichkeit von Staaten für rechtswidriges Verhalten im Zusammenhang mit Aktionen Privater* p. 241 providing for numerous examples of both State practice and judgments supporting this conclusion (at pp. 232–43).

State actors are regulated by the national criminal laws applicable in the State having jurisdiction. Historically there were few instances where private actors could undertake criminal actions against foreign targets while remaining outside of the latter's jurisdiction. An exception to this is the case of crimes against aliens. As a consequence an obligation on the host State to adequately prosecute perpetrators was developed, since the aliens' home State was practically incapable of doing so. Technological developments have however also made such conduct possible in other instances, as for example in internationalised areas outside of singular State jurisdiction. This is the case both for the law of the sea and outer space. Therefore the UN Convention on the Law of the Sea includes provisions for extensive admission, control, and monitoring responsibilities of States for conduct by private actors.[111] These are obligations to exercise due diligence in preventing environmental harm to the environment of other States or other areas beyond the State's jurisdiction. When for example damage is caused by the activities of non-State actors on the seabed and ocean floor, and subsoil thereof, lying beyond the limits of national jurisdiction ('the Area'), the State Party whose nationality the actor has may be liable. This is the case if a State Party fails to carry out its responsibilities under the Convention unless it has taken all necessary and appropriate measures to secure effective compliance with the obligations under the Convention by the non-State actor.[112] The Outer Space Liability Convention in certain cases even establishes a strict liability of the launching or national State for damage caused by space objects also if these are undertaken by private entities.[113] In both cases technological progress has given non-State actors the ability to inflict significant harm on third States while being in an area beyond national jurisdiction. In order to prevent damaged States being left without compensation, these special liability regimes were installed obliging States to diligently supervise the activities of private entities and ultimately bear responsibility for their illegal actions.

A comparable situation exists with malicious cross-border CNOs. While cyberspace is not a sphere sui generis outside of States' jurisdiction but can be 'territorialised', the damaged State mostly lacks the jurisdiction to enforce despite the operations' direct effect on its territory. Notwithstanding these similarities it is unequally more difficult for States in practice to control activities in cyberspace than it is to control the launching of satellites or to monitor activities in the Area. Additionally the latter activities are mostly done with the

111 Arts. 139, 194, 207, 209–211 and 235 UN Convention on the Law of the Sea; Kees 'Responsibility of States for Private Actors' para. 23.

112 Art. 139 UN Convention on the Law of the Sea; see Alena Douhan 'Liability for Environmental Damage' in Rüdiger Wolfrum (ed) *MPEPIL* (OUP Oxford Update 2011) paras. 23–24.

113 Arts. 6 and 7 Convention on International Liability for Damage Caused by Space Objects; Pedrazzi 'Outer Space, Liability for Damage' paras. 2 and 9–11.

intention of generating profits, hence connected to the State's revenue. Ensuing liability for exploitative activities can therefore be regarded as the equitable corollary thereof. The Internet on the other hand has – apart from its role for business – also developed as the primary modern means of communication and is not endowed with original resources that could be exploited, but serves merely as a facilitator for gaining revenue. The liability regimes utilised both in the law of the sea or outer space are hence not suitable for the realm of cyberspace. Nevertheless these regimes show that the due diligence standards for States in connection with the actions of private actors are higher in areas where potentially damaged States are unable to effectively exercise enforcement jurisdiction. This further supports the idea that States are under an obligation to exercise due diligence in the prevention of malicious CNOs by non-State actors within their jurisdiction.

1.2.2.2.5. State Practice

While State practice does not give rise to a specific obligation under customary international law, it nevertheless does give support for the emergence of a general duty of prevention. Several States have in their contributions to the UN Group of Governmental Experts on Information Security indicated their support for an attribution through the obligation of due diligence in preventing CNOs. The Indian representative opined that States have the responsibility to ensure that their ICT infrastructure is not abused by others, either covertly or overtly, to target or attack the ICT infrastructure of other States.[114] A similar opinion was expressed in this forum by China and Russia, which declared respectively that States 'have the responsibilities and rights to take necessary management measures to keep their domestic cyberspace and related infrastructure free from threats, disturbance, attack and sabotage'[115] and 'should bear responsibility at international level for such actions in information space, carried out directly, under their jurisdiction or in the framework of international organisations of their membership'.[116]

A similar point was made by the United States in 2011, qualifying 'cybersecurity due diligence' (defined as the responsibility of States to protect their information infrastructures and national systems from damage and misuse) as an emerging norm.[117]

114 India's contribution to the Report of the UN Group of Governmental Experts on Information Security as cited in Kanuck 'Sovereign Discourse on Cyber Conflict under International Law' p. 1591.

115 China's contribution to the Report of the UN Group of Governmental Experts on Information Security as cited in Kanuck 'Sovereign Discourse on Cyber Conflict under International Law' p. 1591.

116 Russia's contribution to the Report of the UN Group of Governmental Experts on Information Security as cited in Kanuck 'Sovereign Discourse on Cyber Conflict under International Law' p. 1591.

117 The President of the United States of America 'International Strategy for Cyberspace' p. 10.

1.2.2.2.6. Conclusion

There in fact exists an obligation on States to prevent malicious cross-border computer network operations from emanating from networks under their territorial jurisdiction. This is however not a specific obligation created under customary international law but is contained in the general obligation of States not to knowingly allow their territory to be used for acts contrary to the rights of other States. The fulfilment of this obligation, which is at the discretion of States, is evaluated by their exercise of due diligence. While there is no obligation under general international law to introduce specific criminal offences under national law, such can be an indication of diligent behaviour. But States are generally under considerable discretion regarding the realisation of the duty. Knowledge of illegal acts cannot generally be inferred from mere territorial control of a State, an assumption also valid for operations on the Internet. However, such knowledge is presumed when the target State informs the source State of such operations emanating from networks in its territory. It remains the responsibility of each State to designate the appropriate institution for such notifications. Nonetheless, State practice shows that the establishment of national CERTs available on a 24-hours-a-day, seven-days-a-week basis is considered to be the organisational best practice in this regard.

Identifying those individually responsible for CNOs has proven nearly impossible without the cooperation of the source State. This kind of cooperation with the goal of stopping further CNOs is to be seen as diligent behaviour on the part of the source State.[118] In this regard it is important that States cannot invoke conflicting national law as an objection to such cooperation. In cases where due to a lack of cooperation only the source of the operation can be verified to be generally emanating from the territory of a foreign State, it is irrelevant for the latter's responsibility who actually performed the operation. In the case of a State agent, attribution is a given. If undertaken by non-State actors, the source State cannot evade responsibility by simply denying cooperation. This would open the possibility of plausible deniability for every State wishing to undertake CNOs, thus effectively circumventing any State responsibility.

Lastly it must be kept in mind that the obligation of due diligence does not impose the impossible but only those measures disposable to the relevant State. This is of importance as regards the fact that not every CNO can be prevented from the outset. In contrast to more conventional means, CNOs are undertaken instantly and often without detectable preparatory acts. This makes the exercise of due diligence concentrate especially on the acts of the source State after the

118 Similar is seen by the Institut de Droit International in the event of an armed attack by non-State actors. In this case the State from which the attack originates is seen as being under an obligation to cooperate with the target State: Institut de Droit International 'Resolution on Self-Defence' (27 October 2007) 10A Resolution para. 10.

fact. Furthermore it must be taken into account that there will always remain technical possibilities to circumvent obligatory security measures, making total security an unrealistic scenario. However, States are under a duty to provide due diligence to reach this security as far as possible. The principle of proportionality finally serves as the limitation necessary to prevent due diligence obligations from obstructing the freedom of action of States in their Internet policies and the technical functioning of the globally interconnected networks.

2. BREACH OF AN INTERNATIONAL OBLIGATION

The conduct at hand attributed to a particular State must also amount to a breach of an international obligation. The latter is defined by Article 12 ILC Articles as being 'when an act of that State is not in conformity with what is required of it by that obligation, regardless of its origin or character'. In the field of military operations a distinction can generally be drawn between those that are qualifiable as armed force in the sense of Article 2(4) UN Charter and such which lie below that threshold.[119] This is especially important in the case of CNOs as it is conceivable that a considerable number does not easily qualify as armed force. Furthermore, the technical character of CNOs makes them a means not only utilisable by armed forces but also for example by law enforcement authorities and intelligence services. While it is irrelevant from a standpoint of State responsibility which State organ actually executes CNOs, if organs other than the armed forces of a State perform these operations, these might rather belong to the field below the threshold of armed force evaluated in the following.

2.1. COMPUTER NETWORK OPERATIONS BELOW THE LEVEL OF ARMED FORCE

As there exists no singular specific framework applicable to computer network operations undertaken by States, recourse must be made to general principles of international law, first and foremost the prohibition of intervention. Depending on the respective field of application, computer network operations could further conflict with more specific regimes, such as the regimes of international telecommunications and outer space as well as the law of the sea.

119 On the latter see generally Woltag 'Computer Network Operations Below the Level of Armed Force'; and Russell Buchan 'Cyber Attacks: Unlawful Uses of Force or Prohibited Interventions?' (2012) 17 Journal of Conflict and Security Law pp. 212 et seq.

2.1.1. *The Prohibition of Intervention*

The exact content and scope of the principle of non-intervention remains disputed and is mostly contemplated in relation to specific case groups.[120] It has further been alleged that the principle has 'failed to keep pace with technological advancements that render traditional territorial limits irrelevant'.[121] While it is to be admitted that the relevance of the principle is decreasing along with the diminishing domaine réservé of States,[122] it nevertheless provides for a necessary catchall element for the basic protection of State sovereignty.

Today it is generally stipulated that the scope of the non-intervention principle goes beyond the mere prohibition of the use of armed force.[123] The proposition of the PCIJ in the *Lotus Case* of 1927 that it is 'the first and foremost restriction imposed by international law upon a State ... [that] it may not exercise its power in any form in the territory of another State'[124] is still regarded as one of the cornerstones of the international legal order and forms an essential part of the non-intervention principle.[125] A similar point was held by arbitrator Huber in the *Island of Palmas Case* of 1928 where it was stated that '[i]ndependence in regard to a portion of the globe is the right to exercise therein, to the exclusion of any other State, the functions of a State'; this 'principle of the exclusive competence of the State in regard to its own territory' consequently means that 'territorial sovereignty belongs always to one, or in exceptional circumstances to several States, to the exclusion of all others'.[126] These two cases exemplify the interrelation of other general principles which protect a State from external interferences with the non-intervention principle. These are the prohibition of the use of force and the territorial integrity and sovereignty of States.[127] Derived from the sovereign equality of States the principle of non-intervention is a corollary of every State's right to political independence and territorial integrity.[128] The latter refers to the effective control and possession of land

120 Hobe *Einführung in das Völkerrecht* p. 368; Philip Kunig 'Intervention, Prohibition of' in Rüdiger Wolfrum (ed) *MPEPIL* (OUP Oxford Update 2008) para. 1.

121 Simon Chesterman 'Secret Intelligence' in Rüdiger Wolfrum (ed) *MPEPIL* (OUP Oxford Update 2009) para. 23.

122 Dahm, Delbrück & Wolfrum *Völkerrecht vol I/3* p. 815.

123 On the discussion between a wide and narrow interpretation of the scope of intervention see Dahm, Delbrück & Wolfrum *Völkerrecht vol I/3* p. 802.

124 *Lotus Case* p. 18.

125 Armin von Bogdandy & Markus Rau 'Lotus, The' in Rüdiger Wolfrum (ed) *MPEPIL* (OUP Oxford Update 2006) para. 19.

126 *Island of Palmas (Netherlands v United States of America)* (1928) 2 RIAA 829 at p. 838.

127 Dahm, Delbrück & Wolfrum *Völkerrecht vol I/3* pp. 791–92; Christos L. Rozakis 'Territorial Integrity and Political Independence' in Rudolf Bernhardt (ed) *Encyclopedia of Public International Law* vol IV (Elsevier Amsterdam 2000) p. 817.

128 Robert Y. Jennings & Arthur Watts *Oppenheim's International Law* (Longman Harlow 1996) p. 428; Jamnejad & Wood 'The Principle of Non-Intervention' p. 358.

territory, the territorial sea and the seabed and subsoil of the territorial sea.[129] It generally prohibits governmental activities on foreign territory that encroach on the territorial sovereignty of the respective State.[130] Political independence on the other hand 'refers to the autonomy in the affairs of the State with respect to its institutions, freedom of political decisions, policy making, and in matters pertaining to its domestic and foreign affairs'.[131]

These interrelations have prevented the development of a precise definition of the non-intervention principle. Nonetheless, by and large it is defined by the cumulative fulfilment of two conditions: firstly, an interference of one State in the internal or foreign affairs of another State, which is solely the responsibility of inner State actors; and secondly, the interference taking place through the threat or application of coercion, aiming to impose a certain conduct of consequence.[132] Although not explicitly mentioned in the UN Charter, the majority view does, at least partly, derive it from this in one way or another.[133] While references to non-intervention in practice are often of a purely political import without legal relevance, the principle resulting from the sovereign equality of States is in its standing under international law regarded as a fundamental duty of States and part of customary international law.[134]

2.1.1.1. Domaine Réservé in Cyberspace

As the non-intervention principle prohibits the interference in the internal affairs of a State which lie solely in the latter's responsibility, establishing the scope and content of the domestic affairs of a State is of both particular importance but also difficulty. Generally they are regarded as those matters which are not regulated by international law, and are thus dependent on the development and current status of international relations.[135] The advancement of international law into various fields formerly under the sole domestic jurisdiction of States has reduced the sphere of domaine réservé to a large extent in the recent decades.[136] However, the principle of State sovereignty, still

---

129 Samuel KN Blay 'Territorial Integrity and Political Independence' in Rüdiger Wolfrum (ed) *MPEPIL* (OUP Oxford Update 2010) para.1.

130 Dahm, Delbrück & Wolfrum *Völkerrecht vol I/3* p. 792; Stein & Buttlar *Völkerrecht* pp. 187–89.

131 Blay 'Territorial Integrity and Political Independence' para. 1.

132 Kunig 'Intervention, Prohibition of' para. 1; Hobe *Einführung in das Völkerrecht* pp. 366–67.

133 The different approaches to the derivation of the principle from the UN Charter are not of concern here. For a short overview see Kunig 'Intervention, Prohibition of' paras. 9–10 and Dahm, Delbrück & Wolfrum *Völkerrecht vol I/3* pp. 797–98.

134 *Nicaragua Case* para. 202; Jamnejad & Wood 'The Principle of Non-Intervention' p. 358; *Military and Paramilitary Activities in and against Nicaragua (Nicaragua v United States of America) (Dissenting Opinion of Judge Jennings)* [1986] ICJ Rep 528 at p. 534.

135 As already stipulated by the PCIJ in the*Nationality Decrees Issued in Tunis and Morocco (French Zone) (Advisory Opinion)* PCIJ Series B No 4 p. 24.

136 See generally Katja S. Ziegler 'Domain Réservé' in Rüdiger Wolfrum (ed) *MPEPIL* (OUP Oxford Update 2008).

fundamental to international law, does leave a significant margin of areas under the sole competence of States. Whether or not extraterritorial CNOs by one State encroach upon the domaine réservé of a third State may thus be established by determining to what degree State sovereignty also exists on the Internet.

As has already been shown above in relation to jurisdiction in cyberspace, territory is not defined by private law analogies to real property, but by the extent of governmental power capable of being exercised with respect to territory and population.[137] Territorial sovereignty can therefore be understood as governing power with respect to territory.[138] Most recently, the Cybercrime Convention has shown that, by penalising illegal access, interception and interference with computer data, States are very capable of exercising governing power over Internet-related conduct. States regulate the Internet activities of their nationals under the nationality principle, and those of foreign nationals in their territory under the territoriality principle.[139] Jurisdiction over Internet activities of foreigners on foreign territory is increasingly asserted by States through the effects principle.[140] As has been shown above, the idea of a 'borderless cyberspace' or treating the Internet as a common resource is not convincing. Firstly, the infrastructure on which the Internet relies clearly manifests itself in tangible property the location of which is precisely determinable. Secondly, even when regarding cyberspace separately from its infrastructure, a number of States have impressively shown that they are capable of shielding their networks from the general Internet thus creating a virtual corollary to boundaries ultimately contributing to a territorialised Internet.

The same holds true for the case of Internet governance.[141] While at first sight this seems to be solely in the hands of ICANN, and through the oversight of the United States ultimately in the latter's hand, there is nevertheless agreement on certain core components which support the thesis of a territorialised Internet. The UN Tunis Agenda for the Information Society for example stipulates that countries should not be involved in decisions regarding another country's country code top-level domain ('ccTLD'). Regarding decisions affecting ccTLDs, the legitimate interests of the relevant State need to be respected, while the definition of these interests remains with each State individually.[142] While not legally binding, this proposition is in practice adhered to by ICANN, which still holds the ultimate power over the ccTLDs. Firstly the administration of ccTLDs is delegated to national registries. Secondly the recommendations of the Governmental Advisory Committee representing the

---

137 Crawford *The Creation of States in International Law* p. 42; see generally pp. 58 et seq. above.

138 James Crawford 'State' in Rüdiger Wolfrum (ed) *MPEPIL* (OUP Oxford Update 2011) para. 22.

139 Oxman 'Jurisdiction of States' para. 31.

140 See pp. 60 et seq. above; Woltag 'Internet' paras. 18–20.

141 See pp. 62 et seq. above.

142 UN WSIS 'Tunis Agenda for the Information Society (18 November 2005)' para. 63.

interests of States concerning legal and public policy issues have apparently always been adhered to by ICANN.[143] The determination of which entity is afforded its own ccTLD and thus effectively treated as a State is likewise not made by ICANN itself but taken from the designation under the ISO Standard 3166.[144] Despite justified criticism of the role and legitimacy of ICANN, it can therefore be concluded that States in the governance of their networks, hence their 'part of the Internet', effectively retain their sovereignty. This stance is also reflected in the practice of several States. In a statement to the OSCE on the Russian Federation's approach to regulating the security of the information and communications technology sector the Russian representative emphasised that it is a State's sovereign right to independent governance of the Internet at the national level.[145] China opined that 'each country has the right to manage its own cyberspace in accordance with its domestic legislation',[146] which was reiterated by Qatar.[147]

In conclusion it has been established that a certain level of domaine réservé is also retained on the Internet. Firstly, the networks and computer systems located on a State's territory are encompassed under the protection of the latter's territorial integrity. Secondly, this infrastructure on which the Internet is reliant is subject to the jurisdiction of the respective territorial State. This includes the jurisdiction to enforce in regard to Internet service providers, carriers and individuals which create, manage or utilise the information and communications infrastructure. Through the utilisation of the territoriality principle States have clearly rejected the vision of a borderless cyberspace. Hence the regulation both

143 Dederer 'ICANN und die Dominanz der USA: Internet Governance auf dem Weg in die Internationalisierung' p. 384. This is also stipulated in para. 4.1. ICANN Governmental Advisory Committee 'Principles and Guidelines for the Delegation and Administration of Country Code Top Level Domains' (done 5 April 2005). The same document stipulates that under the principle of subsidiarity, ccTLD policy should be set locally in accordance with national law (at para. 1.2.), including delegation and re-delegation of the respective registry (at para. 7.1.). The dispute settlement systems concerning domain names therefore likewise lie in the discretion of the relevant State; Woltag 'Internet' para. 20.

144 John Postel 'Domain Name System Structure and Delegation' (March 1994) Request for Comments 1591, states this principle: 'The IANA [which is operated by ICANN] is not in the business of deciding what is and what is not a country. The selection of the ISO 3166 list as a basis for country code top-level domain names was made with the knowledge that ISO has a procedure for determining which entities should be and should not be on that list' (at para. 4.2).

145 Delegation of the Russian Federation 'Statement by Mr S Shestakov, Representative of the Russian Federation, at the Joint Meeting of the OSCE Forum for Security Co-operation and the OSCE Permanent Council' (10 June 2010).

146 Chinese Statement of 24 May 2006 in UNGA 'Developments in the Field of Information and Telecommunications in the Context of International Security: Report of the Secretary-General' (18 July 2006) at p. 4.

147 Each State 'should have the right to manage its own Internet resources in accordance with domestic legislation'; Statement by Qatar in UNGA 'Developments in the Field of Information and Telecommunications in the Context of International Security: Report of the Secretary-General' (18 July 2008) UN Doc A/63/139 at p. 8.

of activities and content falls within the domaine réservé of the respective State. In practice this approach is also demonstrated in relation to Internet governance which, while being centrally coordinated by ICANN, in effect lies within the competence of each individual State.

2.1.1.2. Means of Interference

State activities are only considered a prohibited intervention into the internal affairs of another State if undertaken by coercive means.[148] Under the classical notion of intervention during the 19th century, protection was merely afforded to the territorial integrity of a State, thus encompassing only armed force as an element of intervention. This concept is hence to an extent congruent with the current prohibition on the use of force. However, during the 20th century, the content of the prohibition of intervention was further developed and expanded in order to also protect States' political independence.[149] The Charter of Economic Rights and Duties of States for example stipulates that outside interference of a State in the affairs of another State in any form whatsoever is forbidden.[150] The ICJ in the *Nicaragua Case* stipulated methods of coercion in regard to choices 'of a political, economic, social and cultural system, and the formulation of foreign policy' to be a prohibited intervention, as these were 'bearing on matters in which each State is permitted, by the principle of State sovereignty, to decide freely'. The element of coercion were to be 'particularly obvious in the case of an intervention which uses force, either in the direct form of military action, or in the indirect form of support for subversive or terrorist armed activities within another State'.[151] With the word 'particularly', the ICJ indicated that the element of coercion need not be of a forceful military nature. Naval demonstrations for example, while generally a prima facie lawful activity, can under certain circumstances be qualified as a (prohibited) military intervention of a non-forcible nature.[152] Ultimately coercion under international law can therefore be defined as an activity of a government 'compelling the government of another State to think or act in a certain way by applying various kinds of pressure, threats, intimidation or the use of force'.[153]

---

148 Kunig 'Intervention, Prohibition of' paras. 5–6.

149 Kunig 'Intervention, Prohibition of' para. 6.

150 UNGA Res 3281 (XXIX) 'Charter of Economic Rights and Duties of States' (12 December 1974) GAOR 29th Session Supp 31 vol 1, 50. The resolution cannot be regarded as reflecting a general consensus on the matter however: Hobe *Einführung in das Völkerrecht* p. 367.

151 *Nicaragua Case* para. 205.

152 Dale Stephens & Tristan Skousgaard 'Naval Demonstrations and Manoeuvres' in Rüdiger Wolfrum (ed) *MPEPIL* (OUP Oxford Update 2009) para. 11; Kunig 'Intervention, Prohibition of' para. 23.

153 Christoph C. Joyner 'Coercion' in Rüdiger Wolfrum (ed) *MPEPIL* (OUP Oxford Update 2006) para. 1.

The requirement of an element of coercion aims at protecting the territorial integrity and political independence of a State.[154] Due to the interrelation between territorial integrity, political independence and the non-intervention principle, an interference in the first two is likewise to be qualified as an interference in the internal affairs of the target State. This results from the fact that territorial integrity and political independence are preconditions for a State to be able to exercise its sovereign powers to the exclusion of others.

Generally a distinction can be made between two types of activities which may potentially infringe on the target State's internal affairs. These are on the one hand sovereign acts which can violate the target State's political independence and on the other hand physical actions or those with a similar effect which are able to interfere with the territorial integrity of States.

2.1.1.2.1. Computer Network Operations as Sovereign Acts

Sovereign acts with effect on foreign territory are those where one State through its actions sets itself in competition to the territorial sovereignty of the target State.[155] Hence, actions taken on foreign territory that do not have an effect therein are permissible, such as for example the signing of laws by State officials on foreign territory which only have an effect in the official's State of origin.[156] State practice offers several examples of activities that have been qualified as illegal sovereign acts with effects on foreign territory.[157] These include the service of process of official documents to private persons on foreign territory if those are of a constitutive quality,[158] as well as the obtaining of evidence on foreign territory.[159] *Weber and Saravia v Germany*, concerning the monitoring of international wireless telecommunications by interception sites located in Germany and the use of the data thus obtained, for example led the ECtHR to find no interference with the territorial sovereignty of foreign States, as the

154 Kunig 'Intervention, Prohibition of' para. 6.

155 Michael Germann *Gefahrenabwehr und Strafverfolgung im Internet* (Duncker und Humblot Berlin 2000) p. 642.

156 Alexander Orakhelashvili 'Governmental Activity on Foreign Territory' in Rüdiger Wolfrum (ed) *MPEPIL* (OUP Oxford Update 2010) para. 15; Dahm, Delbrück & Wolfrum *Völkerrecht vol I/3* p. 792.

157 Examples taken from Dahm, Delbrück & Wolfrum *Völkerrecht vol I/3* p. 792; see also the examples given by Chesterman 'Secret Intelligence' paras. 14–18.

158 Bundesverfassungsgericht (German Constitutional Court) 2 BvR 457/78 'Rechtshilfevertrag' (22 March 1983) BVerfGE 63, 343 at p. 372.

159 A case where such was undertaken by armed forces is the *Corfu Channel Case*; however also the gathering of evidence by regular investigative or law enforcement authorities on foreign territory infringes on the latter State's sovereignty: Barry Sankol 'Verletzung fremdstaatlicher Souveränität durch ermittlungsbehördliche Zugriffe auf E-Mail-Postfächer' (2008) 11 Kommunikation und Recht p. 280; Nicolai Seitz *Strafverfolgungsmaßnahmen im Internet* (Heymanns Köln 2005) p. 364; Orakhelashvili 'Governmental Activity on Foreign Territory' para. 14.

emissions of wireless telecommunications originating abroad were only intercepted within German territory.[160] By emphasising the latter, it can conversely be concluded that an intrusive interception on foreign territory would have been qualified differently by the Court, namely as a violation of the target State's territorial sovereignty.[161] These examples show that it is not necessary for the measure to be of a physically coercive nature. But there are also those – such as transboundary abduction, on the spot extraterritorial police investigations and cross-border assassinations of non-combatants – that qualify as a sovereign act while concurrently having a physically coercive quality.[162] In the absence of host State consent such actions are deemed illegal under international law as has been shown in several cases.[163]

In the case of computer network operations the scenario will mostly involve a State agent executing a cross-border CNO while being located in the territory of his home State. Whether such activity is to be considered a sovereign act depends on its legal character. The access by public authorities to data hosted on servers under a foreign jurisdiction can legally be of both a sovereign and general character. In the latter case the authority acts in the manner of a private individual, which is generally considered to be unproblematic under international law. It is sufficient for an action of a public authority to be of a sovereign character once it is part of the performance of the authority's sovereign functions. It is problematic, however, to define in which cases these acts can be considered to have an effect on the foreign territory. According to one opinion this is the case already where publicly available information is obtained in

160 *Weber and Saravia v Germany* (ECtHR) App 54934/00 para. 88.

161 The placement of malware on foreign systems not causing physical damage (eg malware to monitor foreign activities) constitutes a violation of the target State's sovereignty, as it is an intrusive operation by which the operating State exercises its sovereign powers on foreign territory. Conversely, the group of experts drafting the Tallinn Manual could not achieve consensus in regard to this question: Schmitt (ed) *Tallinn Manual on the International Law Applicable to Cyber Warfare* p. 16 para. 6.

162 Qualifying transboundary abduction as a violation of a State's territorial integrity: Kamminga 'Extraterritoriality' paras. 22–25. Additionally this conduct may also infringe upon the human rights of the abductee, which is however of no concern here; on this see Orakhelashvili 'Governmental Activity on Foreign Territory' paras. 19 et seq.

163 The UN Security Council in Resolution 138 of 23 June 1960 (SCOR 50th Year 4) declared that the abduction of Adolf Eichmann by Israeli agents from Argentina constituted a violation of Argentina's sovereignty. See also generally Stephan Wilske 'Abduction, Transboundary' in Rüdiger Wolfrum (ed) *MPEPIL* (OUP Oxford Update 2009). In case of extraterritorial forcible actions, France acknowledged in the *Rainbow Warrior Case* that its sinking of the ship in a New Zealand harbour – which lead to the death of one person on board – constituted an attack 'in violation of the territorial sovereignty of New Zealand and that it was therefore committed in violation of international law' ('Memorandum of the Government of the French Republic to the Secretary-General of the United Nations' reprinted in *Rainbow Warrior (Ruling by the UN Secretary-General) (6 July 1986) (New Zealand v France)* (1986) 19 RIAA 207 at p. 209.

preparation for a legal procedure against a foreign Internet service provider. This would in turn qualify as a violation of the target State's sovereignty.[164]

This proves to be too narrow. Consequently public authorities would not be able to obtain information via the Internet if this is done in support of their sovereign functions. Determining whether a sovereign act has effects on the foreign territory must take into account the legal quality of these effects. The spirit and purpose of the prohibition on extraterritorial sovereign acts rests on the fundamental protection of a State's territorial sovereignty. Hence only those sovereign acts are prohibited that in their effect encroach on the target State's sovereignty by substituting the latter's powers with its own. However, in the case of CNOs undertaken to gain information by accessing data publicly available on the Internet, the performing State organ does not exercise any power exclusive to the territorial sovereign. Both States and individuals may introduce limitations on access to the data hosted on their systems, for instance through passwords or by generally banning foreign computer systems from access by so-called geolocation.[165] By making the relevant data publicly available, the publisher consents to its general accessibility. This also encompasses foreign public authorities. Data on the other hand which is in some way protected from public access will under most national laws be accessible to a State organ only through the exercise of its public authority, in certain cases conditional upon a court order. The determination of which acts violate the target State's territorial sovereignty is thus to be made with a view to the public availability of the accessed data. This view finds support in the regulation of sovereign measures of law enforcement authorities under the Cybercrime Convention. The Convention generally requires the approval of the State the territory of which the accessed computer system is located on. However, Article 32 Cybercrime Convention allows for this access without an approval by the target State in two circumstances: either if the consent to the access is given by the person having the lawful authority to disclose said data or if it is stored in a publicly available manner. In these cases the authorisation of the other party to the Cybercrime Convention is not needed. Explicitly granting access only in these two cases means in reverse that cross-border access to stored computer data failing authorisation was considered to be contrary to international law by the States Parties.[166]

---

164 Lothar Determann *Kommunikationsfreiheit im Internet: Freiheitsrechte und gesetzliche Beschränkungen* (Nomos Baden-Baden 1999) p. 150.

165 Hoeren 'Zoning und Geolocation – Technische Ansätze zur Reterritorialisierung des Internet' at pp. 3–6 however points out that geolocation does not (yet) function with complete reliability.

166 These two cases were the only ones where the drafters could agree for unilateral action to be permissible: Explanatory Report to the Convention on Cybercrime para. 293.Similarly in relation to the access by law enforcement authorities to the e-mail inbox on servers situated on foreign territory: Sankol 'Verletzung fremdstaatlicher Souveränität durch ermittlungsbehördliche Zugriffe auf E-Mail-Postfächer' p. 282; Björn Gercke 'Kommentierung zu §110

While in cases lacking consent a subsequent approval by the target State can be given this does not mean, as has been opined,[167] that States may temporarily preserve the data acquired in the hope of future approval. This is firstly a circumvention of the relevant agreements on judicial assistance, and secondly sets a scarcely tenable precedent in encouraging States to engage in internationally wrongful conduct.[168] In being directed against the State as such, a subsequent approval by the target State in case of military cross-border CNOs is a fortiori unrealistic.

Despite the author's claim of a territorialised Internet, it is admitted that in practice these different territories are not as easily cognizable as is the case with regular State boundaries. Hence it is not always clear for public authorities to ascertain whether an investigation conducted on the Internet is taking place on systems located on foreign or home territory. Therefore another proposition has been made to consider the element of intent in evaluating a measure's interference with the territorial integrity of the target State.[169] Only in cases where the cross-border activity is of a sovereign character and undertaken with knowledge of the measure's extraterritorial effect shall it be qualified as an illegal interference.

While the State itself as a juridical abstraction is devoid of the condition of intent, the latter may in certain circumstances be required by the agents through which a State acts, which depends on the relevant primary obligation.[170] Yet while the element of intent might be worthy of consideration under national law, as for example in regard to the question of whether information acquired through a computer network operation may be used as evidence in court, under international law it cannot be considered for this case. Under the prohibition of intervention an element of intentional conduct is unnecessary, as the rule's objective – namely to prevent the substitution of the territorial State's sovereignty through a third State – is infringed both by intentional or unintentional conduct. The situation is similar to the treatment of ultra vires acts of State agents: in considering these, a State would have the opportunity to absolve itself of any responsibility as it could either claim its agents to have acted without or in excess of orders or, as in this case, without intent. However, by entrusting their agents with governmental functions States are responsible for any of their conduct. The lack of intent is therefore not to be taken into consideration.

StPO' in Karl-Peter Julius, et al. (eds) *Strafprozessordnung* (CF Müller Heidelberg 2009) p. 584.

167 Wolfgang Bär 'EDV-Beweissicherung im Strafverfahren bei Computer, Handy, Internet: Ermittlungsmöglichkeiten bei Internetstraftaten' (2007) Deutsche Richterzeitung p. 221.

168 Similarly Sankol 'Verletzung fremdstaatlicher Souveränität durch ermittlungsbehördliche Zugriffe auf E-Mail-Postfächer' p. 281.

169 Germann *Gefahrenabwehr und Strafverfolgung im Internet* p. 643.

170 Para. 3 Commentary to Art. 2 UN ILC 'Text of the Draft Articles with Commentaries Thereto: Responsibility of States for Internationally Wrongful Acts'.

In conclusion it can be observed that an interference in the internal affairs of a foreign State with the means of computer network operations exists if these are undertaken by a State organ and qualify as measures of a sovereign character. This is inter alia the case when the data accessed is not publicly available. An element of intent on the part of the State agent is not required. In these instances the executing State infringes the political independence of the target State by exercising enforcement jurisdiction on a foreign territory and thus by attempting to substitute the latter State's sovereignty with its own.

2.1.1.2.2. Computer Network Operations as Physical Acts

Territorial integrity encompasses the freedom from physical impact.[171] Today there are many different activities that may have effects on foreign territory through emissions. This is most prominently the case with transboundary pollution. But there are also other, more technical, activities which may potentially emit on foreign territory: broadcasting (through electromagnetic waves) or weather and climate modification (cloud seeding, storm modifications).[172] Furthermore, there are those activities that are intended to influence the political independence of a State, e.g. by inciting to revolt or civil strife through transborder broadcasts.[173] Lastly, classical intrusions, for instance those of State ships or aircraft into foreign territory without permission, can also be qualified as physical actions.[174]

Activities that have a physical impact on foreign territory have led to the international environmental law maxim sic utere tuo ut alienum non laedas, or the no-harm rule, which has already been established in the *Trail Smelter Case*. Today it is inter alia encompassed in Principle 21 of the 1972 Stockholm Declaration of the UN Conference on the Human Environment stating that: 'States have … the responsibility to ensure that activities within their jurisdiction or control do not cause damage to the environment of other States or areas beyond the limits of national jurisdiction'.[175] While both the *Trail Smelter Case* and the *Affaire du Lac Lanoux* expressly or implicitly provided for a limiting

---

171 Stein & Buttlar *Völkerrecht* p. 189.

172 See generally Jan Willisch *State Responsibility for Technological Damage in International Law* (Duncker & Humblot Berlin 1987) who concludes that physical interference with bodily objects into foreign territory is absolutely prohibited through the protection of the territorial integrity of States (at pp. 73–74).

173 Kunig 'Intervention, Prohibition of' para. 24; Jamnejad & Wood 'The Principle of Non-Intervention' p. 374.

174 As was the case in the shooting or forcing down of several US planes deemed by Russia as flying in Russian airspace unpermitted; see the examples given by Kay Hailbronner & Daniel Heilmann 'Aerial Incident Cases before International Courts and Tribunals' in Rüdiger Wolfrum (ed) *MPEPIL* (OUP Oxford Update 2009).

175 UN Conference on the Human Environment 'Stockholm Declaration of the United Nations Conference on the Human Environment' (16 June 1972) UN Doc A/CONF.48/14/Rev 1, 3; *Trail Smelter (United States of America v Canada)* (1938/41) 3 RIAA 1905; similar can be

criterion as to the intensity of harm incurred – namely only serious consequences[176] – such was omitted in the Stockholm Declaration. The ICJ in the *Use of Nuclear Weapons (Advisory Opinion)* viewed the environmental no-harm principle as a 'general obligation of States' extending not only to neighbour States' territory, but to any 'areas beyond national control' and now forming 'part of the corpus of international law relating to the environment'.[177] However, especially outside of the field of environmental law, the exact content of the no-harm rule, its legal status and relationship to similar concepts such as the abuse of rights and good-neighbourliness are unclear.[178] Some see the rule as also being generally applicable outside of environmental law to all transboundary harm, for example even terrorist acts.[179] In regulations on broadcasting, technical necessities have in fact led to the explicit inclusion of the principle.[180]

The computer network operations considered above under the notion of sovereign acts mostly refer to conduct by authorities other than the armed forces of a State. In the case of (military) CNOs undertaken with a view not to gain information, but rather to alter data on a foreign system – sometimes mistakenly referred to as computer network attacks[181] – these resemble physical actions in that their emphasis lies not on their sovereign character but on the direct negative effects on the target territory. This is underscored by the fact that an alteration mostly brings about more serious direct consequences than illegal access, as one compromised datum may lead to adverse cascading effects on all dependencies thereof. Hence these sorts of CNOs, due to their negative impact on the target systems comparable to that of physical actions, qualify as an interference with the territorial integrity of the target State.

---

found in the *Affaire du Lac Lanoux* (1957) 12 RIAA 281 and *Gabčíkovo-Nagymaros Project (Hungary/Slovakia)* [1997] ICJ Rep 7.

176 *Trail Smelter (United States of America v Canada)* p. 1965; Astrid Epiney 'Lac Lanoux Arbitration' in Rüdiger Wolfrum (ed) *MPEPIL* (OUP Oxford Update 2006) para. 12.

177 *Legality of the Threat or Use of Nuclear Weapons (Advisory Opinion)* [1996] ICJ Rep 226 at para.29; Alexander Proelß 'Raum und Umwelt im Völkerrecht' in Wolfgang Vitzthum (ed) *Völkerrecht* (De Gruyter Berlin 2010) p. 456.

178 See generally Brunnée 'Sic utere tuo ut alienum non laedas' and Willisch *State Responsibility for Technological Damage in International Law* pp. 167–69.

179 Dupuy & Hoss 'Trail Smelter and Terrorism: International Mechanisms to Combat Transboundary Harm' pp. 231–39; Proulx 'Babysitting Terrorists: Should States be Strictly Liable for Failing to Prevent Transborder Attacks?' pp. 659 et seq.

180 See, e.g., Art. 10 International Radiotelegraph Convention (signed 25 November 1927, entered into force 1 January 1929) 84 LNTS 97; and, more recently, Art. 45 Constitution of the International Telecommunication Union (concluded 22 December 1992, entered into force 1 July 1994) 1825 UNTS 331; Francis Lyall 'Broadcasting, International Regulation' in Rüdiger Wolfrum (ed) *MPEPIL* (OUP Oxford Update 2007); Brunnée 'Sic utere tuo ut alienum non laedas' para. 14.

181 'Attack' in this instance is not to be understood as a legal term of art, since the qualification as an attack under international law requires a sophisticated case by case evaluation; see pp. 178 et seq. below. Both in literature and military doctrine such actions are however often entitled computer network attacks (see pp. 20 et seq. above) although from a legal standpoint such a denomination appears oversimplified.

Yet both international environmental law as well as the regulations on international broadcasting have taken into account that a certain level of transborder emissions is unavoidable. Therefore the environmental no-harm principle is subject to some form of limitation as the dispersion of certain pollutants is neither avoidable nor controllable.[182] The threshold for the level of harm which has to be tolerated is to be evaluated from the perspective of the target State, as it is the integrity of this State which is protected by the no-harm rule.[183] In the case of broadcasting the approach is similar: here, an unavoidable 'spill-over' of broadcasts on foreign territory causing interference with those local is treated as acceptable.[184]

The question is thus whether CNOs likewise need to cross a certain threshold in order to be considered significantly harmful. Emissions and Internet activity differ in the avoidability of transboundary effects. In the case of emissions the border crossing is an unavoidable secondary effect of an action which in itself is performed in the home State. The permission of a certain level of transboundary harm is a consequence of States' territorial sovereignty. Otherwise, if all forms of harm were prohibited, States would no longer be free to decide for example to allow certain industries on their territory. CNOs on the other hand necessarily have a transborder quality if the target system is located on foreign territory. However, it has been argued that CNOs share an element similar to the unavoidability of transboundary emissions of pollutants. This is seen in the possible ignorance of the State agent executing a CNO of his action's transboundary quality.[185] This is due to the fact that awareness of the Internet's structure, and ultimately the exact location of the system accessed, is not widespread. While this might be the case for actions of an informatory nature, the conclusion reached before is also valid here: the intent or in this case knowledge of a State actor cannot be taken into consideration when qualifying the activity's legality.[186] A fortiori this is the case where military CNOs are used to alter data as this requires a more thorough examination of the target system, effectively excluding both possibilities.

The expansion of the prohibition's scope in the 20th century was due to the spread of indirect interferences especially targeting the political independence of States. Military computer network operations as used in the 21st century conversely target a State's territorial integrity directly. This is due to the fact that by altering or deleting data on systems in the territory of the target State, its

---

182 Similarly: Proelß 'Raum und Umwelt im Völkerrecht' p. 455; this is also reflected by the no-harm principle in international environmental law being a duty of due diligence (despite certain attempts in the literature arguing for a strict liability) and hence subject to the means available: Brunnée 'Sic utere tuo ut alienum non laedas' para. 12.

183 Epiney 'Lac Lanoux Arbitration' para.12; Proelß 'Raum und Umwelt im Völkerrecht' p. 456.

184 Germann *Gefahrenabwehr und Strafverfolgung im Internet* p. 644.

185 Germann *Gefahrenabwehr und Strafverfolgung im Internet* p. 646.

186 See p. 120 above.

territorial framework is affected in that there is no intermediate step contingent on a target State's action. In this way military computer network operations more closely resemble a use of force than indirect coercive measures aimed at a State's political independence. If they do pass the threshold of armed force in the sense of Article 2(4) UN Charter they are prohibited in any case. But those which do not pass the threshold, do at least qualify as a means of interference in the territorial integrity of a State, hence as an intervention. This also holds true for the case of an interference with a foreign stock exchange system. Even considering that this could potentially lead to enormous monetary losses, such an operation could not qualify as a use of force or even an armed attack, as economic coercion was expressly excluded from the scope of the prohibition on the use of force.[187] Nevertheless these forms of malicious CNOs are different from traditional methods of economic coercion, as they directly affect a foreign institution by altering data within its systems located on foreign territory. It is this direct and unauthorised alteration of data within the victim State's territory that through its physical impact likewise leads to its qualification as an interference in the latter's territorial integrity and hence an intervention. Such an alteration of data always qualifies as a coercive measure, as there ultimately exists no graver form of interference than performing the action by oneself rather than influencing the target State to do so.[188]

2.1.1.2.3. Computer Network Espionage

As demonstrated above, there have been numerous reported instances of computer network espionage activity and the number of unreported cases is estimated to be much higher.[189] But even when qualifying as a mostly severely punishable offence in the majority of national jurisdictions, espionage is commonly regarded as a 'necessary evil' not generally prohibited under international law.[190]

---

187 Concurring: Heintschel von Heinegg 'Automatisierung des Krieges' p. 13; Christopher Greenwood 'Self-Defence' in Rüdiger Wolfrum (ed) *MPEPIL* (OUP Oxford Update 2011) para. 14.

188 Differently: Ziolkowski 'Stuxnet – Legal Considerations' 139– 47, arguing coercion to require 'drastic cases of overwhelming – direct or indirect – force being put upon a State's free and sovereign decision-making process' (at p. 147).

189 See pp. 39 et seq. above. Especially noteworthy are the frequent reports of Chinese cyber espionage programmes; on these see Krekel 'Capability of the People's Republic of China to Conduct Cyber Warfare and Computer Network Exploitation: Prepared for the US-China Economic and Security Review Commission' pp. 51–58.

190 Chesterman 'Secret Intelligence' para. 23; Christian Schaller 'Spies' in Rüdiger Wolfrum (ed) *MPEPIL* (OUP Oxford Update 2009) para. 2; differently: Quincy Wright *Essays on Espionage and International Law* (Ohio State University Press Ohio 1962); Heintschel von Heinegg 'Informationskrieg und Völkerrecht' p. 134. However, espionage activity may in certain circumstances deprive the spy from obtaining a prisoner of war status, see pp. 251 et seq. below.

Yet some regimes do regulate or even prohibit such actions at least in a basic manner. Under Article 19 UN Convention on the Law of the Sea, the right of innocent passage through the territorial sea is limited to activity with a direct bearing on passage, excluding such activity as 'collecting information to the prejudice of the defence or security of the coastal State' or any act 'aimed at interfering with any systems of communication or any other facilities or installations of the coastal State', both of which are to be understood as espionage. The intelligence activities of diplomats and consular agents are also regulated in a rudimentary manner as the law of diplomatic relations has been qualified by the ICJ as a self-contained regime encompassing its own rules and remedies such as the loss of diplomatic status and its privileges.[191]

In the field of arms control in the 1970s, a right to intelligence gathering was more or less provided for in order to verify the antagonist's compliance with the arms control agreements.[192] At that time such intelligence was mostly gathered through photographic or imagery intelligence provided by satellite reconnaissance. In addition to these still important means of intelligence, today it is also possible to gather arms-related information by exploiting military computer systems, for example databases of weapons storage, to identify the location and number of regulated arms. As several arms control agreements have implicitly allowed intelligence gathering as a form of 'national technical means of verification', CNOs that are undertaken for the same goal cannot be regarded as unlawful.

Outside of these limited regimes, the legality of espionage can only be evaluated taking into consideration principles of general international law. In this regard recourse is again to be had to the above-mentioned territorial integrity and sovereignty of the target State which is not suspended for espionage activities. The inviolability of these fundamental principles of international law ultimately lead to the conclusion that an interception of data of whatever quality on the territory of a third State which is not publicly accessible constitutes a breach of said State's

---

Joyner & Lotrionte 'Information Warfare as International Coercion: Elements of a Legal Framework' at p. 855 hold the view that the nature of the information stolen, e.g. classified data vital to national security, could even be qualified as an armed attack evoking the right to self-defence under Art. 51 UN Charter. This view is however clearly in contradiction to State practice as regards espionage activities. Even if such espionage is qualified as a preparation to an attack, the necessary element of immediacy will not be fulfilled.

191 *Tehran Hostages Case* paras. 84–86; Chesterman 'Secret Intelligence' para. 23. The classification of the regime of diplomatic law as a self-contained regime has been criticised in the literature as too broad of a restriction on State's choice of effective remedies: Eckart Klein 'Self-Contained Regime' in Rüdiger Wolfrum (ed) *MPEPIL* (OUP Oxford Update 2006) para. 12.

192 Art. 12 (1) Treaty on the Limitation of Anti-Ballistic Missile Systems (signed 26 May 1972, entered into force 3 October 1972) 944 UNTS 13 paraphrases intelligence gathering by 'national technical means of verification' and explicitly allows such conduct to the parties while at the same time prohibiting interference with the other parties' verification methods; Chesterman 'Secret Intelligence' paras. 12–13.

sovereignty. Regardless of the physical location of the person performing the CNO, while acting as a State agent the operation is to be qualified as a sovereign act. In accessing said data the acting State exercises its public authority on the territory of the target State, thus substituting the latter's powers with its own. The alleged accessing of communications or other data of both citizens and government officials on foreign territory by the NSA is thus to be qualified as illegal, so long as these are not made public but undertaken with an expectation of privacy.

Eavesdropping on communications by senior government officials or heads of State is moreover illegal due to the general inviolability of such communications. Diplomatic law protects the use of encrypted communications by diplomats and consuls and similar protections are afforded to judges of most international courts and tribunals, as well as representatives of members to UN organs.[193] Taken seriously, this right to encrypt and its counterpart, the prohibition to restrict encryption of said persons, a fortiori means that the host State is also prohibited from eavesdropping and decrypting such communication. Otherwise the protection would be deprived of its meaning. Taking into consideration that both the diplomatic bag and official correspondence are likewise inviolable, so would be the regular, unencrypted communication of diplomats.[194] While there is no treaty law on to the privileges and immunities of senior government officials or heads of State, they are generally afforded at minimum the same status as diplomats.[195] This is only because they too, when acting in their official capacity, represent the State. Accordingly, their communications are afforded the same protection as those of diplomats. Interception and eavesdropping on such communication, whether encrypted or unencrypted, is thus likewise prohibited under international law. Although there are apparently numerous such cases of espionage on foreign territory, this has not led to the establishment of relevant customary international law legitimising such operations. For though many States seem to be engaged in these activities, they likewise object to any such actions once they are the target of them,[196] thereby hindering the establishment of a relevant custom.

Given the historic treatment of secret intelligence as a necessary evil, in some cases even acting as a tool of peace-building, and States' general reluctance to

---

193 Woltag 'Coded Communications (Encryption)' para. 4.

194 Art. 27 Vienna Convention on Diplomatic Relations protects the diplomatic bag and official correspondence; see further Jean d'Aspremont 'Diplomatic Courier and Bag' in Rüdiger Wolfrum (ed) *MPEPIL* (OUP Oxford Update 2011).

195 Arthur Watts 'Heads of Governments and Other Senior Officials' in Rüdiger Wolfrum (ed) *MPEPIL* (OUP Oxford Update 2010) para. 16; Arthur Watts 'Heads of State' in Rüdiger Wolfrum (ed) *MPEPIL* (OUP Oxford Update 2010) para. 20. The ICJ has thus afforded these persons full immunity when abroad in order to guarantee their ability to effectively execute State functions: *Arrest Warrant of 11 April 2000 Case (Democratic Republic of the Congo v Belgium)* [2002] ICJ Rep 3 para. 53.

196 BBC News 'Merkel Calls Obama about "US Spying on her Phone"' (23 October 2013) <www.bbc.co.uk/news/world-us-canada-24647268> (date accessed 17 December 2013).

conclusively regulate activities in this field, it is however unrealistic that the number of computer network espionage operations will actually decrease in the future.

2.1.1.3. Conclusion

The PCIJ in the *Lotus Case* stated that a State may not exercise its power in any form in the territory of another State, except by virtue of a permissive rule, providing for a general presumption in favour of territorial supremacy guiding all areas of extraterritorial activity.[197] The above has shown that this likewise applies to computer network operations and their position in regard to the non-intervention principle which has proven to be quite capable of keeping pace with technological advancements. Computer network operations undertaken by State actors can both be qualified as sovereign acts or treated comparably to physical acts. Both may under certain circumstances qualify as an interference in the internal affairs of the target State. Computer network operations that alter or delete data on the target system are readily qualifiable as a violation of the target State's territorial integrity. Due to their intentionally intrusive nature, a comparison of these operations to undirected cross-border emissions is not helpful. For the same reason there is no threshold of harm that needs to be tolerated by the target State. This is emphasised by the designation of such operations as computer network attacks which tend to be utilised by the armed forces of a State. In the case of cross-border operations in which a State organ exercises public authority, their qualification as a violation of the political independence and sovereignty of the target State is dependent on their effect on the foreign territory. If these operations are undertaken by merely accessing publicly available data, the performing State does not substitute the target State's sovereignty on its own. Consequently only those operations that access data not readily available to a foreign State can be considered in their effects to be infringe on the target State's sovereignty and political independence. Acts of computer network espionage are to be treated in the same manner as conventional secret intelligence. While no specific prohibition exists under international law, their execution is ultimately no different from the other operations, whether of a physical or sovereign character.

2.1.2. The Regime of International Telecommunications

Computer network operations which rely on the Internet are inevitably subject to the latter's technical protocols. Depending on the relevant operation, telecommunications cables as well as wireless satellite communications may be

197 *Lotus Case* p. 18; concurring Jamnejad & Wood 'The Principle of Non-Intervention' p. 372; Orakhelashvili 'Governmental Activity on Foreign Territory' para. 36.

utilised to transmit the respective data packets. In practice the lion's share of Internet communication is transmitted via cables, as these provide both for a faster and more reliable connectivity. The Constitution of the International Telecommunication Union – the principal organisation for all types of telecommunication – provides for a regulatory framework for international telecommunications which could possibly constrain computer network operations.

In its preamble the ITU Constitution already 'fully recogniz[es] the sovereign right of each State to regulate its telecommunication'. For this reason Member States are given a wide discretion as regards the stoppage of telecommunications. Article 34 provides for a right to cut off any private communication appearing dangerous to State security or contrary to its laws, public order or decency. Article 35 goes even further by allowing Member States to completely suspend international telecommunications services, whether outgoing, incoming or transit communications. These measures were adopted by Estonia in order to stop the influx of CNOs originating from abroad in the 2007 incident.[198] However only those telecommunications may be suspended that at one point are transmitted through the State's borders. This restriction – basically a corollary of territorial sovereignty – in reverse excludes the possibility of States to influence telecommunications relayed solely in third States.[199]

Article 48 ITU Constitution provides for exceptions for military transmissions. One view regards this as an authorisation for computer network operations conducted by military forces.[200] It is doubtful, however, whether the provisions of Articles 44–48 ITU Constitution (entitled special provisions for radio) are applicable for line-based communications in the first place. The Annex to the ITU Constitution defines radio communication as a 'telecommunication by means of radio waves', hence wireless communications. A telecommunication on the other hand is defined as 'any transmission, emission or reception of signs, signals, writing, images and sounds or intelligence of any nature by wire, radio, optical or other electromagnetic systems'.[201] Communications using the Internet are thus telecommunications. The exception of military transmissions from the prohibition of harmful interference of Article 45 ITU Constitution thus relates only to radio communications.[202] In any case, Article 48(2) demands even from these to observe as far as possible the measures to be taken to prevent harmful

---

198 See pp. 42 et seq. above.

199 Roger D. Scott 'Legal Aspects of Information Warfare: Military Disruption of Telecommunications' (1998) 45 Naval Law Review pp. 63–64.

200 James Terry 'The Lawfulness of Attacking Computer Networks in Armed Conflict and in Self-Defense in Periods Short of Armed Conflict: What Are the Tareting Constraints' (2001) 169 Military Law Review p. 88.

201 Definition of Certain Terms Used in this Constitution, the Convention and the Administrative Regulations of the International Telecommunication Union (ITU Constitution Annex) 1825 UNTS 387.

202 Harmful interference is defined as '[i]nterference which endangers the functioning of a radionavigation service or of other safety services or seriously degrades, obstructs or

interference. This rule depicts the exception of harmful interference of military radio communications not encompassing operations that intentionally target other communications but only those which because of the technology used inevitably cause interference.

This conclusion is supported by the objective of the norms: radio frequencies, which are used for radio transmissions (i.e. broadcasting), are a limited natural resource and must thus be used rationally, efficiently and economically according to Article 44 ITU Constitution. For the Internet, the situation is different. The Internet infrastructure does not make use of a limited natural resource. Hence there is no natural scarcity that needs to be equally distributed, as the infrastructure (cables, routers, etc.) can be expanded anytime to offer more bandwidth for connections. Therefore the danger of interference with other communications that exists for radio transmissions in the limited frequency spectrum does not exist for Internet communications.

The notion of an 'information' or 'electronic blockade' has surfaced in the discussions concerning CNOs which depicts the disruption of all communications into and out of the target State.[203] Jaak Aaviksoo for example, the then Estonian defence minister, in reaction to the CNOs directed against Estonian systems in 2007 stated that cyber war today represents the equivalent threat to a country as a blockade of ports did two hundred years ago.[204] In the terms of naval warfare a blockade is defined as 'the blocking of the approach to the enemy coast, or a part of it, for the purpose of preventing ingress and egress of vessels or aircraft of all States'.[205] Today, aerial blockades are also recognised under Section V of the Manual on Air and Missile Warfare as a valid 'method of warfare exclusively applicable in international armed conflicts.'[206] Both naval and aerial blockades necessarily imply at least a threat to use force, namely by threatening to enforce the blockade against those willing to breach it, and therefore as a means of warfare directed against the enemy's armed forces.[207] For

repeatedly interrupts a radiocommunication service operating in accordance with the Radio Regulations' (ITU Constitution Annex).

203 Barkham 'Information Warfare and International Law on the Use of Force' p. 92; Greenberg, Goodman & Soo Hoo *Information Warfare and International Law* p. 12.

204 NATO Parliamentary Assembly 'NATO and Cyber Defence' (2009) at <www.nato-pa.int/default.asp?SHORTCUT=1782> (date accessed 24 June 2010) para. 59.

205 Louise Doswald-Beck (ed) *San Remo Manual on International Law Applicable to Armed Conflicts at Sea* (CUP Cambridge 1995) p. 176.

206 Program on Humanitarian Policy and Conflict Research (ed) *Commentary on the HPCR Manual on International Law Applicable to Air and Missile Warfare* p. 287. The San Remo Manual already recognised that blockades could also be upheld in the airspace above the sea, in which case the belligerents would also have to abide to the general principles of naval blockade: Doswald-Beck (ed) *San Remo Manual on International Law Applicable to Armed Conflicts at Sea* p. 177; see also Yoram Dinstein 'Air Warfare' in Rüdiger Wolfrum (ed) *MPEPIL* (OUP Oxford Update 2010) para. 40.

207 Concurring: Wolff Heintschel von Heinegg 'Blockade' in Rüdiger Wolfrum (ed) *MPEPIL* (OUP Oxford Update 2009) paras.1 and 25; differently: Oliver Dörr 'Use of Force, Prohibition of' in Rüdiger Wolfrum (ed) *MPEPIL* (OUP Oxford Update 2011) who argues that armed

this reason naval blockades have additionally been qualified as an act of aggression under the UN General Assembly Resolution on the Definition of Aggression.[208]

In the realm of computer network operations, it is generally possible to distinguish between two types of electronic blockades. One possibility is to completely shut off the target State from telecommunications by blocking any data originating from or addressed to computer systems situated inside its territory. This could be achieved by taking control of routers outside of the targeted States and filtering out data en route to the target State. In order to be effective this implies taking control of the majority of routers connecting the target State's networks with those external to it. As in most cases – with the exception of enclaves or small islands – the target State's networks will be connected to several other States; this necessitates control of systems located in those territories, too. The second option is the shutting down of key information and communication infrastructures within the targeted State such as for example Internet exchange points. This would have a similar effect, while additionally also interfering with communications within the targeted State's networks, making the latter option the more serious alternative. The effects of both measures are not readily quantifiable and depend on the target State's reliance on extraterritorial communications including the Internet.

It is questionable, however, whether the traditional rules on blockades can provide any insight for the treatment of 'electronic blockades'. Firstly, if these do not cross the threshold of an armed attack and are taken outside of armed conflict, not as a means of warfare, humanitarian law does not apply. However, as traditional blockades are seen as a means of warfare, the rules applicable to them are influenced by humanitarian law, for instance by providing special rules on the diminishment of negative effects on the civilian population.[209] In situations short of armed conflict there is thus no legal interest in applying these rules. Secondly, electronic blockades are in their mode of operation not comparable to naval or aerial blockades. An electronic blockade does not imply a threat to use force in the event of a breach of the blockade. A necessary condition for an electronic blockade is its execution, hence its 'enforcement' ipso facto. The blockade can either be breached or not, but there are no further means of enforcement if a breach has taken place. Thirdly, there is no lacuna necessary for

force needs to be directed against the territory of a State. In case of a blockade (be it naval or land) the territorial element would be missing as a blockade merely denies the entry to said territory (at para. 23). This view however omits the implicit threat of enforcing the blockade by forceful means.

208 Art. 3 (c) UNGA Res 3314 (XXIX) 'Definition of Aggression' (14 December 1974) GAOR 29th Session Supp 31 vol 1, 142.

209 Rule 157 Program on Humanitarian Policy and Conflict Research (ed) *Manual on International Law Applicable to Air and Missile Warfare* (HPCR Harvard University Cambridge 2009); Rule 102–104 Doswald-Beck (ed) *San Remo Manual on International Law Applicable to Armed Conflicts at Sea*; Heintschel von Heinegg 'Blockade' paras. 49–52.

such an analogy. When undertaken outside of armed conflict the regulations of the ITU Constitution – to which all 192 ITU Member States are bound – apply also to these instances of CNOs. Article 35 allows States to suspend international telecommunications services generally or only for certain communications as long as this is undertaken on their territory. Hence the first option of an electronic blockade would be legitimate as long as it does not interfere with third States' systems. The alternative, namely interfering in telecommunications taking place on foreign territory, is prohibited in any case.

In conclusion the exceptions to military communications under Chapter VII ITU Constitution on the special provisions for radio are not applicable to computer network operations that utilise the Internet. The ITU Constitution does not provide any empowerment to Member States to utilise cross-border computer network operations. In fact the Constitution serves as an example of the recognition of the fact that State sovereignty also encompasses the telecommunications within a State's territory. Consequently a State under the Constitution is allowed to conduct CNOs which stop individual telecommunications or completely suspend telecommunications services on its territory. On the other hand cross-border operations intended to achieve the same goal in foreign territory are implicitly prohibited by Articles 34 and 35 ITU Constitution. For this reason CNOs that have the goal of establishing an 'electronic blockade' in cases short of armed conflict are illicit not due to their designation as a blockade, but in case they stop or suspend telecommunications on foreign telecommunications systems.

2.1.3. The Regime of Outer Space

In some cases computer network operations will make use of satellites located in outer space, which is necessary for example in remote areas with no landline or mobile phone networks. In these cases the legal regime applicable to activities in outer space might impose additional limits on computer network operations.[210] Article 4 Outer Space Treaty provides that 'the moon and other celestial bodies shall be used by all States Parties to the treaty exclusively for peaceful purposes'.[211] Furthermore, weapons of mass destruction may not be stationed in outer space, on celestial bodies or in the earth orbit. If CNOs are undertaken by the armed forces of a State the question arises as to whether outer space may be used for military purposes. Despite the Outer Space Treaty's referral to peaceful purposes it does not regulate the use or stationing of conventional weapons in outer space or in the earth orbit. Article 3 Outer Space Treaty allows States to use

210 As considered by Heintschel von Heinegg 'Informationskrieg und Völkerrecht' pp. 145–47; Stein & Marauhn 'Völkerrechtliche Aspekte von Informationsoperationen' pp. 17–20.

211 Treaty on Principles Governing the Activities of States in the Exploration and Use of Outer Space, Including the Moon and other Celestial Bodies (signed 27 January 1967, entered into force 10 October 1967) 610 UNTS 205.

outer space in accordance with international law, expressly including the UN Charter. Therefore, the stationing of conventional weapons in space is not forbidden, nor is their use in such a case non-compliant with general international law, as for example in a situation of self-defence under Article 51 UN Charter and in conformity with international humanitarian law.[212]

While regular military communications satellites help to communicate with troops geographically far away in a territory that lacks a functioning telecommunications infrastructure, the relevance of satellite communication for computer network operations is marginal. Internet communications are generally transmitted via cable which is inter alia due to the fact that wireless communications are physically limited in their speed, providing for a high latency rate which negatively affects telecommunications.[213] Additionally satellite communications are subject to weather disturbances.

A further limitation on the military use of satellite communications has vanished in the last decade. The regimes of international satellite organisations contained restrictions to the use of their infrastructure for military purposes and thus also to CNOs by armed forces.[214] The former international organisations INTELSAT and EUTELSAT in their respective regimes prohibited the system's use for military purposes.[215] INMARSAT on the other hand only provided for a limitation to 'peaceful purposes', thus allowing military use in conformity with international law as in the case of conventional weapons in outer space.[216] However, all three organisations were privatised in the 2000s. While both INTELSAT and EUTELSAT now provide their services also to the military, INMARSAT Ventures Ltd is still envisaged to continue to act

---

212 Heintschel von Heinegg 'Informationskrieg und Völkerrecht' p. 146. This view is implicitly supported by the practice of the UN General Assembly which inter alia sees the need to 'urge all States ... to contribute actively to the goal of preventing an arms race in outer space' (UNGA Res 65/97 [10 December 2010] UN Doc A/RES/65/97 para. 11). In case of a general prohibition of arms in outer space this appeal would not have been necessary.

213 The latency of Internet telecommunications via satellites lays at around 280 milliseconds one-way. As most Internet communications are undertaken two-way, the latency doubles. Thus, Internet communications via satellite have remained seldom as is expected for the future; Ingo Baumann *Das internationale Recht der Satellitenkommunikation* (Lang Frankfurt am Main 2005) pp. 48–50.

214 This was still the case when the issue was discussed by Stein & Marauhn 'Völkerrechtliche Aspekte von Informationsoperationen' at pp. 18–20.

215 See Art. III (d) and (e) Agreement relating to the International Telecommunications Satellite Organization 'INTELSAT' ([opened for signature 20 August 1971, entered into force 12 February 1973] 1220 UNTS 22) and Art. III (e) and (f) Convention Establishing the European Telecommunications Satellite Organization EUTELSAT (opened for signature 15 July 1982, entered into force 1 September 1985) 1519 UNTS 175.

216 Art. 3 III Convention on the International Maritime Satellite Organization (INMARSAT) ([adopted 3 September 1976, entered into force 16 July 1979] 1143 UNTS 105); on this topic see generally Wolf D. von Noorden 'INMARSAT Use by Armed Forces: A Question of Treaty Interpretation' (1995) 23(1) Journal of Space Law pp. 1 et seq. For a general overview of the interpretation of the concept peaceful purposes see Proelß 'Peaceful Purposes'.

exclusively for peaceful purposes.[217] Be that as it may, States are in any case not prevented from utilising their own satellites. In the end it can be acknowledged that outer space law does not pose any further limits on military computer network operations utilising satellites than those under general international law.[218]

2.1.4. *The Law of the Sea*

The Internet infrastructure to a large degree relies on submarine cables for cross-continental communications. Consequently, depending on the target system, a computer network operation will eventually utilise these. This has led some to conclude that the UN Convention on the Law of the Sea would also be applicable to those CNOs that are routed through submarine cables.[219] Article 17 UN Convention on the Law of the Sea codifies the right of innocent passage through the territorial sea. According to Article 19 a passage can however only be considered innocent as long as it is not prejudicial to the peace, good order or security of the coastal State which includes, inter alia, the collection of information to the prejudice of the defence or security of the coastal State or an interference with its systems of communication. Additionally, Article 113 obliges States to penalise actions that break or injure submarine cables, thus interrupting communications. According to this view, both prohibitions read in conjunction create an obligation for States not to route CNOs through the submarine cables connecting the target coastal State.[220]

This view cannot be supported. The spirit and purpose of the concept of innocent passage is to balance the right to freedom of navigation of third States and the territorial sovereignty of the coastal State, thus forming a compromise between coastal and maritime interests.[221] The limitations on the right of innocent passage through the territorial sea are only imposed on the holder of the right, namely ships. The mere fact of a cable's location in the territorial sea has no bearing on the content transmitted with it. A CNO originating from a land-based system is hence not subject to the limitations of Article 19 UN Convention on the Law of the Sea. The same holds true for Article 113, the telos of which is to protect submarine cables from breaking or damage. The cases

217 Para. 2.3. Public Services Agreement between the International Mobile Satellite Organization, INMARSAT One Ltd, and INMARSAT Two Company (signed 15 April 1999) (1999) 24 Annals of Air and Space Law 493; Francis Lyall 'INMARSAT' in Rüdiger Wolfrum (ed) *MPEPIL* (OUP Oxford Update 2006) para. 16.

218 Similarly Heintschel von Heinegg 'Informationskrieg und Völkerrecht' pp. 146–47.

219 Shackelford 'From Nuclear War to Net War: Analogizing Cyber Attacks in International Law' pp. 227 and 247.

220 Shackelford 'From Nuclear War to Net War: Analogizing Cyber Attacks in International Law' p. 227.

221 Kari Hakapää 'Innocent Passage' in Rüdiger Wolfrum (ed) *MPEPIL* (OUP Oxford Update 2008) para. 44.

leading to damage that were kept in mind during the drafting process were of a merely physical nature, such as the anchoring to pipelines, casting of fishing nets or the exploration by researchers of the areas adjacent to the cables.[222] The damaging of such cables in peacetime is prohibited in general; this would also hold true for a CNO intended to adversely affect these cables. However, cables are merely a medium of transportation, that is to say information carriers not capable of processing data. While they can be destroyed physically by conventional means they are not a viable target for CNOs the purpose of which is to influence a computing process.

The only limitation imposed on computer network operations by the law of the sea concerns the activities of ships during innocent passage. During this phase of sailing a ship is prohibited from launching CNOs targeting the coastal State.[223] Due to the technological disadvantages of satellite communications, and the fact that they are mostly unnecessary, these instances are marginal if they exist at all.

2.1.5. Conclusion

Computer network operations can amount to both a violation of the territorial integrity and political independence of the target State, as well as concurrently to an intervention into its internal affairs. The international telecommunications regime with its explicit recognition of State sovereignty in regard to the stoppage of individual communications and suspension of telecommunications services on its own territory implicitly prohibits States from conducting these kinds of cross-border operations on foreign territory. This encompasses measures establishing a so-called electronic blockade outside of armed conflict.

The regimes applicable to territories other than land territory – the law of the sea and the regime of outer space – do not provide any further limitations than those already existing under general international law, with the exception of the prohibition of conducting computer network operations targeting the coastal State during innocent passage of a vessel.

Further limitations may arise from bilateral treaties, especially status of forces agreements if computer network operations are executed from a base on foreign territory. From the point of view of the host State, the execution of CNOs from its territory by foreign forces might entail its responsibility as a result of its assistance by permitting its territory to be used for such actions.[224] The exact limitations will however depend on the relevant agreement and cannot be generalised.

222 Myron H. Nordquist (ed) *United Nations Convention on the Law of the Sea 1982: A Commentary: Vol 3* (Nijhoff The Hague 1995) p. 268; Lagoni 'Pipelines' para. 18.

223 Similarly: Schmitt (ed) *Tallinn Manual on the International Law Applicable to Cyber Warfare* p. 30 para. 3.

224 Commentary to Art. 16 UN ILC 'Text of the Draft Articles with Commentaries Thereto: Responsibility of States for Internationally Wrongful Acts' para. 8.

2.2. THE PROHIBITION OF THE USE OF FORCEFUL COMPUTER NETWORK OPERATIONS

If computer network operations are undertaken by the armed forces of a State, resort is naturally taken to the prohibition of the use of force. The violation thereof can – just as in case of the non-intervention principle – qualify as a breach of an international obligation invoking State responsibility. Yet as the threshold of the former is higher, the international community generally tends to qualify its violation as a graver breach of international law.[225] It is therefore necessary to further elaborate on the use of force also in cases where an intervention has already been determined. Article 2(4) UN Charter obliges States to refrain from the use of force, or from threatening to do so, in international relations. The main challenge arising out of this prohibition in relation to computer network operations is to determine the threshold that, if exceeded, qualifies the operation to be regarded a use of force. For this purpose it is necessary to at first determine the notion of force and its scope under Article 2(4) UN Charter.

2.2.1. *The Notion of Force*

It is undisputed today that the former liberty to employ inter-State force is obsolete.[226] Considered as one of the cornerstones not only of the UN Charter but also of customary international law the prohibition to use force has been qualified both as containing an obligation erga omnes and ius cogens, hence a peremptory norm of general international law.[227] However, the notion of force as used in Article 2(4) UN Charter has been controversially debated not only during the drafting process of the UN Charter but also in the subsequent literature. The main controversy was – and still is to a certain degree – the scope

---

225 Stelter *Gewaltanwendung unter und neben der UN-Charta* p. 70.

226 Yoram Dinstein *War Aggression and Self-Defence* (CUP Cambridge 2005) p. 92. In the 18th and 19th centuries States were regarded to have full discretion to wage war whenever they considered it fitting, as such freedom was considered an indispensable attribute of statehood and sovereignty, a view which remained prevalent up until World War I; seeAlbrecht Randelzhofer & Oliver Dörr 'Article 2 (4)' in Bruno Simma (ed) *The Charter of the United Nations – A Commentary* (OUP Oxford 2012) paras. 4–8; Cassese *International Law* p. 300; Dinstein *War Aggression and Self-Defence* pp. 75–77; Ian Brownlie *International Law and the Use of Force by States* (Clarendon Oxford 1963) p. 19.

227 *Armed Activities on the Territory of the Congo (Democratic Republic of the Congo v Uganda)* [2005] ICJ Rep 168 para. 148; Dörr 'Use of Force, Prohibition of' paras. 1 and 31–32; Dinstein *War Aggression and Self-Defence* p. 100; Dahm, Delbrück & Wolfrum *Völkerrecht vol I/3* p. 822; UN ILC 'Draft Articles on the Law of Treaties with Commentaries' (1966) vol II UNYBILC p. 247; American Law Institute 'Restatement (Third) of Foreign Relations Law' (1987) §102. The prohibition is likewise to be found in customary international law: *Nicaragua Case* paras. 187 et seq; UN ILC 'Draft Articles on the Law of Treaties with Commentaries' (1966) vol II UNYBILC p. 247.

of the notion of force. The text of Article 2(4) UN Charter itself does not provide for a significant definition thereof. Recourse must therefore be had to interpretation, which according to Article 31 VCLT, denotes that a treaty 'shall be interpreted in good faith in accordance with the ordinary meaning to be given to the terms of the treaty in their context and in the light of its object and purpose'. Therefore it must be considered that a term may have various ordinary meanings, which may also change over time.[228]

2.2.1.1. Armed Force and Economic Coercion

According to the prevailing view, the term is limited only to 'armed force', thereby excluding political, economic and non-military physical force.[229] This is substantiated by several arguments. Firstly, the ordinary meaning of a term must be given in the context of the treaty in its entirety; hence other Charter provisions, especially those related in substance, such as Articles 39, 51 and 53 UN Charter, must also be taken into consideration.[230] Furthermore, object and purpose of the treaty as a whole, which are traditionally stated in the preamble or a general clause at the beginning, help to determine the ordinary meaning of a term.[231] In fact the limited reading of the term force is supported by several Charter provisions: Article 44 and para. 7 of the Preamble of the UN Charter, where it is stipulated that 'armed force shall not be used, save in the common interest' support the view that force in the sense of the UN Charter can only refer to 'armed' force.[232]

Furthermore, one can, according to Article 32 VCLT, also take into account the travaux préparatoires of the UN Charter. These are clear on this issue: a proposal by Brazil to extend the prohibition to economic coercion was rejected during the drafting process.[233] Further support is derived from other international instruments such as the Friendly Relations Declaration of 1970.[234]

---

[228] Mark Eugen Villiger *Commentary on the 1969 Vienna Convention on the Law of Treaties* (Nijhoff Leiden 2009) p. 426.

[229] Randelzhofer & Dörr 'Article 2 (4)' paras. 16–28; Dinstein *War Aggression and Self-Defence* p. 86; Dörr 'Use of Force, Prohibition of' para. 11; seminal: Rolf M. Derpa *Das Gewaltverbot der Satzung der Vereinten Nationen und die Anwendung nichtmilitärischer Gewalt* (Athenaeum Bad Homburg 1970).

[230] Villiger *Commentary on the 1969 Vienna Convention on the Law of Treaties* p. 427; Rüdiger Wolfrum 'The Attack of September 11, 2001, the Wars against the Taliban and Iraq: Is there a Need to Reconsider International Law on the Recourse to Force and the Rules in Armed Conflict?' (2004) 7 Max Planck Yearbook of United Nations Law p. 7.

[231] Villiger *Commentary on the 1969 Vienna Convention on the Law of Treaties* p. 428.

[232] Randelzhofer & Dörr 'Article 2 (4)' para. 18.

[233] United Nations Conference on International Organization *Documents* vol 6 (UN Information Organizations London New York 1945) pp. 334 and 609.

[234] UNGA Res 2625 (XXV) 'Declaration on Principles of International Law concerning Friendly Relations and Co-operation among States in Accordance with the Charter of the United Nations' (24 October 1970) GAOR 25th Session Supp 28, 121.

Herein the prohibition of the use of force is reiterated, and the 'use of economic, political or any other type of measures to coerce another State' is treated as a separate form of coercion to be considered under the principle of non-intervention. The Declaration therefore also utilises a narrow meaning of the notion of force.[235] This position is today shared by the majority view and supported through ICJ jurisprudence.[236] Additionally, the spirit and purpose of the prohibition of force oppose an extensive interpretation as this would strongly restrict States' leverage against other States, in practice preventing any possibility of influence.[237] This influence is however deemed necessary as long as international law does not provide for effective mechanisms to ensure compliance with international law.[238] The Brazilian approach, which was especially supported by developing countries, is nevertheless reflected on a regional level in Article 19 Charter of the Organization of American States and in several UN General Assembly resolutions of the 1960s and 1970s.[239]

While the term force is in a first step defined narrowly by armed force, this restriction is then in a second step interpreted broadly by encompassing all kinds of armed force. Hence the addition in the wording of Article 2(4) UN Charter of force to be directed 'against the territorial integrity or political independence of any state' should not be seen as an indispensable requirement or as a restriction of the prohibition's application. Both the catchall element 'in any other manner

235 Randelzhofer & Dörr 'Article 2 (4)' para. 19; Dörr 'Use of Force, Prohibition of' para. 11.

236 The ICJ did not even consider economic coercion as a breach of the principle of non-intervention in the *Nicaragua Case* paras. 244–45; Derpa *Das Gewaltverbot der Satzung der Vereinten Nationen und die Anwendung nichtmilitärischer Gewalt* p. 136; Brownlie *International Law and the Use of Force by States* p. 435; Dahm, Delbrück & Wolfrum *Völkerrecht vol I/3* p. 833; Stein & Buttlar *Völkerrecht* para. 775; Vaughan Lowe & Antonios Tzanakopoulos 'Economic Warfare' in Rüdiger Wolfrum (ed) *MPEPIL* (OUP Oxford Update 2011) para. 29. Likewise, the Friendly Relations Declaration, while further elaborating on the content and scope of the prohibition of the use of force, did not include economic coercion as falling under the notion of force, as no agreement could be found in the committee responsible: V.S. Mani *Basic Principles of Modern International Law: A Study of the United Nations Debates on the Principles of International Law concerning Friendly Relations and Co-operation Among States* (Lancers Books New Delhi 1993) pp. 12–16. Economic coercion may however violate bilateral or multilateral agreements such as especially the legal framework of the WTO. On this see generally Barry Carter 'Economic Coercion' in Rüdiger Wolfrum (ed) *MPEPIL* (OUP Oxford Update 2009).

237 Randelzhofer & Dörr 'Article 2 (4)' para. 18; Dittmar *Angriffe auf Computernetzwerke: Ius ad bellum und ius in bello* p. 71.

238 Randelzhofer & Dörr 'Article 2 (4)' para. 18.

239 Charter of the Organization of American States (signed 30 April 1948, entered into force 13 December 1951) 119 UNTS 3; as amended by the Protocol of Managua adopted on 10 June 1993; Para. 2 UNGA Res 2131 (XX) 'Declaration on the Inadmissibility of Intervention in the Domestic Affairs of States and the Protection of Their Independence and Sovereignty' (21 December 1965) GAOR 20th Session Supp 14, 11; UNGA Res 42/173 'Economic Measures as a Means of Political and Economic Coercion against Developing Countries' (21 December 1987) GAOR 42nd Session Supp 49 vol 1, 130. Also scholars have in recent times argued in this direction, e.g., Thomas C. Wingfield *The Law of Information Conflict: National Security Law in Cyberspace* (Aegis Falls Church 2000) pp. 89–90.

inconsistent with the Purposes of the United Nations' and the travaux préparatoires demonstrate their inclusion as a mere emphasis of particularly grave forms of prohibited actions.[240] Nor should the particular State organ executing the forceful actions be taken into consideration. As has been shown earlier States are internationally responsible for all actions of their organs even where these are done ultra vires. The term armed force hence does not necessarily imply the action to be undertaken by the official armed forces of a State, but can encompass all sorts of actors as long as the State bears responsibility.[241]

Armed force is not reduced to merely kinetic force, such as to that of fire and explosive weapons. The use of biological and chemical weapons also falls under the notion of force. This is due to their expected effects on humans: to at least damage the health, or even have a lethal impact.[242] The terms armed force, aggression and armed attack commonly feature the idea of force with the use of arms. The definition of the terms arms and weapons is therefore decisive. While originally encompassing objects such as swords or bow and arrow, today any object inflicting damage in a kinetic manner comes into mind, such as handguns, missiles, bombs, etc. For that reason there has never been any discussion of whether for example a newly invented missile would fall under the scope of such a definition, which was automatically assumed. The general possibility to use most objects in a forceful manner and the permanent advancement of new technologies make indispensable the assumption that in order to qualify as arms, it is not the means used that are decisive, but the intentions of the user and the implied effects.[243] This does not lead to an undue expansion of the term to also include economic coercion, as the latter was deliberately excluded from the prohibition's scope in the first place.

2.2.1.2. Physical Force

A connected dispute is whether physical force may fall under the scope of the prohibition. Examples given in this respect mostly involve the unleashing of forces of nature or the modification thereof, such as the diversion of a river

---

240 Dörr 'Use of Force, Prohibition of' para. 14; Randelzhofer & Dörr 'Article 2 (4)' para. 37; Thomas M. Franck *Recourse to Force: State Action against Threats and Armed Attacks* (Cambridge University Press Cambridge 2002) pp. 12–13; Dahm, Delbrück & Wolfrum *Völkerrecht vol I/3* p. 823; Christian J. Tams 'The Use of Force Against Terrorists' (2009) 20 European Journal of International Law p. 364.

241 Brownlie *International Law and the Use of Force by States* p. 361.

242 Brownlie *International Law and the Use of Force by States* p. 362; Derpa *Das Gewaltverbot der Satzung der Vereinten Nationen und die Anwendung nichtmilitärischer Gewalt* p. 25; Michael N. Schmitt 'Angriffe im Computernetz und das ius ad bellum' (1999) 41(5) Neue Zeitschrift für Wehrrecht pp. 183 et seq.; Stein & Marauhn 'Völkerrechtliche Aspekte von Informationsoperationen' p. 6; Schmitt 'Computer Network Attack and the Use of Force in International Law: Thoughts on a Normative Framework' p. 913; Stelter *Gewaltanwendung unter und neben der UN-Charta* p. 67.

243 Stein & Marauhn 'Völkerrechtliche Aspekte von Informationsoperationen' p. 6.

cutting off the downstream State of access to water, or the triggering of incidents comparable to natural catastrophes such as the release of large quantities of water down a valley into a neighbour State or massive cross-border environmental pollution, the causing of forest fires spreading to the neighbouring State and setting off avalanches.[244] While it is mostly admitted that such means may have comparable effects on the foreign territory as armed force of a military nature, both practice and scholarly opinion do not consider physical force to fall under the prohibition of Article 2(4). Its purpose is mainly seen in outlawing solely military armed force to the exclusion of any other forms of force.[245]

The contrary view sees physical force also encompassed under Article 2(4) by arguing with its potential effects, which are considered as similar to, or possibly even graver than, conventional military armed force.[246]

As the travaux préparatoires are silent on the issue of physical force and there is also no clear State practice in this regard, evaluating whether or not physical force is likewise encompassed by the prohibition's scope in the end centres around the principle's underlying question of what form and level of influence States are allowed to exercise between each other. It is helpful in this regard to consider the reasons behind the different treatment of military force and economic coercion. Firstly, military force is generally directly targeted against property and human life,[247] hence against the highest legally protected interest. As the most effective defence against military armed force is by and large to respond in kind, the measure has a high potential for leading to an escalation of a conflict. Economic coercion on the other hand is mostly indirect in that the effects of the economic measures take time to be noticeable on the foreign territory. This provides the target State with more time and opportunities to counterbalance the economic impact. Furthermore, economic measures are increasingly subject to specific frameworks such as that of the WTO which as a self-contained regime provides for its own dispute settlement system. Additionally, economic coercion takes place in a field where negotiations, for instance on the terms of a contract, and attempts to receive preferential treatment are commonplace. In this field coercion can only take place if the target State has already been active on the market, thereby participating in the economic exchange with other States of its own volition. In the case of armed force on the other hand even a State that has chosen complete isolationism and

---

244 Randelzhofer & Dörr 'Article 2 (4)' para. 21.

245 Randelzhofer & Dörr 'Article 2 (4)' para. 21; Dörr 'Use of Force, Prohibition of' para. 12; Michael Bothe 'Friedenssicherung und Kriegsrecht' in Wolfgang Vitzthum (ed) *Völkerrecht* (de Gruyter Berlin 2010) para. 10; critical of the majority opinion: Karl Doehring *Völkerrecht* (CF Müller Heidelberg 2004) pp. 328 et seq.

246 Brownlie *International Law and the Use of Force by States* pp. 362–63 stating that the 'deliberate employment of natural forces by a state … can probably be regarded as a use of force' (at 376); Derpa *Das Gewaltverbot der Satzung der Vereinten Nationen und die Anwendung nichtmilitärischer Gewalt* p. 25, with further references also to State practice.

247 Brownlie *International Law and the Use of Force by States* p. 362.

autarky can be targeted. It is this lack of possibilities of evasion of the victim State which qualifies armed force as a stronger and more irrevocable form of coercion leading to its prohibition, even when in certain cases the consequences of economic coercion can be more dire.

Even proponents of the majority opinion allow for exceptions in case the physical force amounts to an armed attack in the sense of Article 51 UN Charter or merely state that practice so far has not treated physical force under the notion of armed force.[248] By introducing this exemption the focus ultimately all the same lies on the effects of the measure. While it is to be agreed with the majority opinion that Article 2(4) only encompasses military armed force, it should not be overlooked that natural forces may also be utilised in a military fashion. If armed forces utilise a natural force as a means of warfare, as for example through a deliberate flooding of neighbouring territories resulting in a loss of lives, the respective natural force water is ultimately used in a military fashion as a weapon, hence as military armed force. If on the other hand the flooding is caused only due to accidental construction deficits of a dam, the natural force causes identical effects while missing the element of armament. Physical force deliberately utilised by the armed forces or any other State organ is therefore to be qualified as armed force in the sense of Article 2(4) UN Charter.

2.2.2. *Computer Network Operations as Armed Force*

The above has identified the general structure behind the notion of force and the categories associated with it. These shall form the basis of the considerations concerning the encompassment of computer network operations under the scope of the prohibition. Numerous propositions have already been put forward in this regard which will be evaluated in the following. At first it must be considered however whether the prohibition applies to these kinds of operations at all ratione loci.

2.2.2.1. The Applicability Ratione Loci of the UN Charter in Cyberspace

If concurring with the view that to one extent or the other evaluates cyberspace as a kind of 'sphere' lying beyond States' jurisdiction and featuring its own customary rules, it is from the outset already doubtful whether international instruments are at all applicable to this sphere. Some authors compare the sphere they refer to as 'cyberspace' with the high seas or outer space, hence to areas

[248] Randelzhofer & Dörr 'Article 2 (4)' para. 22; Dörr 'Use of Force, Prohibition of' stating that 'computer network attacks against the information systems of another State … may in this respect lead to a different interpretation, given the weapon-like destructive potential which some attacks by means of information technology may develop' (at para. 12); specifically in regard to CNOs: Heintschel von Heinegg 'Informationskrieg und Völkerrecht' pp. 138–40; similarly Bothe 'Friedenssicherung und Kriegsrecht' para. 10.

absent of territorial sovereignty or jurisdiction of one State.[249] Both of these regions are today shaped by customary international law and the relevant frameworks, including the regulation of States' resort to force. For example, the UN Convention on the Law of the Sea allows certain exceptions to the prohibition on the use of force other than those enshrined in the UN Charter, as there exists for example the right of a coastal State of hot pursuit, or the right of visit and seizure of certain vessels under Articles 105–111 UN Convention on the Law of the Sea. These rights can sensibly only be enforced with the use of armed military force or at least the threat of its use.[250] The Outer Space Treaty in its Article 3 stipulates that the UN Charter also applies to States' activity in outer space, thus extending the prohibition on using force to this sphere.[251] This explicit inclusion shows that States saw a necessity to expand the applicability of the UN Charter ratione loci also to this area, or at least recognised a need for clarification.

Yet the aforementioned deconceptualisation of cyberspace as a sphere sui generis results in the acceptance of States' jurisdiction according to the location of the relevant computer system and application of the effects principle over actions undertaken via communications networks.[252] Hence there remains no part which operates in a legal vacuum subject to no jurisdiction. Therefore, in absence of an explicit norm as provided in the Outer Space Treaty, the UN Charter is applicable ratione loci to sovereign cross-border computer network operations utilising the Internet.

2.2.2.2. The Different Approaches of Qualifying Computer Network Operations as Force

A considerable number of authors have put forward propositions of how to qualify computer network operations as a use of force in the sense of Article 2(4) UN Charter. This has been done in order to counter the assumption that CNOs operate in a legal vacuum and as a preliminary step in the assessment of their amounting to an armed attack under Article 51 UN Charter. It is clear from the

---

249 e.g., Johnson and Post come to the conclusion that'[l]aw [in cyberspace] will not, could not, and should not be the same law as that applicable to physical, geographically-defined territories' Johnson & Post 'Law and Borders – The Rise of Law in Cyberspace' at p. 1402; more recently Patrick W. Franzese 'Sovereignty in Cyberspace: Can it Exist?' (2009) 64 Air Force Law Review, stating that while cyberspace is neither immune from State sovereignty nor considerable as a global commons (at p. 40) an international regime were needed for the development of sovereignty in cyberspace (at pp. 27–29).

250 Randelzhofer & Dörr 'Article 2 (4)' para. 41; see also the *M/V 'SAIGA' (No 2) (Saint Vincent and the Grenadines v Guinea) (Merits) (Judgment)* 10, which states that the use of force in the arrest of ships is allowed when unavoidable, provided that certain preliminary warning actions have been undertaken without success (at paras. 153–159).

251 Robert Kolb *Ius contra bellum: le droit international relatif au maintien de la paix* (Helbing & Lichtenhahn Bâle 2009) p. 241; see also pp. 131 et seq. above.

252 See pp. 58 et seq. above.

outset that the UN Charter dating back to 1945 could not include or foresee the development of this new technology. The discussion thus necessarily focuses on the question of whether the notion of force under Article 2(4) UN Charter can be interpreted in such a way as to include CNOs at all and if so, where exactly the threshold for this qualification lies.

The different propositions can be grouped into two main approaches: those that concentrate on the means used in the operation to be evaluated, and those which appraise its effects. However, it will be shown that the two approaches and their respective modifications ultimately more or less follow the same model.

2.2.2.2.1. Instrument-based Approach

The classical definition of armed force concentrates on the type of instrument used for coercion rather than the consequences of the action. This instrument is regularly taken from the field of military weaponry.[253] Proponents of the so-called instrument-based approach see those CNOs as falling under the prohibition if they are comparable to 'traditional' military weapons.[254] Several arguments are put forward to substantiate this claim. Firstly, normatively defining the qualitative or quantitative consequences of an action were too difficult in order for it to be a valid criterion.[255] Secondly, by focusing on the instrument used, economic coercion could be exempted from the prohibition's scope. Solely evaluating the consequences of an action would on the contrary blur the differences between armed and economic coercion as both can have similar effects.[256] Thirdly, only the instrument-based approach could prevent an undue expansion of the scope of the notion of force.[257]

The proponents of the instrument-based approach agree that CNOs can qualify as a military weapon and also their methods of qualifying a concrete operation as a use of armed force are similar. This is achieved by drawing up several criteria that shall signify characteristics of armed force in contrast to economic coercion.

Dittmar uses the criteria of 'directness' and 'predictability of consequences for the attacker' in order to distinguish armed force from political and economic

---

253 Dörr 'Use of Force, Prohibition of' para. 18.

254 See only Dittmar *Angriffe auf Computernetzwerke: Ius ad bellum und ius in bello* pp. 88 et seq; On this see also Schmitt 'Computer Network Attack and the Use of Force in International Law: Thoughts on a Normative Framework' p. 917, who himself however argues for an effects-based approach.

255 Schmitt 'Computer Network Attack and the Use of Force in International Law: Thoughts on a Normative Framework' p. 911.

256 Barkham 'Information Warfare and International Law on the Use of Force' p. 86; Dittmar *Angriffe auf Computernetzwerke: Ius ad bellum und ius in bello* pp. 87 and 92.

257 Schmitt 'Computer Network Attack and the Use of Force in International Law: Thoughts on a Normative Framework' p. 917; Dittmar *Angriffe auf Computernetzwerke: Ius ad bellum und ius in bello* pp. 87 and 92.

coercion.[258] According to this view the criterion of 'directness' is a specific characteristic of armed force, namely the creation of a direct impact without the occurrence of any other factors. Conversely, while economic coercion could likewise cause bodily harm or destruction, this would only be possible over a longer period with the addition of other autonomous factors. This could for example be the case with a CNO that is directed against the national banking and financial sector and which is ultimately – due to a consequential economic crisis – the cause for riots.[259] Closely connected thereto is the criterion of a 'predictability of consequences for the attacker' which is likewise put forward in this regard. The consequences of the use of conventional armed force against a target were easily predictable for the attacker. The destruction of property or the injury of life and limb are for example seen as having a higher predictability when using armed force than in the case of economic coercion. CNOs with a similar degree of directness and predictability of consequences as conventional force would thus have to be considered as armed force in the sense of Article 2(4) UN Charter.[260]

Dittmar provides an overview of several scenarios of malicious CNOs developed in the literature and uses the directness and predictability test for their possible evaluation as armed force.[261] Six scenarios of CNOs are listed, though referring to these as 'attacks': on telecommunications systems; banking and finance systems; satellites; systems relevant to national security such as those of the military; the electricity grid; and traffic control systems. Of these Dittmar only characterises attacks on traffic control systems as comparable to the use of armed force, as only in this case were the destruction of tangible assets and injury of life and limb both a direct cause and predictable outcome of the CNO, as for example through collisions of aircraft or automobiles.[262]

2.2.2.2.2. Effects-based Approach

The second main approach concentrates on the results arising from a computer network operation. It is argued that those operations shall be qualified as armed force the damage of which inflicted has destructive effects.[263] Destruction in this

258 Dittmar *Angriffe auf Computernetzwerke: Ius ad bellum und ius in bello* pp. 99–103.

259 Heintschel von Heinegg 'Informationskrieg und Völkerrecht' p. 138; concurring Dittmar *Angriffe auf Computernetzwerke: Ius ad bellum und ius in bello* p. 100.

260 Dittmar *Angriffe auf Computernetzwerke: Ius ad bellum und ius in bello* p. 101.

261 Dittmar *Angriffe auf Computernetzwerke: Ius ad bellum und ius in bello* pp. 103–09.

262 Dittmar *Angriffe auf Computernetzwerke: Ius ad bellum und ius in bello* p. 109.

263 Wingfield *The Law of Information Conflict: National Security Law in Cyberspace* pp. 123–129; Stelter *Gewaltanwendung unter und neben der UN-Charta* pp. 72 et seq; Yoram Dinstein 'Computer Network Attacks and Self-Defense' in Michael N. Schmitt & Brian T. O'Donnell (eds) *Computer Network Attack and International Law* (Naval War College Newport 2002) p. 103; Stein & Marauhn 'Völkerrechtliche Aspekte von Informationsoperationen' p. 6; Segura-Serrano 'Internet Regulation and the Role of International Law' p. 224; Swanson 'The

context is generally interpreted in comparison with the effects conventional military weaponry has on persons or objects, that is destruction of property or the injury of life and limb.

Several modifications to this approach have been introduced additionally.[264] One view takes into consideration the target of a CNO. If critical infrastructures are targeted the operation shall automatically be qualified an armed attack hence likewise as a use of force.[265] Others put forward the view that CNOs are to be treated analogous to so-called 'physical force'. CNOs could thereby only be considered to fall under the prohibition of the use of force, if their effects were to pass the threshold of an armed attack in the sense of Article 51 UN Charter.[266]

It has further been argued that CNOs which are utilised as a form of economic coercion should – despite the general exemption of economic coercion from the prohibition's scope – nevertheless be treated as armed force. The different treatment shall be justified by the fact that CNOs by their nature require an intrusion into the target State's territory, while traditional economic coercion is induced externally through influencing the markets.[267]

Yet another modification utilises a rather wide interpretation of the effects that should be taken into account. These shall also include such negative effects as the crashing of financial markets or the nuisance caused to the population through an interference with supply chains.[268] A similar view is that which has argued for so-called electronic blockades to qualify as a use of force as their

Era of Cyber Warfare: Applying International Humanitarian Law to the 2008 Russian-Georgian Cyber Conflict' p. 317; Ziolkowski 'Computernetzwerkoperationen und die Zusatzprotokolle zu den Genfer Abkommen – Zum "virtuellen Raum" des Internet und dem Schutzstandard der vor 30 Jahren in Kraft getretenen Protokolle' p. 207. Kanuck 'Information Warfare: New Challenges for Public International Law' evaluates the limitation to armed coercion as too narrow and thus outdated (at p. 289).

264 Most recent with a 'modified effects-based approach': Stephenie Gosnell Handler 'The New Cyber Face of Battle: Developing a Legal Approach to Accommodate Emerging Trends in Warfare' (2012) 48 Stanford Journal of International Law pp. 225 et seq.

265 See the so-called 'strict-liability approach' referred to above at p. 105.

266 Heintschel von Heinegg 'Informationskrieg und Völkerrecht' pp. 139–40; contrary: Ziolkowski 'Computernetzwerkoperationen und die Zusatzprotokolle zu den Genfer Abkommen – Zum "virtuellen Raum" des Internet und dem Schutzstandard der vor 30 Jahren in Kraft getretenen Protokolle' p. 207; Dittmar *Angriffe auf Computernetzwerke: Ius ad bellum und ius in bello* pp. 74–75; Silver 'Computer Network Attack as a Use of Force under Article 2 (4) of the United Nations Charter' p. 83.

267 Todd A. Morth 'Considering Our Position: Viewing Information Warfare as a Use of Force Prohibited by Article 2(4) of the U.N. Charter' (1998) 30(2/3) Case Western Reserve Journal of International Law pp. 592–97; this is seen differently by Dittmar *Angriffe auf Computernetzwerke: Ius ad bellum und ius in bello* who regards any economic coercion of whatever quality as excluded from the prohibition of Art. 2(4) UN Charter (at p. 73).

268 Brown 'A Proposal for an International Convention to Regulate the Use of Information Systems in Armed Conflict' p. 188; Walter Gary Sharp *Cyberspace and the Use of Force* (Ageis Research Corp Falls Church 1999) p. 102.

effects – seriously impairing commerce – were analogous to those of naval blockades.[269]

The most widely cited proposition of an effects-based approach is a seven-stage test introduced by *Schmitt*, which was more or less adopted by the Tallinn Manual as well.[270] The more of the following seven criteria an operation fulfils, the more likely it is to be qualified as a use of armed force:

(1) Severity: the level of physical injury or destruction of property.
(2) Immediacy: the negative consequences of armed coercion usually occur with great timely immediacy, giving the target State or the international community less opportunity to seek peaceful accommodation.
(3) Directness: consequences of armed coercion are more directly tied to the actus reus, rather than depending on multiple contributory factors to operate.
(4) Invasiveness: the harmful measure mostly crosses into the territory of the victim State, thus forming a graver intrusion on the rights of the victim State.
(5) Measurability: consequences of armed coercion are easier to ascertain than those of other forms of coercion.
(6) Presumptive legitimacy: armed coercion is – under international as well as domestic law – mostly deemed illegitimate in absence of a justification such as self-defence, thus following a prohibitory approach. Non-armed versions of coercion rather follow the opposite, permissive approach, that is they are presumptively lawful in absence of a prohibition to the contrary.
(7) Responsibility: acts involving armed force are likelier to be assessed as acts of States than those based on economic or political coercion.

In focusing on the consequences of an action, the criteria of severity, immediacy, directness, invasiveness and measurability ultimately position *Schmitt*'s framework within the effects-oriented approach.[271] The same holds true for Rule 11 Tallinn

---

269 Barkham 'Information Warfare and International Law on the Use of Force' p. 92; Wingfield *The Law of Information Conflict: National Security Law in Cyberspace* pp. 91–92.

270 Firstly introduced as a six-stage test in Schmitt 'Computer Network Attack and the Use of Force in International Law: Thoughts on a Normative Framework' at pp. 914–15, then given the addition of the seventh element, the question of responsibility by Schmitt 'Computer Network Attack: The Normative Software' p. 65.The Tallinn Manual further adds the criterion of the operation's 'military character', ie a nexus between the CNO in question and other military operations:Schmitt (ed) *Tallinn Manual on the International Law Applicable to Cyber Warfare* pp. 48–51.
A comparable approach using the factors of severity, immediacy, directness and effects of the operation has recently been proposed in the International Institute of Humanitarian Law (ed) *Rules of Engagement Handbook* at p. 15. Just as the Tallinn Manual, the handbook neither necessarily reflects customary international law nor the opinion of singular States on the issue.

271 Especially the criterion of severity is ultimately congruent with the approach that demands the effects of a CNO to be comparable to the destructive effects of conventional military

Manual stipulating 'a cyber operation constitutes a use of force when its scale and effects are comparable to non-cyber operations rising to the level of a use of force'.

Schmitt provides an analysis of two fictitious examples of CNOs under his approach: firstly, the interference with an air traffic control service causing a plane to crash; and secondly, operations directed against the military research of a university aimed at diminishing the opponents' abilities on the battlefield. The former qualified as a use of armed force due to the severity and measurability (death of the passengers, destruction of the plane), immediacy and directness (plane crashes shortly after due to the air traffic control system's manipulation). The latter example on the other hand does not qualify as armed force: the desired outcome is remote, not exactly measurable and dependent on several other additional factors.[272] The commentary to the Tallinn Manual evaluates Stuxnet as an example of a use of force.[273]

2.2.2.2.3. Nascent State Practice

A further determinant factor in the consideration of CNOs as armed force under Article 2(4) UN Charter could be derived from State practice if this can be proven to exist at all. State practice, which also forms the objective element of customary international law, can manifest itself in different ways. On the one hand this is expressed in material behaviour through physical acts.[274] Actually conducting CNOs against foreign States would be an example thereof. On the other hand there are statements of positions expressed in various forms and fora.[275] As an element in establishing customary international law applicable to CNOs, the relevant State practice does not necessarily depend on a specific duration. This is the case especially in relation to new technologies which necessarily have to be coped with in a timely manner.[276] However, in such a case, the ICJ requires instead that State practice 'including that of States whose interests are specially affected, should have been both extensive and virtually

---

weaponry; Silver 'Computer Network Attack as a Use of Force under Article 2 (4) of the United Nations Charter' p. 89; concurring: Dittmar *Angriffe auf Computernetzwerke: Ius ad bellum und ius in bello* p. 101.

272 Schmitt 'Computer Network Attack and the Use of Force in International Law: Thoughts on a Normative Framework' p. 916.

273 Schmitt (ed) *Tallinn Manual on the International Law Applicable to Cyber Warfare* p. 45 para. 9. Contrarily, in case there would have been no damage of a physical nature it has also been evaluated as a 'legal masterpiece' not meeting the threshold of illegality: Ziolkowski 'Stuxnet – Legal Considerations' p. 147. This latter view cannot be supported, as at a minimum it is to be qualified as an intervention.

274 Treves 'Customary International Law' para. 27.

275 See the overview of the different forms of State practice given by Michael Wood 'State Practice' in Rüdiger Wolfrum (ed) *MPEPIL* (OUP Oxford Update 2010) paras. 5–25 and Treves 'Customary International Law' para. 26.

276 Examples for this are the rules appertaining to the continental shelf or outer space, necessitated through the development of advanced drilling and space technology; Treves 'Customary International Law' para. 24.

uniform in the sense of the provision invoked'.[277] The fact that CNOs are still a comparatively recent phenomenon does thus not preclude the possibility of customary rules having emerged.

Yet to this day, State practice in the aftermath of CNOs does not show a consensus, neither by victim States, nor by the international community. Although such operations are regularly condemned, there seems to be no uniform position as to their legal qualification or the valid responses thereto.[278]

So far there exists no public knowledge of cases where States have employed CNOs against other States. Only the establishment of units specialising in CNOs within the armed forces of a number of States can be observed, as has been shown above.[279] Yet this is merely a manifestation of the fact that States have begun to consider that warfare may possibly be waged through interconnected networks. It could be argued that the mere establishment of such units would at least manifest the position that the utilisation of CNOs is not contrary to international law per se. Where such units are established to conduct CNOs that have extraterritorial effects, this is a conclusive argument. However, such units can for example also be used solely for passive defence purposes, hence measures that neither qualify as a use of force nor as an intervention as they are only used within the victim State's jurisdiction. Without relevant manuals or directives indicating that their tasks include offensive measures, the mere establishment of units cannot be qualified as the manifestation of a legal position through a physical act.

While there are no physical actions from which to deduce State practice this could likewise be done by examining official statements, manuals, policies and the like. Hence there need not necessarily be any physical conduct at all to establish a customary rule, if the opinio iuris of the relevant States can be sufficiently established.[280]

However, official statements regarding the legal appraisal of CNOs are rare. While some States have declared malicious CNOs to be 'illegal', most statements fail to precisely designate the violation, let alone qualify them as armed force in the sense of Article 2(4). Some US military documents and a statement by US President Obama refer to CNOs as 'weapons'.[281] In the US National Strategy to

277 *North Sea Continental Shelf Cases (Federal Republic of Germany/Denmark; Federal Republic of Germany/Netherlands)* para. 74.

278 Shackelford 'From Nuclear War to Net War: Analogizing Cyber Attacks in International Law' p. 219.

279 See pp. 71 et seq. above.

280 Principle 4 of the ILA Committee on Formation of Customary (General) International Law 'Statement of Principles Applicable to the Formation of General Customary International Law' states that 'Verbal acts, and not only physical acts, of States count as State practice', the commentary of which draws upon PCIJ and ICJ jurisprudence such as the *Lotus Case*, *Nuclear Weapons (Advisory Opinion)* and *Nicaragua Case* (*ibid* p. 14); similarly Treves 'Customary International Law' para. 13.

281 US Joint Chiefs of Staff 'The National Military Strategy of the United States of America' (2004) at <www.defense.gov/news/mar2005/d20050318nms.pdf> (date accessed 11 March 2011) p. 1; Obama 'Remarks by the President on Securing our Nation's Cyber Infrastructure'.

Secure Cyberspace of 2003 it is stated that a diplomatic or military response will follow in the case of a State-sponsored cyber attack.[282] Several high-ranking US military officers (inter alia the Commander of US Cyber Command) have declared that cyber attacks on 'American cyberspace' should trigger a military response including physical force.[283] Most recently Harold Koh, the Legal Adviser of the US State Department in a speech stated that cyber activities qualify as a use of armed force when leading to results comparable to those of kinetic weapons, thereby utilising the effects-based approach.[284] State officials from other countries including Russia, the United Kingdom and Estonia have given similar statements.[285] However, these have remained vague and it remains doubtful whether their phrasing was intended to include a legal evaluation of such operations. The United States has further qualified 'cybersecurity due diligence', which is understood as the responsibility of States to protect their information infrastructures and national systems from damage and misuse as an emerging norm, which is supported by statements of several other major military powers.[286]

There even exist some statements by Russian military officers that try to justify the use of nuclear weapons against the means and forces of information warfare and the source State.[287] However, these statements are not official and are mostly taken from interviews with individuals who do not have the competence to represent the official State policies.

The only attempt ever made to consider regulating or banning CNOs as a means of warfare in the forum of the United Nations was made by the Russian Federation in a draft resolution in 1998,[288] which was however never adopted. In this draft resolution, the Russian Federation considered 'informations weapons' as being capable of having a destructive effect comparable to that of weapons of

---

282 US Department of Homeland Security 'The National Strategy to Secure Cyberspace 2003' p. 28.

283 Several quotations given by Roscini 'World Wide Warfare: Jus ad Bellum and the Use of Cyber Force' pp. 125–26.

284 Harold Hongju Koh 'International Law in Cyberspace' (2012) at <www.state.gov/s/l/releases/remarks/197924.htm> (date accessed 18 December 2013). Providing or an analysis of the speech: Michael Schmitt 'International Law in Cyberspace: The Koh Speech and Tallinn Manual Juxtaposed' (2012) 54 Harvard International Law Journal Online pp. 13 et seq.

285 As reported by Roscini 'World Wide Warfare: Jus ad Bellum and the Use of Cyber Force' pp. 108–09.

286 The President of the United States of America 'International Strategy for Cyberspace' p. 10; and see p. 109 above.

287 Timothy L. Thomas 'Russian Views on Information-based Warfare' (1996) Special Edition 1996 Airpower Journal pp. 25–35.

288 UNGA 'Developments in the Field of Information and Telecommunications in the Context of International Security: Russian Federation: Draft Resolution'; introducing a ban to develop 'informations weapons' remained of special concern for the Russian Federation for some time, seeing such as the major area for international cooperation in the field of information security, as stipulated in the Russian Federation 'Information Security Doctrine of the Russian Federation (approved by President Putin on 9 September 2000)' para. 7.

mass destruction and proposed the establishment of an international centre for monitoring threats to the security of global information and telecommunications systems. However, the concept of information security to which the Russian draft refers apparently is not only a concept to secure the technical integrity of computer systems, but could also legitimise censorship of content on the Internet and may therefore not solely pertain to CNOs. This reading is reiterated by a Russian-drafted Shanghai Cooperation Organization[289] agreement of 2009 which elaborates on the draft resolution and defines information war as a confrontation aimed at undermining political, economic and social systems or mass psychological brainwashing to destabilise society and the State.[290] This concept goes far beyond the traditional understanding of CNOs, which does not concern itself with those operations that utilise the Internet as a means of psychological operations or warfare in order to influence foreign attitudes or behaviour.

Some references to CNOs are also slowly making their way into scholarly handbooks and manuals on the law of armed conflict, as for example the 2010 Manual on International Law of Military Operations, the 2009 Manual on the Law of Air and Missile Warfare, and the 2009 San Remo Rules of Engagement Handbook, which however do not express the views of any government and are not legally binding, but can nevertheless be considered as an attempt to restate current customary international law.[291] However the issue of CNOs is not addressed therein in a comprehensive manner but is restricted to the proclamation of general principles such as 'all information operations conducted by military forces must comply with international law, and, where applicable, domestic law'.[292] The inclusion of this seemingly self-evident rule sets a clear example of the uncertainties still attached to computer network operations. A change has been brought about only through the publication in 2013 of the Tallinn Manual on the International Law Applicable to Cyber Warfare, which can be seen as an attempt to develop a common approach at least in Western literature.[293]

---

289 The current Member States of the Shanghai Cooperation Organization are China, Kazakhstan, Kyrgyzstan, Russia, Tajikistan and Uzbekistan.

290 As cited by Tom Gjelten 'Shadow Wars: Debating Cyber 'Disarmament'' (2010) November/December 2010 World Affairs p. 36.

291 Terry D. Gill & Dieter Fleck (eds) *The Handbook of the International Law of Military Operations* (OUP Oxford 2010) including as an appendix the Manual on International Law of Military Operations, intended to serve as a restatement of the fundamental legal rules and as a best-practice guide; Furthermore, both the Program on Humanitarian Policy and Conflict Research (ed) *HPCR Manual on Air Warfare* and the International Institute of Humanitarian Law (ed) *Rules of Engagement Handbook* likewise include rules on CNOs. On the significance of these manuals see Earle A. Partington 'Manuals on the Law of Armed Conflict' in Rüdiger Wolfrum (ed) *MPEPIL* (OUP Oxford Update 2011) para. 3.

292 Rule 21.02 Manual on International Law of Military Operations.

293 The Tallinn Manual however focuses on the law of armed conflict and does not offer a substantial discussion on CNOs outside of armed conflict and below the level of armed force.

Thus no particular State practice can be observed that would shed light on the question when CNOs qualify as armed force. While several statements denounce the use of this measure in international relations, States fail to classify both which norms of international law are violated by CNOs and the threshold needed in the particular case. This is inter alia due to the still ambiguous definition of the term 'cyber attack' which, though frequently used in statements of the relevant State actors, in most cases remains an empty phrase. Most practice therefore contents itself with general statements such as that of the British Foreign Secretary William Hague who declared that in Britain's view the 'need for governments to act proportionately in cyberspace and in accordance with national and international law' should be a principle underpinning future international norms on the use of cyberspace.[294]

2.2.2.2.4. Conclusion

Due to the lack of a precise definition of force in the UN Charter the term has always remained somewhat ambiguous. While the two UN General Assembly Resolutions on Friendly Relations and on the Definition of Aggression have attempted to clarify its scope and content, they have not managed to definitively solve the controversy.[295] This ambiguity does however have the advantage of a certain flexibility which in turn avoids creating a lacuna by permitting new forms of military means such as CNOs to likewise be encompassed. This is also the most important similarity between the instrument- and effects-based approaches and their respective modifications: neither of them generally excludes CNOs from falling under the scope of the notion of armed force in the sense of Article 2(4).

The criteria of 'directness' and 'predictability of consequences' within the instrument-based approach are in fact intrinsic to conventional weapons. Yet they offer only a limited solution when evaluating CNOs, since these offer a wider spectrum of military possibilities than conventional weapons. Computer viruses can be mentioned as an example of a CNO with a mostly unpredictable outcome, as it depends on the actual spread of the malware. Then there are those operations which are not direct, but rely on additional factors. For conventional weapons this is the case of mines, which are triggered by a certain event, namely contact of a predefined strength. However, not an insignificant number of CNOs

---

This has been criticised by Dieter Fleck 'Searching for International Rules Applicable to Cyber Warfare – A Critical First Assessment of the New Tallinn Manual' (2013) 18(2) Journal of Conflict and Security Law pp. 346 et seq.

294 British Foreign Secretary William Hague 'Security and Freedom in the Cyber Age – Seeking the Rules of the Road (Speech to the Munich Security Conference)' (4 February 2011) at <www.fco.gov.uk/en/news/latest-news/?view=Speech&id=545383882> (date accessed 1 April 2011).

295 Bothe 'Friedenssicherung und Kriegsrecht' p. 650.

are comparable to the laying of mines on foreign soil. These are computer viruses often referred to as 'logic bombs', which remain dormant on the target system until triggered by a predefined event.[296] Furthermore, the high degree of interconnectivity of both military and civilian systems, including those utilised in the control of public infrastructures, leads to a higher potential of cascading effects of CNOs than is the case with conventional weapons that can be confined to an individual target within the theatre of war. This makes the predictability of consequences of a CNO extremely complex. Excluding a severe CNO from the prohibition of the use of force merely due to its unpredictable consequences would however be an untenable result ultimately leading to a rejection of the criterion of predictability of consequences.

The manifold modifications proposed for the effects-based approach do not convince either. Despite the view of some authors to the contrary, the quality of the target – in this case critical infrastructures – cannot automatically qualify a CNO as an armed attack as this requires the crossing of a certain threshold of harm irrespective of the target.[297] Considering the intentional exclusion of economic coercion from the scope of the notion of force, the same must also hold true in the case of CNOs aimed at causing economic damage. CNOs utilised as a means of economic coercion must be treated accordingly, and hence do not fall under the prohibition's scope. Admittedly this is different once the operations are used to destroy economic targets. In these cases, however, one can no longer speak of economic coercion, as the key aspect shifts to the forceful destruction of property.

Electronic blockades likewise do not readily qualify as armed force as they do not include an implicit threat to use force if the blockade is breached. This is due to the fact that they are not readily comparable to their conventional counterparts.[298] Their effects, as for example the obstruction of communications, are to be considered under the ITU Constitution but do not have a bearing on Article 2(4) UN Charter. Only if the blockade is achieved by destruction of the relevant systems can it be considered armed force, but then again the emphasis lies not on the blockade, but on the destructive measures utilised for its implementation.

Within the Schmitt framework, the factors of presumptive legitimacy and responsibility cannot be regarded as valid criteria as they themselves are elements of a legal evaluation of the operation's lawfulness, and can therefore only be considered in a second stage, thus precluding their use as a factor of determining the object of investigation.[299]

296 Pierrot 'Computerviren' para. 118.

297 See pp. 176 et seq. below.

298 See pp. 127 et seq. above.

299 Similarly Ziolkowski 'Computernetzwerkoperationen und die Zusatzprotokolle zu den Genfer Abkommen – Zum "virtuellen Raum" des Internet und dem Schutzstandard der vor 30 Jahren in Kraft getretenen Protokolle' p. 207 at fn. 21.

Ultimately the alleged differences between the two approaches and the manifold modifications they have experienced are not clearly visible. The present work will not make an attempt to introduce yet another approach as this would most likely only increase complexity. It is more appropriate to focus on the similarities of the approaches in order to find a common ground.

As mentioned earlier, both approaches have considerable similarities. While the effects-based approach in any case only evaluates the level of destruction or harm caused by a CNO, the instrument-based approach on the other hand only seemingly focuses on the means utilised. As international law does not provide for a conclusive definition of the term military weaponry, the instrument-based approach is ultimately dependent on the interpretation thereof. It is this interpretation which makes the latter approach able to consider the effects of an operation, showing that the alleged differences between the approaches are artificial. For example, the Oxford English Dictionary defines the term 'weapon' as 'an instrument of any kind used in warfare or in combat to attack and overcome an enemy'.[300] This makes it clear that it is not the object used which is decisive, but the purpose, namely to gain an advantage over the enemy.[301] More or less any object could qualify as a weapon under this definition. The understanding is reflected in the definitions provided in international instruments. For example Rule 1(ff) of the Manual on the Law of Air and Missile Warfare uses the following definition of a weapon:

> 'a means of warfare used in combat operations, including a gun, missile, bomb or other munitions, that is capable of causing either (i) injury to, or death of, persons; or (ii) damage to, or destruction of, objects.'

This rule shows that the main focus lies on the effects of the means utilised, namely those that are capable of causing death, injury, damage or destruction, and not on the particular instrument as such. Whether the effects are the result of a kinetic, electronic, chemical or biological impact is irrelevant. The commentary on the Manual consequently treats what it calls 'computer network attack hardware, software and codes' as 'weapons that can cause such effects through transmission of data streams'.[302]

This is also in accord with the traditional understanding of force under Article 2(4). As has been shown above, the term 'arms' is not confined to conventional kinetic weapons but also encompasses devices with a biological, chemical or nuclear mode of operation. The reason for their inclusion however is their potentially destructive effects on life and limb. A similar opinion has been

---

300 'Weapon, n.', in Oxford English Dictionary Online (September 2011).

301 William H. Boothby 'Weapons, Prohibited' in Rüdiger Wolfrum (ed) *MPEPIL* (OUP Oxford Update 2010) para. 2.

302 Program on Humanitarian Policy and Conflict Research (ed) *Commentary on the HPCR Manual on International Law Applicable to Air and Missile Warfare* p. 55.

expressed by the ICJ, which stated that the choice of weaponry is not relevant for the question of whether armed force or an armed attack has taken place, as neither Article 2(4) nor Article 51 UN Charter refer to any particular type of weapon.[303] The same can also be observed in treaties that outlaw the use of certain weapons which concentrate on the unwanted effects these produce, as for example those deemed excessively injurious or indiscriminate.[304]

What is further ignored by the proponents of an instrument-based approach is the question of whether CNOs can qualify as a 'weapon' at all when considering the traditional understanding of the term. The problem is thus with a feature of the notion of computer network operation: it encompasses a whole operation and not one particular weapon. Every such operation is exercised via and with the help of computer systems and networks, which themselves consist of hard- and software components. A CNO hence utilises several devices which are autonomous from but connected to each other. The software used will need hardware on which it can be executed, and then this hardware has to be connected to a network (generally the Internet) that will ultimately connect the system from which the operation is conducted to the target system. While this setup has been compared to a conventional gun, the bullet in this case being the data packets sent to the target system,[305] the comparison cannot be made that simply. The military use of computer systems and communication networks is only one possible use of many, qualifying them as dual-use goods. A conventional weapon on the other hand – such as the gun in the example given – only has a singular purpose, which is destructive. Admittedly, there exists software which comes close to the traditional understanding of a weapon, namely software the sole purpose of which is malicious, as for example computer viruses. But these are only one of manifold possibilities for conducting CNOs. There are also those cases where due to an insecure target system the manipulation of its data can simply be done by utilising the system's standard tools, so that no special software is needed that could be regarded as a weapon. A CNO must therefore be considered in its entirety and cannot be limited to the particular software used in a fashion comparable to conventional weapons.

Most authors see a need to establish an approach which on the one hand encompasses those computer network operations which in their effects are

303 *Legality of the Threat or Use of Nuclear Weapons (Advisory Opinion)* paras. 38–39.

304 Convention on Prohibitions or Restrictions on the Use of Certain Conventional Weapons Which May Be Deemed to Be Excessively Injurious or to Have Indiscriminate Effects (adopted 10 October 1980, entered into force 2 December 1983) 1342 UNTS 137. Art. 2(1) Agreement between the USA and USSR on the Prevention of Dangerous Military Activities (signed 12 June 1989, entered into force 1 January 1990) 28 ILM 877 designates 'interfering with command and control networks in a manner which could cause harm to personnel or damage to equipment of the armed forces of the other party' as a dangerous military activity prohibited during peacetime.

305 Brown 'A Proposal for an International Convention to Regulate the Use of Information Systems in Armed Conflict' p. 185.

comparable to conventional weapons while on the other hand preventing economic coercion from likewise being encompassed. This concern is explicitly voiced by the critics of the effects-based approach who fear lack of distinction between economic and armed coercion.[306] The history of the prohibition of Article 2(4) UN Charter does not necessitate this, however. Today it is generally settled and accepted that economic coercion is not to be considered as force, making concerns that the effects-based approach would lead to an expansion of the interpretation of the notion of force in order to include CNOs somewhat superfluous. Confirming the applicability of a rule to a new circumstance through interpretation does not mean that disputes generally deemed to be settled automatically need to be reconsidered. The introduction of CNOs does not therefore imply a change in the treatment of economic coercion. The particular use and effect of a CNO is decisive. If it is used to disrupt production in a factory, this might be done under the pretence of an economic coercion; but there is a difference between economic coercion on the market and an intrusive operation directly destroying a production line. While the goal might be the same, only the latter qualifies as a use of force, in that it has destructive effects, thereby shifting the key aspect away from economic and towards armed force.

The approaches presented above do not provide a concise framework of qualification of CNOs as armed force but merely propose different criteria that should be taken into account in the evaluation. While this may seem unsatisfactory at first, it is due both to the specifics of CNOs and the general ambiguity surrounding the term 'force' in Article 2(4) UN Charter. While it might be possible to classify CNOs into several standard categories, their effects are very much dependent on the target system and the particular mode of employment. That is why it is not possible to qualify the deletion or alteration of data by itself as a use of armed force. The processes relying on said data need to be taken into account, that is their functionality after the data has been compromised. Ultimately only those CNOs that have a destructive effect leading to injury of life and limb or destruction of property qualify as armed force. While it has been proposed that only direct and predictable effects may be taken into account, these criteria are too restrictive, especially considering the indirect nature and duration of many CNOs. On the other hand it is clear that not every remote consequence needs to be taken into consideration. Finally it must plainly be admitted that there is no crystal clear dogmatic framework available that would resolve the question of from which point on CNOs are to be definitely qualified as armed force. This is however not unique to the new technology but has gone along with the interpretation of the prohibition of the use of force since its incorporation in Article 2(4) UN Charter.

---

306 Dittmar *Angriffe auf Computernetzwerke: Ius ad bellum und ius in bello* p. 92.

The Operational Law Handbook of the United States Army describes the situation fittingly by predicting that while it was unclear how the international community will apply principles of international law to CNOs:

> '[m]uch will depend on how nations and international institutions react to the particular circumstances in which the issues are raised for the first time. It seems likely that the international community will be more interested in the consequences of an EA [electronic attack] or a CNA [computer network attack] than in the means used. ... This means that the method of IO [information operation] is less important than the effects of a particular IO when establishing the legality of an action.'[307]

3. CIRCUMSTANCES PRECLUDING WRONGFULNESS

In order to establish State responsibility for the breach of an international obligation, no circumstances precluding wrongfulness may be proven to exist. The ILC Articles on State Responsibility envisage six circumstances in this regard, which in their order of appearance in Articles 20–25 ILC Articles are: consent, self-defence, countermeasures, force majeure, distress and necessity.

Actions taken in exercise of a State's right of self-defence under Article 51 UN Charter are a whole issue to themselves and will be dealt with below.[308] The same holds true for countermeasures which are explicitly envisaged by the ILC Articles as a measure for enforcing compliance with a State's obligations under Part II of the ILC Articles.[309] The circumstances of consent, distress and necessity do not pose any new problems in the context of CNOs and will thus not be analysed here.

3.1. FORCE MAJEURE

Invoking force majeure as a preclusion as envisaged in Article 23 ILC Articles in contrast is more realistic in cases of CNOs. The ILC Articles define force majeure as 'the occurrence of an irresistible force or of an unforeseen event, beyond the control of the State, making it materially impossible in the circumstances to perform the obligation'. While it is disputed whether the element of fault is a requirement to establish State responsibility, at any rate it can be considered indirectly if a State contends it did not act willingly but under force majeure.[310]

---

307 US Army *Operational Law Handbook* (The Judge Advocate General's Legal Center & School Charlottesville 2009) pp. 144–45.

308 See pp. 175 et seq. below.

309 See pp. 157 et seq. below.

310 Dahm, Delbrück & Wolfrum *Völkerrecht vol I/3* p. 946; Cassese *International Law* p. 251; according to Crawford & Olleson 'The Nature and Forms of International Responsibility' the

Especially in the case of computer viruses designed to spread over several systems, the question arises as to whether a State could invoke force majeure in cases where the virus spreads in an uncontrolled manner, infecting systems not originally targeted.

In order for side or cascading effects of a CNO to be qualifiable as force majeure, they would have to meet the requirements set out by the ILC Articles: pose an irresistible force or an unforeseen event external to State control, thereby making the performance of the obligation materially impossible.[311] Irresistible force is characterised in the ILC's commentary by a constraint which the State was unable to avoid or oppose by its own means.[312] Such are particularly natural or physical events having an adverse effect on a specific State action; in these cases force majeure presents itself through external circumstances which lead to the wrongful act, as for instance a natural catastrophe causing military craft to illegally arrive on foreign territory. An unforeseen event on the other hand must have been neither foreseen nor easily foreseeable. This criterion focuses on the act itself, as the force majeure is intrinsic to the act which produces the unforeseeable effect, which can also present itself through human intervention.

The preclusion cannot be invoked however, if the situation is due, either alone or in combination with other factors, to the conduct of the State, or if the State has assumed the risk of that situation occurring.[313] For the example of a virus spreading unintentionally to systems that were not targeted, an argument could be made that these effects were unforeseeable. Where the spread is caused by the specific setup of the target system or by a human intervention on the target side, the element of externality could likewise be seen as being fulfilled. However, the acting State bears the burden of proof in this regard and by using a means or method generally known for its side and cascading effects implicitly accepts these risks. States utilising CNOs must therefore take into account the technology's intrinsic risks. In the case of Stuxnet, for example, thousands of systems around the world had been infected although allegedly only one system was the target. This shows the peculiarity of certain CNOs which – if direct access to the target system is not available – spread to an undefined number of systems in order to eventually reach the actual target system. Whether this is done deliberately or not is irrelevant as long as it can be determined that the

ILC Articles do not provide for a presumption either way; this is rather up to the specific context and obligation said to have been breached, which is more likely in cases of omissions than in the case of deliberative actions (at pp. 457–58). Likewise Giuseppe Palmisano 'Fault' in Rüdiger Wolfrum (ed) *MPEPIL* (OUP Oxford Update 2007) paras. 15–19.

311 Sandra Szurek 'Circumstances Precluding Wrongfulness in the ILC Articles on State Responsibility: Force Majeure' in James Crawford Alain Pellet & Simon Olleson (eds) *The Law of International Responsibility* (OUP Oxford 2010) p. 477.

312 Para. 2 Commentary to Art. 23 UN ILC 'Text of the Draft Articles with Commentaries Thereto: Responsibility of States for Internationally Wrongful Acts'.

313 Art. 23(2) UN ILC Articles on State Responsibility.

situation of force majeure is caused by the conduct of the State invoking it.[314] Adducing force majeure as a circumstance precluding the wrongfulness of a CNO is thereby made nearly impossible.

3.2. COMPUTER NETWORK OPERATIONS AS COUNTERMEASURES

A further preclusion of wrongfulness exists if a State resorts to computer network operations as a countermeasure against an internationally wrongful act of another State. This is mirrored in Rule 9 Tallinn Manual, which stipulates that 'a State injured by an internationally wrongful act may resort to proportionate countermeasures, including cyber countermeasures, against the responsible State'.

3.2.1. *The Absence of a Self-Contained Regime Applicable to Computer Network Operations*

As cyberspace does not constitute a new domain outside the reach of public authority, the question arises as to whether a legal regime specific to CNOs has developed under international law, which could qualify or at least come close to a self-contained regime.[315] This is of importance for the possibility of States to utilise CNOs as countermeasures in so far as self-contained regimes are generally considered to be a lex specialis to which the ILC Articles are not applicable.[316] Self-contained regimes are generally defined as regimes which comprise rules regulating a particular field by laying down rights and duties of the relevant actors, while also setting up a system that provides for means and mechanisms to enforce compliance with these rules and settle disputes arising under them. All of this is done with the intention of replacing and excluding the application of general international law at least to a certain extent.[317]

However, there are only very few self-contained regimes. When for example the ICJ in the *United States Diplomatic and Consular Staff in Tehran Case* referred to diplomatic law as a self-contained regime, this was harshly criticised in the literature. Not even the highly detailed European Union legal system is universally accepted to form a self-contained regime.[318] As has been shown

314 Szurek 'Circumstances Precluding Wrongfulness in the ILC Articles on State Responsibility: Force Majeure' p. 478.

315 Denying 'cyberspace' the quality of a self-contained regime: Schmahl 'Zwischenstaatliche Kompetenzabgrenzung im Cyberspace' p. 290.

316 Art. 55 ILC Articles; Klein 'Self-Contained Regime' paras. 7–10.

317 Klein 'Self-Contained Regime' para. 1; Dahm, Delbrück & Wolfrum *Völkerrecht vol I/3* p. 869.

318 In favour: Dahm, Delbrück & Wolfrum *Völkerrecht vol I/3* p. 869; against: Bruno Simma & Dirk Pulkowski 'Of Planets and the Universe: Self-Contained Regimes in International Law'

earlier, there are no specific rules applicable to military CNOs as of now. Nor has there been setup a specific procedure of dispute settlement.[319] The sole quality of the Internet as a new medium for military actions cannot by itself form a self-contained regime. Whether or not countermeasures against CNOs are themselves confined to CNOs therefore ultimately remains a mere question of proportionality.

3.2.2. *Subsidiarity of Countermeasures*

The legal consequences arising from a State's international responsibility for a wrongful act to begin with are the obligations the delinquent State owes towards the injured State. These include first and foremost the cessation and non-repetition of the wrongful act, and further reparation with its sub-categories restitution, compensation and satisfaction.[320] Secondly the injured State may ultimately obtain the right to resort to countermeasures aimed at the enforcement of reparation, subject to certain conditions.[321]

Countermeasures are not intended as a form of punishment for the wrongful conduct but as a means to ensure compliance of the responsible State with the obligations set out in Part II ILC Articles.[322] Hence countermeasures are only to be applied in a subsidiary manner. The first condition imposed on States to be eligible to take countermeasures is to call upon the responsible State for a discontinuance of the still ongoing unlawful act or, if it is non-recurring, to make reparation.[323] Secondly, States have the duty to resort to negotiations, as already provided by the general obligation for States to settle their disputes peacefully.[324] Only if all these attempts fail may a State resort to countermeasures as an ultima ratio.

While computer network operations do not challenge these primary duties, the possibilities for their use specifically as countermeasures need to be determined.

(2006) 17(3) European Journal of International Law pp. 516–19; Eckart Klein & Stefanie Schmahl 'Die internationalen und die supranationalen Organisationen' in Wolfgang Vitzthum (ed) *Völkerrecht* (de Gruyter Berlin 2010) p. 317.

319 The Uniform Domain Name Dispute Settlement system setup by ICANN is extrajudicial and mainly applicable for cases of so-called cybersquatting, not however for issues of security: Woltag 'Internet' para. 21. Therefore it cannot contribute to establishing a self-contained regime for CNOs.

320 Arts. 30–37 UN ILC Articles on State Responsibility.

321 Arts. 28–41 UN ILC Articles on State Responsibility; Dahm, Delbrück & Wolfrum *Völkerrecht vol I/3* pp. 956 et seq; Cassese *International Law* pp. 258–62.

322 Para.1 Commentary to Art. 49 UN ILC 'Text of the Draft Articles with Commentaries Thereto: Responsibility of States for Internationally Wrongful Acts'.

323 Art. 52 ILC Articles; Cassese *International Law* p. 302; Schröder 'Verantwortlichkeit, Völkerstrafrecht, Streitbeilegung und Sanktionen' p. 596; Schmitt (ed) *Tallinn Manual on the International Law Applicable to Cyber Warfare* p. 37 para. 5.

324 Cassese *International Law* p. 302; Dahm, Delbrück & Wolfrum *Völkerrecht vol I/3* pp. 987–89; Schröder 'Verantwortlichkeit, Völkerstrafrecht, Streitbeilegung und Sanktionen' p. 596.

3.2.3. *Possible Computer Network Operation Countermeasures*

Generally, States are free to choose any means as countermeasures. However, countermeasures are subject to limitations, as recognised in Articles 49–53 ILC Articles on State Responsibility. For example, countermeasures are not allowed to violate peremptory norms of international law or fundamental human rights. Countermeasures to acts taken outside of armed conflict that do not qualify as an armed attack may not themselves take recourse to armed force or a threat to do so.[325] This means as a consequence that armed reprisals are prohibited outside of armed conflict.[326] Due regard must also be had to the principle of proportionality, which according to Article 51 ILC Articles on State Responsibility requires countermeasures to be 'commensurate with the injury suffered, taking into account the gravity of the internationally wrongful act and the rights in question'. As a consequence a balance between the different legally protected interests is achieved by resorting to the less harsh of several possible countermeasures able to achieve the pursued ends.[327] Hence, computer network operations are generally qualifiable as a valid means of countermeasures as long as they do not transgress these limitations.

3.2.3.1. Automated Responses

It has been proposed both by legal and computer science scholars that automated responses to hostile computer network operations should be introduced.[328] Automation in warfare is not a peculiarity of CNOs but evolved in the 1960s and 1970s against the background of the policy of nuclear deterrence.[329] The extremely short reaction time available in case of an advancing nuclear strike via

---

325 Art. 50 ILC Articles on State Responsibility; This already stems from the fundamental prohibition of the use of force outside of armed conflict.

326 As stipulated in Principle 1(6) Friendly Relations Declaration and Art. 50(1)(a) UN ILC Articles on State Responsibility; *Legality of the Threat or Use of Nuclear Weapons (Advisory Opinion)* para. 46; Albrecht Randelzhofer & Georg Nolte 'Article 51' in Bruno Simma, et al. (eds) *The Charter of the United Nations – A Commentary* (OUP Oxford 2012) para. 14; in favour of a differentiated approach in relation to armed reprisals in peacetime: Doehring *Völkerrecht* pp. 460–62, arguing that force may be used when the initial wrongful action likewise made use of armed force; similar has been opined by a minority of the group of experts drafting the Tallinn Manual by referencing to the *Oil Platforms (Islamic Republic of Iran v United States of America) (Separate Opinion of Judge Simma)* [2003] ICJ Rep 324 paras. 12–13: Schmitt (ed) *Tallinn Manual on the International Law Applicable to Cyber Warfare* p. 38 para. 5.

327 Dahm, Delbrück & Wolfrum *Völkerrecht vol I/3* p. 990.

328 See only Jensen 'Cyber Warfare and Precautions against the Effects of Attacks' p. 1566; For a view of computer science on active defence see Felix Leder & Tillmann Werner 'Proactive Botnet Countermeasures an Offensive Approach' at <www.ccdcoe.org/publications/virtualbattlefield/15_LEDER_Proactive_Coutnermeasures.pdf> (date accessed 22 June 2011).

329 Olivier Minkwitz 'Ohne Hemmungen in den Krieg? Cyberwar und die Folgen' (2003) at <www.hsfk.de/fileadmin/downloads/report1003.pdf> (date accessed 25 May 2012) p. 29.

intercontinental ballistic missiles (the flight time between launch and impact of such a missile launched in Russia and targeting the US – or vice versa – is approximately half an hour) and the even shorter period – a few minutes – available in the launch phase of an adversary's missile, made the automation of responses necessary in order to keep up an effective deterrence.[330] However, cyber deterrence cannot fully be analogised to nuclear deterrence, especially in those cases where the source cannot be identified with certainty.[331] While most countries are equally vulnerable to a nuclear strike, this is not the case for a malicious CNO. The latter depends on the availability of an information and telecommunication infrastructure and offers more severe consequences the higher the degree of development and connectivity of the target State. This makes less developed States less vulnerable to malicious CNOs, thus decreasing the deterrence posed by automated responses targeting their information infrastructure.

A peculiarity of all computer network operations is their comparably enormous speed, which is in the range of milliseconds. Computer systems in most cases have the capability to respond to inputs instantly. In general, their sole purpose is to process inputs in a pre-defined manner. The question of whether such a computer system is under attack, for example by a CNO, will either be answered by a human, or by the system itself – but based on a program developed by humans. It is thus possible to design a military computer system in such a way that it can counter a hostile CNO instantly and automatically. To achieve this, several conditions can be predefined by the developers which need to be fulfilled in order for the system to execute the response. Typically these conditions will be those which are qualified as a specific characteristic of a hostile CNO.

An automated response could be both of a passive or active nature. A merely passive one, such as for example shutting down the victim system or disconnecting it from external networks, is a completely legitimate measure in that it does not in any way interfere with a foreign system. It would also be possible however to mount a more active response (entitled active defence or 'hack back' by some), as would be the case in a counteroperation targeting the system from which the initial operation originated.[332] One view holds that due

---

330 Holger Iburg *Abschreckung und Software: Computertechnologie als Instrument der amerikanischen Sicherheitspolitik* (Campus-Verlag Frankfurt 1991) pp. 251–66.

331 See also generally Martin Libicki *Cyberdeterrence and Cyberwar* (RAND Santa Monica 2009) pp. 39–74; Hanseman 'The Realities and Legalities of Information Warfare' p. 198; this has been acknowledged by the US Deputy Secretary of Defence William J. Lynn III at a NATO conference, who in consequence stated that 'we have to shift our cyber defence paradigm from assured retaliation to denial of benefit', as quoted in SDA Report 'A Conversation on Cybersecurity' (15 September 2010) <www.securitydefenceagenda.org/Portals/7/2010/Events/lynn/lynn_report.pdf> (date accessed 27 April 2011) p. 3; see also Lynn 'Defending a New Domain: The Pentagon's Cyberstrategy' pp. 99–100.

332 Leder & Werner 'Proactive Botnet Countermeasures an Offensive Approach'.

to the instantaneous nature of CNOs the victim State has the right to 'counterattack' immediately whereas such 'attack' would not be a violation of the host nation's sovereignty as it could in practice not react in a timely manner.[333] This conception of an active response is highly problematic, however, and is likely to meet with criticism. Firstly, there are the aforementioned problems pertaining to the attribution of the operation which could lead an automated response to target systems of an uninvolved State. Secondly, unless the system of origin is a 'familiar' one, as in the case of those analysed via intelligence or otherwise, the foreseeability of the consequences of a CNO directed against it are marginal.[334]

Furthermore, the introduction of an automated system as a measure of deterrence poses legal problems. The automation itself could be qualified as a threat to use force conditional upon the occurrence of a certain event. Under Article 2(4) UN Charter the threat to use force is prohibited in the same manner as its actual use. The ICJ has opined in the *Nuclear Weapons (Advisory Opinion)* that the notions of threat and force 'stand together in the sense that if the use of force itself in a given case is illegal – for whatever reason – the threat to use such force will likewise be illegal'.[335] In the advisory opinion the ICJ dealt with the argument put forward by some States that the mere possession of nuclear weapons constituted in and of itself a threat to use force, as under a policy of deterrence the intention to actually use them must be credible.[336] In the highly contested opinion, the ICJ stated that the use of nuclear weapons could not be concluded to be lawful or unlawful in an extreme case of self-defence, where the very survival of a State would be at stake. Hence nuclear deterrence, that is the threat to use nuclear weapons, was not generally outlawed. This could lead to the assumption that automated responses in form of CNOs are likewise not generally outlawed, especially when considering that their effects will hardly be on the same scale as those of a nuclear weapon.

However, there is a difference between nuclear deterrence and the case of automated CNOs. In nuclear deterrence, there is no automation mechanism as the use of nuclear weapons is conditional on a (human) decision, which will take

---

333 Jensen 'Cyber Warfare and Precautions against the Effects of Attacks' p. 1566; Jensen 'Computer Attacks on Critical National Infrastructure: A Use of Force Invoking the Right of Self-Defense' pp. 238–39, generally arguing that the 'traditional obstacles of attribution, characterisation, and inviolability of neutrals must give way to the need for an immediate self-defense response' (at pp. 239–40); similarly Matthew Hoisington 'Cyberwarfare and the Use of Force Giving Rise to the Right of Self-Defense' (2009) 32 Boston College International and Comparative Law Review p. 453, proposing an exception of the prohibition of the use of force for a State exercising 'active defence measures' in good faith as a response to cyber attacks on critical infrastructures; and Condron 'Getting it Right: Protecting American Critical Infrastructure in Cyberspace' pp. 415–16.

334 Barkham 'Information Warfare and International Law on the Use of Force' p. 83.

335 *Legality of the Threat or Use of Nuclear Weapons (Advisory Opinion)* para. 47.

336 *Legality of the Threat or Use of Nuclear Weapons (Advisory Opinion)* para. 48.

into consideration the legality of the respective action. The proposed automated responses pertaining to 'cyber deterrence', however, include an element which – although being predefined – is of such an instantaneous quality and ultimately executed by a software that a legal attribution can necessarily not take place in a comprehensive manner. Ultimately the concept of automated responses fails to fulfil the requirement of subsidiarity of countermeasures: in being instantaneous, there is no opportunity for the victim State to fulfil its primary duties of calling for discontinuance or demanding reparation from the delinquent State. Automated computer network operations that amount to an internationally wrongful act can therefore not be utilised as legitimate countermeasures that would lead to a preclusion of their wrongfulness under the rules of State responsibility.

3.2.3.2. A Right of 'Cyber Hot Pursuit'?

A further view has been put forward to allow States that have been victims of malicious computer network operations the right to trace the operation back through computer systems and networks located also in foreign jurisdictions.[337] It has been suggested that this right should be treated analogously to that of hot pursuit under the law of the sea. The right of hot pursuit is recognised as customary international law and today also codified in Article 23 Convention on the High Seas and Article 111 UN Convention on the Law of the Sea.[338] It allows a coastal State to pursue a foreign vessel which has violated its laws and regulations within an area under its sovereignty onto the high seas, provided that the pursuit commences immediately after the offence was committed and is not interrupted. The right thus constitutes an exception to the rule of exclusive flag State jurisdiction on the high seas.[339] However, hot pursuit thus far remains a concept unique to the law of the sea. While propositions have been made to also allow hot pursuit by air or on land, these were not accepted by the international community but were rather considered a violation of territorial sovereignty except in cases where the target State consents.[340]

337 Todd 'Armed Attack in Cyberspace: Deterring Asymmetric Warfare with an Asymmetric Definition' pp. 99–100.

338 Convention on the High Seas (done 29 April 1958, entered into force 30 September 1962) 450 UNTS 82.

339 Hugo Caminos 'Hot Pursuit' in Rüdiger Wolfrum (ed) *MPEPIL* (OUP Oxford Update 2009) para. 1.

340 Caminos 'Hot Pursuit' para. 3. An attempt by South Africa to recognise a hot pursuit also on land in cases where due to lack of attribution self-defence is unfeasible was rejected by the Security Council and later abandoned by South Africa itself: UNSC Res 568 'Botswana-South Africa' (21 June 1985) para. 4; Christine D. Gray *International Law and the Use of Force* (OUP Oxford 2008) p. 137; Tams 'The Use of Force Against Terrorists' p. 371 who points out that this denunciation was part of the general practice of condemnation of South Africa's policies under the apartheid regime. However, the denunciation was still based on Art. 2(4) UN Charter.

Hot pursuit is not a typical countermeasure in that it is not necessarily a response to an internationally wrongful act, as the reason for pursuit may lie solely in the violation of domestic laws of the pursuing State by a private vessel. However, a cyber hot pursuit as understood by the proposition is a possibility to provide for unilateral attribution of the attacker – without the cooperation of the source State – as a precursor for further measures.[341] This makes the analogy to hot pursuit under the law of the sea somewhat redundant. From a technical standpoint, there is no 'vehicle' that could be pursued. Rather, what takes place under this concept is a cross-border investigation conducted with CNOs. As has been shown above, these in most cases violate the target State's sovereignty and territorial integrity.[342] If the malicious CNO was undertaken by private individuals located on foreign territory there is already no possibility of invoking countermeasures against them. If undertaken by a State and qualifying as an internationally wrongful act, the subsidiarity of countermeasures must again be taken into account, making a 'hot', that is an instant pursuit without prior milder measures, a wrongful act in itself. Under the law of the sea the vessel to be pursued is the one that has violated domestic law while under the jurisdiction of the coastal State. In recognition of the sovereignty of a coastal State in its territorial sea over all matters, the right of hot pursuit ceases as soon as the vessel pursued enters the territorial sea of its flag State or a third State.[343] However, in the case of a cross-border CNO, the perpetrator is permanently located in a foreign jurisdiction as there are no areas outside the jurisdiction of individual States on the Internet that could be comparable to the area designated as the high seas.[344] All in all, the concept of the right of hot pursuit established under the law of the sea can therefore not be transferred onto computer network operations.

3.2.3.3. Human Rights as Limits to Countermeasures

The choice of means and their utilisation as countermeasures are limited in scope by human rights obligations of the relevant State and by peremptory norms of international law.[345] Yet due to their indeterminate scope and content, neither the non-intervention principle nor that of State sovereignty are regarded by the

341 Todd 'Armed Attack in Cyberspace: Deterring Asymmetric Warfare with an Asymmetric Definition' p. 100.

342 See pp. 117 et seq. above.

343 Art. 111(3) UN Convention on the Law of the Sea; Nordquist (ed) *United Nations Convention on the Law of the Sea 1982: A Commentary: Vol 3* p. 257.

344 See pp. 53 et seq. and pp. 113 above.

345 Art. 50(1) ILC Articles on State Responsibility further lists obligations of a humanitarian character prohibiting reprisals and the obligation to refrain from the threat or use of force as limitations to countermeasures; Dahm, Delbrück & Wolfrum *Völkerrecht vol I/3* p. 988; on this see also Charles Leben 'Obligations Relating to the Use of Force and Arising from Peremptory Norms of International Law' in James Crawford Alain Pellet & Simon Olleson (eds) *The Law of International Responsibility* (OUP Oxford 2010) pp. 1197 et seq.

majority opinion as part of ius cogens, despite their fundamental character for international law.[346] Otherwise States would under no circumstances be eligible to utilise computer network operations as countermeasures, as it has been proven above that in most cases they will qualify as a prohibited intervention.

Already in the *Naulilaa Case*, the arbitral tribunal stated that reprisals were limited by the requirements of humanity.[347] Article 50(1)(b) ILC Articles on State Responsibility likewise stipulates that countermeasures shall not affect obligations for the protection of fundamental human rights. Several human rights treaties identify certain human rights that may not be derogated from, even in times of war, such as those listed in Article 4(2) ICCPR or Article 15 ECHR.[348] Thus, any measures have their limit in these human rights obligations qualifying as ius cogens.[349]

Yet computer network operations taken as countermeasures and hence below the threshold of armed force are more likely to encroach upon those human rights connected to the usage of computer systems and the Internet, namely the freedom of information and communication, the right to privacy and the right to property, which do not qualify as non-derogable rights. Yet these can also be seen as 'fundamental human rights' in the sense of Article 50(1)(b) ILC Articles on State Responsibility. Some view those human rights as fundamental which directly relate to the physical integrity and freedom of a person, thereby excluding for example those of an economic import.[350] Others view all those human rights which are considered to form part of customary international law as fundamental, as their protection is an obligation erga omnes which can generally not be suspended by means of countermeasures as the latter may only be directed against the State which is responsible for an internationally wrongful act.[351] Admittedly there are numerous obligations owed towards the target State that a State may choose to suspend as a form of countermeasure which ultimately might have a negative effect on individuals and therefore also indirectly affect their human rights. This holds especially true in the case of economic sanctions targeting whole sectors of a State's economy. Yet in these cases it is not the individual that is targeted but the State as the subject responsible for an

---

346 Dahm, Delbrück & Wolfrum *Völkerrecht vol I/3* p. 716; Jamnejad & Wood 'The Principle of Non-Intervention' p. 358.

347 *Responsabilité de l'Allemagne à raison des dommages causés dans les colonies portugaises du sud de l'Afrique (sentence sur le principe de la responsabilité) (Portugal contre Allemagne) (Naulilaa Case)* (1928) 2 RIAA 1011 at p. 1026; see also in general Julia Pfeil 'Naulilaa Arbitration (Portugal v Germany)' in Rüdiger Wolfrum (ed) *MPEPIL* (OUP Oxford Update 2007).

348 International Covenant on Civil and Political Rights (adopted 19 December 1966, entered into force 23 March 1976) 999 UNTS 171.

349 Silvia Borelli & Simon Olleson 'Obligations Relating to Human Rights and Humanitarian Law' in James Crawford Alain Pellet & Simon Olleson (eds) *The Law of International Responsibility* (OUP Oxford 2010) pp. 1182 et seq.

350 Dahm, Delbrück & Wolfrum *Völkerrecht vol I/3* p. 989.

351 Borelli & Olleson 'Obligations Relating to Human Rights and Humanitarian Law' pp. 1182–88.

internationally wrongful act, which as an element of implementing State responsibility is the sole purpose of countermeasures. By targeting only the State, the latter is additionally also given the possibility to mitigate the negative effects on her citizens. Ultimately the reason for limiting countermeasures by human rights obligations is to prevent States from using individuals as a bargaining tool by encroaching on human rights afforded to these or threatening to do so in order to coerce the target State to perform certain actions.[352] While indirect negative effects on individuals cannot be completely excluded for all cases of countermeasures, the direct and intentional infringement of individuals' human rights creates a limit on all countermeasures. Allowing these limited negative repercussions on individuals does not also lead to untenable results, as countermeasures are ultimately again limited by the proportionality principle.[353]

While this is not the place to go into the details of human rights law, the cross-border nature of CNOs requires a short overview of the extraterritorial application of the relevant treaties before briefly outlining which human rights are prone to be affected by CNOs.

Internet users enjoy the same freedoms of expression, communication and information when utilising internet services as they do in any other medium. In particular, the right to impart information regardless of frontiers gains new momentum in this regard.[354] Furthermore the right to property and privacy could be infringed by operations which access or alter data on the target system or interfere with its designated functions. In the following, the focus will hence be on these rights and freedoms.

While most of the human rights treaties allow for limitations on those rights which tend to be affected by CNOs, these need not be considered for the case of countermeasures. Seeing that a countermeasure is by definition an internationally wrongful act that becomes lawful only when it is used to implement the international responsibility of the target State, those CNOs which already qualify as a legitimate infringement of the relevant right due to a justification under its limitation clause do not qualify as internationally wrongful acts in the first place and can hence not be deemed a countermeasure.

3.2.3.3.1. Extraterritorial Application of Human Rights Treaties as regards Computer Network Operations

As a consequence of States' jurisdiction extending over those networks and systems located in their territory, cross-border CNOs of States on such foreign

352 Dahm, Delbrück & Wolfrum *Völkerrecht vol I/3* p.989.

353 As stipulated in Art. 51 ILC Articles on State Responsibility; and see Roger O'Keefe 'Proportionality' in James Crawford Alain Pellet & Simon Olleson (eds) *The Law of International Responsibility* (OUP Oxford 2010) pp. 1157 et seq.

354 The right to impart information regardless of frontiers is enshrined in all major human rights instruments except the African Charter on Human and Peoples' Rights.

systems are to be treated as extraterritorial acts.[355] In respect of the potential limitations on CNOs by human rights treaties, the question arises as to whether the latter are also applied extraterritorially, that is whether States are bound by those human rights treaties they are a party to when utilising CNOs against foreign systems.

The extraterritorial applicability of human rights treaties is subject to the existence of jurisdiction of a given State over the particular subject matter. While the relevant treaties provide for obligations on the States Parties to secure the enshrined rights for those persons within their territory or subject to their jurisdiction (as can be seen for example in Article 2 ICCPR, Article 1 ECHR and Article 1 ACHR), it is not sufficiently clear how far the scope of said jurisdiction reaches. Extraterritorial jurisdiction of States is generally accepted by all human rights treaty bodies in two sorts of cases. Firstly in the case of effective overall control over a territory as result of military occupation or on invitation of the other State thereby exercising 'all or some of the public powers normally to be exercised by that government'.[356] In this case the exercise of jurisdiction is expanded spatially into the occupied territory through the specific legal regime pertaining to occupation. The second set of cases is acts taken by a State's diplomatic and consular authorities on foreign territory.[357]

Beyond that, jurisdiction of States is especially disputed in cases where an extraterritorial act of a State by itself allegedly violates the human rights treaty in absence of an occupation. With respect to CNOs this is of particular relevance, as they tend to be used in such a situation as a means of remote and clandestine infiltration of the target systems without ever physically entering the foreign territory. In the *Bankovic Case* concerning the bombing of a building by NATO forces in the former Federal Republic of Yugoslavia, the ECtHR rejected the applicant's argument that the ECHR is applicable in relation to the level of control exercised by a Member State in an extraterritorial situation. Rather, the exercise of effective control by one State over the territory of another was seen as a necessary precondition for the applicability of the ECHR.[358] This stance was to a certain degree mitigated in *Medvedyev v France*, where the Court held that while Article 1 ECHR would not admit of a 'cause-and-effect' notion, excluding instantaneous extraterritorial acts, which the aerial bombardment in *Bankovic v Belgium* was qualified as, de-facto control of a continuous quality was seen as

355 See pp. 116 et seq. above.

356 *Banković v Belgium* (ECtHR) Reports 2001-XII 333 para. 71; Nicola Wenzel 'Human Rights, Treaties, Extraterritorial Application and Effects' in Rüdiger Wolfrum (ed) *MPEPIL* (OUP Oxford Update 2008) paras. 11 and 21.

357 Wenzel 'Human Rights, Treaties, Extraterritorial Application and Effects' para. 21; *Banković v Belgium* paras. 60 and 73.

358 *Banković v Belgium* paras. 70–75.

sufficient to also establish jurisdiction in cases where individuals are detained by a State Party outside its territory.[359]

However, subsequent case law, also of the ECtHR, and several authors argue for the use of a less strict general authority and control test, also applicable in the case of military actions abroad, even if not undertaken in occupied territories.[360] The ECtHR in *Issa v Turkey* for instance held that extraterritorial jurisdiction could also arise in a case where the State temporarily exercises effective control over foreign territory, without this amounting to the status of occupation.[361] Article 1 ECHR could not be interpreted in such a way as to 'allow a State party to perpetrate violations of the Convention on the territory of another State, which it could not perpetrate on its own territory'.[362] A similar point has already been argued by the UN Human Rights Committee in *López Burgos v Uruguay*, where it stipulated that 'it would be unconscionable to so interpret the responsibility under article 2 of the Covenant as to permit a State party to perpetrate violations of the Covenant on the territory of another State, which violations it could not perpetrate on its own territory'.[363] The ICJ in the *Israeli Wall Advisory Opinion* declared that considering the object and purpose of the ICCPR, in cases where the jurisdiction of States is exercised outside the national territory, 'it would seem natural that … States parties to the Covenant should be bound to comply with its provisions', coming to the conclusion that the ICCPR is also applicable to a State's in exercise of jurisdiction outside of its territory.[364]

Linking jurisdiction over extraterritorial acts of a State to the level of control the latter exercises in foreign territory cannot ensure the adherence to human rights treaty obligations by States Parties in their extraterritorial actions. If the authority or control over a person is limited to cases of detention and abduction, that is to instances where State agents perform direct physical control over a person, the modality of delivery would be the decisive factor.[365] Following this view, a State could therefore through its choice of methods and means of action

359 *Medvedyev v France* (Grand Chamber) (ECtHR) App No 3394/03 paras. 64–67; Charlotte Steinorth 'Bankovic Case' in Rüdiger Wolfrum (ed) *MPEPIL* (OUP Oxford Update 2010) para. 24.

360 e.g., Wenzel 'Human Rights, Treaties, Extraterritorial Application and Effects' and Orakhelashvili 'Governmental Activity on Foreign Territory'; Noam Lubell *Extraterritorial Use of Force against Non-State Actors* (OUP Oxford 2010) pp. 219–35.

361 *Issa v Turkey* (ECtHR) Reports 2004-XI 629 para. 74.

362 *Issa v Turkey* para. 71.

363 UN HRC 'Communication No R 12/52, *López Burgos v Uruguay*' (29 July 1981) GAOR 36th Session Supp 40, 176 at para. 12.3.

364 *Legal Consequences of the Construction of a Wall in the Occupied Palestinian Territory (Advisory Opinion)* [2004] ICJ Rep 136 paras. 109 and 111; Orakhelashvili 'Governmental Activity on Foreign Territory' para. 29.

365 Martin Scheinin 'Extraterritorial Effect of the International Covenant on Civil and Political Rights' in Fons Coomans & Menno T. Kamminga (eds) *Extraterritorial Application of Human Rights Treaties* (Intersentia Antwerp 2004) p. 77; Lubell *Extraterritorial Use of Force against Non-State Actors* p. 224.

determine the applicability of a human rights treaty for one and the same outcome: if a person were killed by an air strike in an area not under occupation or effective control of the acting State, the relevant human rights treaty would not be applicable, while the opposite result would arise if the person were detained at the same spot. When taking into consideration the results, the latter view is more convincing. The restrictive view actually encourages States to extraterritorial violative acts against a person rather than to arrest and take into custody the suspect.[366] This would ultimately lead to a circumvention of the obligations Member States of the relevant human rights treaties committed themselves to, which inter alia is already prohibited by the stipulation of Article 5(1) ICCPR that:

> '[n]othing in the present Covenant may be interpreted as implying for any State, group or person any right to engage in any activity or perform any act aimed at the destruction of any of the rights and freedoms recognized herein or at their limitation to a greater extent than is provided for in the present Covenant.'

Connection is therefore to be established by concentrating on the exercise of extraterritorial authority and control by a State agent over the affected individual.[367] This is also the approach of the UN HRC which held that the reference of Article 1 Optional Protocol to the ICCPR to 'individuals subject to its [i.e. that of the State Party] jurisdiction' is not to 'the place where the violation occurred, but rather to the relationship between the individual and the State in relation to a violation of any of the rights set forth in the Covenant, wherever they occurred'.[368]

In the case of CNOs there are only a limited number of variants of control. There are those CNOs which resemble instantaneous extraterritorial acts by targeting one or several systems in a nonrecurring and brief manner, a typical example thereof being a DDoS. At the other end of the spectrum are CNOs which take extensive control of the target system for a considerable period of time. Thus 'control' must be seen from a technical standpoint which will in most cases not mean total control of the system but only the limited level needed to execute the desired operations. This is already necessary for a concealment of the operation in order to avoid technical countermeasures against the intrusion. In these cases control is not exercised over a person directly and in most cases not even over the target system as a whole, but over individual processes running thereon. If this is done over a considerable period of time it can be considered a continuous de facto control of the relevant process which would even under the restrictive view lead to the assumption of an exercise of extraterritorial

366 Wenzel 'Human Rights, Treaties, Extraterritorial Application and Effects' para. 20; Lubell *Extraterritorial Use of Force against Non-State Actors* p. 224.
367 Lubell *Extraterritorial Use of Force against Non-State Actors* pp. 224 et seq.
368 UN HRC 'Communication No R 12/52, *López Burgos v Uruguay*' at para. 12.2.

jurisdiction. Yet this exercise is limited solely to the relevant controlled process and the dependencies thereof. Therefore the individuals utilising said system do not generally come under the control of the acting State but only in their actions that are somehow influenced through the externally controlled process. The same holds true for the case of an instantaneous extraterritorial action except when following the restrictive view requiring an effective control.

Computer network operations can therefore be qualified as the exercise of extraterritorial jurisdiction, but in all cases limited to the processes actually controlled. While this leads to the extraterritorial application of the relevant human rights treaty, the next question pertains to which rights or freedoms might be affected by these cross-border malicious computer network operations.

3.2.3.3.2. Freedom of Information and Communication

On the international level, the freedom of information is enshrined in Article 19 UDHR and Article 19 ICCPR; on the regional level similar guarantees are provided by Article 10 ECHR and Article 13 ACHR, all of which regard the freedom of information as a subcategory of the freedom of expression.[369] Article 9 Banjul Charter provides for a more restricted right to receive information.[370] All forms of communication are protected regardless of frontiers, including the choice of media, hence also communication via the Internet.[371]

However, under international law there exists no general principle of a free flow of information which would oblige States to remit all communications and prohibit any interference therewith.[372] Especially the discussions during the Cold War surrounding the prior-consent concept in satellite broadcasting propagated by socialist and developing States have prevented this principle from being established as customary international law.[373] Hence States have both the

369 UNGA Res 217 A (III) 'Universal Declaration of Human Rights' (10 December 1948) GAOR 3rd Session Part I Resolutions 71; American Convention on Human Rights (signed 22 November 1969, entered into force 18 July 1978) 1144 UNTS 123; Convention for the Protection of Human Rights and Fundamental Freedoms (signed 4 November 1950, entered into force 3 September 1953) 213 UNTS 221.

370 African Charter on Human and Peoples' Rights (adopted 27 June1981, entered into force 21 October 1986) 1520 UNTS 217.

371 Commentary to Art. 10 ECHR, in Jens Meyer-Ladewig *Europäische Menschenrechts-konvention* (Nomos Baden-Baden 2011) para. 5; Commentary to Art. 19 ICCPR, in Manfred Nowak *UN Covenant on Civil and Political Rights: CCPR Commentary* (Engel Kehl 2005) para. 16.

372 Patrick G. Mayer *Das Internet im öffentlichen Recht: Unter Berücksichtigung europarechtlicher und völkerrechtlicher Vorgaben* (Duncker und Humblot Berlin 1999) p. 112; Marina Gets *Meinungsäußerungs- und Informationsfreiheit im Internet aus der Sicht des Völkerrechts* (Berlin Verlag Spitz Berlin 2002) p. 59.

373 Determann *Kommunikationsfreiheit im Internet: Freiheitsrechte und gesetzliche Beschränkungen* pp. 324–25.

right to direct their broadcasts to foreign territory (as long as this is done in compliance with the technical regulations of the ITU) and the right to prevent the reception of foreign broadcasts in their territory.[374] The same holds true for data transmission on the Internet, which de facto is not universally free as the practice of several States of utilising Internet filter techniques shows, and which has even been endorsed by a Council of Europe Committee of Ministers Recommendation in 2008 as a means of protecting children and young people in their use of the Internet.[375] There is not a unique 'right to Internet access' either under international (human rights) law or under most national laws.[376] This was implicitly accepted by the UN Special Rapporteur on the Promotion and Protection of the Right to Freedom of Opinion and Expression who merely stated that ensuring universal access to the Internet should be a priority for States.[377]

Several cases of CNOs directed against websites of non-governmental organisations or individuals hosting content critical of the territorial State have been reported.[378] While the perpetrators of such operations were mostly not identified, the UN Special Rapporteur on the Promotion and Protection of the Right to Freedom of Opinion and Expression did make clear that in his opinion such actions, if undertaken by States, qualified as a violation of the obligation to respect the right to freedom of opinion and expression. Furthermore, according to the Rapporteur, States are obliged to 'protect individuals against interference by third parties that undermines the enjoyment of the rights of freedom of opinion and expression'. Such includes the 'appropriate and effective measures to investigate actions taken by third parties, hold the persons responsible to account, and adopt measures to prevent such recurrence in the future'.[379]

---

374 Rudolf Dolzer 'Wirtschaft und Kultur' in Wolfgang Vitzthum (ed) *Völkerrecht* (de Gruyter Berlin 2010) p. 558; Peter Malanczuk 'Information and Communication, Freedom of' in Rüdiger Wolfrum (ed) *MPEPIL* (OUP Oxford Update 2011) paras. 13–16.

375 At least as long as such filters are compatible with Art. 10(2) ECHR: COE Committee of Ministers Recommendation on Measures to Promote the Respect for Freedom of Expression and Information with Regard to Internet Filters (26 March 2008) CM/Rec(2008)6; see also Mark Bedner '"Deep Packet Inspection" – Technologie und rechtliche Initiativen' (2010) (5) Computer und Recht pp. 339–45; Ulrich Sieber *Verantwortlichkeit im Internet: technische Kontrollmöglichkeiten und multimediarechtliche Regelungen* (Beck München 1999) pp. 43 et seq; Woltag 'Internet' paras. 29 et seq.

376 Segura-Serrano 'Internet Regulation and the Role of International Law' pp. 266–67. However, fundamental rights and freedoms such as the freedom of expression, information and communication are also applicable to activities 'on the Internet'; on the situation under German law see Kai von Lewinski 'Recht auf Internet' (2011) 2(1) Rechtswissenschaft pp. 70 et seq.

377 UNGA 'Report of the Special Rapporteur on the Promotion and Protection of the Right to Freedom of Opinion and Expression, Frank La Rue' (16 May 2011) UN Doc A/HRC/17/27 para. 85.

378 Several cases are listed in the UNGA 'Report of the Special Rapporteur on the Promotion and Protection of the Right to Freedom of Opinion and Expression, Frank La Rue: Addendum: Summary of Cases Transmitted to Governments and Replies Received' (27 May 2011) UN Doc A/HRC/17/27/Add.1.

379 UNGA 'Report of the Special Rapporteur on the Promotion and Protection of the Right to Freedom of Opinion and Expression, Frank La Rue' (16 May 2011) para. 81.

Limitations as to the technical means used to impart information have been qualified as an interference with the right to receive information by the ECtHR.[380] In this case the limitation consisted of a denial of permission necessary for the use of a certain device utilised for telecommunications. However, a limitation can also be of a factual quality, as in the case of CNOs which negatively affect the possibility of a natural or legal person to utilise its computer systems to access information or express an opinion therewith. In both cases the entitled person is unable to exercise his rights in the intended manner. Computer network operations may therefore infringe upon the right to freedom of opinion and expression and the right to receive and impart information, in case they deprive an individual of the actual possibility to utilise the affected system in the designated way.

3.2.3.3.3. Right to Privacy

The right to privacy is enshrined in several human rights documents, most prominently Article 12 UDHR, Article 17 ICCPR, Article 8 ECHR and Article 11 ACHR. Not only do the scope and content of the right differ between the relevant instruments, but also the scope of the notion itself must be developed in line with a changing society. Privacy or private life has accordingly been characterised as a broad term not susceptible to exhaustive definition.[381] For reasons of clarity, reference shall only be made to the ECHR and ICCPR.

Under Article 8 ECHR, private life inter alia encompasses data relating to a person as well as correspondence via e-mail.[382] The protection of correspondence under Article 17 ICCPR is similar in this regard by covering all forms of distance communication, hence also e-mail. By relating to the secrecy of communication, every withholding, censorship or inspection thereof is qualifiable as an interference.[383] The ECtHR regards telephone calls from private as well as business premises to be covered by the notions of private life and correspondence under Article 8(1) ECHR.[384] This coverage shall also apply to e-mails sent and information derived from the monitoring of personal Internet usage. The search and seizure of electronic data hence constitutes an interference with the right to respect for correspondence.[385]

In *Copland v United Kingdom* the ECtHR stipulated that the clandestine collection and storage of personal information relating to e-mail and Internet

380 *Autronic AG v Switzerland* (ECtHR) Series A No 178.

381 *Peck v United Kingdom* (ECtHR) Reports 2003-I 123 para. 57.

382 *Rotaru v Romania* (ECtHR) Reports 2000-V 109 paras. 43–44; *Copland v United Kingdom* (ECtHR) App 62617/00 para. 41.

383 Commentary to Art. 17 ICCPR, in Nowak *UN Covenant on Civil and Political Rights: CCPR Commentary* paras. 47–48.

384 *Amann v Switzerland* (ECtHR) Reports 2000-II 245 para. 44.

385 *Copland v United Kingdom* 62617/00 paras. 41–42; *Wieser and Bicos Beteiligungen GmbH v Austria* (ECtHR) App 74336/01 para. 45.

usage qualifies as an interference with the right to respect for one's private life and correspondence under Article 8 ECHR.[386] It is thus demonstrated that the protection of personal data is likewise encompassed under the right to privacy. This is of importance insofar as personally identifiable information, that is personal data, is expressly protected from State access only in Article 8 Charter of Fundamental Rights of the European Union, which stipulates a right to the protection of one's personal data and the processing thereof on the basis of consent.[387] On an international level, however, there is no comprehensive binding instrument specifically dealing with data protection.[388] It is however generally accepted today that personal data is also protected by the right to privacy under Article 17 ICCPR and Article 8 ECHR.[389] Data protection is thus understood as the safeguarding of the rights, freedoms and interests of individuals in regard to the processing of their personal data and aiming to prevent a misuse thereof.[390]

The German Constitutional Court in 2008 went one step further in this regard by ruling that the general right of personality enshrined in Article 2(1) in conjunction with Article 1(1) German Basic Law encompasses a 'fundamental right to the guarantee of the confidentiality and integrity of information technology systems', thus effectively 'creating' a new fundamental right.[391] While this has not yet been proven to exist by an international court, the case law of the ECtHR in *Copland v United Kingdom* and *Wieser and Bicos Beteiligungen GmbH v Austria* has been analysed as indicating that Article 8 ECHR contains a similar protection.[392]

---

386 *Copland v United Kingdom* (ECtHR) App 62617/00 para. 44.

387 Charter of Fundamental Rights of the European Union (done 7 December 2000, entered into force 1 December 2009) (2001) 40 ILM 266.

388 However, the EU Data Protection Directive (European Parliament and EU Council 'Directive 95/46/EC of 24 October 1995 on the Protection of Individuals with Regard to the Processing of Personal Data and on the Free Movement of such Data' [1995] OJ L128/31) though only being a regional instrument, has also affected legislation in third States. In order to ensure the continuance of the transborder flow of personal data it has likewise led to the conclusion of agreements between third States and the EU providing for the observance of certain privacy principles of these States in relation to personal data originating from the EU Member States; see Commission of the European Communities 'Decision of 26 July 2000 Pursuant to Directive 95/46/EC of the European Parliament and of the Council on the Adequacy of the Protection Provided by the Safe Harbour Privacy Principles and Related Frequently Asked Questions Issued by the US Department of Commerce' [2000] OJ L215/7.

389 Uerpmann-Wittzack 'Internetvölkerrecht' p. 268.

390 Peter Malanczuk 'Data, Transboundary Flow, International Protection' in Rüdiger Wolfrum (ed) *MPEPIL* (OUP Oxford Update 2009) para. 3.

391 Bundesverfassungsgericht (German Constitutional Court) 1 BvR 370/07 (27 February 2008); on this see only: Christoph Herrmann *Das Grundrecht auf Gewährleistung der Vertraulichkeit und Integrität informationstechnischer Systeme: Entstehung und Perspektiven* (Peter Lang Frankfurt am Main 2010); Robert Uerpmann-Wittzack (ed) *Das neue Computergrundrecht* (Lit Berlin 2009).

392 Robert Uerpmann-Wittzack 'Der Schutz informationstechnischer Systeme nach der Europäischen Menschenrechtskonvention' in Robert Uerpmann-Wittzack (ed) *Das neue Computergrundrecht* (Lit Berlin 2009) pp. 99–102.

Computer network operations which target a system of a rights holder in order to gain access either to personal information stored thereupon or to correspondence being exchanged therewith in whatever form, qualify as violations of the right to privacy or a private life. Mere disruptive CNOs on the other hand which do not make any use of personal data cannot be seen as violating the relevant right.

3.2.3.3.4. Right to Property

On the international level a right to property is enshrined only in Article 17 UDHR, but neither in the ICCPR or ICESCR. The regional instruments ACHR, as well as the Banjul Charter and Additional Protocol 1 to the ECHR do protect the right to property however. While Article 1 Additional Protocol 1 to the ECHR does not define the term property, the ECtHR has developed a broad concept which is not limited to ownership of physical goods but contains also other rights and interests as long as these constitute assets.[393] This includes the right to make use of the property as one sees fit.[394]Consequently at least under the ECHR the usage of computer systems is protected under the right to property. CNOs that target said systems in such a way as to constrain their intended use by the proprietor are hence to be seen as an interference. Under the ECHR legal persons also enjoy the right which is in this respect of importance as CNOs have already been used to target industrial control systems, the disruption of which tends cause greater damage to companies than damage resulting from systems operated by individuals.

4. CONCLUSION

The fear has sporadically been expressed that if computer network operations would generally not be considered a use of force, States could only respond in kind, thus leading to the escalation of an 'information war' with the potential of causing grave suffering and even death.[395] Others have argued that States could elude responsibility for violations of international law by entrusting private military companies with the task of computer network operations.[396]

---

393 *Gasus Dosier- und Fördertechnik GmbH v The Netherlands* (ECtHR) App 15375/89 para. 53; Commentary to Art. 1 Additional Protocol to the ECHR, in Meyer-Ladewig *Europäische Menschenrechtskonvention* para. 11; Ursula Kriebaum & August Reinisch 'Property, Right to, International Protection' in Rüdiger Wolfrum (ed) *MPEPIL* (OUP Oxford Update 2009) paras. 34–35.

394 *Chassagnou and Others v France* (ECtHR) Apps 25088/94, 28331/95 and 28443/95 para. 74.

395 Beckett 'New War, Old Law: Can the Geneva Paradigm Comprehend Computers?' p. 50.

396 Compare Geiger *Offensive Informationskriegsführung: Die Joint Doctrine for Information Operations der US-Streitkräfte: Sicherheitspolitische Perspektiven* who states that such conduct is already taking place in all likelihood (at p. 22).

The preceding has shown that these apprehensions are unsubstantiated. Firstly, CNOs not amounting to a use of force are subject to a wide array of frameworks regulating their use. While their use is certainly not comprehensively regulated, there is also no necessity for doing so. It has been demonstrated that State actions in this context which are constrained to non-forcible actions can amount to both a violation of the territorial integrity and political independence of the target State, as well as concurrently to an intervention into its internal affairs. This is also reflected in regulations of the international telecommunications regime.

Secondly, those operations that actually do have destructive effects leading to injury of life and limb or destruction of property can very well be qualified as a prohibited use of force, without necessitating a novel perception of the term armed force in the sense of Article 2(4) UN Charter.

Thirdly, the general regime of State responsibility is also applicable to CNOs that are considered an internationally wrongful act. Consequently a State may not evade responsibility by outsourcing military functions as long as it retains control over them. Due to the technical problems of attributing a CNO to its exact source, the most important and problematic cases in practice are however those where State responsibility is established by an omission of prevention. As it has been shown that States are under an obligation to prevent malicious cross-border computer network operations emanating from their territory as part of the general obligation on States not to knowingly allow their territory to be used for acts contrary to the rights of other States, their failure to exercise due diligence in this regard can establish their international responsibility. While the utilisation of CNOs as automated responses or as a 'cyber hot pursuit' have been shown to be illegal, they may very well be legitimately used as countermeasures, and hence as a means of implementing international responsibility. Due regard must be paid however to human rights obligations which also limit those CNOs undertaken as a countermeasure.

CHAPTER 4

THE JUSTIFIED USE OF FORCEFUL COMPUTER NETWORK OPERATIONS

In between those computer network operations taken outside of armed conflict evaluated above, and those taken within, which will be examined later on, there remain those operations which may be qualified as legitimate uses of force under the ius ad bellum paradigm. This is the case for those operations that are taken within the ambit of the right of self-defence as enshrined in Article 51 UN Charter, which together with enforcement actions decided upon by the UN Security Council under Chapter VII UN Charter and the – now generally considered obsolete[1] – enemy State clauses, form the only generally accepted exceptions to the prohibition of the use of force.[2]

The following section will first determine the possibility of computer network operations giving rise to the right of self-defence by the victim State, followed by an evaluation of them as enforcement measures authorised by the UN Security Council under Chapter VII UN Charter.

1. THE RIGHT OF SELF-DEFENCE

The history of the right of self-defence has to be read together with the prohibition on the use of force. As the freedom of States to wage war was for a long time seen as an essential right, there was no need for a right of self-defence. It was only when the prohibition of war and later of the use of force was recognised, that a right of States to defend themselves against armed attacks in breach of the aforementioned principles was regarded as a necessary exception to

1 Sir Michael Wood 'United Nations Charter, Enemy States Clauses' in Rüdiger Wolfrum (ed) *MPEPIL* (OUP Oxford Update 2006) para. 13; it is also noteworthy in this regard that the ICJ in its *Legality of the Threat or Use of Nuclear Weapons (Advisory Opinion)* does not mention measures against former enemy States as an exception to the prohibition of the use of force (at paras. 38–50), clearly a signal of their redundancy in the present world order.

2 Randelzhofer & Dörr 'Article 2 (4)' para. 44 with reference to further, yet controversial exceptions; Dahm, Delbrück & Wolfrum *Völkerrecht vol I/3* p. 821; Cassese *International Law* p. 56; generally the wrongfulness of an act of a State is precluded if taken in self-defence in conformity with Art. 51 UN Charter, as stipulated in Art. 21 UN ILC Articles on State Responsibility.

the general prohibition on the use of force. In order to abide by the prohibition on the use of force, States needed to justify the use of forceful military countermeasures. But even before the need to legally justify the use of force in the 20th century, States used the argument of self-defence – either for political reasons, or in order to justify acts in situations short of war, such as in the *Caroline Case*.[3] As the concept of self-defence has long been known under national laws, especially criminal law, international law could have recourse to a considerable foundation of the underlying principles developed in the national fora.

For actions to be justified by the right of self-defence, Article 51 UN Charter mainly requires the existence of an armed attack. Two additional questions surrounding this issue shall further be analysed due to their relevance for computer network operations but also their general importance under contemporary international law. These concern the target of actions taken in self-defence, in this particular case non-State actors, and the temporal element of an armed attack, mainly known as the notion of pre-emptive or anticipatory self-defence.

1.1. REQUIREMENTS FOR THE PRESUMPTION OF AN ARMED ATTACK

1.1.1. General Requirements

As Article 51 UN Charter only refers to an 'armed attack', it is clear that not all actions constituting 'force' in the sense of Article 2(4) UN Charter may be seen as such an armed attack. The scope of the term is much narrower compared to that of armed force and requires damages or injuries of a more serious level.[4] Thus, a State is not automatically enabled to react to armed force by using the same in equal measure. In fact, there is a gap in effective possibilities open to States that are the target of armed force of other States not amounting to an armed attack.[5] This has been criticised, as it means that there is not always effective protection available against a State that uses cross-border armed force, as long as it does not meet the threshold of an armed attack.[6] However, this

---

3 Randelzhofer & Nolte 'Article 51' para. 1; Christopher Greenwood 'Caroline, The' in Rüdiger Wolfrum (ed) *MPEPIL* (OUP Oxford Update 2009).

4 Heintschel von Heinegg 'Informationskrieg und Völkerrecht' p. 141; Randelzhofer & Nolte 'Article 51' para. 6; Schmitt 'Angriffe im Computernetz und das ius ad bellum' pp. 191 et seq.; on this see also Karin Oellers-Frahm 'Der IGH und die "Lücke" zwischen Gewaltverbot und Selbstverteidigungsrecht: Neues im Fall "Kongo gegen Uganda"?' (2007) Zeitschrift für europarechtliche Studien pp. 71–92.

5 Dinstein *War Aggression and Self-Defence* p. 193; Randelzhofer & Nolte 'Article 51' paras. 6–8.

6 See Greenwood 'Self-Defence' at para. 12 who sees 'no evident textual reason for holding that the concept of armed attack excludes some attacks which, though armed, fall below an

restraint in the use of efficient military measures to counter such uses of force is not a lapse in drafting the UN Charter, but intent.[7] The gap is to be seen as an attempt to ensure that small-scale uses of force do not automatically escalate into a full-scale war but are to be mitigated by non-violent means.[8] In any case States have the option to enact countermeasures and bring the matter to the attention of the UN Security Council which in turn may qualify the acts as a threat to or breach of the peace or act of aggression in accordance with Article 39 UN Charter.

As in the case of 'force' under Article 2(4) UN Charter, the term 'armed attack' is not defined in the UN Charter so that its meaning has remained somewhat vague, as through interpretation no generally accepted definition has yet been found.[9] The ICJ in its *Military and Paramilitary Activities in Nicaragua Case* took note of this when stating that neither the UN Charter nor treaty law provide for a definition, while nevertheless claiming that 'there appears now to be general agreement on the nature of the acts which can be treated as constituting armed attacks'.[10] This agreement, which is however far from a consensus on the issue, is seen to exist in cases where the use of armed force is on a relatively large scale and with substantial effect, that is crossing a certain scale and degree of gravity.[11] Thus it is – at least since the terrorist attacks on the World Trade Center which utilised unarmed civilian aeroplanes – generally undisputed that it is not the designation or normal use of a device, for example a weapon, that enable it to amount to an armed attack, but the intent with which it is used and its effect.[12] The right of self-defence does not depend on the qualification under international law of a new means of warfare as a weapon, but on the effects on the target State. Article 51 therefore takes account of any kind of force.[13] The condition of an 'armed' attack is thus fulfilled in the event of a

unspecified threshold of intensity of violence'. Furthermore he argues that there is no State practice supporting this view prior to the *Nicaragua Case*. In any case, the limits of necessity and proportionality were sufficient to preclude excessive military responses to minor incidents. Further references for this view are listed by Randelzhofer & Nolte 'Article 51' at para. 8.

7 Randelzhofer & Nolte 'Article 51' para. 8; Stein & Buttlar *Völkerrecht* p. 279; this is however disputed, see only Kranz 'Die völkerrechtliche Verantwortlichkeit für die Anwendung militärischer Gewalt' p. 302 and the different opinions cited therein.

8 Randelzhofer & Nolte 'Article 51' para. 8.

9 Randelzhofer & Nolte 'Article 51' para. 17; Heintschel von Heinegg 'Informationskrieg und Völkerrecht' p. 141; Karl Zemanek 'Armed Attack' in Rüdiger Wolfrum (ed) *MPEPIL* (OUP Oxford Update 2009) para. 2.

10 *Nicaragua Case* para. 195.

11 Randelzhofer & Nolte 'Article 51' para. 20; UNGA Res 3314 (XXIX) 'Definition of Aggression' (14 December 1974), determining a certain amount of gravity needed for armed force to be considered an armed attack (at Art. 2); *Nicaragua Case* para. 195; Institut de Droit International 'Resolution on Self-Defence' para. 5; Zemanek 'Armed Attack' para. 10.

12 Zemanek 'Armed Attack' para. 21.

13 As stated by the ICJ in the *Legality of the Threat or Use of Nuclear Weapons (Advisory Opinion)* while referring to Arts. 2(4), 42 and 51 UN Charter: 'These provisions do not refer to specific

causal and considerable loss of life or extensive destruction of property, regardless of the means utilised.[14]

It is further unclear whether the threshold level for an armed attack may only be examined for each individual incident by itself, or whether a number of smaller incidents can, when regarding them as a whole, be taken together to exceed that threshold. This is maintained by some in cases where the assaults form a distinctive pattern.[15] Critics of this concept warn of its serious side-effects which undermine the temporal element of self-defence, turning it from a temporally limited right to an 'open-ended licence to use force'.[16] The ICJ – despite being confronted with the question – avoided any ruling on the principle, while the practice of the UN Security Council is interpreted differently in the literature.[17] However, the question ultimately is not of a dogmatic nature at all. In the end the qualification of actions will be a matter of the facts of each singular case. Several criteria need to be considered, especially the length of intermediary time between the different actions and their respective level of force. As the scope of what is to be considered an armed attack is far from settled in the first place, Article 51 is certainly not opposed the qualification of several actions as amounting to an armed attack.

1.1.2. Computer Network Operations as an Armed Attack

At present there is no documented case in which a government has officially put forward the argument it had fallen victim to an armed attack in the sense of Article 51 UN Charter due to a malicious computer network operation.[18] Nevertheless it is undisputed that CNOs have the potential to qualify as an armed attack.[19] The United States in their 2011 International Strategy for Cyberspace has for example asserted that 'certain aggressive acts in cyberspace' may trigger the right of self-defence under Article 51 UN Charter; something

---

weapons. They apply to any use of force, regardless of the weapons employed. The Charter neither expressly prohibits, nor permits, the use of any specific weapon, including nuclear weapons. A weapon that is already unlawful per se, whether by treaty or custom, does not become lawful by reason of its being used for a legitimate purpose under the Charter' (at para. 39).

14 Zemanek 'Armed Attack' para. 21.

15 Dinstein *War Aggression and Self-Defence* pp. 230–31.

16 Tams 'The Use of Force Against Terrorists' p. 389; likewise rejecting this doctrine: *Oil Platforms (Islamic Republic of Iran v United States of America) (Separate Opinion of Judge Simma)* para. 14.

17 *Oil Platforms (Islamic Republic of Iran v United States of America)* [2003] ICJ Rep 161 para. 64; Gray *International Law and the Use of Force* pp. 155–56.

18 In the Estonian case of 2007, the Estonian government reportedly contemplated at first to invoke the collective defence mechanism of Art. 5 NATO Treaty: Shackelford 'State Responsibility for Cyber Attacks: Competing Standards for a Growing Problem' p. 204. According to others this was never seriously considered however: Tikk, Kaska & Vihul *International Cyber Incidents: Legal Considerations* pp. 25–26.

19 Randelzhofer & Nolte 'Article 51' para. 43.

similar has been stated by the legal advisor of the US Department of State.[20] The exact threshold required remains unclear, however. Just as in the case of armed force under Article 2(4) UN Charter, most scholars argue for an effects-based approach which considers CNOs to only be able to amount to an armed attack if the consequences are manifested in human casualties. A mere disruption or destruction of the information infrastructure would not be sufficient, neither would cyber espionage activities.[21] Rule 13 Tallinn Manual utilises the same approach by stipulating 'whether a cyber operation constitutes an armed attack depends on its scale and effects'. The literature has provided for several hypothetical examples where a CNO would amount to an armed attack. Dinstein names: fatalities caused by loss of computer-controlled life-support; the flooding of inhabited areas caused by the shutting-down of computers controlling waterworks and dams; aircraft crashes caused by a manipulation of the software of steering computers; and the causing of a core-meltdown in a nuclear power plant resulting in the release of radioactive material or an explosion.[22] The group of experts drafting the Tallinn Manual agreed that CNOs which injure or kill persons or damage or destroy property would qualify as an armed attack, but brief interruption of non-essential cyber services would however not. Yet it was admitted that the law is unclear as to the precise threshold needed to reach the level of an armed attack.[23]

But it has also been argued that the stealing of data vital to national security – for example troop location or codes for a nuclear weapon's launch instruments – could be considered an armed attack.[24] Others even see the threshold as being crossed by targeting a State's major stock exchange and causing it to crash.[25] It has further been proposed that a State that falls victim to a CNO which targets critical national infrastructure should be given the right of self-defence even if the operation could not be qualified as an armed attack under Article 51 UN Charter.[26] It must be clearly stated however that these latter views are all inconsistent with current international law. Espionage is not generally treated internationally as an armed attack, regardless of the quality of the acquired information.[27] The manipulation of a stock exchange system does not cause

20 The President of the United States of America 'International Strategy for Cyberspace' p. 10; Koh 'International Law in Cyberspace' (Answer 4).

21 Stein & Marauhn 'Völkerrechtliche Aspekte von Informationsoperationen' p. 8; concurring Stelter *Gewaltanwendung unter und neben der UN-Charta* p. 213.

22 Dinstein 'Computer Network Attacks and Self-Defense' p. 105.

23 Schmitt (ed) *Tallinn Manual on the International Law Applicable to Cyber Warfare* pp. 55–56 paras. 6–7.

24 Joyner & Lotrionte 'Information Warfare as International Coercion: Elements of a Legal Framework' pp. 855–56.

25 Sharp *Cyberspace and the Use of Force* p. 117.

26 Jensen 'Computer Attacks on Critical National Infrastructure: A Use of Force Invoking the Right of Self-Defense' p. 209.

27 See pp. 124 et seq. above.

direct physical destruction or human casualties but is treated under the notion of economic coercion, measures intentionally excluded from the scope of the prohibition on the use of armed force and consequently also from that of armed attack.[28] The targeting of critical infrastructure does not in itself have any consequences as long as the operation does not exceed the classical threshold of an armed attack. This however cannot already be the case when the sovereignty, territorial integrity or political independence of the target State are being violated, as has been suggested.[29] While an armed attack will in most cases also violate these fundamental principles of international law there also needs to be a certain degree of destruction in order for an operation to qualify as an armed attack.

What has caused a considerable amount of confusion in the literature is the provision of Article 41 UN Charter. According thereto measures not involving the use of armed force include, inter alia, the complete or partial interruption of telegraphic, radio and other means of communication. The Internet infrastructure as the modern means of communication most certainly falls under this scope. If in conclusion the interruption of a State's networks would not be considered as armed force, it can hardly be qualified as an armed attack in the sense of Article 51 UN Charter. This reasoning has been put forward several times to back up the argument the UN Charter is an outdated instrument not capable of dealing with the modern threats of cyberspace.[30] This interpretation is too short-sighted, however, or rests on a misunderstanding of the technical side of CNOs. Article 41 UN Charter generally does not encompass the authorisation of military actions, but rather economic measures such as embargos, which are by their nature not a direct intrusion into the target State. In fact, the article refers to situations where the communications to and from a particular State are cut on the outside without any direct intrusive action. While this can both be achieved through CNOs or conventional means, such as through the destruction of the major cross-border cable connections of the target State, these actions do not directly interfere with systems under the sovereignty of the target State. Intrusive computer network operations into critical infrastructure systems such as telecommunications networks which are located in the territory of the target State are however not covered by Article 41 UN Charter at all and can hence not support a view which regards them as not qualifying either as armed force or as an armed attack.[31] This does not mean

---

28 See pp. 135 et seq. above.

29 Stein & Marauhn 'Völkerrechtliche Aspekte von Informationsoperationen' p. 7.

30 Westby 'Stabilität statt Cyberkrieg' p. 68; generally calling for a convention dealing with conduct of CNOs during armed conflict: Brown 'A Proposal for an International Convention to Regulate the Use of Information Systems in Armed Conflict' pp. 177 et seq.; Hollis 'Why States Need an International Law for Information Operations' pp. 1023 et seq.; Hoisington 'Cyberwarfare and the Use of Force Giving Rise to the Right of Self-Defense' pp. 439 et seq.

31 Woltag 'Cyber Warfare' para. 8.

however that cutting off all communication routes will inherently have to be qualified as an armed attack, as has been suggested.[32] The crucial point is whether these disruptions are caused by an intrusive CNO that targets systems in the target State's territory. Only then may CNOs that disrupt communications networks be qualified as armed attack once they meet the scale and degree of gravity necessary. A mere impairment of telecommunications in the target State cannot be qualified as sufficient, however. A fortiori this is not the case where the infrastructure is not destroyed irreversibly, but can be reinstated by removing the malware on the targeted systems.

1.1.3. The Gathering of Evidence in Proof of a Claim to Act in Self-Defence

While the meaning of the term 'armed attack' has drawn considerable attention both in literature and jurisprudence and has certainly led to common understandings of its core substance, there is still room left for interpretation. Ultimately it is the victim State itself which has to determine whether it has been subject of an armed attack.[33] However, this decision can be subject to a judicial review by international courts and tribunals. Problematic in this regard is the presentation of evidence linking a foreign State to a CNO. The procedure of inter-State disputes is generally based on the principle of actori incumbit probatio, that is the party alleging a fact carries the burden of proof.[34] Hence the State that seeks to justify military actions with the right of self-defence must provide proof of the existence of its requirements.[35] Due to a lack of strict rules regarding the admissibility of evidence, States thus enjoy considerable freedom in the submission of what they deem to be relevant evidence, which can inter alia be submitted through documents or expert testimonies.[36] If a victim State evaluates solely a CNO as an armed attack, without the additional use of any conventional armed force, evidence linking a source State to the operation will be hard to come by as will be shown in the following examples.

In the *Tehran Hostages Case* the ICJ referred to facts which it considered to be 'matters of public knowledge which have received extensive coverage in the world

---

32 This has been given as an example for a blockade qualifying as an impairment comparable to a military invasion thus constituting an armed attack by Randelzhofer & Nolte 'Article 51' para. 24.

33 Stanimir A. Alexandrov *Self-Defense against the Use of Force in International Law* (Kluwer The Hague 1996) p. 98; concurring Zemanek 'Armed Attack' para. 2.

34 *Avena and Other Mexican Nationals (Mexico v United States of America)* [2004] ICJ Rep 12 para. 55; Markus Benzing *Das Beweisrecht vor internationalen Gerichten und Schiedsgerichten in zwischenstaatlichen Streitigkeiten* (Springer Heidelberg 2010) pp. 670–71; Rüdiger Wolfrum 'International Courts and Tribunals, Evidence' in Rüdiger Wolfrum (ed) *MPEPIL* (OUP Oxford Update 2006) para. 69. The rules are different at international criminal courts, which are not of concern here however.

35 *Oil Platforms (Islamic Republic of Iran v United States of America)* para. 57.

36 Art. 43(1) ICJ Statute; Wolfrum 'International Courts and Tribunals, Evidence' para. 23.

press and in radio and television broadcasts from Iran and other countries'.[37] This was unproblematic as it included Iranian sources; but most decisively, after having been communicated to the Iranian government, the latter did not make 'any denial or questioning of the facts alleged'.[38] However, in the *Nicaragua Case* the Court stated that '[w]idespread reports of a fact may prove on closer examination to derive from a single source, and such reports, however numerous, will in such case have no greater value as evidence than the original source'.[39] Similarly, in the *Oil Platforms Case*, the ICJ valued the public sources which the US cited as being 'by definition secondary evidence; and the Court has no indication of what was the original source, or sources, or evidence on which the public sources relied'.[40]

Public knowledge is likewise unlikely to play a role as evidence in the case of CNOs. As these are by their nature clandestine and provide many opportunities to conceal the true identity of the original source, the public in neither the target nor the source State will not necessarily be able to gain knowledge of the operation at all. The Estonian incident is an example where secondary evidence multiplied exponentially although only a few official and original sources existed in the beginning. While it was an undisputed fact that CNOs were targeted at Estonian systems, official allegations that Russia was the source of the operations were not put forward. Nevertheless the generally tense relationship between the two countries and the fact that software performing these operations was available on servers located in Russia led to numerous media reports that suggested Russia was the source of the operations. However, under adjudication these secondary reports could not have been admitted as permissible evidence.

A crucial measure for a target State to gain evidence could be to access foreign computer systems for a forensic investigation. As has been shown above, such cross-border access would however in most cases qualify as a wrongful act.[41] A similar problem of obtaining evidence was already before the ICJ in the *Corfu Channel Case* where it admitted that the 'exclusive territorial control exercised by a State within its frontiers has a bearing upon the methods of proof available to establish the knowledge of that State as to such events'.[42] This led the ICJ to demand a relaxed standard of proof from States encountering this problematic. As in these cases a State 'is often unable to furnish direct proof of facts giving rise to responsibility', it 'should be allowed a more liberal recourse to inferences of fact and circumstantial evidence'.[43] The granting of this so-called indirect evidence does not however imply a right of a State to gather evidence in foreign territory as a measure of self-help. This was attempted by the United

37 *Tehran Hostages Case* para. 12.
38 *Tehran Hostages Case* para. 13.
39 *Nicaragua Case* para. 63.
40 *Oil Platforms (Islamic Republic of Iran v United States of America)* para. 60.
41 See pp. 116 et seq. above.
42 *Corfu Channel Case* p. 18.
43 *Corfu Channel Case* p. 18.

Kingdom in the incident which led to the *Corfu Channel Case*, but was rejected by the ICJ as it nevertheless amounted to a prohibited intervention.[44] Consequently a State may likewise not use CNOs to gain access to log-files or other data on foreign systems that could provide evidence for the source of a CNO. However, by granting indirect evidence as a relaxed standard of proof, it is up to the respondent State to provide evidence that it was not involved, in the event that the victim State provides evidence that the operations originated from a particular State, for instance through IP addresses in log-files. Yet despite the fact that under the principle of free assessment of evidence international judges enjoy a wide discretion,[45] this cannot go so far as to override the fact that from a technological perspective it is extremely difficult to conclusively provide evidence of the source of a CNO. This difficulty however needs to be taken into consideration by the relevant court, making indirect evidence an indispensable part of being able to build a case for the victim of a computer network operation.

1.2. SELF-DEFENCE AGAINST NON-STATE ACTORS

Apart from a plethora of other legal questions, international terrorism has raised the question of whether actions against a State may also be qualified as an armed attack when launched by non-State actors from foreign territory. This involves the issue of whether an action taken in self-defence may then also be directed against these actors on foreign territory or against other legally protected interests by the source State.

The traditional restrictive view holds that an armed attack in the sense of Article 51 UN Charter cannot be committed by private groups or organisations as such but solely by States. Therefore only an attribution of these acts to a State could lead to their qualification as armed attacks.[46] This attribution is reached by examining the level of support given by the State to the non-State actors, the degree of which naturally remains disputed. The ICJ in the *Nicaragua Case*, by having recourse to Article 3(g) Definition of Aggression, has required the State to be at least 'substantially involved' in the actions of the non-State actors.[47] Despite growing criticism, also voiced in several dissenting and separate opinions, the ICJ upheld this requirement in the *Armed Activities on the Territory of the Congo Case* and the *Israeli Wall Advisory Opinion*.[48]

44 *Corfu Channel Case* pp. 34–35; Waibel 'Corfu Channel Case' paras. 14–16.

45 Wolfrum 'International Courts and Tribunals, Evidence' para. 2.

46 Randelzhofer & Nolte 'Article 51' para. 37; Bothe 'Friedenssicherung und Kriegsrecht' pp. 651 and 658; for a summary of the discussion see Tams 'The Use of Force Against Terrorists' pp. 359–97.

47 *Nicaragua Case* para. 195.

48 *Armed Activities on the Territory of the Congo (Democratic Republic of the Congo v Uganda)* paras. 146–47; *Legal Consequences of the Construction of a Wall in the Occupied Palestinian Territory (Advisory Opinion)* para. 139; for the opposing view held by several ICJ judges see

The opposing expansive view inter alia makes reference to the classic *Caroline Case* of 1841 wherein both the United States and the United Kingdom apparently took for granted that the right of self-defence also extends to threats from non-State actors.[49] This view was also shared by the majority of the group of experts drafting the Tallinn Manual.[50] In addition, more recent State practice manifested in the reaction of the international community to the terrorist attacks on the United States of September 11, 2001 are cited as proof that non-State actors are also regarded as legitimate targets of measures taken in self-defence.[51] The terrorist attacks were inter alia qualified by the United States, the North Atlantic Council and the Organization of American States as an armed attack invoking the right to self-defence.[52] And while it remains disputed as to whether or not the UN Security Council in its Resolutions 1368 and 1373 of September 2001 authorised the use of military force by the United States and its allies against targets in Afghanistan,[53] the claims by the US-led coalition were nevertheless not contested by an overwhelmingly large majority of other States. This acquiescence is especially telling as at that point in time the attributability of the attacks by Al-Qaeda to the Afghan State was far from firmly established.[54] The Resolution on Self-defence by the Institut de Droit International points in a

---

only *Armed Activities on the Territory of the Congo (Democratic Republic of the Congo v Uganda) (Separate Opinion of Judge Simma)* para. 12; and Arthur Watts 'Israeli Wall Advisory Opinion (Legal Consequences of the Construction of a Wall in the Occupied Palestinian Territory)' in Rüdiger Wolfrum (ed) *MPEPIL* (OUP Oxford Update 2007) stating that Art. 51 UN Charter 'refers simply to an armed attack occurring against a Member State of the UN, without any indication of the nature of the entity mounting the attack, or of the attack's geographical origins' (at para. 42).

49 Correspondence between Great Britain and the United States, respecting the Arrest and Imprisonment of Mr. McLeod, for the Destruction of the Steamboat Caroline (March, April 1841) (1840–41) 29 BSP 1126; Greenwood 'Caroline, The' para. 10.

50 Schmitt (ed) *Tallinn Manual on the International Law Applicable to Cyber Warfare* p. 59 para. 17.

51 Dinstein *War Aggression and Self-Defence* p. 208; Jochen Abr. Frowein 'Der Terrorismus als Herausforderung für das Völkerrecht' (2002) 62(4) Zeitschrift für ausländisches öffentliches Recht und Völkerrecht p. 887; Markus Krajewski 'Selbstverteidigung gegen bewaffnete Angriffe nicht-staatlicher Organisationen: Der 11. September 2001 und seine Folgen' (2002) 40(2) Archiv des Völkerrechts p. 198.

52 UNSC 'Letter Dated 7 October 2001 from the Permanent Representative of the United States of American to the United Nations Adressed to the President of the Security Council' (7 October 2001) (2001) 40 ILM 1281, containing the report of actions taken by the United States and its allies in the exercise of their right of individual and collective self-defence as obliged by Art. 51 UN Charter; NATO 'Statement by the North Atlantic Council' (12 September 2001) (2001) 40 ILM 1267; OAS 'Resolution on Terrorist Threat to the Americas' (21 September 2001) (2001) 40 ILM 1273.

53 Strongly arguing in the affirmative: Dinstein *War Aggression and Self-Defence* p. 207; differently: Cassese *International Law* pp. 473–74; see also generally Rüdiger Wolfrum & Christiane E. Philipp 'The Status of the Taliban: Their Obligations and Rights under International Law' (2002) 6 Max Planck Yearbook of United Nations Law p. 587.

54 Greenwood 'Self-Defence' para. 17; Proulx 'Babysitting Terrorists: Should States be Strictly Liable for Failing to Prevent Transborder Attacks?' p. 636.

similar direction by envisaging the right of self-defence against armed attacks by non-State actors launched 'from an area beyond the jurisdiction of any State'.[55]

The next question concerns the addressees of the relevant measures taken under the right of self-defence, namely whether these can be directed against the territory or other legally protected interests by the State from where the non-State actors have instigated their actions. When following the expansive view, measures against non-State actors in areas beyond the jurisdiction of a third State would be viable, as also stated in the Resolution on Self-defence by the Institut de Droit International. These cases are however in the minority and apply especially to the high seas. It cannot however be construed that cyberspace is such an area beyond the jurisdiction of any State from which non-State actors could launch attacks. The aforementioned deconceptualisation of cyberspace as a sphere sui generis has shown the contrary, namely that any Internet-related case does fall under the jurisdiction of some State.[56]

It is however possible to also direct measures against targets on the territory of a third State. Several arguments have been put forward in this regard. One view makes use of an analogy to Article 16 ILC Articles on State Responsibility which stipulates an attribution of an internationally wrongful act of one State to another if the latter provided aid or assistance in its commission.[57] While this rule does not directly apply to the case of a State giving aid or assistance to non-State actors, the underlying principle of attribution through aid and assistance is argued to also be applicable here. This is exemplified by the case of the acts of the United States directed against the Taliban, which were declared as being undertaken resorting to the right of self-defence, despite the Taliban being an actor different to the perpetrators of the 9/11 terrorist attack, Al Qaeda. This was justified by arguing that the assistance given by the Taliban to Al Qaeda enabled the attribution, thus invoking said underlying principle of Article 16 ILC Articles on State Responsibility.[58] Otherwise a State would be privileged in these cases in comparison to those where the executor is a subject of international law.[59] The conduct at hand lies therein, that a 'subject of international law deliberately

55 Institut de Droit International 'Resolution on Self-Defence' para. 10.

56 See pp. 53 et seq. above.

57 Rüdiger Wolfrum 'The Attack of September 11, 2001, the Wars against the Taliban and Iraq: Is there a Need to Reconsider International Law on the Recourse to Force and the Rules in Armed Conflict?' (2003) 7 Max Planck Yearbook of United Nations Law p. 37; concurring Lehto *Indirect Responsibility for Terrorist Acts: Redefinition of the Concept of Terrorism Beyond Violent Acts* p. 400.

58 Wolfrum 'The Attack of September 11, 2001, the Wars against the Taliban and Iraq: Is there a Need to Reconsider International Law on the Recourse to Force and the Rules in Armed Conflict?' p. 37.

59 Wolfrum & Philipp 'The Status of the Taliban: Their Obligations and Rights under International Law' p. 595; Wolfrum 'The Attack of September 11, 2001, the Wars against the Taliban and Iraq: Is there a Need to Reconsider International Law on the Recourse to Force and the Rules in Armed Conflict?' p. 37; following this approach: Lehto *Indirect Responsibility for Terrorist Acts: Redefinition of the Concept of Terrorism Beyond Violent Acts* p. 400.

created a situation which was a necessary precondition for a later event … provided that event was not beyond reasonable probability and constituted a breach of international law'.[60] In addition, the ICJ in the *Bosnian Genocide Case* considered Article 16 ILC Articles in relation to a case of alleged State assistance to non-State actors in an international crime, while however clarifying it was not directly relevant to the case.[61]

A similar reasoning is given by those arguing that the provision of a safe haven or the unwillingness or inability to stop non-State actors from performing armed attacks from the State's territory, may make the latter a valid target of measures undertaken in self-defence.[62] This is underscored inter alia by taking recourse to the laws of neutrality, under which neutral States are obliged to prevent their territory from being used by parties to the conflict, also requiring the use of force if necessary.[63] These are further obliged to intern belligerents captured on their territory.[64] If a neutral State does not fulfil these obligations it risks losing its neutral status, making it a legitimate target for the opposing belligerent party. The same should apply for the case of the provision of a safe haven for non-State actors which is nothing other than a specific form of giving aid and assistance, hence an unneutral behaviour. If a State does not fulfil its duties as a neutral, or in this case its duty to prevent its territory from being utilised for acts contrary to the rights of other States,[65] it cannot refer to its rights as a neutral State or the preservation of its territorial integrity and political independence in case the aggrieved State takes action against the relevant actors on its territory.[66] Just as under the laws of neutrality, these defensive measures

---

60 Wolfrum 'The Attack of September 11, 2001, the Wars against the Taliban and Iraq: Is there a Need to Reconsider International Law on the Recourse to Force and the Rules in Armed Conflict?' pp. 37–38.

61 *Genocide Convention Case* paras. 419–20.

62 In this direction: Walter 'Terrorism' para. 78; Greenwood 'Self-Defence' para. 18; this view was also shared by the majority of the group of experts drafting the Tallinn Manual: Schmitt (ed) *Tallinn Manual on the International Law Applicable to Cyber Warfare* p. 61 para. 22.

63 Art. 5 Convention respecting the Rights and Duties of Neutral Powers and Persons in Case of War on Land (signed 18 October 1907, entered into force 26 January 1910) (1908) 2 AJIL Supp 117; Michael Bothe 'Neutrality, Concept and General Rules' in Rüdiger Wolfrum (ed) *MPEPIL* (OUP Oxford Update 2011) paras. 33 et seq.; Thomas Bruha 'Gewaltverbot und humanitäres Völkerrecht nach dem 11. September 2001' (2002) 40(4) Archiv des Völkerrechts p. 408.

64 Peter Hostettler 'Neutrals, Disarming and Internment of Belligerents' in Rüdiger Wolfrum (ed) *MPEPIL* (OUP Oxford Update 2009) para. 8.

65 *Corfu Channel Case* p. 22. The Friendly Relations Declaration reiterates this stance in stating that States have the duty to refrain from acquiescing in organised activities within their territories that are directed towards the commission of civil strife or terrorist acts involving the use or threat of force, a position which was seen as declaratory of customary international law by the ICJ in *Armed Activities on the Territory of the Congo (Democratic Republic of the Congo v Uganda)* at para. 162; and see already pp. 99 et seq. above.

66 Bruha 'Gewaltverbot und humanitäres Völkerrecht nach dem 11. September 2001' p. 408; Blay 'Territorial Integrity and Political Independence' para. 55; likewise arguing in that direction is Walter 'Terrorism' para. 78; Krajewski 'Selbstverteidigung gegen bewaffnete Angriffe nicht-staatlicher Organisationen: Der 11. September 2001 und seine Folgen' p. 203.

are restricted to being directed solely against the perpetrators of the armed attack, hence non-State actors, but not against the host State as such.

While there are different methods of justifying the use of force against non-State actors on foreign territory and also without the authorisation of the target State, the majority opinion today together with State practice supports an expansive interpretation of the right of self-defence. This is to be agreed with. Only the expansive view makes it possible to take into account the changes brought about by transnational conflicts between States and private terrorist actors and the general 'individualization of international relations'.[67] The opposite view preferred by a majority of ICJ judges, as manifested most recently in the *Armed Activities on the Territory of the Congo Case*, harshly restricts a State's possible reactions to armed attacks by non-State actors. This results in a hardly tenable outcome which leaves States in the event of inactivity of the UN Security Council in a situation that allows no defensive military actions whatsoever. In particular, recent State practice of the last decade has shown that the international community is not willing to accept this lacuna in the right of self-defence against non-State actors. The wording of Article 51 UN Charter which refers only to an armed attack against a State while not qualifying the source of the attack likewise allows such an interpretation.[68] Measures taken in self-defence against non-State actors are however restricted to target only these, not the host State as such. This may only be done if the actions are directly attributable to the State, making it legally responsible for the armed attack. For this to happen there is a higher threshold in place which requires more than the passive provision of a safe haven. The duty of cooperation between the aggrieved State and the State from which the attack originates coupled with the requirement of inability or unwillingness of the host State to take action against the non-State actors are sufficient safeguards against a misuse or erosion of the right of self-defence. If however a State refrains from cooperating with the victim State, this may be an indication of the State's unwillingness to prevent its territory from being used contrary to the right of the aggrieved State. That sort of behaviour defies the protective purpose both of the laws of neutrality and the rights of a sovereign State in respect to its territorial integrity.

The peculiarities of the underlying technology make a simple counterattack against the (alleged) source a legally questionable option, as the identification of the individual perpetrators of computer network operations is extremely difficult

67 Wolfrum 'The Attack of September 11, 2001, the Wars against the Taliban and Iraq: Is there a Need to Reconsider International Law on the Recourse to Force and the Rules in Armed Conflict?' pp. 35–36; Bruha 'Gewaltverbot und humanitäres Völkerrecht nach dem 11. September 2001' pp. 393–95.

68 Frowein 'Der Terrorismus als Herausforderung für das Völkerrecht' p. 888; Bruha 'Gewaltverbot und humanitäres Völkerrecht nach dem 11. September 2001' p. 394; Walter 'Terrorism' para. 78; Greenwood 'Self-Defence' para. 17.

if not impossible without the cooperation of the source State.[69] This already makes a reasonable level of cooperation a diligent behaviour on the part of the source State to which it is obliged already in cases not amounting to an armed attack.[70] Otherwise States would be given the possibility to evade responsibility for any CNOs originating from their territory by denying cooperation thus allowing for a plausible deniability of any involvement. The same duty exists in cases where CNOs surpass the threshold required under Article 51 UN Charter. The differences thus are the possible countermeasures the aggrieved State may take. Under the right of self-defence these go further, ultimately entailing the use of force against non-State actors inn a third State's territory.

This does not mean that a failure of States to effectively secure their computer systems could be imputed as a limitation on their right of self-defence, as has been suggested.[71] While it could be considered that States are under a due diligence obligation to secure their systems in order for these not to be abused by third actors for malicious CNOs against other States, this is only due to the obligation of States not to allow their territory to be utilised for acts contrary to rights of other States.[72] There does not however exist a general obligation of self-defence, for instance by maintaining armed forces, contempt of which could lead to a forfeiture of the right, and neither can exist for the protection of computer systems.[73] The situation where a State has been attacked by non-State actors from systems located in a third State is to be solved by cooperation between the two States, to which the host State is obliged, and ultimately allows the aggrieved State to take action against hijacked systems or the non-State actors in the territory of the third State, but not against other targets.

1.3. ANTICIPATORY AND PRE-EMPTIVE SELF-DEFENCE

Another controversial question generally surrounding the right of self-defence also in the absence of a computer network operation concerns the temporal

69 See pp. 28 et seq. above. This has not deterred senior military leaders from stating that firing back directly, even when the identity of the attacker is unknown, were a viable option: 'Military Asserts Right to Return Cyber Attacks' (14 April 2010) The Washington Post; available at <www.washingtonpost.com/wp-dyn/content/article/2010/04/14/AR2010041400264.html> (date accessed 20 April 2010).

70 See pp. 102 et seq. above.

71 Stelter *Gewaltanwendung unter und neben der UN-Charta* p. 214.

72 See pp. 99 et seq. above.

73 This can already be seen by the possibility for States to declare themselves as permanently neutral and maintaining no armed forces, such as Costa Rica. While this might lead a belligerent to not consider the State neutral anymore once its opponent makes use of its territory, this only results in a right of the belligerent to target belligerent forces also on the neutral States territory, but not to directly target the neutral State as such. The neutral hence does not forfeit its right of self-defence but only its territorial integrity in respect to the region where the belligerents are operating from. See also Bothe 'Neutrality, Concept and General Rules' paras. 34–35.

emergence of the right of self-defence. The traditional view asserts that self-defence is permissible only after an armed attack has already been launched.[74] This narrow reading is justified by the object and purpose of Article 51 UN Charter which were to cut the unilateral use of force by States to a minimum. A more expansive view allows for anticipatory self-defence, the concept of which is already disputed by its proponents,[75] while again others, especially in recent years, argue for the right of pre-emptive self-defence.[76] Proponents of anticipatory self-defence argue that a State need not wait until the enemy fires the first shots, but may resort to self-defence under the conditions set forth by the *Caroline* case, as proclaimed in the so-called Webster formula. According to this formula, armed force can be utilised in self-defence when the necessity thereof is instant, overwhelming and leaving no choice of means, and no moment for deliberation, namely when an armed attack is imminent.[77] The more extensive view of pre-emptive self-defence even sees the factor of imminence as being too restrictive, advocating for the right of pre-emptive action which may arise in situations prior thereto, pushing the temporal condition of self-defence even further away from the actual outbreak of the attack.

However, the concepts are not precisely defined but are rather interpreted differently. Further difficulty arises through the differences in the evaluation of at what point in time exactly an armed attack begins. By expanding the temporal spectrum in which an armed attack occurs even proponents of the traditional narrow interpretation can in effect come to the same conclusion provided by anticipatory self-defence.[78] For example, the Institut de Droit International in its Resolution on Self-defence states that there is no basis in international law for the doctrines of preventive self-defence. However, the existence of a manifestly imminent armed attack may suffice for an armed response, thereby distinguishing between the concepts of 'imminent attack' and 'anticipatory self-

74 For an overview of the discussion see Randelzhofer & Nolte 'Article 51' paras. 50 et seq.

75 See, e.g., Franck *Recourse to Force: State Action against Threats and Armed Attacks* p. 105; Dinstein 'Computer Network Attacks and Self-Defense' p. 111.

76 This view was especially put forward in the document: The President of the United States of America 'The National Security Strategy of the United States of America' (September 2002) at <www.au.af.mil/au/awc/awcgate/nss/nss_sep2002.pdf> (date accessed 7 April 2011), parts of which are commonly also referred to as the 'Bush doctrine'. Israel, in 1981, justified its bombardment of an Iraqi nuclear reactor under construction with the concept of pre-emptive self-defence. The Security Council however condemned the action as an illegal act in the unanimously adopted Resolution 487 of 19 June 1981.

77 The Webster formula, named after the United States Secretary of State Daniel Webster, is found in the Correspondence between Great Britain and the United States, respecting the Arrest and Imprisonment of Mr McLeod, for the Destruction of the Steamboat Caroline (March, April 1841) at p. 1138; Greenwood 'Self-Defence' para. 45; see also Rule 15 Tallinn Manual.

78 Greenwood 'Self-Defence' paras. 41–42.

defence'.[79] Others again try to strike a balance by qualifying anticipatory self-defence as legally prohibited in general, while admitting that certain actions taken under that justification will simply be condoned by the international community.[80] At present the majority opinion seems to crystallise in the position that a State does not need to wait to suffer the first damage or casualties in order to resort to measures under the right of self-defence. It can react once the armed attack is imminent.[81] Whether or not one describes such a situation as for example anticipatory self-defence is irrelevant. It nevertheless leaves open the question of when exactly 'imminence' is reached.

It is doubtful, however, if the concept of anticipatory self-defence plays a role at all in the case of computer network operations. If a CNO is part of an overall armed attack using traditional forms of warfare, the addition of a CNO does not add any new questions to the general debate concerning anticipatory self-defence. For proponents of this concept the CNO will have to be seen as part of the general armed attack, thus making anticipatory measures available. The same holds true for the traditional view, which in any case opposes this concept in the first place, regardless of the weapons or means utilised.

If it is only the utilisation of CNOs that amounts to the armed attack, it is the technology itself that excludes anticipatory self-defence. CNOs are in their execution not comparable to traditional kinetic military operations. Supporters of anticipatory self-defence give as examples for the latter the positioning of enemy forces in strategic positions in preparation of an attack, or the locking on to a target of a missile site or military aircraft in a similar situation.[82] These sorts of preparations are more or less easily detectable by radar, remote sensing and other intelligence measures, giving the soon-to-be victim State the opportunity for timely military defensive measures. A hostile CNO, on the other hand, is not that easily detectable beforehand.[83] The characteristic of a CNO in comparison to the more traditional forms of force as described above is its swiftness. As the time-span between launching and impact lies within milliseconds, a situation comparable to that of missiles being detected and destroyed by the attacked State in the air is hardly relevant. This does not change

---

79 Institut de Droit International 'Resolution on Self-Defence' para. 6.

80 Cassese *International Law* p. 362.

81 UN High-Level Panel on Threats, Challenges and Change 'A More Secure World: Our Shared Responsibility' (2 December 2004) UN Doc A/59/565, 8 para. 188; UN Secretary-General 'In Larger Freedom: Towards Development, Security and Human Rights for All: Report of the Secretary General' (21 March 2005) UN Doc A/59/2005 paras. 124–25; Elizabeth Wilmshurst 'The Chatham House Principles of International Law on the Use of Force in Self-Defence' (2006) 55(4) International and Comparative Law Quarterly p. 968; Greenwood 'Self-Defence' para. 45.

82 Dinstein 'Computer Network Attacks and Self-Defense' p. 111; Aldrich 'How Do You Know You Are at War in the Information Age' p. 240; Marco Benatar 'The Use of Cyber Force: Need for Legal Justification?' (2009) 1 Göttingen Journal of International Law p. 389.

83 Similarly: Terry D. Gill & Paul A.L. Ducheine 'Anticipatory Self-Defense in the Cyber Context' (2013) 89 International Law Studies p. 466.

in cases where malware, such as Stuxnet, lies dormant on the target system or needs months to fulfil its purpose.[84] While in this case the time between the beginning of the operation and the effect may be months, the armed attack begins with the first execution of the malware if it operates as autarkically as the Stuxnet worm does. Anticipatory or even pre-emptive measures therefore do not play a role in defending against those CNOs that qualify as an armed attack.

1.4. LIMITS TO THE RIGHT OF SELF-DEFENCE

In addition to the aforementioned limitation on the addressees of measures taken under the right of self-defence, these are generally limited by the principles of necessity and proportionality, or as stated by the ICJ 'measures which are proportional to the armed attack and necessary to respond to it'.[85] Further, States are obliged to report measures taken in self-defence against an armed attack to the UN Security Council.

While the duty to report has in the past been denoted as being of 'limited practical significance',[86] it could eventually gain importance if CNOs are utilised in self-defence. As their targets and effects are not readily identifiable, the duty to report could help to overcome clandestine actions. Yet as long as identification of the attacker is difficult or impossible, the obligation will depend on a State's willingness to disclose its defensive measures which in most cases will be limited as long as it can claim plausible deniability of any such actions.

The use of armed force taken in self-defence must be necessary to respond to the armed attack. Hence the goal pursued may not have been achieved without recourse to armed force.[87] They must further be proportionate to the degree of the armed attack they are a response to.[88] What is proportionate in this regard is not evaluated by comparing the degree of the initial use of force and that of the actions taken in self-defence; rather, the measures have to be required in order to reverse the effects of the initial armed attack, even if this implies the utilisation of a higher degree of force, thus making the element of proportionality a forward-looking one.[89]

---

84 See pp. 47 et seq. above.

85 See generally Emily Crawford 'Proportionality' in Rüdiger Wolfrum (ed) *MPEPIL* (OUP Oxford Update 2011) para. 10; Randelzhofer & Nolte 'Article 51' paras. 45–46; *Nicaragua Case* para. 176; *Legality of the Threat or Use of Nuclear Weapons (Advisory Opinion)* para. 41; *Armed Activities on the Territory of the Congo (Democratic Republic of the Congo v Uganda)* para. 147; *Oil Platforms (Islamic Republic of Iran v United States of America)* paras. 73 et seq; Rule 14 Tallinn Manual.

86 Randelzhofer & Nolte 'Article 51' para. 56.

87 Greenwood 'Self-Defence' para. 27.

88 Ipsen 'Bewaffneter Konflikt und Neutralität' p. 1094.

89 Greenwood 'Self-Defence' para. 28.

What is necessary and proportionate depends on the specific case at hand in the case of CNOs too. In order to achieve the goal of self-defence, which is to reverse the effects of the initial attack, the aggrieved State is free to choose the most appropriate means as long as these are necessary. Hence the victim State need not respond in kind through a CNO but may utilise conventional force. This stems from the fact that some States lack the possibilities to respond in kind or even if available these may not necessarily be able to reverse the effects of the initial attack. The limitations on CNOs under taken in self-defence are hence no different to those for conventional weapons.

2. UN SECURITY COUNCIL ENFORCEMENT MEASURES

The UN Security Council is vested with the primary responsibility for the maintenance of international peace and security.[90] For this purpose the UN Security Council is provided with the power to decide on measures to be taken in pursuance of this task, including inter alia military sanctions and the authorisation of Member States or regional organisations to use armed force. Subject to the preconditions of Chapter VII UN Charter, this gives the UN Security Council the ability to also authorise the use of computer network operations both as non-forceful and forceful means, as also stipulated in Rule 18 Tallinn Manual.

2.1. THE PREREQUISITES FOR A DECISION OF THE UN SECURITY COUNCIL

The UN Security Council can authorise States to take action that would normally qualify as an internationally wrongful act, such as for example an intervention. In order to do so, the Council must first determine the existence of a 'threat to the peace, breach of the peace, or act of aggression' under Article 39 UN Charter, whereby it is regarded as enjoying a large margin of discretion.[91] This is

---

90 Art. 24(1) UN Charter.

91 Nico Krisch 'Article 39' in Bruno Simma (ed) *The Charter of the United Nations – A Commentary* (OUP Oxford 2012) para. 4; this was also stated by the ICTY Appeals Chamber in the *Prosecutor v Tadić (Decision on the Defence Motion for Interlocutory Appeal on Jurisdiction)* IT-94–1 (2 October 1995) at paras. 31–32, adding though that the Security Council had to remain within the limits of the purposes and principles of Art. 39 UN Charter (at para. 24). The nature of the Security Council's discretion in the determination of a threat to the peace and the justiciability thereof nevertheless remains disputed. On this see Erika de Wet & Michael Wood 'Peace, Threat to' in Rüdiger Wolfrum (ed) *MPEPIL* (OUP Oxford Update 2009) paras. 16–20.

substantiated by Articles 40 and 42 UN Charter in enabling the UN Security Council to 'call upon the parties concerned to comply with such provisional measures as it deems necessary or desirable' or to 'take such action … as may be necessary to maintain or restore international peace and security'.

Although there are three different prerequisites in Article 39 UN Charter, the one most widely used in practice is the concept of a threat to the peace. This does not come as a surprise, as it is by far the broadest and most vague of the three. Besides, it will regularly appear in the forefront of a breach of the peace, making it in any case practical for the UN Security Council to take measures based 'only' upon a threat to the peace. The UN Security Council has over the years increasingly broadened the scope of the concept so that it is now interpreted to encompass internal conflicts, widespread deprivations of human rights, humanitarian disasters, and serious threats to democratic government.[92] Hence a threat to the peace is interpreted by the UN Security Council to also be able to exist in cases not involving the use of inter-State force.[93]

The occurrence of cross-border CNOs can therefore, regardless of whether or not they qualify as forceful, potentially be qualified as a threat to the peace in the sense of Article 39 UN Charter. This has already been acknowledged in a report of the UN Group of Governmental Experts on Developments in the Field of Information and Telecommunications in the Context of International Security which concluded that the Internet has become an arena for disruptive activity the motives of which being inter alia the extension of State conflict, making it utilisable in a way to pose a threat to international peace.[94]

But neither the Internet as such, nor specific malware or hardware utilised for military CNOs may per se be qualified as constituting a threat to the peace. This is due to the generally accepted position that States are by and large free in their choice of armaments. This has been recognised by the ICJ in the *Nicaragua Case* where it opined, that 'in international law there are no rules, other than such rules as may be accepted by the State concerned, by treaty or otherwise, whereby the level of armaments of a sovereign State can be limited, and this

92 Michael J Matheson *Council Unbound: The Growth of UN Decision Making on Conflict and Postconflict Issues after the Cold War* (United States Institute of Peace Washington 2006) p. 233; other examples include: illicit trafficking in small arms and light weapons, as well as proliferation of weapons of mass destruction. A new development is the determination of generic threats to the peace as, e.g., acts of international terrorism which were regarded as generally, that is also in the future, constituting a threat to the peace by UNSC Res 1373 of 28 September 2001.

93 Tams 'The Use of Force Against Terrorists' p. 376.

94 UNGA 'Report of the Group of Governmental Experts on Developments in the Field of Information and Telecommunications in the Context of International Security' (30 July 2010) UN Doc A/65/201 para. 4; similar has been stated by the Delegation of the Russian Federation 'Statement by Mr S Shestakov, Representative of the Russian Federation, at the Joint Meeting of the OSCE Forum for Security Co-operation and the OSCE Permanent Council' (10 June 2010).

principle is valid for all States without exception'.[95] Nevertheless the UN Security Council has already qualified the proliferation of weapons of mass destruction as constituting a threat to international peace and security, albeit not in general but with a view towards particular States.[96] This is likewise applicable to the field of CNOs, wherein which States are generally free to choose to establish 'cyber units' within their armed forces and develop tools and techniques for military CNOs. Depending on the circumstances at hand, for example a general fragility in the relevant geographical region or prior aggressions by the target State, the UN Security Council may yet also in these cases implement measures preventing a proliferation of components required for CNOs. Controlling a readily available dual-use technology such as information and communications technology components will prove difficult if not impossible in practice, however.

Once the UN Security Council has established the existence of a threat to the peace, or one of the other two prerequisites of Article 39 UN Charter, it may make recommendations or decide on the measures under Articles 41 or 42. Both articles contain an enumeration of possible measures generally considered as non-exhaustive. Therefore the utilisation of cross-border CNOs as a measure of both Articles 41 42 UN Charter could potentially be authorised by the UN Security Council. In this regard, the forceful measures taken under Article 42 are subsidiary to those of Article 41, as they may only be taken if non-military measures are expected to be ineffective. Because the decision contains the element of prognosis, forceful measures can be decided upon instantly without the need for an unsuccessful implementation of non-forceful measures, if these deemed to be the only viable option to maintain or restore international peace and security.[97]

2.2. COMPUTER NETWORK OPERATIONS AS MEASURES UNDER CHAPTER VII

While the wording of Article 42 UN Charter, which includes blockades as an example of a forceful measure, seems fitting for those CNOs which have by some been called 'electronic blockades',[98] this is not the case. Firstly, at the time of drafting of Article 42 electronic blockades were unheard of. Further, naval as well as land and aerial blockades inherently imply a threat to use force, as this is a necessary means for enforcing the blockade in case it is breached.[99] Most

95 *Nicaragua Case* para. 269.

96 UNSC 'Note by the President of the Security Council' (31 January 1992) UN Doc S/23500 p. 4; UNSC Res 1172 'International Peace and Security' (6 June 1998) SCOR 53rd Year 104; Krisch 'Article 39' para. 16.

97 Krisch 'Article 42' para.19.

98 See pp. 129 et seq. above.

99 Differently Dörr 'Use of Force, Prohibition of' who regards naval blockades as not qualifying as a prohibited use of force, as it were not directed against the territory of a State (at para. 23).

prominently though it is Article 41 UN Charter which includes the example of a complete or partial interruption of means of communication as a measure not involving the use of armed force, which is just a synonym for an electronic blockade. Therefore electronic blockades are not subject to the customary rules applicable to naval blockades, which is supported by the fact that these rules are established as part of humanitarian law. Yet the existence of an armed conflict which would give rise to the applicability of this body of international law need not exist for the UN Security Council to decide on measures under Chapter VII. Considering the vulnerability of modern information and communication technologies to CNOs, electronic blockades may very well be the most effective measure to interrupt communications without an use of conventional weapons.

A further, more intrusive form of CNOs could be chosen as a measure for example to prevent the incitement of racial hatred in conflict situations. Historically it was primarily the radio which was used to incite racial hatred, from Nazi Germany to Bosnia and Rwanda.[100] Today the Internet has arguably replaced the radio as the primary means of mass communication, and incitement to (not only) racial hatred can likewise be spread via news websites, services or social networking platforms. In the case of radio transmissions, radio jamming – that is the emission of electromagnetic radiation to reduce or prevent hostile use of the electromagnetic spectrum – is one way to stop such broadcasts with technical means. Where the incitement is spread via the Internet, techniques comparable to those of radio jamming might be utilised. This may include filtering techniques which can be used to filter out content designated as illegal by the respective Resolution, or distributed denial of service attacks in order to shut down the major source of dissemination.

It has to be kept in mind in this respect however that radio broadcasts are more easily controllable by governments, which generally also impose licensing schemes on broadcasters. This is due to the fact that the number of radio broadcasts is naturally limited by the number of available frequencies and is more cost intensive as regards the equipment needed. As a consequence there is a relative scarcity of radio broadcasts in comparison to websites. Radio stations may thus more easily gain a dominant position and be politically aligned than news websites or other platforms, especially those of social networking. It is consequently much more difficult for a news website to be in a position comparable to an ubiquitous radio station as was the case with the station Radio-Télévision Libre des Mille Collines in Rwanda. Nevertheless, from a technical standpoint it is possible for a State to establish news websites that de facto control public opinion. This could inter alia be done by blocking all other news websites,

100 On Rwanda and the Radio-Télévision Libre des Mille Collines broadcasts see *Prosecutor v Nahimana (Judgment)* ICTR-99-52-T (3 December 2003), especially paras. 1031–34; furthermore Jamie Frederic Metzl 'Rwandan Genocide and the International Law of Radio Jamming' (1997) 91(4) American Journal of International Law pp. 628 et seq.

especially from foreign sources (as is partly already being done today in China, so-called geolocation or zoning),[101] or by providing news content in the local language with the simultaneous absence of an alternative in that language. In this case the news website or other platform may have a similar position and thus a comparable potential to be used for incitement as was the case of the Radio-Télévision Libre des Mille Collines during the Rwandan genocide. In this position a news website could pose a legitimate target for computer network operations utilised as sanctions under Chapter VII UN Charter.

3. CONCLUSION

The utilisation of computer network operations can be justified both by their being taken as a measure of self-defence under Article 51 UN Charter or with authorisation from the UN Security Council under Chapter VII UN Charter. Both these instances have prerequisites which may themselves be triggered by CNOs. A computer network operation may amount to an armed attack which in turn allows the victim State to respond with a similar operation but also with conventional military force. In this respect these new forms of military operations do not pose different challenges than those utilising conventional kinetic weapons. Attaining evidence to attribute a CNO to a specific State has proven to be one of the major challenges of the new technology. As States are barred from gathering evidence in foreign territory as a measure of self-help, which is necessary however in the case of tracing back a CNO, the allowance of indirect evidence as a relaxed standard of proof before international courts is to be granted to victim States.

In the case of armed attacks by non-State actors, the aggrieved State is not left without redress but can ultimately respond by targeting non-State actors in foreign territory. However, this only as a measure of last resort if the host State has failed to comply with its obligation of cooperation.

Anticipatory or pre-emptive self-defence against computer network operations is inherently limited by the technology itself as their generally clandestine nature and extreme swiftness make imminent attacks hardly detectable. This contested issue therefore does not play a role in self-defence against malicious computer network operations.

Due to the wide margin of discretion afforded to the UN Security Council, computer network operations can also be utilised as measures under Chapter VII UN Charter. In this regard they could be a valuable tool of pressure against aggressor States which increases proportionally not only to the dependence on the Internet of the State itself, but also to its proliferation and utilisation among the general public.

---

101 Hoeren 'Zoning und Geolocation – Technische Ansätze zur Reterritorialisierung des Internet' p. 4.

CHAPTER 5

COMPUTER NETWORK OPERATIONS DURING AN INTERNATIONAL ARMED CONFLICT

1. INTRODUCTION

In relation to the history of warfare the codification of humanitarian law is still a rather new phenomenon. However, the sources of international humanitarian law reach far back into religion, philosophy or chivalry of many cultures, emphasising that humanitarian law is a common theme of all humankind. Although these instruments show that this body of law is highly codified, customary international law still plays a major role therein.[1] This is emphasised by the fact that most of the major States recently participating in international armed conflicts have not ratified the Additional Protocol I to the Geneva Conventions of 1949, although it has otherwise gained a high ratification record of 170 States.[2]

The applicability of humanitarian law – or ius in bello – is activated by the factual existence of an armed conflict, as stated in common Article 2 Geneva Conventions of 1949, which due to their ratification by practically all States are universally binding. In renunciation of the just-war theory, the ius ad bellum does not have an effect on the ius in bello. Both frameworks must rather be treated completely separately, providing for the full equality of both sides during an armed conflict, whatever the reason or justifications put forward for the outbreak. Actions taken in self-defence under recourse to Article 51 UN Charter can thus nevertheless still qualify as illegal under humanitarian law.[3] Naturally, the question arises as to what scope the term 'armed conflict' has. This question was and still is highly disputed regarding traditional warfare. When it comes to conflicts solely confined to computer network operations exclusive of

1 Jean Marie Henckaerts 'The Development of International Humanitarian Law and the Continued Relevance of Custom' in Howard M. Hensel (ed) *The Legitimate Use of Military Force: The Just War Tradition and the Customary Law of Armed Conflict* (Ashgate Aldershot 2008) p. 129.

2 A (non-exhaustive) enumeration of States not having ratified Additional Protocol I includes the United States, Israel, Iraq, Iran, Pakistan, Turkey and the Philippines.

3 Greenwood 'Self-Defence' para. 4.

kinetic weapons, the existence of an armed conflict – cyber warfare – will be even more difficult to establish.

The term 'armed conflict' was intentionally substituted for the term 'war' in international instruments since the 1949 Geneva Conventions. This was done in order to prevent States from claiming that a forceful action would not qualify as a war in the sense until then accepted.[4] The wider definition of armed conflict makes any situation formerly termed 'war' a fortiori qualify as an armed conflict. Oppenheim defined war as a 'contention between two or more States through their armed forces, for the purpose of overpowering each other and imposing such conditions of peace as the victor pleases'.[5] Although this definition requires a contention, that is a violent struggle, it is generally accepted that a state of war can also exist through the mere declaration of war, without any exchange of violence, a situation labelled as war in the technical sense.[6] Therefore a belligerent occupation may also activate the substantive rules of the 1949 Geneva Conventions even when the victim State does not offer any resistance.[7] The complete body of humanitarian law is applicable during that time, although the majority of rules apply to the actual conduct of hostilities, which do not take place in these instances.

This broad understanding of 'armed conflict' is also reflected in the ICRC Commentary on the 1949 Geneva Conventions which proposes that it means 'any difference arising between two States and leading to the intervention of armed forces … no difference how long the conflict lasts, or how much slaughter takes place'.[8] In the respective ICRC commentary to Additional Protocol I, it is defined even more broadly as 'any dispute between two States involving the use of their armed forces'.[9] Lastly, the ICTY in the *Tadic Case* gave the definition 'whenever there is a resort to armed force between States or protracted violence between governmental authorities and organised armed groups or between such groups within a State'.[10]

International humanitarian law applies from the initiation of the armed conflict, until a general conclusion of peace or peaceful settlement is reached.[11]

---

4 Jean Pictet (ed) *The Geneva Conventions of 12. August 1949: Commentary* (ICRC Geneva 1952–1960) vol. 1 p. 32.

5 L. Oppenheim & H. Lauterpacht *International Law vol. 2: Disputes, War and Neutrality* (Longmans Green London 1952) p. 202.

6 Dinstein *War Aggression and Self-Defence* p. 9.

7 Emily Crawford 'Armed Conflict, International' in Rüdiger Wolfrum (ed) *MPEPIL* (OUP Oxford Update 2011) para. 1.

8 Pictet (ed) *The Geneva Conventions of 12. August 1949: Commentary* vol. 1 p. 32.

9 Yves Sandoz, Christophe Swinarski & Bruno Zimmermann (eds) *Commentary on the Additional Protocols of 8 June 1977 to the Geneva Conventions of 12 August 1949* (Martinus Nijhoff Publishers Geneva 1987) para. 62.

10 *Prosecutor v Tadić (Decision on the Defence Motion for Interlocutory Appeal on Jurisdiction)* IT-94-1 (2 October 1995) para. 70.

11 *Prosecutor v Tadić (Decision on the Defence Motion for Interlocutory Appeal on Jurisdiction)* IT-94-1 (2 October 1995) para. 70.

The pivotal role lies therefore, just as in Article 2(4) UN Charter, in the use of armed force. However, not all engagements of armed forces with their counterparts have been regarded as causing an armed conflict. For example small scale border clashes are only regarded as so-called closed incidents short of war.[12] The exclusion of these incidents demonstrates that a certain intensity of hostilities must be reached, although no clear-cut threshold has been agreed upon.[13] Most attempts to qualify the level of force needed utilise criteria such as the spatiality in terms of geographic expansion of the conflict, its duration, quantity and quality in terms of destruction through military operations.[14] As the purpose of humanitarian law in general is to guarantee certain core humanitarian values during hostilities in order to reduce unnecessary human suffering and to protect civilian life,[15] it becomes clear that the discretion in evaluating the threshold of armed conflict must in cases of doubt be at the lower rather than higher level.

In the case of computer network operations accompanying conventional warfare the qualification of the existence of an armed conflict can be solved through the analysis of the latter. However, CNOs may also be used exclusively thus necessitating the appraisal of their potential ability to call an armed conflict into existence. Their potential to qualify both as a use of force and even an armed attack in the sense of Article 51 UN Charter has been shown above, despite of the lack of a dogmatic definition.[16] This allows CNOs to likewise constitute an armed conflict by themselves absent the utilisation of traditional kinetic weapons. As territoriality is not alien to cyberspace the qualification of an armed conflict as international cannot be excluded merely by reference to cyberspace as lying outside of State authority. As soon as two or more States are involved in the exchange of cross-border CNOs, the conflict is of an international character.

---

12 Dinstein *War Aggression and Self-Defence* p. 11; Michael N. Schmitt 'Wired Warfare: Computer Network Attack and Jus in Bello' (2002) 84(846) International Review of the Red Cross p. 372.

13 International Law Association Committee on the Use of Force 'Initial Report on the Meaning of Armed Conflict in International Law' (2008) at <www.ila-hq.org/en/committees/index.cfm/cid/1022> (date accessed 20 September 2009) p. 23. Critical as to the criterion of gravity as not suitable for practical purposes: Kranz 'Die völkerrechtliche Verantwortlichkeit für die Anwendung militärischer Gewalt' p. 303.

14 Dinstein *War Aggression and Self-Defence* p. 11.

15 *Legal Consequences of the Construction of a Wall in the Occupied Palestinian Territory (Advisory Opinion)* para. 162; Christopher Greenwood 'The Law of Weaponry at the Start of the New Millenium' in Michael N. Schmitt & Leslie C. Green (eds) *The Law of Armed Conflict: Into the Next Millennium* (Naval War College Newport 1998) p. 189.

16 See pp. 150 et seq. and pp. 176 et seq. above. Differently: Gaycken *Cyberwar: Das Internet als Kriegsschauplatz* at p. 198, who argues that CNOs by themselves cannot amount to an armed attack so that consequently there could likewise never exist the right of self-defence against a CNO absent a formal declaration of war.

2. THE APPLICABILITY OF INTERNATIONAL HUMANITARIAN LAW TO MILITARY COMPUTER NETWORK OPERATIONS

Despite the potential of computer network operations to constitute an armed conflict this does not by itself mean that the rules of humanitarian law are applicable to this new form of warfare. It has for example been put forward in the literature that the rules of humanitarian law do not encompass the actors, means and methods of CNOs; violations of humanitarian law were not recognisable and the assumed involvement of non-military authorities would blur the distinction between combatants and civilians.[17] The following will therefore first demonstrate the applicability of current humanitarian law also to computer network operations. Secondly, both the general principles of humanitarian law and the specific rules on the methods and means of warfare will be examined as regards their compatibility with this new form of warfare.

2.1. GENERAL APPLICABILITY OF HUMANITARIAN LAW TO NEW WEAPONS

In order to exploit the enemy's vulnerabilities, the employment of new strategies, tactics or methods not envisaged by the opponent is an essential characteristic for any war since ancient times.[18] Humanitarian law has however set up limitations on States' freedom of choice in the use of weapon systems. Article 22 Hague Regulations of 1907 but also Article 35(1) Additional Protocol I already stipulate the principle that the choice of methods and means of warfare is not unlimited.[19] Additionally a variety of treaties have been developed which prohibit or restrict the use of specific weapons. These range from the 1868 St Petersburg Declaration Prohibiting the Use of Explosive Projectiles under 400 Grammes Weight,[20] to recent codifications dealing with newly developed technologies, such as the 1995 Protocol on Blinding Laser Weapons to the Convention on Prohibitions or Restrictions on the Use of Certain Conventional

---

17 Geiger *Offensive Informationskriegsführung: Die Joint Doctrine for Information Operations der US-Streitkräfte: Sicherheitspolitische Perspektiven* p. 23.

18 See already the earliest known treatise on the subject dating from approximately 500 BCE: Sun Tzu *The Art of War* (Clarendon Press Oxford 1963) Chapter VI paras. 24–31; or the other classical work from 1832: Carl von Clausewitz *Vom Kriege* (Hedrich Leipzig 1832) Book 3, Chapters 9–10.

19 Convention concerning the Laws and Customs of War on Land and its Annex: Regulations Respecting the Laws and Customs of War on Land (signed 18 October 1907, entered into force 26 January 1910) (1907) 205 CTS 277.

20 Declaration Renouncing the Use, in Time of War, of Explosive Projectiles Under 400 Grammes Weight 1868 (signed 11 December 1868) (1907) 1 AJIL Supp 95–96 (Declaration of St Petersburg).

Weapons which may be Deemed to be Excessively Injurious or to Have Indiscriminate Effects.[21] However, there is no international instrument dealing specifically with military computer network operations and the means associated therewith. Thus, recourse can only be had to the general codifications of humanitarian law and the customary rules developed thereto. These are especially the 1907 Hague Conventions, the 1949 Geneva Conventions and their Additional Protocols. There will also be scrutiny of the Tallinn Manual.

In general, the fact that methods and means of cyber warfare are not specifically regulated in a humanitarian law instrument, does not mean them being exempt from the coverage of the rules of humanitarian law. Article 1(2) Additional Protocol I for example, which is considered to represent customary international law[22] and to be a modified version of the Martens Clause,[23] stipulates that:

> '[i]n cases not covered by this Protocol or by other international agreements, civilians and combatants remain under the protection and authority of the principles of international law derived from established custom, from the principles of humanity and from dictates of public conscience.'

While there are different interpretations regarding the scope of the Martens clause's applicability, its content is generally agreed to mean at the very least that what is not prohibited by treaty may not necessarily be lawful.[24] A similar requirement has been stipulated by the ICJ in the *Nuclear Weapons (Advisory Opinion)* by stating that 'the entire law of armed conflict ... applies to all forms of warfare and to all kinds of weapons, those of the past, those of the present and those of the future'.[25] Therefore, all military operations during armed conflict need to comply with humanitarian law principles.[26]

But in a much earlier step States were already obliged to assess the legality of a weapon. Two international instruments make reference to the importance of

---

21 Convention on Prohibitions or Restrictions on the Use of Certain Conventional Weapons which may be Deemed to be Excessively Injurious or to have Indiscriminate Effects: Protocol IV: Protocol on Blinding Laser Weapons (issued 13 October 1995, entered into force 30 July 1998) 35 ILM 1218.

22 *Legality of the Threat or Use of Nuclear Weapons (Advisory Opinion)* para. 84.

23 The original Martens Clause with similar meaning is to be found in the preamble of the Convention with Respect to the Laws and Customs of War by Land and its Annex: Regulations Respecting the Laws and Customs of War on Land (signed 29 July 1899, entered into force 4 September 1900) (1898–99) 187 CTS 429. It is likewise to be found in the 1949 Geneva Conventions I–IV and further treaty law.

24 Theodor Meron 'The Martens Clause, Principles of Humanity, and Dictates of Public Conscience' (2000) 94(1) American Journal of International Law p. 87; for an overview of the different interpretations: Jochen von Bernstorff 'Martens Clause' in Rüdiger Wolfrum (ed) *MPEPIL* (OUP Oxford Update 2009) para. 13.

25 *Legality of the Threat or Use of Nuclear Weapons (Advisory Opinion)* para. 86.

26 Schmitt 'Wired Warfare: Computer Network Attack and Jus in Bello' p. 369.

reviewing the legality of weapons, means or methods of warfare already in the stage of their development. The St Petersburg Declaration Renouncing the Use, in Time of War, of Explosive Projectiles Under 400 Grammes Weight of 1868, is the first such international instrument.[27] It is stated therein:

> 'The Contracting or Acceding Parties reserve to themselves to come hereafter to an understanding whenever a precise proposition shall be drawn up in view of future improvements which science may effect in the armament of troops, in order to maintain the principles which they have established, and to conciliate the necessities of war with the laws of humanity.'

The only other reference in this regard is Article 36 Additional Protocol I which states that:

> '[i]n the study, development, acquisition or adoption of a new weapon, means or method of warfare, a High Contracting Party is under an obligation to determine whether its employment would, in some or all circumstances, be prohibited by this Protocol or by any other rule of international law applicable to the High Contracting Party.'

The referral by Article 36 to both weapons and means or methods of warfare gives the provision a broad spectrum, making the distinction under which category activities in the field of cyber warfare fall somewhat superfluous, especially as it is unclear how the term 'means of warfare' differs from 'weapons'.[28] The reference to 'some or all circumstances' does not mean an obligation to analyse all possible misuses of a weapon, but only the employment for its normal or expected use, as it is clear that all objects can be used in a prohibited manner.[29] This is especially important regarding dual-use software products that may enable their user to attack other systems, but which are not specifically designed for this purpose.

It has been criticised that the provision has not been given the required attention by States, as only few have adopted measures on a national level to undertake the necessary thorough legal reviews of weapons.[30] During the

---

27 Isabelle Daoust, Robin Coupland & Rikke Ishoey 'New Wars, New Weapons? The Obligation of States to Assess the Legality of Means and Methods of Warfare' (2002) 84(846) Revue internationale de la Croix-Rouge p. 346.

28 Daoust, Coupland & Ishoey 'New Wars, New Weapons? The Obligation of States to Assess the Legality of Means and Methods of Warfare' p. 352 fn. 19.

29 Michael Bothe, Karl Josef Partsch & Waldemar A. Solf *New Rules for Victims of Armed Conflicts: Commentary on the Two 1977 Protocols Additional to the Geneva Conventions of 1949* (Nijhoff The Hague 1982) p. 200.

30 Daoust, Coupland & Ishoey 'New Wars, New Weapons? The Obligation of States to Assess the Legality of Means and Methods of Warfare' pp. 346 and 361; Bothe, Partsch & Solf *New Rules for Victims of Armed Conflicts: Commentary on the Two 1977 Protocols Additional to the Geneva Conventions of 1949* p. 200; see also the listing of some States that do provide for such

drafting of the article a proposition to establish a special international body with the task of creating a prohibited weapons or methods list was rejected.[31] While the criticism holds true from a practical perspective, legally it does not make a difference whether or not a prior national review has been conducted for the assessment of a new weapon or method of warfare as illegal under humanitarian law. Article 36 Additional Protocol I as a catch-all clause links the rules of Additional Protocol I to any new type of weapon, means or method of warfare.[32] States cannot evade the rules of humanitarian law or international responsibility for their actions, neither by introducing new weapons or methods of warfare, nor by declaring a certain type of weapon or method as legal as a result of their national review procedure.[33] Therefore military computer network operations are subject to the rules of humanitarian law just as any other new weapon before.[34] Article 36 Additional Protocol I also imposes an obligation for the evaluation of the legality of software designed for CNOs at all stages, from its study and research phase, development and testing phase, or acquisition from a third State or private vendor.[35] At each stage the future use of the software should be taken into consideration. The same holds true for CNOs that do not make use of specific software, but for example utilise generic commands of widely used programmes. While such may not be qualified as a weapon, they are

---

a review mechanism: ICRC *A Guide to the Legal Review of New Weapons, Means and Methods of Warfare* at <www.icrc.org/eng/assets/files/other/icrc_002_0902.pdf> (date accessed 4 June 2012) pp. 5–6.

31 This idea which was important especially to smaller States could not reach stronger support as it would in fact mean disarmament, which was a topic not considered to be discussed by the conference; Sandoz, Swinarski & Zimmermann (eds) *Commentary on the Additional Protocols of 8 June 1977 to the Geneva Conventions of 12 August 1949* para. 1463; Marie Jacobsson 'Modern Weaponry and Warfare: The Application of Article 36 of Additional Protocol I by Governments' in Anthony M. Helm (ed) *The Law of War in the 21st Century: Weaponry and the Use of Force* (Naval War College Newport 2006) p. 184.

32 Sandoz, Swinarski & Zimmermann (eds) *Commentary on the Additional Protocols of 8 June 1977 to the Geneva Conventions of 12 August 1949* para. 1466.

33 Similarly the ICJ in the *Legality of the Threat or Use of Nuclear Weapons (Advisory Opinion)* para. 86.

34 Knut Dörmann 'Applicability of the Additional Protocols to Computer Network Attacks' (2004) at <www.icrc.org/eng/assets/files/other/applicabilityofihltocna.pdf> (date accessed 23 March 2011) p. 2; see also Rule 20 Tallinn Manual: 'cyber operations executed in the context of an armed conflict are subject to the law of armed conflict'. The wording 'in the context of' was a compromise formula, as the group of experts drafting the Manual could not agree upon the nature of the nexus required between cyber activity and the armed conflict. One view held that only those activities are meant that are directed against the enemy and in order to contribute to the originator's military effort: Schmitt (ed) *Tallinn Manual on the International Law Applicable to Cyber Warfare* p. 76 para. 5. This view cannot be shared, as it bears the danger of belligerents arguing an operation were not contributing to its military effort in order to achieve the inapplicability of humanitarian law. Rather all military operations during armed conflict which are somehow directed against the enemy need to be in compliance thereto.

35 Seminal: ICRC *A Guide to the Legal Review of New Weapons, Means and Methods of Warfare* pp. 23–24.

nonetheless a specific method of warfare subject to legal scrutiny if undertaken during armed conflict by the armed forces.

2.2. THE SPATIAL APPLICABILITY OF HUMANITARIAN LAW: THE REGION OF WAR

Technical developments in the 20th century allowed armies utilising modern warfare to bridge vast distances. Air, naval and especially missile warfare allow actors to strike targets anywhere in the world. While the actual theatre of operations might be confined to a relatively small area, humanitarian law allows the parties to the conflict a much wider region to wage war. This so-called region of war consists of the parties' territories, the high seas, exclusive economic zones (even of neutral States) and outer space, albeit limited to a certain degree through the Outer Space Treaty.[36] Irrespective of the location of the actual theatre of operations, humanitarian law is applicable in this entire region of war.[37]

The laws of war classically made a tripartition between land, naval, and air warfare, in which the origin of the attack, not the location of its effects, constitute the criterion for distinguishing between the different theatres of war.[38] This distinction gains importance when determining the applicable law. While the rules on land warfare are codified to a great extent, the rules for naval and air warfare mostly derive from customary law.[39] Article 49(3) Additional Protocol I extends the general protection of civilians against the effects of hostilities to all attacks from the sea or from the air against objectives on land, however leaving a lacuna with respect to air-to-air and ship-to-ship combat. This limitation is a reference to the view supported by many countries during the drafting process that it was too difficult and undesirable to review and revise the law applicable to armed conflict at sea and in the air.[40] Additionally civilians are not as vulnerable to the effects of these forms of warfare compared to that on land.

In relation to CNOs, the question arises as to whether the region of war constrains the belligerents in their choice of targets or in the manner cyber warfare is conducted. Additional Protocol I only makes reference to the media

---

36 Dinstein *War Aggression and Self-Defence* pp. 19–24. The Outer Space Treaty limits the use of the moon and other celestial bodies to peaceful purposes. However, the land-to-land firing of missiles flying through outer space is considered to not be forbidden (*ibid* at p. 24).

37 Julia Breslin 'Region of War' in Rüdiger Wolfrum (ed) *MPEPIL* (OUP Oxford Update 2010) para. 14.

38 Robin Geiß 'Land Warfare' in Rüdiger Wolfrum (ed) *MPEPIL* (OUP Oxford Update 2009) para. 1.

39 Dinstein 'Air Warfare' para. 3.

40 Bothe, Partsch & Solf *New Rules for Victims of Armed Conflicts: Commentary on the Two 1977 Protocols Additional to the Geneva Conventions of 1949* pp. 290–91; Sandoz, Swinarski & Zimmermann (eds) *Commentary on the Additional Protocols of 8 June 1977 to the Geneva Conventions of 12 August 1949* paras. 1895–98.

water, land and air. If cyberspace were to be understood as a completely new medium, it could also be seen as constituting a new theatre of war, as for example in case of a 'cyberspace-to-cyberspace' attack.[41] In this case one could argue that civilians could not benefit from the protections afforded under Article 49(3) Additional Protocol I. But although cyberspace may be seen as a new 'medium' or social sphere of some sort, the infrastructure whereupon the data is stored is still made up of physically tangible objects. Any targeted data must thus be stored on one or several systems located on some State's territory and hence under its jurisdiction. This is the reason for the traditional concepts of jurisdiction and territoriality to also be applicable to cyberspace, as has been shown above.[42] Being applicable in the entire region of war, humanitarian law utilises the traditional geographic connection to its subject matter in order to be effective and reach its addressees. Therefore there is no genuine geographical region that may be termed cyberspace existing outside of the boundaries posed by the traditional region of war. The legal rules of land warfare are thus also applicable to cyber warfare. As a consequence, computer systems located in the area traditionally qualifying as the region of war can potentially pose valid military targets.[43] A computer system inside a military base on the territory of one of the belligerents will thus be attackable via CNOs. This result is also in accordance with the aim of humanitarian law: the protection of non-combatants. As the number of people utilising computer systems is significantly higher than that of those utilising naval or aerial craft, a lacuna for 'cyberspace' would leave a large number of systems and accordingly also their users unprotected.

2.3. THE QUALIFICATION OF MILITARY COMPUTER NETWORK OPERATIONS AS AN ATTACK UNDER INTERNATIONAL HUMANITARIAN LAW

In order for most rules of Additional Protocol I and customary international humanitarian law to be applicable, CNOs must fall under the definition of the term 'attack' in the meaning of humanitarian law. This notion differs from other branches of international law, especially the notion of armed attack under

41 It has for example been put forward that cyberspace is a region of its own, which cannot qualify as a war zone; Michael Hoffman 'The Legal Status and Responsibilities of Private Internet Users under the Law of Armed Conflict: A Primer for the Unwary on the Shape of Law to Come' (2003) 2 Washington University Global Studies Law Review p. 419.

42 See pp. 53 et seq. above.

43 A further question is posed through the possible utilisation of computer resources located on the territory of a State not party to the conflict. How to deal with extraterritorial computer systems and their utilisation by belligerents is however a question of the laws of neutrality and will be answered below at pp. 259 et seq.

Article 51 UN Charter.[44] Article 49(1) Additional Protocol I defines attacks as 'acts of violence against the adversary, whether in offence or in defence'. As the objective of Additional Protocol I – the protection of the civilian population in an armed conflict – is at risk both from offensive and defensive military actions, the definition of attack was decided to be broad in scope encompassing all combat action.[45] A classification between cyber defence or offence operations is thus of no concern in their qualification as an attack.

Nonetheless, acts of violence during armed conflict are also generally seen as only encompassing physical force, thereby excluding actions pertaining to psychological, political or economic warfare.[46] CNOs that amount to physical damage to objects – beyond the mere destruction of data on computer systems – or persons will therefore have to be seen as an attack under Article 49 Additional Protocol I. Similar is stipulated in the commentary to the Manual on Air and Missile Warfare, which regards attacks to 'also cover "non-kinetic" attacks (i.e. attacks that do not involve the physical transfer of energy, such as certain CNAs [i.e. computer network attacks] ... that result in death, injury, damage or destruction of persons or objects'.[47]

The majority of CNOs are however likely to involve more subtle effects without any physical destruction. Whether these can be qualified as violence in the context of humanitarian law is more controversial. Reference is made hereby to the deletion or manipulation of stored data or the writing of such on belligerent computer systems. The effect of such measures will – from a technical standpoint – most likely be a mere alteration of the magnetisation or electric charge of the memory used. This is an operation making a designated use of the target device without doing any physical harm to the system as such. Nevertheless, one result of these actions could be the rendering useless of the whole system or parts of its functions. According to the group of experts responsible for drafting the Manual on Air and Missile Warfare, CNOs that result in a mere inconvenience, such as temporary denial of Internet access, should be excluded from the definition of attack.[48] Schmitt on the other hand regards violence as referred to in Article 49 Additional Protocol I to also

---

44 Dörmann 'Applicability of the Additional Protocols to Computer Network Attacks' p. 3; Program on Humanitarian Policy and Conflict Research (ed) *Commentary on the HPCR Manual on International Law Applicable to Air and Missile Warfare* pp. 27–28.

45 Sandoz, Swinarski & Zimmermann (eds) *Commentary on the Additional Protocols of 8 June 1977 to the Geneva Conventions of 12 August 1949* para. 1880.

46 Bothe, Partsch & Solf *New Rules for Victims of Armed Conflicts: Commentary on the Two 1977 Protocols Additional to the Geneva Conventions of 1949* p. 289.

47 Program on Humanitarian Policy and Conflict Research (ed) *Commentary on the HPCR Manual on International Law Applicable to Air and Missile Warfare* p. 28.

48 Program on Humanitarian Policy and Conflict Research (ed) *Commentary on the HPCR Manual on International Law Applicable to Air and Missile Warfare* p. 28; similarly: Schweizer Bundesamt für Justiz und EDA 'Gutachten über Rechtsgrundlagen für Computernetzwerkoperationen durch Dienststellen des VBS' at p. 168. According to Swanson 'The Era of Cyber Warfare: Applying International Humanitarian Law to the 2008 Russian-

encompass the causation of damage to what he identifies as 'intangible assets with a tangible meaning' such as currency or stock.[49]

Military forces are generally not restricted to physically destroying targets. A military advantage may also be gained by capturing or neutralising military objectives, as acknowledged in Article 52(2) Additional Protocol I. Neutralisation refers to an attack for the purpose of denying the adversary the use of the object without actually destroying it.[50] Article 52(2) states, inter alia, that the attack of military objectives is limited to those, the neutralisation of which offers a military advantage. Hence Additional Protocol I assumes that neutralisation may be caused by an attack. An example of this, using more traditional forms of warfare, is the laying of land mines on a field or the causing of artillery gun crews to seek shelter by firing antipersonnel munition. This does not directly cause injuries to enemy combatants or damage to the artillery as such, but effectively denies the enemy the use both of the field and the artillery.[51] The comparable scenario is the shutting down of the electricity grid without destroying it. This, it has been argued, should also be qualified as an attack.[52] In cyber warfare, the scenario will have to be rewritten to take account of actions rendering adversary computer systems useless by either taking control or manipulating them in such a way as to cause malfunctions. Neither destroys the systems, but they will at least deny the adversary use of the systems for a certain amount of time, and hence neutralise them. For that reason CNOs not amounting to physical damage outside of the computer system must also be qualified as an attack in the definition of Article 49 Additional Protocol I.[53] In any case this does not lead to untenable results. The qualification of an action as an attack by itself does not per se make it illegal. The latter is a question of how the attack is performed and on which target. Excluding CNOs as a form of attack would simultaneously also deny the applicability of most rules protecting civilians and civilian objects, a result contrary to the very essence of humanitarian law.

The same discussion is mirrored in Rule 30 Tallinn Manual and the commentary thereto. Rule 30 Tallinn Manual stipulates its own definition of cyber attack which is seen as 'a cyber operation, whether offensive or defensive, that is reasonably expected to cause injury or death to persons or damage or destruction to objects'. Controversy arose regarding the qualification of

Georgian Cyber Conflict' these sorts of CNOs were utilised in the Russian-Georgian conflict making them 'permissible attacks' (at p. 323).

49 Schmitt 'Computer Network Attack: The Normative Software' p. 77.

50 Bothe, Partsch & Solf *New Rules for Victims of Armed Conflicts: Commentary on the Two 1977 Protocols Additional to the Geneva Conventions of 1949* p. 325.

51 Bothe, Partsch & Solf *New Rules for Victims of Armed Conflicts: Commentary on the Two 1977 Protocols Additional to the Geneva Conventions of 1949* p. 325.

52 Dörmann 'Applicability of the Additional Protocols to Computer Network Attacks' p. 4.

53 Contrarily: Döge 'Cyber Warfare: Challenges for the Applicability of the Traditional Laws of War Regime' p. 499.

interferences with the functionality of an object as damage and hence an attack. The majority opinion within the group of experts drafting the Manual was that once restoration of functionality requires replacement of physical components, such an action is to be considered as damage, thus as a cyber attack.[54] This is to be agreed with, as obviously a replacement of a component is only done once it is defective, hence damaged. Yet only a minority opinion held that irrespective of how an object is disabled, its loss of usability in all cases constitutes the requisite damage.[55] As stated above, those CNOs not amounting to physical damage outside of the computer system must be qualified as an attack in order for the substantive rules protecting civilians from armed conflict to be applicable. Only then can each individual case be evaluated as to whether the attack was illegal or not. Under the Tallinn Manual the principle of distinction (Rule 31), the precautionary principle (Rules 53–59) as well as the prohibition to attack civilians (Rule 32) and civilian objects (Rule 37) shall apply only for 'cyber attacks' in said sense of Rule 30. Excluding some forms of malicious CNOs from the definition of cyber attack as so understood by the majority opinion drafting the Tallinn Manual results in the untenable result that such operations could be intentionally directed against civilians or civilian objects, independent of their participation in hostilities, as long as the malfunctions caused do not necessitate the exchange of hardware components. While the consequences for civilians would of course by no means be as detrimental as those from actual cyber attacks as understood by the majority opinion, it remains unanswered why civilians and their objects should be allowed to be wilfully targeted at all, even if only on a very low level of scale and effects.

3. THE RULES OF HUMANITARIAN LAW AS APPLIED TO MILITARY COMPUTER NETWORK ATTACKS

After having established the applicability of humanitarian law to military computer network operations, its individual rules will be analysed as to their influence on the usage of computer network attacks (CNAs) during armed conflict.

3.1. THE RULES CONCERNING THE METHODS OF COMPUTER NETWORK ATTACKS

One of the fears associated with cyber warfare is similar to that expressed by UN Special Rapporteur Alston on drones: they could make killing easier, with only a limited risk to a State's forces, tempting policy makers and commanders to

[54] Schmitt (ed) *Tallinn Manual on the International Law Applicable to Cyber Warfare* p. 108.
[55] Schmitt (ed) *Tallinn Manual on the International Law Applicable to Cyber Warfare* p. 109.

interpret the legal limitations on who can be targeted, and under what circumstances, too expansively. Moreover, the team operating a drone or instigating a CNA located in a remote position may be at an even greater human intelligence disadvantage than the ground forces, who themselves are often unable to collect reliable intelligence.[56] Drones can be operated remotely by a team thousands of miles away from the place of action. It is this remote control of military actions, which are entirely executed via a computer with remote audio and video feeds, that has prompted critics to fear the risk of developing a 'PlayStation', or in other words a computer game, mentality to killing through the use of remote controllers.[57] The same holds true for CNAs. These can be performed remotely from a computer lab located anywhere in the world. In comparison to drones, the target is not even visible or audible via a video or audio uplink and in most cases there will be no ground forces to verify the target or success of the operation. This is due to the genuine technicalities of CNAs. The system targeted may be physically visible; but it is not the computer system as such that is targeted, but the programmes and databases running thereon. A manipulation will therefore not necessarily be noticeable instantly. This could lead operators of CNAs to act comparatively recklessly.

The legal situation for the deployment of both drones and computer network operations during international armed conflict is the same. Both technologies, due to the remoteness of their operators, pose new challenges for the gathering of intelligence on the ground. Either might cause the operator to act more recklessly than an infantryman who immediately feels and sees with his own eyes the consequences of his actions. Yet the sophistication and duration of highly developed CNAs as could be seen in the case study of the Stuxnet malware, mostly does not allow an operator to develop a 'PlayStation' attitude towards the operation, as most of the work is spent in the programming and not execution of the software, making it a rather tedious task. Nevertheless the results achieved by both means of warfare in the end are no different than those of a conventional attack.[58] As long as the technology does not per se qualify as an indiscriminate and hence prohibited weapon, these new challenges can only be solved by addressing them in the training of the forces. In most cases it is the employment and not the nature of a weapon that determines a lawful or unlawful outcome.[59] The normal rules of humanitarian law are in place to keep excessive attacks to a

56 Philip Alston 'Report of the Special Rapporteur on Extrajudicial, Summary or Arbitrary Executions: Study on Targeted Killings (UN Doc A/HRC/14/24/Add.6)' (28 May 2010) paras. 80–82.

57 Alston 'Report of the Special Rapporteur on Extrajudicial, Summary or Arbitrary Executions: Study on Targeted Killings (UN Doc A/HRC/14/24/Add.6)' para. 84.

58 For the example of drones see Alston 'Report of the Special Rapporteur on Extrajudicial, Summary or Arbitrary Executions: Study on Targeted Killings (UN Doc A/HRC/14/24/Add.6)' paras. 79 et seq.

59 Yoram Dinstein 'Warfare, Methods and Means' in Rüdiger Wolfrum (ed) *MPEPIL* (OUP Oxford Update 2009) para. 2.

minimum. If used in accordance with these rules, computer network attacks are a valid means of warfare just like any other.

3.1.1. *Precautions before Launching Computer Network Attacks*

Before starting any attack, combatants are under the general obligation stipulated in Article 57 Additional Protocol I that 'constant care shall be taken to spare the civilian population, civilians and civilian objects'. Before utilising CNAs several questions need to be considered in order to adhere to this precautionary principle, which is also reflected in customary international law.[60] An attack which may be expected to cause loss or injury of civilian life or damage to civilian objects shall not be undertaken if it is excessive in relation to the military advantage anticipated.[61] Thus the margin of appreciation of those who plan or decide upon an attack is considered to be broad in regard to the standard of what may be expected.[62] Yet a military commander must use this discretion in good faith.[63] This however is sufficient, so that a later appraisal of a military action must be based on the circumstances and combat situation ruling at the time of the decision, thus assuming an ex-ante view, as stipulated in Article 86(2) Additional Protocol I and reflected in customary international law.[64]

One possibility to ensure these precautions has been included in Article 57(2)(c) Additional Protocol I and Rule 58 Tallinn Manual by requiring the attacker to warn the possibly affected civilian population in advance of the attack. When flying bombing raids, some militaries notify the population by radio of the imminent attack; during the Gaza conflict in 2008/09 the Israeli Defence Forces used so-called 'roof knocking' (that is, the firing of non-explosive missiles on the roofs of targets to be bombed and warning calls by phone) to warn of an imminent attack. In the case of a CNA, one could think of a prior warning of a disturbance

---

60 See Jean-Marie Henckaerts & Louise Doswald-Beck (eds) *Customary International Humanitarian Law Volume I: Rules* (Cambridge University Press Cambridge 2005) Rules 15 et seq. with further references to relevant State practice also of non-State Parties to Additional Protocol I. With Rules 52–59 the Tallinn Manual incorporates a whole section on precautions.

61 Art. 57(2)(a)(iii) Additional Protocol I; similar holds true for customary international law: Henckaerts & Doswald-Beck (eds) *Customary International Humanitarian Law Volume I: Rules* (Rule 18) and Rule 55 Tallinn Manual.

62 Sandoz, Swinarski & Zimmermann (eds) *Commentary on the Additional Protocols of 8 June 1977 to the Geneva Conventions of 12 August 1949* para. 2210.

63 Yoram Dinstein 'Military Necessity' in Rüdiger Wolfrum (ed) *MPEPIL* (OUP Oxford Update 2009) para. 28.

64 See eg the *Hostage Case (United States v List) (Judgment)* (19 February 1948) in *Trials of War Criminals before the Nuernberg Military Tribunals* vol 11 (US Government Printing Office Washington DC 1950) wherein the tribunal states it were 'obliged to judge the situation as it appeared to the defendant at the time' (at p. 1296); Henckaerts & Doswald-Beck (eds) *Customary International Humanitarian Law Volume I: Rules* accompanying pages 54–55 to Rule 15.

in Internet connectivity, which in certain instances of real-time applications can cause monetary damages and communication interruptions. However, due to the military necessity of an element of surprise for certain attacks to be successful, there may be a derogation if circumstances do not permit such prior warning.[65] As in most cases CNAs are undertaken clandestinely and with the element of surprise, prior warnings of CNAs will rarely play a role during cyber warfare.

Modern technology has on the one hand allowed weapons systems to become more accurate, for example through precision guided munitions. On the other hand, the fear has been voiced that the growing intelligence of weapons systems has lessened the efforts required by humans in preparation and execution of an attack. To take a practical example, in the accidental bombing of the Chinese embassy in Belgrade by United States forces during the Kosovo conflict, the geographical coordinates communicated were allegedly those of a Yugoslavian arms agency.[66] In this case, the aircrew relied on the coordinates provided, without any visual confirmation of the target. This instance shows that the precautions that must be taken prior to an attack have to a certain degree shifted from those executing the attack to those gathering information to identify a target. In these cases the precautions that needed to be taken concentrate on assuring the accuracy of data used by the 'intelligent' weapons system. Just as this was the case in the Chinese embassy bombing, it will also play an important role in the case of CNAs. A commander is under an obligation to assess the risks involved in launching a CNA. Thus the obligation to take all feasible precautions overrides the need for swift decision-making, as the latter is an inherent feature of most operations.[67] The risks of attacking the wrong target are especially high when actively defending against a hostile CNA. As stated above, the traceability of CNAs is rather low, depending on the level of its sophistication.[68] The mere reliance on remote intelligence gathered via computer network exploitation may not be enough but should be accompanied by additional intelligence sources.[69]

Unexpected consequences, so called second and third-tier effects, are evaluated as being more probable in the case of CNAs than when using kinetic

---

65 Sandoz, Swinarski & Zimmermann (eds) *Commentary on the Additional Protocols of 8 June 1977 to the Geneva Conventions of 12 August 1949* para. 2223; the same derogation rule is established under customary international law: Henckaerts & Doswald-Beck (eds) *Customary International Humanitarian Law Volume I: Rules* (Rule 20) and in Rule 58 Tallinn Manual and accompanying commentary: Schmitt (ed) *Tallinn Manual on the International Law Applicable to Cyber Warfare* p. 175 para. 8.

66 Jack M. Beard 'Law and War in the Virtual Era' (2009) 103 American Journal of International Law p. 440.

67 Pointing this out for the case of air warfare: Dinstein 'Air Warfare' para. 33.

68 See pp. 28 et seq. above.

69 Louise Doswald-Beck 'Some Thoughts on Computer Network Attack and the International Law of Armed Conflict' in Michael N. Schmitt & Brian T. O'Donnell (eds) *Computer Network Attack and International Law* (Naval War College Newport 2002) p. 170.

force.[70] In contrast to conventional attacks, preliminary considerations therefore need to especially concentrate on the cascading effects a CNA could generate on connected systems and eventually on the Internet as a whole. Therefore the quality of the targeted system and its operation must be studied, as well as the system's connection to third systems and their dependencies on each other in order to give a prognosis on the probability of larger cascading effects.[71] Rule 59 Tallinn Manual, by encompassing solely 'cyber attacks' in the sense of its Rule 30 under the precautionary principle, again leads to the problem that for example the effects of viruses that would spread to civilian systems need not be taken into account, as long as these merely disrupt, yet do not lead to the need to physically exchange hardware components.[72] This cannot be supported for the reasons given above.[73]

As weapon systems have become more and more precise, several views have been voiced that a State which is in possession of precision guided munitions has a duty to utilise such over conventional munitions in order to minimise collateral damage.[74] The existence of this duty has been contested by many States and there is no State practice which could support the creation of any customary rule on the issue.[75] Yet while there is no obligation to generally make use solely of precision munitions, such a duty may be developed from different widely

---

70 Eric Talbot Jensen 'Unexpected Consequences from Knock-on Effects: A Different Standard for Computer Network Operations?' (2003) 18(5) American University International Law Review pp. 1175–78.

71 O'Donnell & Kraska 'Humanitarian Law: Developing International Rules for the Digital Battlefield' p. 159. Robin Geiß & Henning Lahmann 'Cyber Warfare: Applying the Principle of Distinction in an Interconnected Space' (2012) 45 Israel Law Review at pp. 395 et seq. arrive at the same conclusion yet via the principle of proportionality.

72 Only a minority of the group of experts understands all operations and not only cyber attacks to be encompassed also by the precautionary rule: Schmitt (ed) *Tallinn Manual on the International Law Applicable to Cyber Warfare* p. 177 para. 5.

73 See pp. 208 et seq. above.

74 Seeing such a duty as established: Stuart Walters Belt 'Missiles over Kosovo: Emergence, Lex Lata, of a Customary Norm Requiring the Use of Precision Munitions in Urban Areas' (2000) 47 Naval Law Review pp. 115–75 arguing that State practice has modified the principle of proportionality to include a newly developed customary norm on the use of precision weaponry in urban settings. Wolfrum 'The Attack of September 11, 2001, the Wars against the Taliban and Iraq: Is there a Need to Reconsider International Law on the Recourse to Force and the Rules in Armed Conflict?' at p. 51 sees an obligation to use precision weapons in certain cases but concludes that it 'remains doubtful whether the rule only to use weapons which, from a technological point of view, are the most accurate ones has been fully implemented'. Concurring in this regard is Michael N. Schmitt 'Precision Attack and International Humanitarian Law' (2005) 87(859) International Review of the Red Cross at p. 461, who sees no foundation to claims that States possessing precision weapons must always use them.

75 US Department of Defense Office of General Counsel 'An Assessment of International Legal Issues in Information Operations' (1999) at <www.au.af.mil/au/awc/awcgate/dod-io-legal/dod-io-legal.pdf> (date accessed 27 April 2011) p. 24; giving an overview of (missing) State practice as to the use of precision guided munitions: Christopher B. Puckett 'In this Era of "Smart Weapons", Is a State under an International Legal Obligation to Use Precision-Guided Technology in Armed Conflict?' (2004) 18(2) Emory International Law Review pp. 688–700.

recognised principles of humanitarian law: the prohibition of indiscriminate attacks, the principle of proportionality and the duty to take precautions in attack.[76] While these may not create a general duty, they nevertheless need to be taken into account in each individual attack. If a precision guided munition for example has a higher probability of not causing collateral damage, its use is made obligatory by the precautionary rule of Article 57 Additional Protocol I.

The same result is achieved considering the proportionality principle inter alia stipulated in Article 51(5)(b) Additional Protocol I. According to this, 'an attack which may be expected to cause incidental loss of civilian life, injury to civilians, damage to civilian objects, or a combination thereof' is forbidden where this loss 'would be excessive in relation to the concrete and direct military advantage anticipated'. If the same military advantage can be achieved by a precision weapon that poses a smaller risk of civilian casualties the attacker is obliged to utilise it. It can therefore be concluded that while a general duty to use precision weapons does not exist, in individual cases their application may nevertheless be compulsory in order to comply with particular rules of humanitarian law. This applies, however, only to those weapons a State actually has in its possession, meaning that there is no obligation to replace older munitions with those that are precision guided.[77] This results from the fact that such an obligation would in effect deny poorer countries the possibility to defend themselves without committing war crimes as they are not able to purchase highly developed munitions. With respect to CNAs, this means that States which have acquired the capability to conduct cyber warfare must consider this new means in accordance with the precautionary principle when planning an operation, while they are not obliged to establish new units specialising in this type of warfare.

3.1.2. *The Principle of Distinction*

The principle of distinction as incorporated in Article 48 Additional Protocol I has been identified by the ICJ in the *Legality of the Threat or Use of Nuclear Weapons (Advisory Opinion)* as a cardinal principle of humanitarian law, thus constituting customary international law also binding for non-parties to Additional Protocol I.[78] Article 48 states that:

> '[i]n order to ensure respect for and protection of the civilian population and civilian objects, the Parties to the conflict shall at all times distinguish between the civilian population and combatants and between civilian objects and military objectives and accordingly shall direct their operations only against military objectives.'

---

76 Schmitt 'Precision Attack and International Humanitarian Law' pp. 454–66.

77 Christopher Greenwood 'Legal Issues Regarding Explosive Remnants of War (UN Doc CCW/GGE/I/WP.10)' (23 May 2002) para. 17; Schmitt 'Precision Attack and International Humanitarian Law' p. 460.

78 *Legality of the Threat or Use of Nuclear Weapons (Advisory Opinion)* paras. 78–79.

According to the ICJ, the principle prohibits 'methods and means of warfare, which would preclude any distinction between civilian and military targets, or which would result in unnecessary suffering to combatants'.[79] Thus the purpose of the principle is to give effect to the general protection of civilians against the dangers arising from military operations as incorporated in Article 51(1) Additional Protocol I. The subsequent targeting rules of Additional Protocol I must therefore be interpreted in light of this principle classified as a basic rule of humanitarian law.

It is to a large degree due to the evolution of the principle of distinction that the use of biological and chemical weapons has been forbidden, as these have a high probability of causing indiscriminate effects and unnecessary suffering.[80] Computer network attacks may paradoxically be seen both as a weapon completely in compliance with the principle of distinction, while at the same time having the potential for an indiscriminate spread comparable to that of a biological virus. A CNA regularly targets one or several particular computer systems. Unlike a conventional weapon being fired on a target, the CNA is at least from a technical standpoint unable to 'miss' its target. Any error in targeting will ultimately rest within the responsibility of the programmer or executor of the operational programme. A CNA could therefore theoretically solely target a computer system purely in military use, thus excluding the possibility of collateral damage. This however depends on the type of CNA used. After all, there exist numerous forms of malware which spread uncontrollably from one system to another and it is no coincidence that the term computer virus is derived from its biological counterpart. The design of computer viruses, particularly in their dissemination, produces effects on computer systems that are comparable to those virus diseases have on biological organisms. But just as there are numerous different kinds of conventional weapons and ammunition, the same holds true for the arsenal of CNAs. For example, a distributed denial of service attack against a purely military target will only cause the specific system (and any dependent on it) to be affected. Forwarding a computer virus on the other hand can lead to its spreading out from purely military to civil systems. Thus, due to the interdependence of civil and military networks, and the unintelligible results an attack on military network infrastructure may have on those of civilians, the principle of distinction is of particular importance in evaluating the legality of computer network attacks.

3.1.2.1. The Prohibition of Indiscriminate Attacks

The rather broad principle of distinction is rendered more precisely in the prohibition of indiscriminate attacks enshrined in Article 51(4) Additional

---

79 *Legality of the Threat or Use of Nuclear Weapons (Advisory Opinion)* para. 95.

80 On the evolution of the principle of distinction and its influence on indiscriminate weapons starting with the Lieber Code of 1863 see William H. Boothby *Weapons and the Law of Armed Conflict* (OUP Oxford 2009) pp. 69–85.

Protocol I. These are defined as attacks which are not directed at a specific military objective, employ a method or means of combat which cannot be directed in that way, or the effects of which cannot be limited as required by Additional Protocol I. Ultimately they are of such a nature as to strike military objectives and civilians or civilian objects alike without distinction. As military CNAs qualify as an attack under humanitarian law, this rule clearly also applies to their usage. Whether or not CNAs abide by this regulation cannot be answered in general but depends on the type of means used. Computer viruses in particular tend to be difficult to control considering the intertwinement of military and commercial computer networks.[81] For example in February 2009, computer systems of the French, British and German armed forces were reported to have been massively infected by the so-called 'Win32/conficker' worm, a program setting up a botnet that is believed to be capable of controlling up to nine million computer systems in over 120 States.[82] Although this worm was first detected in commercial systems several months earlier, as it was probably not intentionally directed against military systems, the incident shows how heavily connected military computer systems have become with the public Internet, causing malicious software to be easily disseminated from one network to the other. Even if such programmes were directed only against a single military computer system, it will sometimes be impossible to predict which other systems are linked thereto and to what degree. In these cases it may well be that the effects of the original attack may not be limited only to the target system, but eventually also spread uncontrollably into high-value civilian systems, such as air traffic control, telecommunications infrastructure or power generation facilities. In these cases, the effects of the attack are clearly not limited as required by the Protocol. It thus follows that the use of such a CNA is prohibited as indiscriminate.[83] The launching of a CNA utilising viruses or similar means is thus subject to a heightened review under the precautionary principle. Due regard must be given to the assessment of experts in information

81 Dörmann 'Applicability of the Additional Protocols to Computer Network Attacks' p. 5; similarly Döge 'Cyber Warfare: Challenges for the Applicability of the Traditional Laws of War Regime' p. 494.

82 Wegener 'Der unsichtbare Feind: Die neuen Gefahrenlagen im digitalen Raum' p. 53; Heise Security 'Hunderte Bundeswehr-Rechner von Conficker befallen' (14 February 2009) at <www.heise.de/security/meldung/Hunderte-Bundeswehr-Rechner-von-Conficker-befallen-195953.html> (date accessed 3 January 2012); Gaycken *Cyberwar: Das Internet als Kriegsschauplatz* reports the 2009 botnet 'Mariposa' to even have infected thirteen million systems (at p. 147).

83 Schmitt 'Wired Warfare: Computer Network Attack and Jus in Bello' p. 389; similarly Terry 'The Lawfulness of Attacking Computer Networks in Armed Conflict and in Self-Defense in Periods Short of Armed Conflict: What Are the Tareting Constraints' pp. 86–87; differently: Hanseman 'The Realities and Legalities of Information Warfare' who states that it would be 'unreasonable to prevent commanders from launching … attacks because they cannot be completely certain what the ancillary consequences of the attack will be' (at p. 187).

technology of the possible effects of such attacks and the level of their controllability.[84]

A further specification of the principle of distinction rests in the prohibition of acts or threats of violence the purpose of which is to spread terror among the civilian population stipulated in Article 51(2) Additional Protocol I. As an armed conflict is mostly likely to spread terror among the population in any case, the prohibition only refers to such acts that are intentionally directed at the civilian population without providing for any substantial military advantage.[85] It has been argued that the blocking or shutting-down of computer systems of a company operating on a worldwide basis, such as Google, could be qualified as a prohibited spread of terror.[86] What is meant by this is the denial of services accessible via the Internet which can be considered as being of such a high importance to civilians that their outage could actually spread terror. Such a reading however overstretches the meaning of terror in the sense of Article 51(2) Additional Protocol I. Despite the fact that the goal of humanitarian law is to protect civilians from the effects of armed conflict, its occurrence will in all cases at least cause nuisance to the public in one way or another. Actions that could qualify as a prohibited spreading of terror need to manifest themselves in a more physical way or at least threaten to do so. Otherwise any conflict would qualify as the spreading of terror as there are many side-effects of military operations that do not pose a clear military advantage but cause detriment to the civilian population. This is also supported by State practice and several ICTY judgments in which examples for terrorising the population were always of a physically violent nature such as mass killings of and using snipers on civilians.[87] In any case the targeting of civilian infrastructure such as the computer systems of Google would be an indiscriminate attack, hence there is no reason to strive towards their qualification as a spread of terror.

3.1.2.2. The Wearing of Uniform

Another aspect falling under the scope of distinction is the wearing of uniforms by members of the armed forces. The traditional goal for wearing these was to create a bond between troops and maintain discipline, but also to help identify one's own troops.[88] But in addition to that it also allows the belligerents to easily

---

84 Boothby *Weapons and the Law of Armed Conflict* p. 237.

85 Sandoz, Swinarski & Zimmermann (eds) *Commentary on the Additional Protocols of 8 June 1977 to the Geneva Conventions of 12 August 1949* para. 1940.

86 Döge 'Cyber Warfare: Challenges for the Applicability of the Traditional Laws of War Regime' p. 499.

87 Henckaerts & Doswald-Beck (eds) *Customary International Humanitarian Law Volume I: Rules* Rule 3, p. 11.

88 Dale Stephens & Tristan Skousgaard 'Flags and Uniforms in War' in Rüdiger Wolfrum (ed) *MPEPIL* (OUP Oxford Update 2009) para. 1.

distinguish themselves from the civilian population. However, such attire is not considered the only or a sufficient means of distinction.[89] That is why under codified humanitarian law there is no provision obliging members of armed forces to wear a complete uniform or a definition what such shall comprise.[90] Nevertheless Article 44(7) recognises a 'generally accepted practice of States with respect to the wearing of the uniform by combatants'. As suggested by the reading of Article 44(3) second sentence Additional Protocol I, the carrying of arms openly is the minimum requirement.[91] Although it is common practice to wear uniforms in combat, this is mostly done to provide camouflage and to distinguish friendly troops from enemy combatants. Thus, very few military manuals impose a duty to wear uniform without reservation, especially due to particularities special forces pose to the wearing of uniforms.[92]

It could therefore be assumed that operators performing a CNA need not wear a uniform or carry a distinctive emblem. This presumption gains even more weight when considering that the operator does not need to be active directly on the battlefield. In most instances he will be located in some military complex equipped with the relevant infrastructure and connection to the public Internet. Most likely a direct encounter with an enemy combatant will therefore never occur, not only because of the distance to the target, but also because combatants can in any case not be targeted directly through a CNA. Nevertheless the duty to provide for distinction in these cases obliges the operator to wear a distinctive emblem. This is due to the fact that he cannot carry his weapon openly as for example an infantryman can. The weapon of an operator of CNAs is a computer system equipped with the relevant software. This system is either not portable, but even if so, not identifiable as a weapon due to its dual-use nature. Therefore the only way to provide for distinction in this case actually is the wearing of at least a distinctive emblem, if not a uniform.

3.1.2.3. The Duty to Separate Military from Civilian Targets

From the outset it is clear that technically it is possible to establish military networks which are completely independent from the public networks.[93]

---

89 Toni Pfanner 'Military Uniforms and the Law of War' (2004) 86(853) International Review of the Red Cross p. 123.

90 Stephens & Skousgaard 'Flags and Uniforms in War' para. 4.

91 Bothe, Partsch & Solf *New Rules for Victims of Armed Conflicts: Commentary on the Two 1977 Protocols Additional to the Geneva Conventions of 1949* p. 253.

92 Giving an overview of the different military manuals in this regard: Pfanner 'Military Uniforms and the Law of War' p. 103; for the problems concerning special forces attires see W. Hays Parks 'Special Forces' Wear of Non-Standard Uniforms' in Richard B. Jaques (ed) *Issues in International Law and Military Operations* (Naval War College Newport 2006) p. 90.

93 This is the case only for completely, ie physically, separated networks. So-called virtual private networks cannot be qualified as establishing such an independence, as they still rely on infrastructure external to the network.

However, this is currently not the case in practice. The dependence of military networks on those in the public or private domain is due to practical and economic reasons. In the drafting of Additional Protocol I it was already made clear that the dependence of civilians on modern infrastructure made it impossible to avoid collateral effects.[94] Nevertheless it has been argued that humanitarian law obliges States to distinguish their military networks from that of the public.[95]

Support for this contention could be seen in Article 58(b) Additional Protocol I which provides for the parties to 'avoid locating military objectives within or near densely populated areas' limited though 'to the maximum extent feasible'. This precautionary principle against the effects of attacks is also listed as a rule of customary international law in the relevant ICRC study.[96] As discussed during the deliberations of the responsible working group and as indicated in several declarations by the States Parties to Additional Protocol I, 'feasible' in this regard is to be seen as meaning practicable or practically possible, based on the conditions and situation prevailing at the time.[97] Of concern in this regard was that especially in densely populated areas it would be impossible to separate military objects from civilian ones. This was seen by delegates of such densely populated countries as limiting their right to self-defence and by others as posing an excessive economic burden.

Network infrastructures become more effective the higher their degree of interconnection. At the same time this makes a network less vulnerable, as the disconnection of one system or a whole network can be circumvented by utilising a different network. This is the very essence of the global Internet and effectively forces militaries to also make usage thereof for their communications. This is especially the case for those armies operating abroad. It is practically untenable to oblige States operating on this basis to install their own telecommunications infrastructure from their home base as far as to their foreign bases. The mere possibility of creating a military network independent of

---

94 Bothe, Partsch & Solf *New Rules for Victims of Armed Conflicts: Commentary on the Two 1977 Protocols Additional to the Geneva Conventions of 1949* pp. 371–72.

95 Heintschel von Heinegg 'Informationskrieg und Völkerrecht' p. 151; similarly Döge 'Cyber Warfare: Challenges for the Applicability of the Traditional Laws of War Regime' arguing for an obligation to separate military and civilian networks 'as much as possible' (at p. 495). Geiß & Lahmann 'Cyber Warfare: Applying the Principle of Distinction in an Interconnected Space' at pp. 390–95 investigate several possibilities of deriving an obligation to disentangle military and civilian networks from current international humanitarian law, yet with a negative outcome.

96 Henckaerts & Doswald-Beck (eds) *Customary International Humanitarian Law Volume I: Rules* (Rule 22).

97 Bothe, Partsch & Solf *New Rules for Victims of Armed Conflicts: Commentary on the Two 1977 Protocols Additional to the Geneva Conventions of 1949* pp. 373–74; Sandoz, Swinarski & Zimmermann (eds) *Commentary on the Additional Protocols of 8 June 1977 to the Geneva Conventions of 12 August 1949* paras. 2198 and 2245.

the public networks can thus not be seen as practicable.[98] In that case the military would also be obliged to build its own road networks for transportation in order to not make public roads valid military targets. An obligation to separate military from civil communications networks can thus not be proven to exist.[99]

However, it has been argued that States, which due to this infeasibility cannot separate military from civilian objects, are at least under a duty to protect dual-use networks under their control according to Article 58(c) Additional Protocol I.[100] Control under Article 58 is to be understood in a territorial, hence geographical, sense, applicable to all territory under the effective de facto control of a State Party. Consequently it is also applicable to occupied territory.[101] Therefore the worldwide Internet which is not under the control of one singular State need not be protected by a State utilising it for its armed forces. But in cases where a government takes control over specific networks or computer systems, the relevant resource is under control of the State Party in the sense of Article 58(c). This can be the case during armed conflict in order to safeguard systems or networks of particular importance for the communication of the armed force.[102] In these cases the State would be under the obligation to protect that resource. Despite suggestions to the contrary, this does not include the protection of civilian communications traffic that takes place via this network.[103] Protection is only afforded to the system or network as these are the only objects controlled by the State. Private communications are voluntary acts of those communicating free from any State control. Only the infrastructure needed for these communications is to be protected, which in practice will mostly guarantee these private communications. Nevertheless it makes a difference as a State could after taking control over the infrastructure impose limitations under national law on the infrastructure's usage during armed conflict. Were a State obliged to protect the communications as such, it would be contrary to international law to limit these under national law.

By including a precautionary approach, Article 58(c) obliges States to take precautions even before the outbreak of armed conflict.[104] It has therefore been

98 Similarly: Jensen 'Cyber Warfare and Precautions against the Effects of Attacks' p. 1535.

99 Similarly: Eric Talbot Jensen 'Cyber Attacks: Proportionality and Precautions in Attack' (2013) 89 International Law Studies p. 213.

100 Jensen 'Cyber Warfare and Precautions against the Effects of Attacks' pp. 1552–55.

101 Bothe, Partsch & Solf *New Rules for Victims of Armed Conflicts: Commentary on the Two 1977 Protocols Additional to the Geneva Conventions of 1949* p. 373; Sandoz, Swinarski & Zimmermann (eds) *Commentary on the Additional Protocols of 8 June 1977 to the Geneva Conventions of 12 August 1949* para. 2239.

102 Jensen 'Cyber Warfare and Precautions against the Effects of Attacks' p. 1554.

103 As suggested by Jensen 'Cyber Warfare and Precautions against the Effects of Attacks' p. 1554.

104 For example through the construction of shelters and the establishment of civil defence organisations. Art 58(c) is considered as reflecting customary international law: Henckaerts

suggested that States are furthermore under the obligation to also secure private sector computer systems in peacetime. In this respect it is regarded as insufficient to allow the private sector to merely voluntarily assent to security policies developed by the State as only binding laws would guarantee a comprehensive protection of the civilian information infrastructure.[105] The issuing of laws obliging the private sector to technically secure the information infrastructure is truly a feasible and effective precaution in order to prevent these systems from being the subject of foreign CNAs. As it is already in the self-interest of the private sector to do so, most companies have long since taken the appropriate steps. An obligation for States to enact laws obliging the private sector to do so can however not be read from the wording of Article 58(c). The obligation in its precautionary element applies only to cases where there is sufficient certainty for the civilian objects to come under the control of the State during armed conflict. If a State has for example developed a contingency plan or orders for the case of an outbreak of armed conflict which include taking over control over information infrastructures, there is sufficient certainty. In this case the relevant State is actually obliged by Article 58(c) to develop precautions for these private sector systems even before the outbreak of armed conflict. But this case is the only instance, whereas there are no general obligation for States to precautionarily secure all private systems and infrastructures within their territory.

A related proposition effectuating the separation of military and civilian objects is to make the installation of unique electronic identifiers on computer systems mandatory in order for combatants conducting CNAs to be able to distinguish between valid military objectives and civilian objects.[106] These could be used to identify a system as military or not, comparable to the wearing of uniform or other significant signs or emblems of identification. In this way the computer systems of specially protected objects such as hospitals or constructions containing dangerous forces could also be identified and the respective tools launching an attack modified in such a way as to omit such systems. Again, if put into effect this proposal would make military and civilian systems distinguishable from each other. However, it is first and foremost the obligation of the attacker not to attack indiscriminately.[107] An obligation to mark military objectives would basically deny militaries the possibility of concealing and camouflaging these. The obligation to separate military from

---

& Doswald-Beck (eds) *Customary International Humanitarian Law Volume I: Rules* Rule 22 at pp. 68–71.

105 Jensen 'Cyber Warfare and Precautions against the Effects of Attacks' p. 1561–62; an overview of initiatives in the United States to protect civilian information infrastructure is given at pp. 1555–63.

106 Brown 'A Proposal for an International Convention to Regulate the Use of Information Systems in Armed Conflict' p. 196.

107 See also Art. 57 Additional Protocol I and pp. 210 et seq. above.

civilian objects does not go so far as to supersede requirements of military necessity. This evaluation is already contained in the limitation of the obligation to those actions that are feasible. While unique identifiers may be installed there does not exist an obligation under international law to do so.

3.1.3. *Perfidy and Ruses in Cyber Warfare*

There are those computer network attacks which from a technical standpoint are merely regular communications requests. In the case of distributed denial of service attacks their accumulation leads to the targeted computer system to eventually either shutdown or at least not be able to function in its designated manner.[108] It has been argued that by using such 'innocent requests for information' the attacker would act comparably to a soldier feigning a civilian status on the battlefield, as the attack comes in the disguise of a valid communications request.[109] This would be a prohibited behaviour as Article 37 Additional Protocol I explicitly prohibits the use of perfidy in armed conflict.[110]

Perfidy is defined in Article 37(1) as an act:

> 'inviting the confidence of an adversary to lead him to believe that he is entitled to, or is obliged to accord, protection under the rules of international law applicable in armed conflict, with intent to betray that confidence.'

However, the resort to perfidious acts is explicitly prohibited under the Protocol only in those cases where they are used to kill, injure or capture an adversary. Hence not in operations resulting in a mere damage or destruction of property.[111] At first glance this seems to exclude CNAs due to their 'virtual' character from being able to be qualified as perfidious acts.[112] After all, these can only be directed against computer systems and not directly at combatants. If

---

108 See pp. 26 et seq. above.

109 Shackelford 'From Nuclear War to Net War: Analogizing Cyber Attacks in International Law' pp. 241–42.

110 Perfidy is not prohibited per se, but only such perfidious acts that are the proximate cause of the capture, injury, or killing; Bothe, Partsch & Solf *New Rules for Victims of Armed Conflicts: Commentary on the Two 1977 Protocols Additional to the Geneva Conventions of 1949* p. 204. The rule is also considered as reflecting customary international law: Henckaerts & Doswald-Beck (eds) *Customary International Humanitarian Law Volume I: Rules* pp. 221 et seq. and incorporated in Rule 60 Tallinn Manual. The majority of the group of experts drafting the Manual however opined that customary international law does not encompass a prohibition to capture in a perfidious manner: Schmitt (ed) *Tallinn Manual on the International Law Applicable to Cyber Warfare* p. 181 para. 2.

111 Schmitt (ed) *Tallinn Manual on the International Law Applicable to Cyber Warfare* p. 182 para. 10.

112 Some of the group of experts drafting the Tallinn Manual were of the opinion, that the notion of confidence presupposes direct human involvement and not merely influencing a machine's processes: Schmitt (ed) *Tallinn Manual on the International Law Applicable to Cyber Warfare* p. 182 para. 9. This view must be rejected, as the processes which computers utilise are merely

however a causal link between a perfidious CNA and the killing, injuring or capturing of adversaries can be proven to exist, such action is likewise covered the prohibition.[113] Additionally there is also a more expansive view according to which perfidy is per se prohibited, hence also in cases not resulting in killing, injury or capture, which would lead to the inclusion of more forms of CNAs under the prohibition. This view is however contrary to the clear wording of Article 37(1) Additional Protocol I.[114]

CNAs may therefore potentially be utilised in a perfidious manner. This is not however the case merely due to the fact that CNAs utilise the Internet as a dual-use infrastructure or appear as regular communications. Perfidy involves the creation of confidence in order to gain a military advantage with the intent of later betraying it.[115] However, neither a seemingly regular communication nor the utilisation of the public Internet can build confidence in the potential victim of attack or give evidence as to the intent of the attacker to betray it. Firstly, there is no voluntary act of disguise by the attacker in cases where it is solely the technology dictating how to carry out the attack. If the Internet needs to be utilised for a CNA the attacker has simply no other option than to adhere to this technological necessity. The element of intent is therefore missing. Secondly, treating each communication as separate from each other in the case of distributed denial of service attacks would in fact disrupt a single set of circumstances, as the decisive element in this sort of attack is the preferably large amount of communications sent. The fact that an individual communication does not cause any damage is irrelevant as the massive application thereof no longer appears as a regular communication which could build confidence in the victim. On the contrary, it is a very open attack, the effects of which are noticeable instantly. Consequently, distributed denial of service attacks cannot qualify as perfidious acts despite the fact that their elements are regular communication requests.

Article 37(1)(d) Additional Protocol I further characterises the feigning of a protected status of neutrals or other States not parties to the conflict as perfidy. Likewise, Article 39 Additional Protocol I prohibits the use of flags or military emblems, insignia or uniforms of neutral States during armed conflict, while the use of such of the adverse party is only prohibited while engaging in an attack or other military operations. As mentioned earlier, it is already difficult to ascertain

---

manifestations of a predefined will of humans, such as who is legitimately entitled to access a specific computer resource.

113 For further critique on the restrictive scope of Art. 37 Additional Protocol I: Michael Bothe, Knut Ipsen & Karl Josef Partsch 'Die Genfer Konferenz über humanitäres Völkerrecht: Verlauf und Ergebnisse' (1978) 38 Zeitschrift für ausländisches öffentliches Recht und Völkerrecht p. 25, likewise seeing the possibility of a causal link between preparatory non-prohibited perfidious acts and final non-perfidious combat action assisted hereby.

114 Providing for an overview of the discussion: Vera Rusinova 'Perfidy' in Rüdiger Wolfrum (ed) *MPEPIL* (OUP Oxford Update 2011) paras. 11–13 and 21.

115 See generally Rusinova 'Perfidy' paras. 4–7.

the origin of a CNA, while the practice of criminal individuals in the past has shown that it is fairly easy to further conceal the origin by masking the attack as one originating from a completely different, mostly foreign source. Furthermore, it is conceivable that a State might take advantage of the more developed infrastructure of a neutral third State for launching a CNA. This approach would especially in the case of distributed denial of service attacks even be a necessity in order for the attack to be effective.

The prohibition of perfidy further sets limits on the possibilities of masking an attack as originating from a different actor by prohibiting an attack from being intentionally masked or routed through networks of neutral States in order for the CNA to seemingly originate from that State.[116] The purpose of this rule is inter alia to avoid a spreading of the conflict to neutral States, as the wearing of uniform of a neutral party could lead the adversary to believe the neutral State had given up its neutral status.[117] The view that the prohibition would only encompass the usage of concretely visible objects hence not the merely 'virtual' masking of CNAs to originate from neutral parties can therefore not convince.[118] After all, the danger for neutral parties is equally high in both instances.

A similar situation holds true for one of the major strategies to spread computer viruses, namely the distribution via e-mail attachment or embedded code. As an unwitting assistance of the target system's operator is needed, this type of attack exploits the confidence or naivety of the target computer system's operator. Given that the sender of an e-mail can be easily forged, the attacker has numerous options to mask his true identity. But the prohibition of perfidy limits the choices of forging. Already the explicit prohibition of Article 37(1)(d) Additional Protocol I makes clear that the feigning of the e-mail to originate from a sender that enjoys a protected status under humanitarian law by using protected emblems is prohibited.[119] The feigning of the sender to be a member of the armed forces of the target State bears resemblance to the improper use of the national flag, military insignia or uniform of the enemy which is prohibited by Article 23(f) Hague Regulations and considered customary law. This is the case however only in regard to situations of actual fighting on the battlefield.[120] Communicating false information via a CNO while feigning the status of the enemy is therefore a permitted ruse of war as it cannot be considered part of

116 Doswald-Beck 'Some Thoughts on Computer Network Attack and the International Law of Armed Conflict' p. 171.

117 Bothe, Partsch & Solf *New Rules for Victims of Armed Conflicts: Commentary on the Two 1977 Protocols Additional to the Geneva Conventions of 1949* p. 213.

118 As proposed by Dittmar *Angriffe auf Computernetzwerke: Ius ad bellum und ius in bello* p. 217.

119 Such as feigning an e-mail to originate from the ICRC; Mark R. Shulman 'Discrimination in the Laws of Information Warfare' (1999) 37(3) Columbia Journal of Transnational Law p. 959 and see Rules 62 and 63 Tallinn Manual.

120 Stephens & Skousgaard 'Flags and Uniforms in War' para. 7.

the actual fighting.[121] This approach is also mirrored in Rule 64 Tallinn Manual.[122]

Besides the feigning of protected status through the use of emblems or signs this can also be achieved merely by feigning that the sender to qualifies as a protected person, for example a civilian. In this respect it has been argued that the feigning of an e-mail originating from a software company should not be treated differently than when acting under the false pretence of the ICRC.[123] Others argue that such a company was afforded no protected status under IHL so that the feigning of a non-government source coming from within the region of war would not be prohibited.[124] While the forged sender would invite the confidence of the recipient with an intention of a later betrayal, it would not lead the recipient to accord any special protection to the sender.[125]

The legal problem behind this question lies in the feigning of civilian status. Additional Protocol I is rather clear in this regard by explicitly listing the feigning of civilian, non-combatant status as an example of perfidy in Article 37(1)(c). Concurrently, Article 44(3) Additional Protocol I obliges combatants to 'distinguish themselves from the civilian population while they are engaged in an attack or in a military operation preparatory to an attack'. In addition, the exception in Article 44(3) second sentence, which allows a deviation from the obligation of combatants to distinguish themselves from civilians as long as they carry their arms openly during combat, is not applicable. Firstly, operators of CNOs are technically not able to carry their arms openly. Secondly, this exception was primarily introduced as a reaction to guerrilla fighters, and to resistance and liberation movements fighting in effectively occupied territories.[126] Therefore it is generally understood as applying only to such fighters but not to regular armed forces and only in occupied territories.[127]

---

121 Similarly Dittmar *Angriffe auf Computernetzwerke: Ius ad bellum und ius in bello* p. 215.

122 Rule 64 reads: 'It is prohibited to make use of flags, military emblems, insignia, or uniforms of the enemy while visible to the enemy during an attack, including a cyber attack'. A minority was of the opinion that the limitation of visibility should not apply, yet this view does not take into account the requirement of a connection to the battlefield: Schmitt (ed) *Tallinn Manual on the International Law Applicable to Cyber Warfare* p. 189 para. 4.

123 Shulman 'Discrimination in the Laws of Information Warfare' p. 959.

124 As put forward both by Brown and Wingfield, strongly opposing the assessment of Shulman; Brown 'A Proposal for an International Convention to Regulate the Use of Information Systems in Armed Conflict' pp. 204–05 and Wingfield *The Law of Information Conflict: National Security Law in Cyberspace* p. 169.

125 Brown 'A Proposal for an International Convention to Regulate the Use of Information Systems in Armed Conflict' p. 205 at fn. 115.

126 Sandoz, Swinarski & Zimmermann (eds) *Commentary on the Additional Protocols of 8 June 1977 to the Geneva Conventions of 12 August 1949* para. 1692; Bothe, Partsch & Solf *New Rules for Victims of Armed Conflicts: Commentary on the Two 1977 Protocols Additional to the Geneva Conventions of 1949* p. 253.

127 As cited in Bothe, Partsch & Solf *New Rules for Victims of Armed Conflicts: Commentary on the Two 1977 Protocols Additional to the Geneva Conventions of 1949* at p. 253, referring to the Conférence Diplomatique sur la Réaffirmation et le Développement du Droit International

At a first glance, the feigning of a sender of an e-mail as coming from a civilian will seemingly always qualify as an act of perfidy, since Article 37(1)(c) explicitly lists this behaviour as an example. This assumption, however, fails to take into account the purpose of the prohibition on feigning a protected status. If this were a permitted ruse of war, disguised combatants could not be distinguished from civilians, making the latter generally fall under the suspicion of being a combatant. Ultimately this would lead to an erosion of the principle of distinction which lies at the very heart of humanitarian law. An e-mail that appears to be from a civilian does not however implicate that person into the battlefield at all. The response of the recipient to a malicious e-mail is to not accept or open it in the future, but not to kill or injure the sender. The protected status of civilians is therefore not endangered by forging e-mails to appear to emanate from this protected class of persons. This especially holds true in cases where the feigned name is fictitious. Feigning a civilian sender for the transmission of malicious e-mails hence merely belongs to the expressly permitted ruses of war.[128]

The use of so-called Trojan horse software against military systems during armed conflict similarly qualifies as a legal ruse of war.[129] The same also applies to modifications of enemy databases containing information about the adversary's force strength, location or movement, just as the transmission of false orders to enemy forces.[130] On the other hand, modifying an enemy targeting database in such a way as to make military objectives appear as objects with a protected status, such as for instance hospitals, would be a case of prohibited perfidy.[131]

It is common knowledge that almost any software even after its release contains security vulnerabilities which are gradually discovered and repaired via

---

Humanitaire Applicable dans les Conflits Armés (1974–1977 Genève) *Official Records of the Diplomatic Conference of the Reaffirmation and Development of International Humanitarian Law Applicable in Armed Conflicts. Geneva, 1974 1977* (Federal Political Department Bern) Doc/III/SR 55 paras. 12 and 54; Sandoz, Swinarski & Zimmermann (eds) *Commentary on the Additional Protocols of 8 June 1977 to the Geneva Conventions of 12 August 1949* para. 1698. This leaves a marginal number of instances in which CNAs are actually capable of being encompassed by the exception. However the missing capability of carrying the arms openly prevents the exception from being applicable in the first place.

128 Ruses of war are defined by Art. 37(2) Additional Protocol I as 'acts which are intended to mislead an adversary or to induce him to act recklessly', while not inviting 'the confidence of an adversary with respect to protection under that law'. See also Knut Ipsen 'Ruses of War' in Rüdiger Wolfrum (ed) *MPEPIL* (OUP Oxford Update 2010) and Rule 61 Tallinn Manual.

129 Joyner & Lotrionte 'Information Warfare as International Coercion: Elements of a Legal Framework' p. 859.

130 Michael Schmitt, Heather Harrison & Thomas Wingfield 'Computers and War: The Legal Battlespace' (2004) at <http://ihl.ihlresearch.org/_data/n_0002/resources/live/schmittetal.pdf> (date accessed 4 June 2012) p. 10; Dittmar *Angriffe auf Computernetzwerke: Ius ad bellum und ius in bello* p. 215.

131 Blaise Cathcart 'Legal Dimensions of Special Forces and Informations Operations' in Terry D. Gill & Dieter Fleck (eds) *The Handbook of the International Law of Military Operations* (OUP Oxford 2010) p. 412.

updates. In most cases these vulnerabilities are unintentional flaws in the programme's code. But software developers are time and again under the suspicion of intentionally including backdoors into their products in order to provide for access of intelligence services onto systems running these programmes.[132] It has been argued that such actions could be qualified as perfidious behaviour, as they were a deliberate breach of faith and a calculated violation of trust.[133] However, this tactic again only qualifies as a ruse of war. If a backdoor is voluntarily, or due to legal obligations, installed by the developer and later during armed conflict exploited by the foreign armed forces or intelligence service, there again is no feigning of protected status that would lead to endangering protected civilians. Again the reaction of the attacked would be to remove the malware from his systems and not to attack the software vendor as such. Additionally, in these cases the attacker merely has the intention of making the buyer believe the obtained software is secure and free of backdoors but not that the software as such is given a protected status.

Belligerents are consequently afforded considerable freedom when feigning sender names of e-mails or using backdoors of programmes installed on target systems. Only in cases where the feigning puts protected persons or neutral States in danger of being subject to attack are these operations to be qualified as prohibited perfidy. This is the case for those computer network attacks against which the defensive reaction is a counterattack, as here the feigned person or State is in danger of being drawn into the conflict.

3.1.4. *The Principle of Proportionality in Cyber Warfare*

The principle of proportionality known under general international law also exists in humanitarian law. Inter alia it is codified in Article 51(5)(b) Additional Protocol I which prohibits 'an attack which may be expected to cause incidental loss of civilian life, injury to civilians, damage to civilian objects, or a combination thereof, which would be excessive in relation to the concrete and direct military advantage anticipated'. It has also acquired the status of customary international law and is referred to in Rule 51 Tallinn Manual.[134]

In the proportionality test of Article 51(5)(b) the principle of humanity is balanced against military necessity. As a result civilian casualties can actually be lawful if outweighed by the military advantage of the attack.[135] The evaluation of

---

132 Chinese and Israeli companies are denounced in this regard by Rieger 'Angriff ist besser als Verteidigung'.

133 Streltsov 'International Information Security: Description and Legal Aspects' p. 12.

134 Henckaerts & Doswald-Beck (eds) *Customary International Humanitarian Law Volume I: Rules* Rule 14, pp. 46–50; Geiß 'Land Warfare' para. 15.

135 Dittmar *Angriffe auf Computernetzwerke: Ius ad bellum und ius in bello* p. 259; Dominik Steiger 'Civilian Objects' in Rüdiger Wolfrum (ed) *MPEPIL* (OUP Oxford Update 2011) para. 9; James H. Doyle 'Computer Networks, Proportionality, and Military Operations' in

the anticipated military advantage – which in any case is never allowed to be insignificant – and the expected civilian casualties necessarily takes place in advance of the attack. The yardstick in this regard is not the actual result of the attack but the objective expectation of a reasonable commander based on information reasonably available at the time of the attack.[136] Thus it is not merely the isolated attack that needs to be considered but also its role for a broader strategic purpose which can consist of several operations.[137]

Despite all this it is clear that an assessment necessarily carries a subjective element, as there is no mathematical formula or other objective standard for the appraisal of the relation of the expected collateral damage as excessive to the military advantage anticipated.[138] In the end it is a decision to be made on a case-by-case basis by commanders acting in good faith. In this regard it is especially the precautionary principle of Article 57 Additional Protocol I that again merits consideration.[139]

In the case of CNAs negative effects on civilians will mostly concentrate on damages to civilian objects, namely civilian computer systems ranging from individual systems to whole information infrastructures belonging to the private sector. Planners of CNAs must therefore especially take into consideration the interdependencies of military targets with civilian systems. This includes the evaluation of potential cascading effects of an attack.[140] Particular care needs to be given to dual-use targets such as communications infrastructures or the national power grid. In these cases the mere loss of functionality of civilian systems also needs to be considered in the proportionality test.[141] However, any loss of functionality of a networked device is not to be equated with damage to it. From the outset it is clear that the civilian population will in all cases of armed conflict have to bear certain inconveniences as an indirect result of the lawful

---

Michael N. Schmitt & Brian T. O'Donnell (eds) *Computer Network Attack and International Law* (Naval War College Newport 2002) p. 156.

136 Steiger 'Civilian Objects' para. 9; Greenwood 'Legal Issues Regarding Explosive Remnants of War (UN Doc CCW/GGE/I/WP.10)' para. 23.

137 Doswald-Beck 'Some Thoughts on Computer Network Attack and the International Law of Armed Conflict' p. 170; and see the relevant State practice cited in Henckaerts & Doswald-Beck (eds) *Customary International Humanitarian Law Volume I: Rules* p. 49.

138 Geiß 'Land Warfare' para. 29; Nils Melzer 'Civilian Participation in Armed Conflict' in Rüdiger Wolfrum (ed) *MPEPIL* (OUP Oxford Update 2010) para. 9; Schmitt 'Wired Warfare: Computer Network Attack and Jus in Bello' p. 392.

139 After all, the wording of both principles is identical by intention of the Drafting Committee: Sandoz, Swinarski & Zimmermann (eds) *Commentary on the Additional Protocols of 8 June 1977 to the Geneva Conventions of 12 August 1949* para. 1976.

140 See generally Jensen 'Unexpected Consequences from Knock-on Effects: A Different Standard for Computer Network Operations?' pp. 1145–88; Dittmar *Angriffe auf Computernetzwerke: Ius ad bellum und ius in bello* p. 251; Schmitt 'Wired Warfare: Computer Network Attack and Jus in Bello' pp. 390–93; Geiß & Lahmann 'Cyber Warfare: Applying the Principle of Distinction in an Interconnected Space' pp. 395 et seq.

141 Geiß & Lahmann 'Cyber Warfare: Applying the Principle of Distinction in an Interconnected Space' p. 397.

targeting of military objectives.[142] Thus only grave consequences inflicted upon the civilian population through the loss of functionality will play a role in the proportionality test.

Conversely, CNAs may provide for a less invasive measure than conventional weapons as the same result can be achieved by a deactivation of the target without necessarily destroying the object and its surroundings. In this respect CNAs have the same beneficial potential as precision munitions.[143] Situations may therefore arise in which CNAs would have to be given precedence over conventional methods of warfare due to reasons of proportionality. In the end it is again the employment of the weapon that is crucial in the assessment of the proportionality of an attack. The discovery and further development of computer network attacks as a means and method of warfare has nevertheless widened the range of possibilities available to military decision makers. From a humanitarian perspective CNAs can consequently be considered an advancement.

3.2. VALID TARGETS OF COMPUTER NETWORK ATTACKS, THEIR CONTROL AND ABANDONMENT

3.2.1. The Military Objectives of Cyber Warfare

The principle of distinction makes it necessary to define which targets may lawfully be attacked by whatever means of warfare including computer network attacks. In Additional Protocol I this is done by firstly defining which targets are exempt from attack – civilians and civilian objects – as the instrument has as its goal the protection of these regular victims of armed conflict. A similar approach is utilised in Rules 37–39 Tallinn Manual. Historically, the rule of only attacking military objectives was created as a reaction to the developments in the field of warfare. Through the emergence of bombers and long-range weapons, it became easier to reach distant targets whilst their reconnaissance became somewhat more difficult, which made the sole prohibition on attacking undefended towns insufficient.[144] Nevertheless it is an old principle of humanitarian law that the only legitimate aim of warfare is to weaken the military forces of the enemy.[145]

---

142 Schmitt (ed) *Tallinn Manual on the International Law Applicable to Cyber Warfare* p. 160 para. 5. For the discussion surrounding the qualification of interference with the functionality of an object as a damage see pp. 205 et seq. above.

143 Schmitt 'Wired Warfare: Computer Network Attack and Jus in Bello' p. 394; Dittmar *Angriffe auf Computernetzwerke: Ius ad bellum und ius in bello* p. 251.

144 Marco Sassòli 'Military Objectives' in Rüdiger Wolfrum (ed) *MPEPIL* (OUP Oxford Update 2007) para. 2.

145 Sassòli 'Military Objectives' para. 31. This principle was first codified in the St. Petersburg Declaration of 1868, but earlier elements can already be found in 500 BCE in Sun Tzu *The Art of War*, where it is stipulated that '[g]enerally in war the best policy is to take a state intact; to

Article 52(2) Additional Protocol I defines military objectives as:

> 'objects which by their nature, location, purpose or use make an effective contribution to military action and whose total or partial destruction, capture or neutralization, in the circumstances ruling at the time, offers a definite military advantage.'

Thus, any object – with the exception of certain specially protected objects[146] – can turn into a military objective once it fulfils the two-tiered test of Article 52(2) Additional Protocol I. Firstly, it must make an effective contribution to military action of the enemy, secondly its destruction must offer a definitive military advantage. Both requirements must be fulfilled cumulatively. The precondition is that the person contemplating the attack in his particular circumstances and with the information available to him reasonably believes that the requirements of the two-tiered test of Article 52(2) are fulfilled.[147] The definition which is widely reflected in military manuals of non-States Parties to Additional Protocol I is considered customary international law.[148]

However, the further definition of the terms 'effective contribution' and 'definite military advantage' has proven more controversial. According to a wider reading the definition provides for 'economic objects of the enemy that indirectly but effectively support and sustain the enemy's war-fighting capability' to also be lawfully attackable.[149] This wider reading is restated in the United

ruin it is inferior to this' and 'to subdue the enemy without fighting is the acme of skill' (at Chapter III).

146 Cf Arts. 53–56 Additional Protocol I protecting cultural objects and places of worship, objects indispensible for the civilian population as well as works and installations containing dangerous forces.As these special protections are generally afforded during international armed conflict they must also be respected during cyber warfare. The examples of opening the floodgates of dams and dykes which are often drawn upon in the discourse of cyber warfare are thus illegal in the most cases (Art. 56(2)(a) Additional Protocol I contains an exception for dams and dykes under certain circumstances). See already Dittmar *Angriffe auf Computernetzwerke: Ius ad bellum und ius in bello* p. 262. However, this rule does not reflect customary international law according to the respective ICRC study: Henckaerts & Doswald-Beck (eds) *Customary International Humanitarian Law Volume I: Rules* (Rule 42). Rule 80 Tallinn Manual adopts a view similar to the ICRC study, namely that only 'particular care' must be taken when attacking such installations. Generally, the Internet as such cannot qualify as indispensible for the civilian population. This could only be the case if other infrastructure indispensible to the population would solely function when connected thereto: Schmitt (ed) *Tallinn Manual on the International Law Applicable to Cyber Warfare* p. 227.

147 *Prosecutor v Galić (Judgment and Opinion)* IT-98-29-T (5 December 2003) para. 51; Michael Schmitt 'Targeting in Operational Law' in Terry D. Gill & Dieter Fleck (eds) *The Handbook of the International Law of Military Operations* (OUP Oxford 2010) p. 255.

148 Henckaerts & Doswald-Beck (eds) *Customary International Humanitarian Law Volume I: Rules* p. 30; *Partial Award: Western Front, Aerial Bombardment and Related Claims Eritrea's Claims 1, 3, 5, 9–13, 14, 21, 25 & 26 between the State of Eritrea and the Federal Democratic Republic of Ethiopia* Eritrea-Ethiopia Claims Commission (19 December 2005) (2006) 45 ILM 396 para. 113; Sassòli 'Military Objectives' para. 8.

149 As argued in the US Department of the Navy *The Commander's Handbook on the Law of Naval Operations (July 2007 Edition NWP 1-14M)* (Navy Warfare Library 2007) para. 8.2.5.

States Military Commission Instruction No. 2, in which the definition of a military objective requires merely a military advantage, thus omitting the 'definite' limitation of Article 52 Additional Protocol I.[150] Thus an object's potential for military usage is already seen as sufficient to qualify it a military objective, if the likelihood of military use is reasonable and not remote in the context of the particular conflict under way, even if it is currently used solely for civilian purposes.[151]

This expansive view cannot be shared. The rebuttable presumption of Article 52(3) Additional Protocol I stipulates that in cases of doubt the usage of a civilian object is to be presumed not to make an effective contribution to military action. As military usage is not confined to weaponry only, most objects have the potential of eventually being used by the military at some point in order to make an effective contribution. The wording in the definition of military objectives that the object should 'make' (in the present tense) an effective contribution likewise points into that direction by excluding possible future military uses of an object.[152] A different interpretation would strongly delimit the protection of civilian objects in a manner contrary to Article 52(3). Objects making an effective contribution can therefore only be those that are directly or intended to be used by the armed forces, such as weapons, equipment, transports, fortifications and the like. By requiring a definite military advantage, Article 52 Additional Protocol I prohibits launching an attack which only offers potential or indeterminate advantages, thus according to the principle of limited warfare.[153]

As long as certain hard- and software may be destined only for military purposes, for example those that are specifically used only by the military, such objects qualify as a military objective even before their delivery. Some of these items are explicitly listed in the Munitions List of the Wassenaar Arrangement, an arms control regime.[154] However, most soft- and hardware produced by the private sector is of such a generic nature that it is usable by the civilian and military sector alike. For these so-called dual-use objects it is not their designation but application by the military which renders them military

---

150 US Department of Defense 'Military Commission Instruction No. 2' (30 April 2003) at <www.fas.org/irp/doddir/dod/milcominstno2.pdf> (date accessed 7 January 2012) p. 3.

151 Schmitt 'Wired Warfare: Computer Network Attack and Jus in Bello' p. 385.

152 Sassòli 'Military Objectives' para. 15; Sandoz, Swinarski & Zimmermann (eds) *Commentary on the Additional Protocols of 8 June 1977 to the Geneva Conventions of 12 August 1949* para. 2022.

153 Sandoz, Swinarski & Zimmermann (eds) *Commentary on the Additional Protocols of 8 June 1977 to the Geneva Conventions of 12 August 1949* paras. 2020–24; Wolfrum 'The Attack of September 11, 2001, the Wars against the Taliban and Iraq: Is there a Need to Reconsider International Law on the Recourse to Force and the Rules in Armed Conflict?' pp. 47–49.

154 The Wassenaar Arrangement on Export Controls for Conventional Arms and Dual-Use Goods and Technologies (as of 3 December 2008) <www.wassenaar.org/controllists/index.html> (23 September 2009).

objectives, as also stipulated in Rule 39 Tallinn Manual. In this regard, objects of a dual-use character are subject to the same two-tiered test of Article 52(2) and may thus become a military objective despite their use by civilians. Civilian use of such dual-use goods will nevertheless have to be considered in the planning of an attack under the proportionality and precautionary principles.[155]

Further, only material, tangible things are considered to qualify as a military objective but not notional targets such as 'civilian morale' or 'victory'.[156] This is of importance insofar as otherwise civilian objects could be attacked in order to indirectly shatter the military objective of civilian morale. This does not conflict with the general possibility of conducting CNAs against computer systems. While one can argue that the initial operation only manipulates 'immaterial' data, it is the result of this action which shows the required tangible effect. Only a minority of the group of experts drafting the Tallinn Manual understands data to per se qualify as an object. The majority was of the contrary opinion, with the caveat that once affecting the functionality of computer systems, the alteration of data could also qualify as an attack.[157] The latter majority opinion leads to the same result as already criticised in connection to the understanding of 'cyber attack' under Rule 30 Tallinn Manual,[158] namely the possibility of targeting civilian datasets independent of their value or import as long as this does not affect the functionality of the computer system. According to this understanding, social networks could be targeted even if these were not utilised for military purposes.[159] This can similarly not be supported as it hollows out the principle of distinction and enables belligerents to intentionally draw civilians into the conflict.

The public Internet in its quality as an infrastructure is to be treated as analogous to the power grid or a public telecommunications network. The dual-use character of those computer systems and the software running thereon is undisputed at least in industrialised countries, where the military makes heavy use of this infrastructure. It is estimated for example that 98% of US government communications are routed via the privately owned and operated networks, including intelligence and information reports or military orders.[160] The possibility of effectively cutting off all Internet connections in a single country was demonstrated by the Mubarak regime in Egypt in 2011 as a reaction to

---

155 Sassòli 'Military Objectives' para. 13; similarly also Geiß & Lahmann 'Cyber Warfare: Applying the Principle of Distinction in an Interconnected Space' pp. 395 et seq.

156 Sassòli 'Military Objectives' para. 9.

157 Schmitt (ed) *Tallinn Manual on the International Law Applicable to Cyber Warfare* p. 127 para. 5.

158 See the discussion concerning the qualification of CNOs as an attack in the sense of humanitarian law at pp. 205 et seq. above.

159 As implied in Schmitt (ed) *Tallinn Manual on the International Law Applicable to Cyber Warfare* p. 135 para. 4.

160 Jensen 'Cyber Warfare and Precautions against the Effects of Attacks' p. 1542.

growing protests in the country.[161] While this was done by simply ordering the Egyptian Internet service providers to shut down their networks, a CNA could also achieve similar effects against the will of the respective providers. Hence these dual-use communications networks may qualify as valid military objectives if their destruction results in a definitive military advantage. The structure of the Internet poses a significant problem in this regard, however. The outage of singular systems does not result in the total breakdown of the Internet, as smaller deficiencies are automatically counterbalanced by the re-routing of traffic along functioning routes. A CNA that is intended to cause a breakdown of Internet connectivity in a whole country must therefore target those main systems vital to the regional Internet in the targeted area such as Internet exchange points. Individual dual-use systems, the outage of which can easily be balanced, do not therefore qualify as military objectives, as their outage does not bring about a military advantage.

3.2.2. *Controlling Military Objectives via Cyber Warfare*

It has been shown that belligerent computer systems can qualify as military objectives. Especially in the case of CNAs the latter need not be neutralised or even destroyed but can also be controlled, for example when utilising so-called Trojan horse programmes.[162] This could be done in order to further attack other such systems, or to take advantage of the system's functions for the attacker's own use. The question in this regard is whether such a hijacking or 'virtual occupation' of a belligerent system could have further legal limitations than those included in the rules on targeting. A comparison could be drawn with traditional occupation by military land forces. Were the regime of occupation to also apply to the control of belligerent computer systems this would have grave consequences for the attacker, such as for example the extraterritorial applicability of the human rights treaties it is a party to.[163] This is especially relevant for States Parties to human rights treaties providing for a court system featuring the possibility of individual complaints by those negatively affected by the takeover of a system.

The existence of a traditional belligerent occupation consists of two conditions, the first being that the ousted government is unable to exercise its authority in the given area. The second condition is disputed: for some, the foreign army must have actually substituted its own authority for that of the ousted government, while for others the army's potential ability to do so would

---

161 Ryan Singel 'Egypt Shut Down Its Net With a Series of Phone Calls' (28 January 2011) at <www.wired.com/threatlevel/2011/01/egypt-isp-shutdown/> (date accessed 7 January 2012).

162 On Trojan horse software see p. 27 above.

163 The applicability of human rights treaties in occupied territories is admittedly disputed inter alia by Israel and the United States; see Eyal Benvenisti 'Occupation, Belligerent' in Rüdiger Wolfrum (ed) *MPEPIL* (OUP Oxford Update 2009) para. 13.

be sufficient.[164] However, this dispute is irrelevant with regard to the situation at hand. For a situation to be qualified as an occupation, the computer systems and networks of a belligerent would have to be of such a great importance that losing control thereof would likewise cause the loss of authority in the respective area by the government. At least today, there is no such situation imaginable, as public authority is not mainly exercised via computer networks. This is also rather unrealistic in the future, as the enforcement of laws will in the end always have to rely on physical force executed via the relevant authorities such as the police. In conclusion, a 'virtual occupation' cannot be treated as analogous to a traditional belligerent occupation making the respective regime inapplicable.

3.2.3. *The Clearance of Remnants Caused by Cyber Warfare*

After termination of an armed conflict large territories have often been left contaminated by land mines and explosive or other remnants of war. The situation can be similar in respect of malware utilised in CNAs that also remains on the infected computer systems after termination of armed conflict. All of these means of warfare share the similarity of having a high potential of indiscriminate effects if not used in a controlled manner. In an effort to diminish the dangers to civilians several instruments have been adopted since the 1980s. These are the Protocol II to the Conventional Weapons Convention on Prohibitions or Restrictions on the Use of Mines, Booby-Traps and Other Devices (amended in 1996), the Convention on the Prohibition of the Use, Stockpiling, Production and Transfer of Anti-Personnel Mines and on Their Destruction and the 2003 Protocol V to the Conventional Weapons Convention on Explosive Remnants of War.[165]

The common ground of these instruments is the goal of limiting the negative effects of the relevant subject matter to civilians, especially also after termination of armed conflict. For example under the Amended Protocol II to the Conventional Weapons Convention a party that has laid mines in areas over

164 The first view is shared by the ICJ in *Armed Activities on the Territory of the Congo (Democratic Republic of the Congo v Uganda)* at paras. 173 and 177; the second view has been supported by Judge Kooijmans in his Separate Opinion to the case, as well as in *Tzemel Adv v Minister of Defence and Commander of the Antzar Camp* Israel Supreme Court (1983) 13 Israel Yearbook on Human Rights 360; see also generally Benvenisti 'Occupation, Belligerent' paras. 4–5 and Adam Roberts 'Occupation, Military, Termination of' in Rüdiger Wolfrum (ed) *MPEPIL* (OUP Oxford Update 2009) para. 4–5.

165 Convention on the Prohibition of the Use, Stockpiling, Production and Transfer of Anti-Personnel Mines and on Their Destruction (concluded 18 September 1997, entered into force 1 March 1999) 2056 UNTS 211; Protocol on Prohibitions or Restrictions on the Use of Mines, Booby-Traps and Other Devices as Amended on 3 May 1996 (adopted 3 May 1996, entered into force 3 December 1998) 2048 UNTS 93; Protocol on Explosive Remnants of War to the Convention on Prohibitions or Restrictions on the Use of Certain Conventional Weapons which may be deemed to be Excessively Injurious or to have Indiscriminate Effects (Protocol V) (adopted 28 November 2003, entered into force 12 November 2006) UN Doc CCW/MSP/2203/2.

which it no longer exercises control must provide to the party in control of the area technical and material assistance necessary for mine removal.[166] A fortiori the party is obliged to reveal where mines have been placed. The Anti-Personal Mines Ban Treaty introduces the most extensive framework with a general prohibition on using, acquiring, developing or producing such devices, limited however to anti-personnel mines.

The Protocol on Explosive Remnants of War introduced obligations in post-conflict situations regarding the clearance, removal or destruction of conventional munitions containing explosives that were either abandoned by the party using them or remained unexploded. Remnants of war in general refer to the residuum left in a territory after the end of an armed conflict, while the Protocol specifically excludes land mines from its scope.[167] Therefore only those explosive remnants are included which involuntarily remain dangerous, mostly due to technical insufficiencies, as for example submunitions of cluster bombs.

There are several means of cyber warfare which can be compared to these explosive remnants of war. For example there exists malware which is installed on belligerent systems with the aim of controlling these for a longer period of time. If not properly removed beforehand, this type of malware might sustain the possibility of remote control even in post-conflict situations. Then there are those types which are triggered by a specific event or command, often referred to as logic-bombs. In both cases the danger exists in the potential access of third actors to the programmes and the infected systems. Both these examples feature malware that is intentionally designed in such a way as to be accessible or dormant for a longer period of time. Their functionality also after the end of an armed conflict is thus not the consequence of a flawed design, but intentional. As a consequence, this kind of malware resembles land mines rather more closely than munitions that fail to explode. Then there are those CNAs which utilise computer viruses that spread from one system to another with the danger of doing so uncontrollably. If this spread continues especially also after termination of the armed conflict, they more closely resemble munitions that fail to explode due to the element of uncontrollability.

In comparison to land mines or explosive remnants of war, treaty law does not impose an obligation on the State which causes cyber remnants of war to remove them after the conflict from systems it does not control, nor does it require it to pay the cost of doing so. And from the outset it is clear that malware does not fall under the scope of any of the above-mentioned instruments which due to conclusive definitions are restricted in their applicability. However, where a party to the conflict has utilised CNAs indiscriminately, or in any other

166 Art. 10(3) amended Protocol II to the Conventional Weapons Convention; Knut Dörmann 'Land Mines' in Rüdiger Wolfrum (ed) *MPEPIL* (OUP Oxford Update 2011) para. 33.

167 Gabriella Blum 'Remnants of War' in Rüdiger Wolfrum (ed) *MPEPIL* (OUP Oxford Update 2010) paras. 1–2.

manner violating humanitarian law, it is obliged to make reparation irrespective of the weapon used according to Article 91 Additional Protocol I.[168] The obligation primarily consists of restoring the situation existing prior to the violation, as monetary compensation is only due if the case so demands.[169] For the case of cyber remnants of war, this implies the removal of the malware or cooperation and assistance therein.

More problematic is the question of obligations concerning the clearance of remnants that arise from an attack in compliance with humanitarian law. Outside the scope of the specific regimes on land mines or explosive remnants of war, there exists no obligation for States to remove the munitions it used or to pay for this.[170] And while the ICRC study on customary international law has identified the customary rule that after termination of active hostilities 'a party to the conflict which has used landmines must remove or otherwise render them harmless to civilians, or facilitate their removal',[171] this is not applicable to cyber remnants of war, as a customary rule cannot be applied by analogy to similar circumstances.[172] Furthermore, the exclusion of anti-vehicle mines from most restrictions of the relevant treaties shows their intended limitation to the subject matters explicitly listed therein. And by introducing obligations concerning the clearing and reporting of land mines and explosive remnants of war, the State parties implicitly denied the existence of prior customary law in this respect. Therefore there is no obligation of clearance in the case of cyber remnants of war which have emerged from a permissible employment of CNAs during armed conflict.

The result is nevertheless more tenable than was the case with anti-personnel land mines before the creation of the relevant treaties. The clearing of infected computer systems is much easier to facilitate than the complex, dangerous and costly clearing of explosive remnants, which has led large territories to be contaminated for decades. Even the reporting by the source State on how to detect and remove the malware will be sufficient in most cases for the target State to be able to clear its systems of malware. Providing this information for the State of origin is neither costly nor dangerous, meaning that it is realistic to include appropriate passages in peace treaties or UN Security Council resolutions. In

168 This rule is also considered reflecting customary international law: Henckaerts & Doswald-Beck (eds) *Customary International Humanitarian Law Volume I: Rules* Rule 150 at p. 537.

169 Sandoz, Swinarski & Zimmermann (eds) *Commentary on the Additional Protocols of 8 June 1977 to the Geneva Conventions of 12 August 1949* para. 3655.

170 Greenwood 'Legal Issues Regarding Explosive Remnants of War (UN Doc CCW/GGE/I/WP.10)' para. 27.

171 Henckaerts & Doswald-Beck (eds) *Customary International Humanitarian Law Volume I: Rules* Rule 83 at pp. 285–86; Dörmann 'Land Mines' para. 11.

172 Wolff Heintschel von Heinegg 'Die weiteren Quellen des Völkerrechts' in Knut Ipsen (ed) *Völkerrecht* (Beck München 2004) pp. 245–46; differently Silja Vöneky 'Analogy in International Law' in Rüdiger Wolfrum (ed) *MPEPIL* (OUP Oxford Update 2008) who does not see the will of the subjects of international law as decisive for the creation of customary international law (at para. 20).

cases where the malware belongs to its regular arsenal a State will however be more reluctant to disclose removal tools as these could easily spread, thereby making the malware useless for a future CNA even in a different armed conflict.

3.3. THE STATUS OF ACTORS IN CYBER WARFARE

Next to military objectives, combatants are the only other permissible target for an attack.[173] Furthermore, civilians may likewise be a valid target of attack despite not qualifying as combatants. This is the case as long as they directly participate in hostilities, thereby losing their protected status. Combatant status is further of importance as regards the right to participate in armed conflict. Only when given this right may a person perform actions which during peacetime would qualify as a punishable offence, limiting the prosecution of actions by combatants to violations of humanitarian law. For the case of cyber warfare the question arises as to how persons performing CNAs in whatever capacity shall be categorised in order for them to be a valid target of attack or legitimately take part in hostilities and qualifying as prisoners of war if captured.

3.3.1. *Combatants in Cyber Warfare*

3.3.1.1. Regular Members of Armed Forces

Combatants are generally defined by Articles 3 Hague Regulations and 43(2) Additional Protocol I as members of the armed forces of a party to an international armed conflict and in this particular instance also referred to as de iure combatants. The question of combatancy is therefore at first linked to the definition of armed forces. Generally States have the discretion to organise the internal structure of their armed forces as they wish. However, whatever this internal organisation may be, what is decisive for humanitarian law is only the definition under international law. Article 43(1) Additional Protocol I defines armed forces as consisting of:

> 'all organized armed forces, groups and units which are under a command responsible to that Party for the conduct of its subordinates, even if that Party is represented by a government or an authority not recognized by an adverse Party. Such armed forces shall be subject to an internal disciplinary system which, inter alia, shall enforce compliance with the rules of international law applicable in armed conflict.'

---

[173] For some, combatants also fall under the category of military objectives: Anthony P.V. Rogers *Law on the Battlefield* (Manchester University Press Manchester 2004) p. 63; Yoram Dinstein *The Conduct of Hostilities under the Law of International Armed Conflict* (CUP Cambridge 2010) p. 92. This classification does ultimately not make any difference however and will therefore not be considered here.

Hence police or paramilitary forces may also belong to the armed forces under the scope of humanitarian law, be it through a formal act under national law, or by fulfilling the criteria of Article 43 Additional Protocol I. Under the manifold different branches within the armed forces one can roughly distinguish between persons that actually take an active part in hostilities and those which give assistance in one way or the other while refraining from engaging in combat action. However, today it is generally understood that all members of the armed forces qualify as combatants, irrespective of their individual function – with certain exceptions for specially protected persons such as medical and religious personnel.[174] They may thus be targeted and are afforded the privileges just as any other combatant, for example prisoner of war status once captured. These interrelated definitions of armed forces and combatants under Article 43 Additional Protocol I are also considered to reflect customary international law.[175] Individuals may not become combatants of their own volition, but must belong to a group belonging to a party to the international armed conflict.[176] Personnel performing CNAs or providing assistance therein – called 'information warriors' by some[177] – while being members of the armed forces of a party to the conflict are thus combatants just like any other members. They may lawfully be attacked at any time and anywhere within the region of war while simultaneously enjoying combatant privileges such as the right to participate in hostilities.

3.3.1.2. The Utilisation of Individuals who are not Regular Members of the Armed Forces of a State

Determination of combatant status is highly disputed in relation to persons that in one way or another are not regular members of armed forces. Several categories are discussed of which some are reflected in codified humanitarian

174 Knut Ipsen 'Combatants and Non-Combatants' in Dieter Fleck & Michael Bothe (eds) *The Handbook of International Humanitarian Law* (OUP Oxford 2008) p. 98; Marco Sassòli 'Combatants' in Rüdiger Wolfrum (ed) *MPEPIL* (OUP Oxford Update 2007) para. 5; Rogers *Law on the Battlefield* p. 31; Sandoz, Swinarski & Zimmermann (eds) *Commentary on the Additional Protocols of 8 June 1977 to the Geneva Conventions of 12 August 1949* para. 1677; Dinstein *The Conduct of Hostilities under the Law of International Armed Conflict* p. 33. Some States in their military manuals have included more members of the armed forces that are deemed to not qualify as combatants, namely those members which do not have any combat mission, as for example the German manual: Bundesministerium der Verteidigung *Humanitäres Völkerrecht in bewaffneten Konflikten: Handbuch* (Bundesministerium der Verteidigung 1992) para. 313.

175 Sassòli 'Combatants' paras. 4 and 14; Jean-Marie Henckaerts 'Armed Forces' in Rüdiger Wolfrum (ed) *MPEPIL* (OUP Oxford Update 2010) para. 12; Henckaerts & Doswald-Beck (eds) *Customary International Humanitarian Law Volume I: Rules* (Rule 3) with reference to the relevant State practice.

176 Sassòli 'Combatants' para. 4.

177 Dittmar *Angriffe auf Computernetzwerke: Ius ad bellum und ius in bello* pp. 218 et seq.

law – such as mercenaries – while others are novelties intended to cope with the appearance of novel actors and conflicts – such as so-called unlawful or unprivileged combatants. Likewise belonging to this discussion is the legal classification of private military companies and their members during armed conflict. The latter discussion in particular gains new relevance in relation to cyber warfare as many functions and services in connection to the maintenance of military information infrastructure have been outsourced to private contractors and many predict this trend as also growing in relation to the actual performance of CNAs.[178] Other cases exist where the operational basis for CNAs rests within government agencies not designated as armed forces.[179] The focus shall therefore in the following be on the question of the status of private information technology security companies utilised in some way by a party to an international armed conflict. The issue of so-called unlawful combatants shall not be reproduced here as it mostly discusses the treatment of armed groups that act independently from a State.[180]

Recent years have witnessed an expansion in commercial military activity through the proliferation of so-called private military companies.[181] This development is envisaged to grow with regard to CNAs, inter alia also due to a replacement of the military as a driving force of technological progress by the commercial sector. Although the development of the Internet was to a large extent triggered by the US military, the rising demands for high-tech industrial production, private consumer goods and services has to a certain extent superseded the military sector as such moving power. Consequently, in the field of information technology the military is to a much higher degree dependent on dual-use technology than in the field of conventional weaponry.[182] Furthermore, it is not only the technology by itself but also the operational techniques of CNAs which are widely known in the commercial sector as a consequence of the permanent defence readiness against cybercrime. Having resort to this substantial knowledge both of the IT security sector and also hackers is therefore advantageous for militaries. The hiring of individuals or companies from the

---

178 Brown 'A Proposal for an International Convention to Regulate the Use of Information Systems in Armed Conflict' pp. 182–83.

179 As apparently the case in the USA, according to Sean Watts 'Combatant Status and Computer Network Attack' (2010) 50 Virginia Journal of International Law pp. 407–11.

180 On this see generally Knut Dörmann 'Combatants, Unlawful' in Rüdiger Wolfrum (ed) *MPEPIL* (OUP Oxford Update 2011) pointing out the ambivalences of the notion; and Dinstein *The Conduct of Hostilities under the Law of International Armed Conflict* arguing in favor of the distinction between lawful and unlawful combatants (at pp. 33 et seq.) and Yoram Dinstein 'Unlawful Combatancy' (2002) 32 Israel Yearbook on Human Rights pp. 247–70.

181 Chia Lehnhardt 'Private Military Companies' in Rüdiger Wolfrum (ed) *MPEPIL* (OUP Oxford Update 2011) paras. 2–3; Tina Roeder 'Zum Kriterium der "unmittelbaren Kampfteilnahme" bei der humanitärrechtlichen Einordnung privater Konfliktdienstleister im internationalen bewaffneten Konflikt' (2010)(4) Humanitäres Völkerrecht pp. 173 et seq.

182 Similarly: Ralf Hoffmann 'Information War: Tendenzen – Optionen – Perspektiven' (2002) 15(3) Humanitäres Völkerrecht p. 160.

private IT sector by militaries then again makes their status during armed conflict questionable, resuming the general discussion concerning the status of members of private military companies.

Humanitarian law does not provide for any specific regulation of private military companies, although commercial undertakings during armed conflict can be traced back to the privateers of the 13th century.[183] With Article 47 Additional Protocol I there does exist a rule on mercenaries, however, with which private military companies have in the past often been compared.[184] Therein, mercenaries are defined as persons who (1) are specially recruited to fight in an armed conflict and factually take a direct part in the hostilities, (2) are motivated primarily by private gain and are granted compensation by a party to the conflict which is substantially in excess to that afforded to comparable ranks of the party's regular armed forces, (3) are neither nationals nor residents of territory, nor members of the armed forces of a party to the conflict, and (4) have not been sent by a State not party to the conflict on official duty as a member of its armed forces. Most importantly, the rule affords mercenaries neither combatant nor prisoner of war status, which is also considered to reflect customary international law.[185] Consequently, Article 47 does not prohibit mercenaries per se, but highly disapproves of their employment by making their actions punishable under criminal law due to their deprivation of combatant privileges.

Members of private military companies can therefore qualify as mercenaries if they fulfil the conditions of Article 47 Additional Protocol I. But by requiring the criteria to be fulfilled cumulatively, the definition is extremely narrow, thus averting such permanent groups as the French Foreign Legion from being qualified as mercenaries.[186] The definition has further been severely criticised as unworkable from a practical standpoint. This is due to the fact that the stigma of mercenarism can simply be avoided by declaring the individuals to be part of the armed forces. Moreover, the subjective element of a motivation of financial gain and payment in excess to a comparable rank will mostly be impossible to prove in practice.[187] The status of members of private military companies is therefore in most cases determined without recourse to mercenarism.

---

183 Lehnhardt 'Private Military Companies' para. 2.

184 There further exist two conventions on mercenaries, both of which however only have around 30 States Parties: International Convention against the Recruitment, Use, Financing and Training of Mercenaries (signed 4 December 1989, entered into force 20 October 2001) 2163 UNTS 75; OAU Convention for the Elimination of Mercenarism in Africa (signed 3 July 1977, entered into force 22 April 1985) 1490 UNTS 89.

185 Sassòli 'Combatants' para. 17; Henckaerts & Doswald-Beck (eds) *Customary International Humanitarian Law Volume I: Rules* Rule 108 with relevant State practice at pp. 391 et seq. The United States do not consider the rule to reflect customary international law (*ibid* p. 392).

186 Ipsen 'Combatants and Non-Combatants' p. 84; similarly Robert M. Chesney 'Prisoners of War' in Rüdiger Wolfrum (ed) *MPEPIL* (OUP Oxford Update 2009) para. 22.

187 Holger P. Hestermayer 'Mercenaries' in Rüdiger Wolfrum (ed) *MPEPIL* (OUP Oxford Update 2010) para. 13; Dinstein *The Conduct of Hostilities under the Law of International Armed*

From a historical perspective, Article 1 Hague Regulations and Article 4A(2) Geneva Convention III distinguished between regular and irregular armed forces, the latter consisting of militias, volunteer corps and organised resistance movements.[188] Members of the irregular units should only be granted combatant status if they fulfil six criteria: (1) forming an organised group, (2) that belongs to a party to the conflict, (3) commanded by a person responsible for his subordinates, (4) wearing a fixed distinctive and recognisable emblem, (5) carrying their arms openly and (6) abiding by the laws and customs of war. Members of the regular armed forces were regarded as in any case fulfilling these criteria.[189] Both Additional Protocol I and customary international law have brought about a change in these rules however. Today it is no longer necessary to distinguish between regular and irregular units as all units fulfilling the conditions set out in Article 43 Additional Protocol I are considered members of the armed forces, hence combatants. These are individuals or units under a command responsible to a party to the armed conflict for the conduct of its subordinates, a rule which is considered by some to reflect customary international law, but is however contested by others.[190] In this regard the definition of combatants has been expanded in comparison with the more restrictive criteria of the Hague Regulations and Geneva Convention III. Nevertheless, the latter criteria have not lost their relevance as they are applicable in determining the prisoner of war status, which can be divergent from combatant status.

Ultimately the controversy over the definition of combatants is not of so much relevance for the case of cyber warfare, as the definition of combatants both under the Hague Regulations and Geneva Convention III on the one hand, and Additional Protocol I on the other, are similar for the case of individuals conducting CNAs. The criterion of an organised group belonging to a party to the conflict is easily met by private military companies through their organisational structure. The contract with a party to the conflict constitutes the necessary association needed to consider the company to be fighting on behalf of one party.[191] The criterion of a command responsible for its subordinates is a necessary

---

Conflict p. 59; Lehnhardt 'Private Military Companies' para. 4; Dittmar *Angriffe auf Computernetzwerke: Ius ad bellum und ius in bello* p. 229; Doehring *Völkerrecht* p. 259.

188 Geneva Convention relative to the Treatment of Prisoners of War (adopted 12 August 1949, entered into force 21 October 1950) 75 UNTS 135.

189 Henckaerts 'Armed Forces' para. 7.

190 Arguing for its status as customary international law: Henckaerts 'Armed Forces' para. 12; Henckaerts & Doswald-Beck (eds) *Customary International Humanitarian Law Volume I: Rules* Rules 3 and 4 at pp. 11 et seq. with further references to supporting State practice; concurring: Imke-Ilse Drews *Die völkerrechtlichen Dimensionen des staatlichen Einsatzes privater Militärfirmen* (Nomos Baden-Baden 2011) p. 109. Differently, especially due to the criticism by several States in regard to Art. 44 (3) second sentence Additional Protocol I: Sassòli 'Combatants' para. 7; similarly Watts 'Combatant Status and Computer Network Attack' pp. 416–17.

191 Chia Lehnardt *Private Militärfirmen und völkerrechtliche Verantwortlichkeit: Eine Untersuchung aus humanitär-völkerrechtlicher und menschenrechtlicher Perspektive* (Mohr

condition in both cases. Due to the fact that those conducting CNAs cannot from a practical standpoint carry their arms openly, the wearing of a fixed distinctive and recognisable emblem is an obligation they have to fulfil in any case, derived from the principle of distinction.[192] Therefore there is only one criterion, namely abiding by the laws and customs of war, which distinguishes the definition of combatant status in the two different frameworks. While Article 44(2) Additional Protocol I obliges combatants to comply with the rules of humanitarian law, non-compliance does not lead to a loss of combatant status with the exception of not carrying arms openly and providing for distinction from the civilian population as stipulated in Article 44(3) Additional Protocol I. Conversely, in the Hague Regulations and Geneva Convention III this criterion is of a constitutive quality for combatant status. However, practical considerations have led to a restrictive interpretation of the criterion through which disregard only of the most fundamental rules of humanitarian law leads to loss of combatant status as there are numerous rules solely of marginal character, the non-observance of which does not justify the loss of combatant privileges.[193]

Members of private IT security companies under contract to a party to the conflict qualify as combatants if they become members of the armed forces through a formal act of incorporation.[194] While their qualification as mercenaries is generally possible, it is of little practical relevance. Ultimately it lies in the hands of each State to formally incorporate private military companies into their armed forces to relieve their members from mercenary status. The requirement for a mercenary to be paid more than a member of the regular armed forces of a comparable rank further leads to the questionable result that States which provide for a comparably high remuneration for their armed forces can use those private military companies which are available for lesser payment without their falling under the definition of mercenaries, while poorer States are completely deprived of this possibility.[195] The criterion of an organised group with State affiliation is easily fulfilled by private military companies. For those States arties to Additional Protocol I – or when considering its Article 43(1) as customary international law – the decisive criterion is being under a command which is responsible to a party to the armed conflict for the conduct of its subordinates that determines combatant status. This responsibility can only arise out of contractual liability under civil law in case of violations of directions. While such

Siebeck Tübingen 2011) pp. 150 et seq; Chia Lehnardt 'Private Military Companies' in Rüdiger Wolfrum (ed) *MPEPIL* (OUP Oxford Update 2011) para. 10.

192 See above pp. 216 et seq.

193 Sassòli 'Combatants' paras. 11–12; Drews *Die völkerrechtlichen Dimensionen des staatlichen Einsatzes privater Militärfirmen* p. 125.

194 Similarly Drews *Die völkerrechtlichen Dimensionen des staatlichen Einsatzes privater Militärfirmen* p. 126.

195 Lehnardt *Private Militärfirmen und völkerrechtliche Verantwortlichkeit: Eine Untersuchung aus humanitär-völkerrechtlicher und menschenrechtlicher Perspektive* p. 122.

is always less assertive than military orders which can be tried under military jurisdiction, the element of responsibility should not be considered too restrictive. After all, the ratio of the rule is to award prisoner of war and combatant status to those individuals which are under a command that ensures compliance with humanitarian law. As the incentive of members of private military companies in most cases is monetary gain, the impending contractual liability – which in itself is of a monetary character – is of a sufficient grave detriment to qualify the command as responsible to a State.[196] Both the company and its members will under these circumstances in most cases abide by their contractual obligations.

In all other cases the decisive element is the observance of the fundamental rules of humanitarian law under Article 4A(2) Geneva Convention III and Article 1 Hague Regulations. As it is a collective criterion, the failing of the group as a whole to fulfil this requirement makes all members lose both their combatant and prisoner of war status.

Current humanitarian law consequently adequately addresses the status of persons conducting CNAs who do not belong to the 'regular' armed forces of a party to the conflict but to private IT security companies that can very well also be labelled private military companies if their services are attacks in the sense of humanitarian law.[197]

3.3.2. *Civilian Participation in Cyber Warfare*

Alongside the potentially developing market for IT security companies to provide services so far reserved to traditional private military companies, the easy and comparably cheap access to computer systems capable of undertaking CNAs that can result in military harm likewise gives a vast number of civilians the possibility to participate in hostilities by using this dual-use technology during armed conflict. According to Article 51(3) Additional Protocol I, civilians, when and as long as the have a direct part in the hostilities, lose their protection under Articles 48–67 Additional Protocol I and may thus be lawfully targeted although not qualifying as combatants. This rule is also considered as reflecting customary international law.[198] Participation may range from support

---

196 Drews *Die völkerrechtlichen Dimensionen des staatlichen Einsatzes privater Militärfirmen* pp. 120–21; Lehnardt 'Private Military Companies' para. 12; Michael N. Schmitt 'Humanitarian Law and Direct Participation in Hostilities by Private Contractors or Civilian Employees' (2005) 5(2) Chicago Journal of International Law pp. 529 et seq.; Roeder 'Zum Kriterium der "unmittelbaren Kampfteilnahme" bei der humanitärrechtlichen Einordnung privater Konfliktdienstleister im internationalen bewaffneten Konflikt' p. 175.

197 As has been shown above, already those CNOs not amounting to physical damage outside of the computer system can qualify as an attack under the definition of Art. 49 Additional Protocol I: see pp. 205 et seq. above.

198 Henckaerts & Doswald-Beck (eds) *Customary International Humanitarian Law Volume I: Rules* Rule 6 at pp. 19–24; Melzer 'Civilian Participation in Armed Conflict' para. 4; Rule 29 Tallinn Manual.

actions such as recruitment or reconnaissance to actual offensive actions against target systems.[199] In this regard the Georgian and Estonian incidents set a clear example that the willingness of parts of the population to participate in such a way exists. Whether or not these civilians are aware that their conduct possibly qualifies as a direct participation and what consequences this has is a different question. However, the loss of protection is not a sanction for criminal conduct but a concession to military necessity.[200] In the short time span available for targeting decisions it is impossible to reliably determine the subjective motives of a civilian to carry out a specific act. Therefore the civilian's awareness of actually participating in hostilities does not have to be taken into account in the actual targeting decision.[201] The rule is further applicable to those cases where members of private military companies as shown above do not qualify as combatants meaning that they can only be treated as civilians.[202]

First it is to be determined whether those persons conducting CNAs qualify as civilians or combatants. In cases of doubt, Article 50(1) Additional Protocol I provides for an assumption of the civilian status. Once a civilian status is assumed, the criterion of their direct participation in hostilities must then be evaluated. As the conduct of CNAs can take place from any location, proximity to the theatre of war is not a prerequisite for the determination of participation. The launching of CNAs is rather to be compared to the launching of missiles, where it is sufficient to program the target computer with the target's coordinates and initiate the launch sequence in order to directly participate in the hostilities. While there is no clear textual definition as to what constitutes such participation, State practice, legal doctrine, treaty interpretation and jurisprudence have outlined certain elements the fulfilment of which is a necessity in order to judge civilians as directly participating in hostilities.[203]

Firstly, the action must amount to a certain level of military harm, namely such that adversely affects the military operations of a party to the conflict.[204]

---

199 An overview of the different possibilities available for civilian participation is given by Ottis 'From Pitchforks to Laptops: Volunteers in Cyber Conflicts' pp. 97–109 and Schmitt (ed) *Tallinn Manual on the International Law Applicable to Cyber Warfare* p. 120 para. 5.

200 Melzer 'Civilian Participation in Armed Conflict' para. 4.

201 During the expert meetings leading to the ICRC's Interpretive Guidance there was almost unanimous agreement that the subjective motives of a civilian cannot serve as criterion for targeting decisions: Nils Melzer *Interpretive Guidance on the Notion of Direct Participation in Hostilities under International Humanitarian Law* (ICRC Geneva 2009) fn. 40.

202 The controversy surrounding the so-called unlawful combatants shall not be addressed here. Rather, the traditional distinction between combatants and civilians is supported here. On the problem see generally Dinstein 'Unlawful Combatancy' pp. 247–70 and Knut Dörmann 'The Legal Situation of "Unlawful/Unprivileged Combatants"' (2003) 85(849) International Review of the Red Cross pp. 45–74.

203 Melzer 'Civilian Participation in Armed Conflict' para. 7.

204 The ICRC Commentary to Art. 51 Additional Protocol I speaks of 'acts of war which by their nature or purpose are likely to cause actual harm to the personnel and equipment of the enemy armed forces'; Sandoz, Swinarski & Zimmermann (eds) *Commentary on the Additional Protocols of 8 June 1977 to the Geneva Conventions of 12 August 1949* para. 1944.

This can inter alia be achieved by disturbing military communications. In this regard, the harmful effects must not yet have materialised, it suffices that such may be expected in all likelihood. Secondly, a direct connection between the civilian's action and the military harm inflicted is needed, thereby excluding indirect activities building up or sustaining the military capacity such as the production of weapons and the like.[205] Thirdly, there must be a nexus to the actual conduct of hostilities. This requires the act to have been designed to inflict harm onto one party to a conflict while thereby supporting the other party. Here the subjective or hostile intent of the civilian is generally not of concern.[206] Under certain circumstances, however, for instance when a civilian is totally unaware of the role he is playing in the conduct of hostilities, or totally deprived of any physical freedom as in the case of coerced human shields, the belligerent nexus can be called into question. In these cases the civilian could be regarded as not performing an action in a meaningful sense.[207]

While direct participation always requires an element of support for one party to the conflict, civilian actions can generally be divided into those that are taken in voluntary cooperation with the military and those taken independently thereof. It is further possible that the traditional exception existing in situations of a levée en masse is applicable to also instances of civilian-authored CNAs, thereby offering civilians under certain circumstances the status of combatants and prisoners of war once captured.

3.3.2.1. Actions Taken in Cooperation with the Armed Forces

Civilians may on the one hand merely support the military effort of a party to the conflict by providing for auxiliary services not directly connected to the actual conduct of hostilities in the theatre of war. Traditionally these are weapons engineers or workers in a factory producing weapons. Engineers of generic software used for CNAs are the equivalent thereof. In both cases there is no direct connection between the programming of the software or production of the weapon and the damage caused through its subsequent utilisation by a member of the armed forces. These measures merely establishing a general capacity to carry out unspecified operations are generally not considered a direct participation but merely a participation in the war effort.[208] Similar holds true

---

205 *Prosecutor v Strugar (Judgment)* IT-01-42-A (17 July 2008) paras. 172–79.

206 Melzer *Interpretive Guidance on the Notion of Direct Participation in Hostilities under International Humanitarian Law* pp. 46–64.

207 Melzer *Interpretive Guidance on the Notion of Direct Participation in Hostilities under International Humanitarian Law* p. 60.

208 Melzer 'Civilian Participation in Armed Conflict' para. 18; Sandoz, Swinarski & Zimmermann (eds) *Commentary on the Additional Protocols of 8 June 1977 to the Geneva Conventions of 12 August 1949* para. 1945; Schmitt (ed) *Tallinn Manual on the International Law Applicable to Cyber Warfare* p. 120 para. 5.

for persons accompanying the armed forces without actually being members thereof which under Article 4A(4) Geneva Convention III qualify as prisoners of war when captured by the adversary while not having combatant status. The list of persons included in Article 4A(4) encompasses those that provide the armed forces with technical assistance, like for instance maintenance works, or services for the welfare of the forces. Computer technicians working on the maintenance of the military networks and weapons systems are therefore neither combatants nor civilians directly participating in hostilities but nevertheless enjoy prisoner of war status.[209]

In order for a CNA to be most effective, generic software will however only play a marginal and supportive role. The higher the number of different types of computer systems and programmes that are used by the designated target, the more the complexity of an attack grows. In these cases, generic software is mostly not sufficient to achieve the desired results. Rather, a specific software will have to be designed or at least adapted to the specific target system, as was the case with Stuxnet.[210] In these instances, software engineers will need to closely cooperate with the armed forces in order to identify the features needed by the military and to closely survey the peculiarities of the target systems. Mapping and scanning the enemy's systems as a preparation for a later attack may also imply an intrusion into the systems due to technical necessities. Accordingly, the question arises as to whether actions of external software engineers are to be treated as a direct participation in the hostilities in these situations.

Rule 29 (iii) HPCR Manual on Air and Missile Warfare lists

> 'engaging in electronic warfare or computer network attacks targeting military objectives, combatants or civilians directly participating in hostilities, or which is intended to cause death or injury to civilians or damage to or destruction of civilian objects'

as an example of an act constituting a direct participation in hostilities (subject to the circumstances ruling at the time). It is simultaneously conceded however,

---

209 Similarly: Dittmar *Angriffe auf Computernetzwerke: Ius ad bellum und ius in bello* p. 260; Schmitt 'Wired Warfare: Computer Network Attack and Jus in Bello' p. 384. One example for such a service can be seen in a US $5.8 million contract awarded to Lockheed Martin which is to maintain US Pentagon electronic messaging systems including virus and spam protection as well as directory, security and configuration management support <www.lockheedmartin.com/news/press_releases/2008/0820_pentagon-netcents-contract.html> (12 January 2011).

210 As stated for a comparable case in the expert survey prepared for the German Constitutional Court on the technical aspects of the remote search and surveillance of computer systems by the Federal Criminal Police Office; Dirk Fox 'Stellungnahme zur "Online-Durchsuchung": Verfassungsbeschwerden 1 BvR 370/07 und 1 BvR 595/07' (2007) at <www.secorvo.de/publikationen/stellungnahme-secorvo-bverfg-online-durchsuchung.pdf> (date accessed 23 April 2010) pp. 5 et seq.

that by merely hacking into the intranet of a military base a civilian should not automatically be considered as directly participating in hostilities.[211] While this is correct, it is not a characteristic of CNOs but of the rules pertaining to civilian participation in general. The HPCR Manual on Air and Missile Warfare – like the ICRC Study on Customary Law – draws up a threshold for civilian participation depending on the level of harm likely to be expected from the operation.[212] Hence it is this 'level of harm threshold' that generally needs to be reached independently of the type of action performed by the civilian. Supportive acts such as the participation in target acquisition or planning of an (air) attack are given as examples in Rule 29 HPCR Manual as amounting to a direct participation. Generally if a civilian engages in CNOs as a supportive role to the armed forces, the level of harm, direct connection and nexus requirements demanded by the ICRC study will more easily be fulfilled than in the case of autonomous actions by civilians. Hence the qualification of 'hacking into' a military network by a civilian depends on the consequences resulting therefrom and undertaken by the military. In the event that such a CNO leads to the acquisition of material used in an attack by the armed forces, the civilian action may very well be qualified a supportive act and thus a direct participation.

Persons compiling and interpreting computer data, for example to verify the character of a system as a military objective likewise directly participate in hostilities if this target information is then immediately used for an attack against said system. The same holds true for computer network exploitation in order to obtain such information, even if data on the target system is not modified. Such activity is to be regarded as military reconnaissance.[213] Here the military harm lies in the subsequent attack undertaken by the armed forces but directly based on the information gathered by civilians. In these cases a targeting of the systems of those civilians directly participating may be done in order to disable their further ability to do so.

Network security technicians who actively defend networks under their supervision against a belligerent CNA likewise directly participate once they actively take defensive measures against this targeting, as humanitarian law does not distinguish between defensive and offensive attacks.[214]

---

211 Program on Humanitarian Policy and Conflict Research (ed) *Commentary on the HPCR Manual on International Law Applicable to Air and Missile Warfare* p. 122.

212 Melzer *Interpretive Guidance on the Notion of Direct Participation in Hostilities under International Humanitarian Law* p. 50.

213 Dale Stephens & Tristan Skousgaard 'Military Reconnaissance' in Rüdiger Wolfrum (ed) *MPEPIL* (OUP Oxford Update 2009) para. 18; Doswald-Beck 'Some Thoughts on Computer Network Attack and the International Law of Armed Conflict' p. 172.

214 This shall already apply for merely repairing military equipment in the midst of hostilities: Bothe, Partsch & Solf *New Rules for Victims of Armed Conflicts: Commentary on the Two 1977 Protocols Additional to the Geneva Conventions of 1949* p. 304.

3.3.2.2. Actions by Civilians Taken Independently from the Armed Forces

During the expert meetings in preparation of the ICRC study on direct participation in hostilities, the use of CNAs by civilians that are likely to inflict death, injury or destruction was regarded as part of the hostilities and hence a direct participation therein.[215] This was seen as generally including the causation of military harm to the adversary in a situation of armed conflict such as the neutralisation of an enemy computer network via a CNA.[216]

When acting independently from the armed forces of a party to the conflict civilians cannot however directly participate by, for example, merely gathering information without transmitting it to the armed forces in order for the armed forces to gain a military advantage from it, as the criteria of military harm or belligerent nexus are not fulfilled. Yet in the limited time of decision-making during armed conflict it will be difficult to ascertain the civilian's motives. As the decision to attack is based on the circumstances and combat situation at the time of the decision, this ambiguity is ultimately to the detriment of the civilian, as he can ultimately nevertheless be subject to a legitimate attack in this situation. The same holds true in those cases where civilians take part in a concerted attack consisting of several smaller actions – typically a distributed denial of service attack as demonstrated in the Estonian and Georgian case studies – each individual act in itself is already to be regarded as a direct participation even if the respective part of the overall operation could not cross the threshold of military harm necessary. This is achieved through a reciprocal attribution of the concerted actions as in the case of complicity. The necessity of such an approach lies in the fact that otherwise there would be no valid possibility of active defence against such a concerted attack consisting of an amassment of small scale operations. Due regard must however be had to the proportionality principle in this regard in order to limit the scale of defensive reactions against such low level attacks.

It has also been argued that civilians who spread false information or rumours over the Internet in order to undermine military or related national security efforts of the enemy could run the risk of being regarded as combatants.[217] This view must be rejected. First and foremost, combatant status cannot be acquired by civilians of their own volition. Moreover such behaviour

---

215 ICRC 'Direct Participation in Hostilities under International Humanitarian Law: First Expert Meeting Summary Report' (2003) at <www.icrc.org/Web/eng/siteeng0.nsf/htmlall/direct-participation-report_res/$File/2003-03-report-dph-2003-icrc.pdf> (date accessed 3 November 2009) p. 5; Melzer 'Civilian Participation in Armed Conflict' para. 17.

216 ICRC 'Third Expert Meeting on the Notion of Direct Participation in Hostilities: Summary Report' (2005) at <www.icrc.org/eng/assets/files/other/2005-09-report-dph-2005-icrc.pdf> (date accessed 25 November 2010) p. 14.

217 Hoffman 'The Legal Status and Responsibilities of Private Internet Users under the Law of Armed Conflict: A Primer for the Unwary on the Shape of Law to Come' p. 425.

cannot even qualify as a direct participation in hostilities. The spreading of information in itself cannot qualify as an attack under humanitarian law as there is neither actual military harm to persons or equipment nor a direct connection between action and intended result.

Civilian participation may not only entail consequences for this class of persons, but also for the State they are nationals of. Common Article 1 Geneva Conventions I–IV and Article 1 Additional Protocol I oblige the States Parties to 'ensure respect' for the conventions in all circumstances. This has been interpreted as being able to trigger State responsibility for breaches of humanitarian law by private actors, if the State fails to exercise due diligence in preventing such actions by individuals.[218] However if the State has no indications that individuals are actually performing CNAs on their behalf during armed conflict, the provision of an effective penalisation of these actions under domestic law is to be regarded as sufficient.

3.3.2.3. Cyber Levée en Masse

Past conflicts have shown that civilians may engage in defensive measures instantaneously and independent from the armed forces. As an old rule of humanitarian law, the civilian population of a non-occupied territory is afforded the right to spontaneously take up arms to resist the invading forces, when having had no time to form themselves into regular armed units, provided they carry arms openly and respect the laws and customs of war. Members of this so-called levée en masse are to be treated as combatants and afforded prisoner of war status according to Article 2 Hague Regulations of 1907 and Article 4A(6) Geneva Convention III. Inhabitants of already occupied territories do not enjoy these rights. Despite some occasional instances of levée en masse these uprisings have however remained very isolated in recent times.[219]

Considering the events related to the Russian-Georgian conflict of 2008, it is not out of question that, in the event of a conventional armed conflict, the civilian population will make use of the Internet as a means of resistance. The capability of regular computer systems to undertake CNAs, the ease of doing so and the seeming anonymity of the attacker can make this sort of resistance far more attractive than physically taking up arms and fighting enemy soldiers in combat. The question thus arises as to whether such a 'cyber resistance' could legally be qualified as a cyber levée en masse with the respective implications as to the status of the civilians. The levée en masse is considered to be a longstanding rule of customary international law already recognised in

---

218 Koivurova 'Due Diligence' para. 32.

219 As has been the case in some instances in the former Yugoslavia, as acknowledged in *Prosecutor v Orić* (Judgment) IT-03-68-T (30 June 2006) para. 136; this uncommonness has led some to characterise this category of combatants as 'pertinent for historical reasons only': Crawford 'Armed Conflict, International' para. 14.

Articles 49 and 51 Lieber Code and repeated until today in many military manuals.[220] Members of a levée en masse are considered to be allowed only to fight against an invading enemy, but not against a retreating one nor to attack units on the homeland of the attacker.[221] These criteria raise a number of problems in connection with cyber warfare, yet Rule 27 Tallinn Manual also grants civilians this special protection when performing CNOs. According to one view, the concept of a cyber levée en masse is however an 'unworkable anachronism whose application diminishes various protections afforded both civilians and conflict participants in armed conflicts'.[222] The traditional criteria of a spontaneous mass uprising, the protection of non-occupied territory and carrying arms openly are hereby seen as unworkable in the field of cyberspace. It is true that carrying the computer openly, when understood as a weapon, is a superfluous criterion, as most individuals will sit inside houses and can from the outside not be distinguished from regular civilians. This carries with it the danger of uninvolved civilians being targeted. Further, most targets typically vulnerable to CNAs will be located on the territory of the attacker, for example government and military communications servers. Under the traditional concept of levée en masse they would not be valid targets. Targets could only be computer systems under control of the attacker already located in the territory of the attacked. Conceivable scenarios in this respect are hard to come by. The attacker would have to be in control of the local network infrastructure. Due to the technical requirements this scenario is probably only thinkable in a time of occupation. However, in this situation the possibility of a levée en masse is already precluded in the first place. The only scenarios where a cyber levée en masse is possible seem to be the cases where civilians defend computer systems located on their State territory against CNAs or target command and control infrastructure of the attacker which is already located in the territory of the attacked. This cannot however amount to attacking the source systems if these are located on foreign territory as the purpose of granting the levée en masse combatant privileges is solely to expel an intruding force without attacking its home territory.[223] The prerequisites for a cyber levée en masse are thus so high that

---

220 Henckaerts & Doswald-Beck (eds) *Customary International Humanitarian Law Volume I: Rules* p. 18; UK Ministry of Defence *The Manual of the Law of Armed Conflict* (OUP Oxford 2004) para. 4.8; US Department of the Navy *The Commander's Handbook on the Law of Naval Operations (July 2007 Edition NWP 1-14M)* para. 5.4.1.1.

221 Sandoz, Swinarski & Zimmermann (eds) *Commentary on the Additional Protocols of 8 June 1977 to the Geneva Conventions of 12 August 1949* para. 1704; Brown 'A Proposal for an International Convention to Regulate the Use of Information Systems in Armed Conflict' p. 192; Hoffman 'The Legal Status and Responsibilities of Private Internet Users under the Law of Armed Conflict: A Primer for the Unwary on the Shape of Law to Come' p. 423.

222 David Wallace & Shane R. Reeves 'The Law of Armed Conflict's "Wicked" Problem: Levée en Masse in Cyber Warfare' (2013) 89 International Law Studies p. 664.

223 Generally opposed to any kind of cyber levée en masse: Brown 'A Proposal for an International Convention to Regulate the Use of Information Systems in Armed Conflict' pp. 191–92 who argues that it would further erode the barrier between combatants and non-

the granting of this specific form of civilian status will be of a marginal role during cyber warfare. It has therefore been put forward to disregard this traditional category altogether for cases of CNOs and rather utilise those of militias or organised resistance movements.[224] As a consequence these groups would then be able to also take action on occupied territory. The problem with this approach is however that militias require a command structure and the wearing of a fixed distinctive sign recognisable at a distance.[225] These criteria are likewise unrealistic when civilians are involved in the cyber context. The Georgian case for example, where malware was readily available worldwide to anyone wishing to take action against predefined Georgian targets, has shown that it neither needs a command structure nor special IT knowledge to take part in hostilities. It is not unlikely that cases like this will proliferate in the future, which can especially be seen in the decentralised structure of the group 'Anonymous', which has neither some sort of membership nor hierarchy. Denying civilians participating in combat the privileged status of being part of a levée en masse ultimately has the potential to be more detrimental to their protection than the risk of not being able to distinguish between civilians performing CNOs with their computers and those using them for peaceful means.

A disputed yet majority opinion of the group of experts engaged with the Tallinn Manual considered the concept of a levée en masse to require a physical 'conventional' invasion of national territory.[226] Attacks undertaken solely by CNOs without a physical presence could not give rise to a levée en masse. This view cannot be shared. The ratio behind the concept is to afford civilians who feel a duty to defend their country combatant status. Therefore it is only granted as long as the actions are of a defensive quality, namely on territory not yet occupied and a fortiori not on foreign territory. These defensive situations can also occur when attacks are merely performed by CNOs without a physical military presence. If a system is under attack by a remote CNO a cyber levée en masse can initiate countermeasures in order to repel said CNOs, as long as this does not mean transgressing into foreign territory.

Irrespective of these differing views, it must be acknowledged that the applicability of this old concept in the field of CNOs will ultimately remain rare. Simply put, there are just not that many viable targets available under the current understanding of the concept.

---

combatants, make civilian network infrastructure a legitimate target also of conventional attack and would, in any case, not be viable as it were only targeted at information structures within the attacking State's territory.

224 Wallace & Reeves 'The Law of Armed Conflict's "Wicked" Problem: Levée en Masse in Cyber Warfare' p. 664.

225 Art. 4 A(2) Geneva Convention III.

226 Schmitt (ed) *Tallinn Manual on the International Law Applicable to Cyber Warfare* p. 103.

3.3.3. *Spies and Computer Network Espionage*

As already seen above, espionage is not prohibited per se under general international law.[227] Nevertheless being qualified as a spy may have negative repercussions during armed conflict to the individual. According to Article 46(1) Additional Protocol I, members of the armed forces qualifying as spies do not enjoy the status of prisoners of war when captured, in fact they may be tried for domestic law violations.[228] The definition of 'spy' under Article 29 Hague Regulations of 1907 refers to persons that, by acting clandestinely or on false pretences, obtain or endeavour to obtain information in the zone of operations of a belligerent, with the intention of communicating it to the hostile party. The zone of operations in this connection encompasses all territory controlled by the enemy, hence also occupied territory.[229]

When carrying out their activities openly individuals are however not considered to be spies, nor are soldiers wearing their uniforms while so acting.[230] The ratio behind the differentiation between clandestine and open conduct lies in the close connection of the clandestine operation to the prohibited act of perfidy in the sense of Article 37 Additional Protocol I.[231] Military reconnaissance in the enemy territory is thus a lawful method of warfare when carried out openly and affords the operators the status of prisoners of war.[232] Usually the test of whether or not a member of the armed forces is gathering information clandestinely or openly will depend on the wearing of uniform at the relevant point in time. However, airmen are for example not required to wear uniform during flight.[233] This is not required insofar as the necessary markings of the military aircraft are sufficient indication of combatant status, while the duty of the airmen to distinguish themselves from the civilian population is no different from that of other members of armed forces, once they leave the aircraft.[234]

How does intelligence gathering on computer systems fit into these rules? It seems clear that the gathering of information via the Internet of freely available sources cannot be considered as espionage. First and foremost, the publisher has

---

227 See pp. 39 et seq. above.

228 This rule is considered as customary international law by both: Henckaerts & Doswald-Beck (eds) *Customary International Humanitarian Law Volume I: Rules* Rule 107 at pp. 389–91; and the Program on Humanitarian Policy and Conflict Research (ed) *HPCR Manual on Air Warfare* Rules 118–122. It is also incorporated in Rule 66 (b) Tallinn Manual.

229 Schaller 'Spies' para. 5.

230 Art. 46(2) Additional Protocol I.

231 Sandoz, Swinarski & Zimmermann (eds) *Commentary on the Additional Protocols of 8 June 1977 to the Geneva Conventions of 12 August 1949* para. 1776. On perfidy see already pp. 221 et seq. above.

232 Stephens & Skousgaard 'Military Reconnaissance' para. 18.

233 Dinstein 'Air Warfare' para. 69.

234 Program on Humanitarian Policy and Conflict Research (ed) *Commentary on the HPCR Manual on International Law Applicable to Air and Missile Warfare* p. 257.

implicitly given free access to anybody; secondly, the gathering of data is done openly.[235]

The situation is different however if the information gathered is not freely available but can only be accessed after circumventing or breaching security measures such as passwords or exploiting vulnerabilities of the target system. Comparable actions of traditional espionage for example would be to infiltrate foreign buildings in order to get access to secret documents stored therein, thus amounting under most jurisdictions at least to the crime of trespassing – if specific espionage laws are not directly applicable. A similar situation holds true for those cases where security measures need not be circumvented, for example when security vulnerabilities of software are exploited to gain access to data. A comparable action would be infiltrating a building through a window carelessly left open – an action likewise mostly qualifying as trespassing. The common feature in all these cases is the access to data without the necessary authorisation. But while being a spy in the sense of Article 29 Hague Regulations meant obtaining information while physically being in the zone of operations of the belligerent and Article 46 Additional Protocol I requires the person to be caught while engaging in espionage, the situation in modern cyber espionage is different, as CNOs also during wartime do not have to be conducted from within the enemy's territory. On the one hand the operator may as a person be located anywhere in the world, while the data that is being accessed in some way or another may be stored on a computer system physically located within the enemy territory. On the other hand though, such computer system can also be located in the territory of a neutral State, or when considering cloud computing, spread over diverse computer systems around the world. This allows the operator to remain in the territory of his own State while remotely gathering the data stored in the zone of operations. The question is thus whether a person must personally and physically be within the enemy territory while obtaining the information in order to be treated as a spy, or if the obtainment of information from within said territory suffices.

Some suggest that this sort of espionage should be treated as being analogous to remote sensing which is not considered to be prohibited.[236] Others have taken recourse to Article 24 Hague Regulations which states that 'the

---

235 This argument is further strengthened when considering that also under Art. 32 COE Cybercrime Convention a party may, without the authorisation of another party, access publicly available computer data, regardless of where the data is stored geographically, or such where the person who has the lawful authority to disclose the data has given his lawful and voluntary consent.

236 Doswald-Beck 'Some Thoughts on Computer Network Attack and the International Law of Armed Conflict' p. 172; the remote sensing via satellites is seen as not being considerably limited or restricted under public international law by Jana Kristin Hettling *Satellite Imagery for Verification and Enforcement of Public International Law* (Heymanns Köln 2008), Chesterman 'Secret Intelligence' para. 17 and Mahulena Hofmann 'Remote Sensing' in Rüdiger Wolfrum (ed) *MPEPIL* (OUP Oxford Update 2011).

employment of measures necessary for obtaining information about the enemy and the country are considered permissible'. The commentary to the Manual on Air and Missile Warfare concludes these permissible activities to also include CNOs designed to exploit data resident in enemy computer networks.[237] Both approaches are questionable, however, as computer espionage cannot be easily equated either with remote sensing, or with surveillance or reconnaissance missions. Both of these operations merely obtain information that is plainly visible. A related technique of data acquisition would only be to gather information freely accessible which per se cannot qualify as espionage. Furthermore, remote sensing is generally understood as only applying to the observation for purposes of natural resources and land management, as well as environmental protection.[238] However, computer network exploitation also entails accessing non-freely available data by hacking into secured systems. By actively circumventing defences this means more closely resembles an attack than a mere passive remote sensing or reconnaissance.

While leading to the same result, attention should rather be given to the traditional definition of a spy and the ratio of the accompanying norm which is sufficient to also deal with computer espionage during armed conflict. Article 46(1) Additional Protocol I requires the alleged spy to fall 'into the power of an adverse Party while engaging in espionage', hence during the operation itself. Instances where this might happen will probably remain purely academic as there is nearly no chance of apprehending such persons during the act while in the safety of their home territory. Further the purpose of the disadvantageous treatment of spies requires consideration. Ultimately it is yet another regulation intended to safeguard civilians. Only those persons can qualify as a spy that operate clandestinely, hence do not show their allegiance to the enemy party. This in itself is already a violation of the principle of distinction and a dangerous activity with respect to civilians, as it may lead the adverse party to accidently take measures against its own nationals when assuming an infiltration of spies. If undertaken from foreign territory the espionage activity does not lead to this mixture of civilians and spies hence not endangering the former. The mere 'virtual' presence on foreign territory is thus not sufficient for a qualification of an individual as spy.[239] Only those persons conducting cyber espionage while physically located in the adversary's territory are to be given this status, while those who remain on their party's territory retain combatant status if belonging

---

237 Program on Humanitarian Policy and Conflict Research (ed) *Commentary on the HPCR Manual on International Law Applicable to Air and Missile Warfare* p. 259.

238 Principle 1(a) UNGA Res 41/53 'Principles Relating to Remote Sensing of the Earth from Space' (3 December 1986) GAOR 41st Session Supp 53, 115. For a differentiation between remote sensing and military reconnaissance see Hofmann 'Remote Sensing' paras. 1–2.

239 Concurring: Dittmar *Angriffe auf Computernetzwerke: Ius ad bellum und ius in bello* p. 227; Brown 'A Proposal for an International Convention to Regulate the Use of Information Systems in Armed Conflict' p. 189.

to the armed forces. Computer network espionage during armed conflict carried out between the belligerents is therefore permissible.[240] After all, the usually conflicting non-intervention principle is inapplicable in this situation.

Nevertheless one cannot generally rule out the necessity of conducting computer network espionage also from within the zone of operations of the enemy. This could be the case for example where the target system is not connected to the public Internet – which for example in the case of Stuxnet led to the distribution of the malware via USB sticks – so that an infiltration must be undertaken from a system connected to the local network to which the target system is likewise connected to. Certain CNAs may possibly even require the operator to have direct access to the target system, which necessarily presupposes the physical presence in the foreign territory in which the system is located. This may be the case both when the target system is not connected to any network, or when a hardware device needs to be installed for example as a measure of surveillance. In these cases the persons may very well be qualified as spies under humanitarian law, if they operate clandestinely and are apprehended during their engagement.

4. LIMITS: HUMAN RIGHTS

The applicability of human rights law during a period of time where the regime of international humanitarian law applies has proven to be one of the most heavily-debated issues of international law in the second half of the 20th century. International humanitarian law developed in a time which was still dominated by military thinking, culminating in the famous German phrase used by writers during that time, '*Kriegsräson geht vor Kriegsmanier*', meaning that military necessity takes precedence over the rules of warfare.[241] However, this is a very outdated concept, as current humanitarian law is regarded a product of reconciliation between military necessity and humanitarian considerations.[242]

Traditionally, the concept of a separation between human rights law and international humanitarian law prevailed, a view that is today held inter alia by Israel.[243] While disputes remain, the prevailing opinion describes the

240 Rule 66(a) Tallinn Manual therefore rightly states that 'cyber espionage and other forms of information gathering directed at an adversary during an armed conflict do not violate the law of armed conflict'. The Tallinn Manual differs between computer network exploitation and cyber espionage. The first is understood as those operations originating from beyond enemy territory via remote access, the latter as those behind enemy lines.

241 Christian Tomuschat 'Human Rights and International Humanitarian Law' (2010) 21(1) European Journal of International Law p. 17; providing for references of several German authors: Oppenheim & Lauterpacht *International Law vol. 2: Disputes, War and Neutrality* p. 231.

242 Dinstein 'Military Necessity' para. 2.

243 Proponents for such a view were, inter alia, Alfred Verdross *Völkerrecht* (J. Springer Berlin 1937) p. 293. Israel held in its report to the Human Rights Committee, that the Committee's

relationship as a situation of progressive interpenetration, making both bodies of law applicable in the context of armed conflict.[244] The ICJ was able to elaborate on the issue both in the *Nuclear Weapons Advisory Opinion* and in the *Israeli Wall Advisory Opinion*. In the first advisory opinion the ICJ used language that proved to be quite contradictory as both interpretations could be derived therefrom.[245] However, in the *Israeli Wall Advisory Opinion* the ICJ identified three possible situations for the relationship between the two bodies of law: 'some rights may be exclusively matters of international humanitarian law; others may be exclusively matters of human rights law; yet others may be matters of both these branches of international law'.[246] Nonetheless, humanitarian law was explicitly denominated as lex specialis to human rights law by the ICJ.[247] However this has generally been understood not to mean lex specialis in the formal sense, hence providing for a complete separation, but as a requirement for human rights norms to be read in conjunction with those of humanitarian law during armed conflict. Otherwise the ICJ would have contradicted its own statement of a 'continuity of human rights in wartime'.[248] The ECtHR has likewise dealt with cases arising from the internal armed conflict in Chechnya concerning the right to life. Therein, the Court did not question the applicability ratione materiae of the ECHR also during armed conflict.[249]

The differences between humanitarian and human rights law should however not be overstated. In regard to the right to life, for example, human rights law is

mandate could not relate to the events in the West Bank and Gaza Strip, as they were 'part and parcel of the context of armed conflict as distinct from a relationship of human rights' UN Human Rights Committee 'Government of Israel: Second Periodic Report (UN Doc CCPR/C/ISR/2001/2)' (4 December 2001) para. 8.

244 Robert Kolb 'Human Rights and Humanitarian Law' in Rüdiger Wolfrum (ed) *MPEPIL* (OUP Oxford Update 2006) para. 44; Alston 'Report of the Special Rapporteur on Extrajudicial, Summary or Arbitrary Executions: Study on Targeted Killings (UN Doc A/HRC/14/24/Add.6)' para. 29; Dagmar Richter 'Humanitarian Law and Human Rights: Intersecting Circles or Separate Spheres?' in Thomas Giegerich (ed) *A Wiser Century? Judicial Dispute Settlement, Disarmament and the Laws of War 100 Years after the Second Hague Peace Conference* (Duncker & Humblot Berlin 2009); Kranz 'Die völkerrechtliche Verantwortlichkeit für die Anwendung militärischer Gewalt' p. 307; Hans-Joachim Heintze 'Theorien zum Verhältnis von Menschenrechten und humanitärem Völkerrecht' (2011) 24 Humanitäres Völkerrecht p. 11.

245 *Legality of the Threat or Use of Nuclear Weapons (Advisory Opinion)* para. 25; pointing this out: Tomuschat 'Human Rights and International Humanitarian Law' p. 17.

246 *Legal Consequences of the Construction of a Wall in the Occupied Palestinian Territory (Advisory Opinion)* para. 106.

247 *Legal Consequences of the Construction of a Wall in the Occupied Palestinian Territory (Advisory Opinion)* para. 106; critical to this approach: Kolb 'Human Rights and Humanitarian Law' para. 36.

248 Tomuschat 'Human Rights and International Humanitarian Law' p. 18. This has been classified as the 'renvoi approach' by Kolb 'Human Rights and Humanitarian Law' paras. 35–37.

249 See *Isayeva v Russia* (24 February 2005) (ECtHR) App 57950/00; further examples given by Tomuschat 'Human Rights and International Humanitarian Law' at pp. 19–20.

not necessarily considered to be more protective than humanitarian law. This is due to the fact that under human rights law the use of lethal force is possible against any person if absolutely necessary for a legitimate purpose, while under humanitarian law only civilians are generally exempt from being attacked directly.[250]

Article 15 ECHR includes derogations from most of the Convention's rights in a time of war or other public emergency, in any case during international armed conflict.[251] The same holds true for the ICCPR, which contains a similar clause in Article 4(1). While not every armed conflict is automatically seen as involving a threat to the life of the nation that cannot be contained using normal legal measures, States are afforded a wide margin of appreciation.[252] And while there are certain non-derogable rights, these do not include the freedom of expression or information or the right to privacy, which in any case are already outside of armed conflict subjectable to limitations. As these are the relevant human rights affected by cyber warfare operations, they can hardly pose significant limitations on measures involving CNOs as long as these are strictly required by the exigencies of the situation. Hereby the requirement resembles those limitations already existing under humanitarian law, namely the principle of proportionality. As emergency derogations of human rights under the relevant regimes do not imply a suspension of other international obligations of the State, the rules of humanitarian law remain applicable in any case.

5. CONCLUSION

Humanitarian law is applicable both to new weapons and methods of warfare, hence also to computer network operations, regardless of their particular execution. This holds true in the event of a conflict utilising different types of warfare, as well as in the event of it being fought purely utilising this novel form of warfare. As cyberspace does not constitute a new region of war, the traditional rules of land warfare are also applicable to cyber warfare. Specifically, computer network operations also can qualify as an attack in the sense of humanitarian law if they do not cause physical destruction noticeable outside of the targeted computer system. Therefore the entire framework of humanitarian law is applicable to all forms of military computer network operations undertaken during an international armed conflict.

---

250 Nils Melzer *Targeted Killing in International Law* (OUP Oxford 2008) p. 384.

251 Para. 6 Commentary to Art. 15 ECHR, in Jochen Abr. Frowein & Wolfgang Peukert *Europäische Menschenrechtskonvention* (Engel Kehl am Rhein 2009) p. 422.

252 At least under the ECHR as stated by the ECtHR: David Kretzmer 'Emergency, State of' in Rüdiger Wolfrum (ed) *MPEPIL* (OUP Oxford Update 2008) paras. 7–14.

Several rules of humanitarian law require specific attention in connection with the means of cyber warfare. Under the precautionary principle the probability of cascading effects of an attack need to be particularly taken into consideration by studying the targeted system's operations, its connections to third systems and their dependencies on each other. The principle further requires a heightened review of the effects of those operations utilising viruses or similar means especially in regard to the level of controllability of their spread.

The principle of distinction requires military personnel conducting computer network attacks to at least wear a distinctive emblem due to the fact that they are not able to carry their arms openly in a manner for the enemy to be able to distinguish them from civilians. As regards the communications infrastructure, an obligation to separate military from civil communications networks cannot be proven to exist because of the lack of feasibility of this measure. During armed conflict States are however obliged to protect the communications infrastructure they utilise for conducting computer network operations as these are thereby put under their control. This does not however lead to an obligation during peacetime to secure private sector computer systems unless there is sufficient clarity that the military will take control of these during armed conflict. Nor does the principle of distinction in its form of a duty to separate military from civilian targets go so as far as to oblige belligerents to mark systems qualifying as military objectives with an identifier, as it primarily remains the obligation of the attacker not to attack indiscriminately.

When in use by the armed forces, civilian infrastructure obtains a dual-use character thereby making it a military objective despite its use by civilians. The latter will nevertheless have to be considered in the planning of an attack both under the proportionality principle and precautionary approach. Yet since their legitimate destruction requires a definitive military advantage, individual dual-use systems, the outage of which can be balanced due to the technical architecture of the Internet, do not qualify as military objectives.

While computer network attacks have the potential to be utilised in a perfidious manner, the prohibition only applies to those cases in which they result in the killing, injuring or capturing of adversaries, thereby excluding a significant number of operations. Ultimately there are in any case not many instances imaginable in which computer network attacks betray the confidence of an adversary as a necessary element of a perfidious act. This holds true for the case of distributed denial of service attacks as their malicious intention is readily detected. The feigning of sender names of e-mails or using backdoors of programmes installed on target systems can only qualify as perfidy if it puts protected persons or neutral States at risk of being subject to a counterattack as a defensive measure and thereby being drawn into the conflict.

If computer network attacks are utilised in contravention of humanitarian law, the State responsible is obliged to make reparation by restoring the situation that existed prior to the violation, which can include the malware's removal or cooperation and assistance therein. If their utilisation was in accord with the law, there does not exist such obligation, however.

With respect to the actors in cyber warfare it is evident that the members of armed forces performing computer network attacks are to be treated as combatants. Members of IT security companies providing services to a belligerent party likewise qualify as combatants if they are under a command which is responsible to a party to the armed conflict. While contractual liability under domestic law in case of violations of directions is less assertive than military orders which can be tried under military jurisdiction, the element of responsibility should not be considered too restrictive. As the incentive of members of these companies in most cases is monetary gain, the impending contractual liability is of a sufficient grave detriment to ensure compliance with humanitarian law which ultimately stands behind the requirement of responsibility. If civilians individually decide to engage in computer network attacks during armed conflict it is especially exceeding the level of harm threshold as well as the criteria of direct connection and nexus to the battlefield that qualify their actions as a direct participation in hostilities, which are all more easily fulfilled once a civilian directly supports the armed forces for example by transmitting his findings. The prospect of civilians attaining the status of a cyber levée en masse is unrealistic, however, due to its high prerequisites.

Espionage conducted with the means of computer network operations during armed conflict will only have the negative ramification for its performers of being qualified as spies while they are physically located in the adversary's territory.

Lastly cyber warfare operations are not significantly limited by human rights regimes, as the relevant rights are all derogable during armed conflict while their protective aim is in any case warranted by the rules of humanitarian law.

CHAPTER 6
NEUTRALITY IN CYBER WARFARE

The principle of neutrality obliges States not involved in an armed conflict to maintain impartiality and non-discrimination towards the conflict parties, while in turn ensuring that neutral States will kept out of the conflict. In the relations between belligerents and neutral States a courant normal – the continuance of the commercial relations existing before the armed conflict – shall be observed.[1] As a result, the law applicable between the conflict parties and the neutral State is not that of armed conflict but of general international law, modified by certain regulations arising from the laws of neutrality.[2] The neutral status of a State is considered to emerge ipso iure at the outbreak of armed conflict, whereas the degree of armed force necessary to reach the threshold of an armed conflict under the laws of neutrality remains disputed.[3] The two 1907 Hague Conventions (V and XIII) relating to the rights and duties of neutrals in case of war on land and naval warfare, respectively, are the latest codifications on the topic, though further provisions dealing with neutrality are included in the more recent Geneva Conventions of 1949 and Additional Protocol I thereto.[4] Given the small number of ratifications of the Hague Conventions and subsequent State practice, this hardly supports the thesis that the Conventions state current customary international law on the issue of neutrality.[5] The essential aspects of the laws of neutrality have rather been developed through State practice, while under

1 Michael Bothe 'The Law of Neutrality' in Dieter Fleck & Michael Bothe (eds) *The Handbook of International Humanitarian Law* (OUP Oxford 2008) para. 1116.

2 Stein & Buttlar *Völkerrecht* p. 460; Wolfgang Vitzthum (ed) *Völkerrecht* (de Gruyter Berlin 2010) pp. 723 et seq; Bothe 'The Law of Neutrality' para. 1101.

3 A prior notification of the existence of a state of war to the neutral States as required by Art. 2 Convention respecting the Rights and Duties of Neutral Powers and Persons in Case of War on Land was already at that time generally regarded as constituting only a protection of confidence; see also Stefan Oeter *Neutralität und Waffenhandel* (Springer Berlin 1992) p. 37. It remains disputed where the threshold for the applicability of the law of neutrality lies. Some see a parallel with the threshold of the applicability of the laws of armed conflict between the conflict parties, while others call for a certain duration and intensity of the conflict so that the applicability of the law of neutrality can be justified with its spirit and purpose; on this see: Stein & Buttlar *Völkerrecht* p. 460; Oeter *Neutralität und Waffenhandel* pp. 73–86; Bothe 'The Law of Neutrality' para. 1106.

4 Convention respecting the Rights and Duties of Neutral Powers in Naval War (signed 18 October 1907, entered into force 26 January 1910) (1908) 2 AJIL Supp 202.

5 Oeter *Neutralität und Waffenhandel* p. 219.

certain circumstances both the UN Charter and UN Security Council decisions may provide for modifications.[6] Studies attempting to restate customary international law of naval and aerial warfare likewise include rules on neutrality in the respective frameworks, and the Tallinn Manual has also incorporated relevant rules.[7] Obviously the Hague Conventions could not take into account the revolution in communications technology in the past decades and thus do not expressly include computer network operations. Their specific regulations are thus not directly applicable to CNAs, but as they depict particularities of the general principles of neutrality law they can be drawn upon in a subsidiary manner when addressing new forms of warfare.[8] In any case it is undisputed that the duty to respect the integrity of neutral States during armed conflict exists for all kinds of warfare, hence also cyber warfare.[9]

In general the law of armed conflict supports the continuation of communications between the conflict parties. Although a neutral State may restrict the use of its telecommunications infrastructure to the belligerents on a non-discriminatory basis, it is expressly stated in Article 8 Hague Convention V that a 'neutral power is not required to forbid or restrict the use, in behalf of belligerents, of telegraph or telephone cables or wireless telegraph apparatus belonging to it or to companies or private individuals'. What is prohibited, though, is to 'erect on the territory of a neutral Power a wireless telegraphy station or other apparatus for the purpose of communicating with belligerent forces on land or sea', or to 'use any installation of this kind established by them before the war on the territory of a neutral Power for purely military purposes, and which has not been opened for the service of public messages'.[10] As CNAs necessarily utilise communications infrastructures, in addition to the general principles these are the rules which form the basis for an analysis of neutrality during cyber warfare.

1. NO PROHIBITION ON ROUTING CNAs THROUGH NEUTRAL STATES' TERRITORY

According to Article 2 Hague Convention V belligerents are 'forbidden to move troops or convoys of either munitions of war or supplies across the territory of a

---

6 Bothe 'The Law of Neutrality' paras. 1102–03.

7 There exists Doswald-Beck (ed) *San Remo Manual on International Law Applicable to Armed Conflicts at Sea* and the Program on Humanitarian Policy and Conflict Research (ed) *HPCR Manual on Air Warfare* which are seen by many to partly reflect customary international law. Whether Schmitt (ed) *Tallinn Manual on the International Law Applicable to Cyber Warfare* of 2013 can attain the same reputation will remain to be seen over the years to come.

8 Similarly: Dittmar *Angriffe auf Computernetzwerke: Ius ad bellum und ius in bello* p. 283.

9 Similarly: Schmitt (ed) *Tallinn Manual on the International Law Applicable to Cyber Warfare* pp. 248–49.

10 Art. 3 of the 1907 Hague Convention V.

neutral Power'. The same holds true for aerial warfare, including overflight, which is not allowed to take place in the airspace of neutral territories.[11] The question thus arises as to whether States are prohibited to route a CNA through the territory of a neutral State. By qualifying those data packets that transmit a CNA as weapons, one view holds that routing them through neutral territory is comparable to the prohibited movement of troops or munitions, thus being in violation of Article 2 Hague Convention V.[12] Yet another view holds that only the transmission of 'cyber weapons' (hence for example malware) across neutral territory is prohibited by Article 2 Hague Convention V, whereas the utilisation of the public Internet for military purposes does not violate the laws of neutrality.[13] The opposing view holds that such routing were merely a legitimate use of the neutrals' communications infrastructure in the sense of Article 8 Hague Convention V and at any rate not comparable to the movement of troops.[14] The Internet as a network of an inherently transnational nature could hardly fit under the rules developed in the context of the traditional territoriality principle.[15]

Only the latter view both correctly interprets the rules of neutrality and leads to practicable results. Firstly it must be borne in mind that the utilisation of foreign telecommunications services is part of the commercial relations between States, irrespective of whether CNAs or malware is routed. The general principle of a courant normal is thus of special importance in this regard. If one party to the conflict has already used the communications infrastructure of the – now neutral – State before the outbreak of armed conflict, it is not prevented from making further use this during armed conflict. Nor is the neutral obliged to prevent such use by the belligerent State.[16] Yet a neutral may not provide one party to the conflict with communications services that were not available to it

11 Dinstein 'Air Warfare' para. 75; Rule 167(a) HPCR Manual on Air and Missile Warfare.

12 Jeffrey Kelsey 'Hacking into International Humanitarian Law: The Principles of Distinction and Neutrality in the Age of Cyber Warfare' (2008) 106 Michigan Law Review pp. 1443–45; concurring therewith: Korns & Kastenberg 'Georgia's Cyber Left Hook' p. 62 and Kastenberg 'Non-Intervention and Neutrality in Cyberspace: An Emerging Principle in the National Practice of International Law' pp. 56–57. Proposing a distinction between un- and intentional routing, wherein intentional routing through neutral States should be prohibited: Brown 'A Proposal for an International Convention to Regulate the Use of Information Systems in Armed Conflict' p. 210. A minority of the group of experts drafting the Tallinn Manual were of the similar opinion, as they did not see Art. 8 Hague Convention V as applicable to cyber communications systems: Schmitt (ed) *Tallinn Manual on the International Law Applicable to Cyber Warfare* p. 251 para. 4.

13 This was the majority view of the group of experts drafting the Tallinn Manual: Schmitt (ed) *Tallinn Manual on the International Law Applicable to Cyber Warfare* pp. 251–52 paras. 4–5.

14 Schmitt, Harrison & Wingfield 'Computers and War: The Legal Battlespace' p. 15; Döge 'Cyber Warfare: Challenges for the Applicability of the Traditional Laws of War Regime' p. 497; Rule 167(b) HPCR Manual und Air and Missile Warfare.

15 Heintschel von Heinegg 'Informationskrieg und Völkerrecht' p. 153.

16 Bothe 'The Law of Neutrality' para. 1116; Dittmar *Angriffe auf Computernetzwerke: Ius ad bellum und ius in bello* p. 286.

before the beginning of hostilities, if this is done on a discriminatory basis. One can therefore speak of a principle of network neutrality resulting from the courant normal before the outbreak of hostilities.

In addition, outside of humanitarian law the term 'network neutrality' characterises the routing techniques underlying the Internet. Traditionally, the Internet infrastructure transports data indiscriminately by the so-called best-effort principle. Data packets are thus transferred without any prioritisation according to content, sender or addressee. Recently however, network operators and Internet service providers have sporadically abandoned these principles and made use of their ability to discriminate in the transfer of data according to its content.[17] This is done mainly for economic reasons, as it for example makes it possible to suppress certain competing services provided by third-party businesses in order to force users to only utilise those services offered by the provider or its partners. It is likewise possible to alter the content of data transferred; this has reportedly already occurred in the United States for political considerations.[18] Once a State gains neutral status during armed conflict it is prohibited from discriminating between data transmitted to or from one of the belligerents as long as this was not part of the courant normal before the outbreak of hostilities.

Data of a CNA which is being transmitted by the neutral's infrastructure cannot readily be compared to communications of a mere informatory character, as in itself it is an operation that qualifies as an attack under humanitarian law. This does not however change the qualification of routing services as a mere commercial activity subject to the courant normal. In the transmission of CNAs or malware by belligerents, neutral States are in a similar situation as domestic Internet service providers are with the transmission of illegal content by their customers. For example under European Union law the transfer of illegal content by Internet service providers does not make them liable for the illegal information transmitted, if it remains in a mere conduit thereof. This is justified by the fact that the activity is of a mere technical, automatic and passive nature, which implies that the service provider has neither knowledge of nor control over the information which is transmitted or stored.[19] Service providers shall likewise not be obliged to monitor traffic they transmit or store.[20] Besides the obvious implications for privacy rights, such a privilege meets the concerns that

---

17 Illustrative in this regard: Holznagel 'Netzneutralität als Aufgabe der Vielfaltssicherung' pp. 95–100.

18 Holznagel 'Netzneutralität als Aufgabe der Vielfaltssicherung' p. 97.

19 Recital No 42 to Directive 2000/31/EC of the European Parliament and of the Council of 8 June 2000 on Certain Legal Aspects of Information Society Services, in Particular Electronic Commerce, in the Internal Market [2000] OJ L178/1.

20 See Arts. 12 and 15 of Directive 2000/31/EC of the European Parliament and of the Council of 8 June 2000 on Certain Legal Aspects of Information Society Services, in Particular Electronic Commerce, in the Internal Market.

a filtering of content by the service providers is nearly impossible.[21] The same also holds true for neutral States.

Such a reading is further supported by Rule 167(b) of the recent Manual on International Law Applicable to Air and Missile Warfare which states that:

> 'when Belligerent Parties use for military purposes a public, internationally and openly accessible network such as the Internet, the fact that part of this infrastructure is situated within the jurisdiction of a Neutral does not constitute a violation of neutrality.'[22]

Forming part of the general rules on neutrality identified in the HPCR Manual, this rule is not limited to air and missile warfare. However, neither express treaty law nor customary international law could be identified to substantiate Rule 167(b). But the Rule's drafters according to the commentary to the Manual deemed Article 8 Hague Convention V to also be applicable to the Internet, while further stating that:

> '[g]iven the complexity and interdependence of an openly accessible network such as the Internet, it is impossible for any State to effectively control or interfere with communications over such a network. After all, most Internet communications are not traceable, since they are transmitted over lines of communications and routers passing through various States before reaching their ultimate destination. Therefore, the mere fact that military communications, including CNAs, have been transmitted via a router situated in the territory of a Neutral is not to be considered a violation of neutrality.'[23]

Overall it must be contended that a suppression of the routing of CNAs or malware through a particular territory is in practice nearly impossible. An obligation for States to do so is therefore hardly justifiable.

Most strikingly, the data packets while en route neither pose a danger to the neutral State, nor are they themselves attackable. This holds true for the transmission of both CNAs or malware that might be qualified as a weapon. The risk to the neutral of being dragged into a conflict merely as a result of routing CNAs or malware through its networks is thus much lower than is the case with regular troop movements in its territory, if it exists at all. As this risk is the ratio for prohibiting the transfer of conventional weapons and troops over neutral

---

21 Sieber *Verantwortlichkeit im Internet: technische Kontrollmöglichkeiten und multimedia-rechtliche Regelungen* pp. 231–33; a recent example for a similar treatment is given in the case *Roadshow Films Pty. Ltd. v. iiNet Limited* decided by the Federal Court of Australia on 4 February 2010, wherein the court ruled that the Internet service provider was not liable for copyright infringements of its subscribers.

22 Program on Humanitarian Policy and Conflict Research (ed) *HPCR Manual on Air Warfare*.

23 Program on Humanitarian Policy and Conflict Research (ed) *Commentary on the HPCR Manual on International Law Applicable to Air and Missile Warfare* pp. 309–10.

territory in the first place, its elimination makes the comparison of routing and troops transfer somewhat poor. Rule 8 Tallinn Manual likewise provides support for this view by stating that 'the fact that a cyber operation has been routed via the cyber infrastructure located in a State is not sufficient evidence for attributing the operation to that State'. It is thus reasonable to qualify the routing of CNAs or malware through neutral networks as a legitimate use thereof which cannot be compared to the sending of armed troops.

2. THE PROHIBITION ON MASKING CNAs AS ORIGINATING FROM A NEUTRAL STATE

As has been pointed out before, CNAs are regularly routed through systems located on the territory of States neutral to the conflict due to the architecture of the Internet. A more invasive possibility would be to rent or hijack systems within the territory of a neutral State in order to provide a subsequent opportunity to use them during cyber warfare with a third State.[24] Furthermore, it is possible to mask the source of a CNA to make it appear to be within a neutral State while actually being conducted by the armed forces of a belligerent party in its territory. This can be done for two reasons: firstly in order to mask the origin of the attack and thus the perpetrator State's involvement; and secondly it can also have as its goal implying the involvement of a third State or even aim at causing a counterattack of the victim State on the alleged attacker. Such an action is however prohibited by the general rule of neutrality that declares the territory of a neutral State to be inviolable, which includes any act of hostility within that State.[25] The launching of any kind of attack from neutral territory, irrespective of the means utilised, is therefore forbidden.

While this rule appertaining to the inviolability of the territory of the neutral State cannot be invoked for the case where CNAs are masked as originating therefrom, the latter are likewise prohibited by fundamental principles of neutrality. As neutral States are to be kept outside of the armed conflict, belligerents are also prohibited from generally implying a neutral State's involvement against its will. This is inter alia stipulated in the inclusion of feigning a protected status by the use of emblems, flags or uniforms of a neutral State as a prohibited act of perfidy under Article 37(1)(d) Additional Protocol I, which is also considered customary international law.[26] Similar rules

24 Brown 'A Proposal for an International Convention to Regulate the Use of Information Systems in Armed Conflict' pp. 209–10.

25 Art. 1 Hague Convention V and XIII; Bothe 'Neutrality, Concept and General Rules' para. 30.

26 Henckaerts & Doswald-Beck (eds) *Customary International Humanitarian Law Volume I: Rules* Rule 63 p. 218.

apply to aircraft.[27] Warships on the other hand are exceptionally allowed to fly a false flag. However, while doing so they may not launch an attack.[28] It can therefore be inferred from these rules that while engaging in attack the source State may not feign a neutral status in any way whatsoever. States are therefore likewise prohibited from feigning that a CNA originates from a system of a neutral State.

3. OBLIGATIONS OF NEUTRAL STATES

By stating that the territory of neutral powers is inviolable, Article 1 Hague Convention V stipulates the most fundamental provision intended to assure that neutral States are kept out of armed conflict. This prohibition encompasses not only intentional violations but also collateral effects of the hostilities to the detriment of the neutral State's territory.[29] The complement to this right is the obligation on neutrals to refrain from taking any part in hostilities. Under certain circumstances this might even oblige neutral States to use armed force in order to defend their neutrality. As has been shown above, the utilisation of the Internet for CNAs, that is their routing through network infrastructure located on the territory of a neutral State, is not a violation of said State's neutrality. Hence the neutral State does not act contrary to its duties if it has knowledge of this and is not obliged to prevent such from happening.[30]

Articles 4 and 5 Hague Convention V of 1907 prohibit a neutral State from tolerating the establishment of corps of combatants to assist a belligerent in the neutral State's territory.[31] It must therefore likewise prevent the establishment on its territory of corps that undertake CNAs on behalf of a belligerent party. By contrast it is not called upon to prevent its nationals from joining the armed forces of a party to the conflict if this is done of their own volition. Another duty of prevention exists in respect of attacks that are launched by a party to the conflict from the neutral's territory. This can be the case when a party to the conflict violates the neutrality by sending troops into the neutral's territory or using it as a base for further attacks. But it can likewise include CNAs originating from systems located on the neutral's territory. In these cases the neutral State is

27 Rule 112(d) HPCR Manual on Air and Missile Warfare; Dinstein 'Air Warfare' para. 70.

28 Doswald-Beck (ed) *San Remo Manual on International Law Applicable to Armed Conflicts at Sea* Rules 109 and 110 pp. 184 et seq.

29 Bothe 'The Law of Neutrality' para. 1108.

30 Due to the technological complexities and questionable benefits involved in analysing all Internet traffic States will mostly not have knowledge of the paths of routing. As the routing in most instances is more or less randomly depending on load sharing of networks and the location of the target system, the routing of a CNA through a neutral State cannot serve as a prejudice to the effect that the perpetrator State intentionally routes through the neutral State's networks.

31 Bothe 'Neutrality, Concept and General Rules' para. 44.

obliged to prevent its territory from being used by a belligerent with all means at its disposal, including military means. These are limited to those measures of defence that are feasible for the neutral State to prevent it from being obliged to destroy itself.[32] Nonetheless, neutral States remain bound by the prohibition on the use of armed force and may thus only resort to it if the actions of one of the belligerents against the neutrality of the State qualify as an armed attack. The latter can generally be assumed to exist in situations where one belligerent party tries to take parts of the neutral's territory as a basis for hostilities.[33] Neutrals are therefore under an obligation to prevent computer systems on their territory from being used by the parties to a conflict to launch CNAs. As these systems are located within their territory, neutral States are generally free to choose the relevant measures.[34]

Ultimately the limitation created by the general prohibition on use of force also applicable to States defending their neutrality does not play an important role in preventing computer systems in the neutral's territory from being utilised by parties to the conflict for CNAs. As the physical control over these systems rests with the neutral, the final and also most simple measure is to disconnect or shut down the relevant systems even if this might cause monetary damage.[35] In the end neutral States are free to decide how to fulfil their preventive obligation. States will therefore employ defensive measures out of self-interest in order to secure the functionality of their systems and the data stored thereon. Nevertheless there exists no general obligation for States to make use of a certain type of military defence or to secure their computer systems.[36]

---

32 Bothe 'Neutrality, Concept and General Rules' para. 33; seeing a similar limitation conditioned on the neutral's ability to detect and counter CNAs: George K. Walker 'Neutrality and Information Warfare' in Michael N. Schmitt & Brian T. O'Donnell (eds) *Computer Network Attack and International Law* (Naval War College Newport 2002) p. 242. This approach is reflected in Rule 93 Tallinn Manual and the accompanying commentary: Schmitt (ed) *Tallinn Manual on the International Law Applicable to Cyber Warfare* p. 253.

33 Bothe 'The Law of Neutrality' paras. 1107 and 1109; Arts. 5 and 10 Hague Convention V.

34 Bothe 'Neutrality, Concept and General Rules' para. 35.

35 Under domestic law some already see an obligation to disconnect critical infrastructures from the public Internet as the ultima ratio if traditional protective measures fail in preventing CNAs. For the case of Germany: Gaycken & Karger 'Entnetzung statt Vernetzung: Paradigmenwechsel in der IT-Sicherheit' pp. 3–8; This stands in stark contrast however to the concept of co-dependency which promotes a high level of interconnectedness as the ultimate deterrence against CNAs: the higher the level of interconnectedness, the more likely it is that the attacker is deterred by the prospect of adverse effects on his own IT-infrastructure through his own attack: Constanze Kurz 'Sicherheit im Netz? Nur durch Vernetzung!' in *Frankfurter Allgemeine Zeitung* of 6 August 2010 p. 31.

36 Similarly in this regard: Dittmar *Angriffe auf Computernetzwerke: Ius ad bellum und ius in bello* who currently sees no obligation of States to secure their systems, but considers the establishment of such an obligation for the future, as the UNGA Resolutions on the 'developments in the field of information and telecommunications in the context of international security' would hint to that direction (at p. 169).

If an officially neutral State is proven to have sponsored an attack from its territory, or to have been unable or unwilling to stop it, it is argued that the victim State may defend itself by also attacking those units located in the neutral's territory.[37] Consequently the same holds true if a neutral State does not fulfil its obligation to prevent one party to the conflict from using systems on its territory as a source for CNAs. In this case the victim State may react by eliminating the source of the attack even if this includes a violation of the neutral's territorial integrity.[38] Due regard must however be given in this respect to the swiftness of CNAs and the possibility of their detection by the neutral State. The latter will mostly not be able to gain knowledge of the preparation of CNAs from systems on its territory.[39] Once the attack stops – regardless of whether it was successful or not – the victim State has no right to attack the neutral State and nor is there a military necessity to do so.

4. THE HOSTING OF GOVERNMENT WEBSITES ON FOREIGN SERVERS

During the Georgian-Russian conflict of 2008, several servers hosting government websites were targeted by DDoS attacks, rendering these resources unavailable.[40] The Georgian government reacted by moving the respective websites to servers located in the United States. Some authors have asked whether such a relocation amounts to a violation of the neutrality of the host State, hence that of the United States.[41] In this regard it was opined that these actions could firstly be in breach of the neutral status of the US by violating Article 3 Hague Convention V, which prohibits the erection of an apparatus for communication by the belligerent on neutral territory or the use of such erected prior to the conflict. Secondly, the inaction of the US, which did not require the companies involved to terminate Internet services for the Georgian government, 'could be interpreted as a violation of Hague V in that they formed a quasi-corps of cyber combatants on behalf of the US government to protect Georgia's

---

37 Stein & Marauhn 'Völkerrechtliche Aspekte von Informationsoperationen' p. 11; Kees 'Responsibility of States for Private Actors' paras 17–18; Bothe 'Neutrality, Concept and General Rules' paras. 34–35; Dittmar *Angriffe auf Computernetzwerke: Ius ad bellum und ius in bello* p. 288.

38 Similarly: Rule 94 Tallinn Manual.

39 Stein & Marauhn 'Völkerrechtliche Aspekte von Informationsoperationen' p. 11.

40 See p. 45 et seq. above.

41 Kastenberg 'Non-Intervention and Neutrality in Cyberspace: An Emerging Principle in the National Practice of International Law' pp. 60–62. The relocation was apparently done after an offer for assistance by the owner of TSHost, an US resident of Georgian origin, who was in Georgia during the time of conflict.

Internet assets'.[42] Moreover, servers that host this sort of data could be regarded as a military objective by the opposing party to the conflict.[43]

These assumptions cannot be confirmed. First and foremost there is so far no evidence that the CNAs were instigated by Russian State actors. The laws of neutrality are however not applicable in instances of attacks by civilians. But even if they were actually initiated by State actors, the conclusion is no different. The prohibition of Article 3 Hague Convention V is limited to the erection, after the outbreak of hostilities, for the 'purpose of communicating with belligerent forces'. An apparatus erected prior to the conflict may however be used by the belligerent if it has been opened to the general public.[44] While from the outset it is clear that the hosting of websites or other services is not what was originally meant by the 'erection of an apparatus for communication', the situations are admittedly quite similar. One must distinguish, however, between the hosting of websites merely intended for purposes of information and communication or database services. The mere hosting of websites containing plain information, as was done in the Georgian case – at least according to what is publicly known – is not a form of communication, but a merely one-sided type of information similar to a radio broadcast. In any case it was not used as a form of communication with the Georgian armed forces. These sorts of websites rather aim at informing the general public, equally in times of conflict.

Moreover, Georgia did not set up the server itself, but merely utilised a pre-existing server that was also open to a general public. There is moreover no evidence indicating that these services were exclusively provided for the Georgian government and not to the general public, hence potentially also Russia. In this regard it is irrelevant that the hosting in the US was done by private companies without specific State approval, as a State has the duty to ensure that private companies likewise provide or deny their services impartially.

The inaction by the US as to the hosting of Georgian government websites – regardless of whether by intent or negligence – can therefore not be qualified as a violation of its neutral duties as the hosting itself was not contrary to the rules of neutrality. Nor does it set a precedent for future belligerents in cyber warfare. The principle of impartiality, fundamental to the rules of neutrality and stipulated in Article 9 Hague Convention V, only applies to the treatment of belligerents in a continuing armed conflict. It cannot however be interpreted that in a future armed conflict the neutral State will have to treat other belligerents in the same manner. This is due to the aim of protection which only intends a neutral State to be impartial during an armed conflict but not to shape

42 Kastenberg 'Non-Intervention and Neutrality in Cyberspace: An Emerging Principle in the National Practice of International Law' p. 62; Korns & Kastenberg 'Georgia's Cyber Left Hook' p. 69.

43 Kastenberg 'Non-Intervention and Neutrality in Cyberspace: An Emerging Principle in the National Practice of International Law' p. 64.

44 Art. 3(b) Hague Convention V.

the future obligations of a State. Neither the text of Article 9 Hague Convention V nor State practice point in this direction.

Lastly the servers hosting Georgian government websites could not be qualified as a military objective. While such could be argued as long as the servers were located on Georgian territory, the neutral status of the United States prevents any objects on its territory from becoming military objectives. While this certainly holds true for example for embassies of belligerents, it is likewise the case for enemy property on neutral territory. A fortiori this is the case for a website or service hosted by a server on neutral territory, as long as these by themselves are not contrary to the laws of neutrality.

The conclusions drawn from the Georgian case can also be generalised. As long as a neutral State itself – or private companies within its jurisdiction – impartially provide services or infrastructure to a party to a conflict which are not specifically created for this purpose and do not by themselves qualify as taking part in hostilities, this does not qualify as an unneutral action. The conclusion is different if services are either provided partially only to one belligerent, or if the services are of a military character. The first instance is an unneutral service a State must also prevent private companies from offering. The latter is likewise, but moreover also an active participation in hostilities. In both instances the victim State may resort to reprisals for an unneutral service, though limited by the prohibition on the use of force.[45]

This is also important for the recent phenomenon of so-called cloud computing which has been brought about by the ever-increasing interconnectivity of networks. The term refers to computing operations that use shared resources, software or information on remote systems. It is thus foreseeable that computer systems are actively utilised in an armed conflict which are not – or not entirely – physically located in the territory of a belligerent party. Even today the utilisation of large global botnets for cybercrimes can be seen as an example thereof. As long as no new customary rules emerge from State practice the above is also applicable to this case. Cloud computing that utilises resources in neutral States may therefore also be utilised by armed forces as long as these are impartially available. It is still prohibited, however, to use those resources for CNAs as this means launching attacks from neutral territory. The utilisation of transnational botnets must therefore be seen as a violation of the neutrality of the respective States. This is only logical considering that the target State, in order to defend itself against such CNAs, could potentially counter-attack those systems located in neutral territory.

45 Bothe 'Neutrality, Concept and General Rules' paras 28–29 pointing to the different levels in legal analysis of the laws of neutrality and the UN Charter framework on the use of force.

5. CONCLUSION

The laws of neutrality do not provide express rules on cyber warfare. Yet neither is the case concerning aerial warfare, and even the rules on land and naval warfare mostly rely on the general principles of neutrality, especially as the relevant Hague Conventions have only been ratified by a small number of States. Just as this has not prevented the emergence of frameworks for conventional forms of warfare, so is this the case for neutrality in cyber warfare. The general principles of neutrality are sufficient to regulate most forms of cyber warfare and also lead to tenable results. The apprehension that the laws of neutrality are too 'border-centric' to relate to the notion of a 'borderless Internet' as the structural basis for cyber warfare is therefore unsubstantiated.[46]

The laws of neutrality do not make the utilisation of CNAs impossible, in that their routing over the infrastructure of neutral States is not prohibited. This is not only a concession to the technological necessity of doing so, but is also in conformity with the fundamental rule of neutrality, namely to keep neutral States out of the conflict. As routing of CNAs does not negatively affect neutral States, its prohibition would not offer any increase in their protection. By contrast, the masking of CNAs to originate from a neutral State is clearly a violation as in this case the neutral State might be drawn into the conflict due to a deception of the target State. The general obligations of neutral States already known under the frameworks of neutrality in other forms of warfare likewise apply to cyber warfare: neutral States must prevent belligerents from launching attacks from systems within their jurisdiction limited however by the element of feasibility. Lastly, neutral States and companies within their jurisdiction are allowed to offer information and communications services to the belligerents as long as these are provided impartially and within the courant normal of economic relations so not to favour one party to the conflict over the other.

---

[46] As voiced by Kastenberg 'Non-Intervention and Neutrality in Cyberspace: An Emerging Principle in the National Practice of International Law' p. 64.

PART III

CONCLUSION

COMPUTER NETWORK OPERATIONS RESTRAINED

The goal of this study was to show that both general international law as well as international humanitarian law provide a framework to adequately constrain States in their application of military computer network operations during and outside of international armed conflict. The emergence of the technical infrastructure referred to as the Internet, or a social sphere considered as cyberspace, has not led actions performed in connection therewith to take place in a legal vacuum. On the contrary, the existing rules governing State conduct on the international level and during warfare are applicable thereto just as in other fields. This proves the assertions voiced both in legal scholarship and in the media, but also by several States, arguing for a requirement of an international cyber warfare convention or code of conduct, to have been made prematurely.

The inherent flexibility of international law allows it to regulate this novel instrument, as shown initially by demonstrating that the jurisdiction of States also extends over all activities performed via the Internet. For this purpose the Internet has been identified as a physical infrastructure territorialised along State boundaries. Further, it has been shown how States implicitly assert jurisdiction with respect to actions performed via the Internet. Since it is imbedded within all national jurisdictions it was also shown that the Internet cannot qualify as an international commons, and never has been. On the one hand this reveals that the Internet is not devoid of the exercise of State sovereignty. On the other hand the limitation of a potentially infinite jurisdiction granted by the effects principle through the requirement of a genuine link simultaneously illustrates that States are vested with governing power primarily only over those systems located within their territory and the operations running thereon. Operations on foreign systems only under special circumstances may be subject to the jurisdiction of a third State, thereby showing that State sovereignty and their sovereign equality is also to be respected in cyberspace. From this the concept of a territorial fragmentation of the Internet can be deduced.

Drawing upon this concept, the study developed the idea that even outside of armed conflict States can incur international responsibility for cross-border computer network operations. While it is clear that the established rules of attributing wrongful acts to a State also apply to these operations, the major problem in this regard has been shown to be the insufficient technical capacity to track and trace hostile computer network operations to their source systems. As a consequence the legal attributability of the operation is similarly inadequate. This problem of non-attributability – whether due to technical complexities or the operations being conducted by non-State actors – has been solved by holding that States are generally under an obligation to prevent malicious computer network operations from emanating from networks under their jurisdiction. In this context the failure to exercise due diligence in order to prevent such operations occurring has been qualified as a sufficient basis of attribution. Yet it was likewise shown that no such obligation has been specifically created or established under customary international law, but can only be derived from the general obligation of States not to knowingly allow their territory to be used for acts contrary to the rights of other States. While a growing international consensus could be shown to exist in the field of combating cybercrime both in regard to its material and procedural aspects, this could however not be proven to exist with regard to cross-border computer network operations undertaken by the armed forces of a State or other organs. However, the non-legally binding standards and recommendations given in soft law instruments can through their qualification as best practices clarify the due diligence obligations of States in respect of their duty of prevention.

As States generally have considerable discretion over the realisation of the duty to exercise due diligence, mere territorial control cannot establish a presumed knowledge of illegal acts. This must be presumed however as soon as the victim State informs the source State of relevant operations emanating from networks under its jurisdiction. State practice shows that the establishment of national CERTs available at all times is considered to be organisational best practice for this form of cooperation. Cooperating with the victim State in identifying the perpetrator of a malicious CNO is further to be seen as diligent behaviour on the part of the source State. In contrast the source State cannot evade international responsibility by simply refusing to cooperate or asserting conflicting national laws as a justification. This would open the possibility of plausible deniability for every State wishing to undertake computer network operations, thus effectively circumventing any State responsibility. Nevertheless States are obliged to only carry out those measures available to them in the particular case, which due to the operations' technicalities makes the exercise of due diligence concentrate especially on the acts of the source State after the fact, namely cooperation with the victim State.

Computer network operations have been proven to be able to amount to both a violation of the territorial integrity and political independence of the victim State, as well as concurrently to an intervention into its internal affairs. Reference was further made to the international telecommunications regime which implicitly prohibits States from conducting these kinds of cross-border operations on foreign territory. This encompasses measures establishing a so-called electronic blockade outside of armed conflict. On the other hand the regimes applicable to territories other than land territory, namely the law of the sea and the regime of outer space, have been shown not to provide any further limitations, with the exception of the prohibition on conducting malicious computer network operations targeting the coastal State during innocent passage of a vessel.

The qualification of a computer network operation as a form of armed force in the sense of the UN Charter has been shown not to be susceptible to a schematic classification. There are several criteria that can be used as an evaluative indicator, while in this regard the target system must always be seen in its entirety together with the processes running thereon, as well as the cascading effects on dependent systems. Yet it ultimately remains necessary to evaluate the crossing of the threshold in each individual case, bearing in mind elements of a political decision and considerations of opportunity. Taking into account the history of the prohibition on the use of force and its interpretation in respect of conventional weapons, only those operations that have a destructive effect leading to injury of life and limb or destruction of property readily qualify as armed force.

Just as computer network operations can be imbedded within the regime of State responsibility, international law likewise is able to provide justifications for their use. This is the case when taken as a countermeasure, as a means of self-defence, or with UN Security Council authorisation. The trigger for these situations may itself lie in the occurrence of a computer network operation. As these may also amount to an armed attack, the victim State itself can answer with a similar operation as well as with conventional military force. In this respect these new forms of military operations do not pose different challenges from those utilising conventional kinetic weapons. However, as States are barred from gathering evidence on foreign systems as a measure of self-help, which is necessary for being able to traceback a computer network operation, the allowance of indirect evidence as a relaxed standard of proof before international courts is to be granted to the victim State.

The regime of international humanitarian law is also applicable to this novel means of warfare thereby limiting the course of action of States during an international armed conflict in order to protect both civilians and neutral States. Several rules are of special concern in this regard: the precautionary principle and that of distinction. The former obliges commanders to take the probability of cascading effects of a computer network attack into consideration by studying the targeted system's operations, its connections to third systems and their dependencies on each other. Additionally the controllability of the malware utilised needs to be taken into account beforehand. As a consequence of the principle of distinction, military personnel conducting computer network attacks are required to wear at least a distinctive emblem due to the fact that they are not able to carry their arms openly in a manner for the enemy to be able to distinguish them from civilians. States are not obliged however to separate military from civil communications networks as this is not feasible.

As regards the actors in cyber warfare it is evident that the members of armed forces who perform computer network attacks are to be treated as combatants. Yet members of IT security companies providing services to a belligerent party have been shown to qualify as combatants as well if they are under a command which is responsible to a party to the armed conflict. In this regard contractual liability is a sufficient basis for establishing responsibility. Furthermore, civilians are able to directly participate in the hostilities by engaging in computer network attacks during armed conflict, thereby making themselves able to be subjected to counter-attacks.

Several rules of humanitarian law have been proven to play only a marginal role in conjunction with computer network attacks. An example of this is the prohibition of perfidy which only applies in instances where the feigning endangers protected persons or neutral States by putting them at risk of attack. This can be the case where a defensive reaction usually consists of a counter-attack, as here the deceived person or State is in danger of being drawn into the conflict. Due to the operations' technicalities these instances are however marginal. The same holds true for cases of cyber espionage, the actors of which will during armed conflict in most cases not qualify as spies, thereby avoiding the status' negative ramifications. Cyber warfare operations are moreover not significantly limited by human rights regimes, as the relevant rights are all derogable during armed conflict, while their protective aim is in any case warranted by the rules of humanitarian law.

Under the laws of neutrality States are not prohibited from routing computer network attacks through the infrastructure of neutral States, as neutral States are not negatively affected by this. However, the masking of attacks so as to deceive the target State into believing these to originate from a neutral State violates the fundamental principle of preventing neutrals from being drawn into the conflict.

A specific treaty-based regulation of computer network operations by States does not exist in even a nascent state and any attempted developments on this issue have so far met with strong resistance. This ambiguity as to the status of computer network operations has been remedied by this study which ultimately establishes that all kinds of computer network operations must comply with traditional rules of international law. This is the case regardless of their effects, or whether they are undertaken during or outside of an international armed conflict. Both the detailed provisions of humanitarian law, and general international law, have proven to be sufficiently flexible to regulate this novel means.

Ultimately militaries have gained yet another means and method of warfare. Yet as with any weapon it is the utilisation in each individual case that will decide its legality. Computer network operations as a means of warfare or sovereign measure outside of armed conflict can therefore potentially lead to a proliferation of low-level conflicts promoted by their characteristic of being a clandestinely operating instrument, or lead to adverse effects on civilian infrastructure. However, the operations likewise provide a tool that allows militaries to merely neutralise and not destroy targets, possibly even preventing the outbreak of more serious conventional hostilities by decapacitating the adversaries' command and control systems. When conducted in conformity with humanitarian law, this novel form of warfare can actually be considered as an improvement from a humanitarian perspective.

BIBLIOGRAPHY

LITERATURE

MONOGRAPHS

Abbate, Janet *Inventing the Internet* (MIT Press Cambridge 2000)

Alexandrov, Stanimir A. *Self-Defense against the Use of Force in International Law* (Kluwer The Hague 1996)

Baslar, Kemal *The Concept of the Common Heritage of Mankind in International Law* (Nijhoff The Hague 1998)

Baumann, Ingo *Das internationale Recht der Satellitenkommunikation* (Lang Frankfurt am Main 2005)

Benzing, Markus *Das Beweisrecht vor internationalen Gerichten und Schiedsgerichten in zwischenstaatlichen Streitigkeiten* (Springer Heidelberg 2010)

Berkowitz, Bruce *The New Face of War: How War Will be Fought in the 21st Century* (Free Press New York 2003)

Boothby, William H. *Weapons and the Law of Armed Conflict* (OUP Oxford 2009)

Bosselmann, Klaus *The Principle of Sustainability: Transforming Law and Governance* (Ashgate Aldershot 2008)

Bothe, Michael, Partsch, Karl Josef and Solf, Waldemar A. *New Rules for Victims of Armed Conflicts: Commentary on the Two 1977 Protocols Additional to the Geneva Conventions of 1949* (Nijhoff The Hague 1982)

Brenner, Susan W. *Cyberthreats: The Emerging Fault Lines of the Nation State* (OUP Oxford 2009)

Brownlie, Ian *International Law and the Use of Force by States* (Clarendon Oxford 1963)

Brownlie, Ian *Principles of Public International Law* (OUP Oxford 2008)

Brunst, Phillip W. *Anonymität im Internet – rechtliche und tatsächliche Rahmenbedingungen zum Spannungsfeld zwischen einem Recht auf Anonymität bei der elektronischen Kommunikation und den Möglichkeiten zur Identifizierung und Strafverfolgung* (Duncker & Humblot Berlin 2009)

Cassese, Antonio *International Law* (OUP Oxford 2005)

Clausewitz, Carl von *Vom Kriege* (Hedrich Leipzig 1832)

Crawford, James *The Creation of States in International Law* (Clarendon Oxford 1979)

Dahm, Georg, Delbrück, Jost and Wolfrum, Rüdiger *Völkerrecht vol I/3* (de Gruyter Berlin 2002)

Dahm, Georg, Delbrück, Jost and Wolfrum, Rüdiger *Völkerrecht vol I/2* (de Gruyter Berlin 2002)

Delibasis, Dimitrios *The Right to National Self-Defence in Information Warfare Operations* (Arena Books Bury St Edmunds 2007)

Derpa, Rolf M. *Das Gewaltverbot der Satzung der Vereinten Nationen und die Anwendung nichtmilitärischer Gewalt* (Athenaeum Bad Homburg 1970)

Determann, Lothar *Kommunikationsfreiheit im Internet: Freiheitsrechte und gesetzliche Beschränkungen* (Nomos Baden-Baden 1999)

Dinstein, Yoram *War Aggression and Self-Defence* (CUP Cambridge 2005)

Dinstein, Yoram *The Conduct of Hostilities under the Law of International Armed Conflict* (CUP Cambridge 2010)

Dittmar, Falko *Angriffe auf Computernetzwerke: Ius ad bellum und ius in bello* (Duncker & Humblot Berlin 2005)

Doehring, Karl *Völkerrecht* (CF Müller Heidelberg 2004)

Doria, Avri and Kleinwächter, Wolfgang *Internet Governance Forum (IGF): The First Two Years* at <www.intgovforum.org/cms/hydera/IGFBook_the_first_two_years.pdf> (date accessed 29 April 2012)

Drews, Imke-Ilse *Die völkerrechtlichen Dimensionen des staatlichen Einsatzes privater Militärfirmen* (Nomos Baden-Baden 2011)

Eckert, Claudia *IT-Sicherheit: Konzepte – Verfahren – Protokolle* (Oldenbourg München 2009)

Epiney, Astrid *Die völkerrechtliche Verantwortlichkeit von Staaten für rechtswidriges Verhalten im Zusammenhang mit Aktionen Privater* (Nomos Baden-Baden 1992)

Ernst, Stefan *Hacker,, Cracker & Computerviren: Recht und Praxis der Informationssicherheit* (Schmidt Köln 2004)

Fleisch, Elgar and Mattern, Friedemann *Das Internet der Dinge: Ubiquitous Computing und RFID in der Praxis* (Springer Heidelberg 2005)

Franck, Thomas M. *Recourse to Force: State Action against Threats and Armed Attacks* (Cambridge University Press Cambridge 2002)

Frowein, Jochen Abr. and Peukert, Wolfgang *Europäische Menschenrechtskonvention* (Engel Kehl am Rhein 2009)

Fuchs, Christian *Internet and Society: Social Theory in the Information Age* (Routledge New York 2008)

Gaycken, Sandro *Cyberwar: Das Internet als Kriegsschauplatz* (Open Source Press München 2011)

Geiger, Gebhard *Offensive Informationskriegsführung: Die Joint Doctrine for Information Operations der US-Streitkräfte: Sicherheitspolitische Perspektiven* (SWP Berlin 2002)

Genoni, Maurizio A. M. *Die Notwehr im Völkerrecht* (Schulthess Polygraphischer Verlag Zürich 1987)

Germann, Michael *Gefahrenabwehr und Strafverfolgung im Internet* (Duncker und Humblot Berlin 2000)

Geschonneck, Alexander *Computer-Forensik* (Dpunkt Heidelberg 2008)

Gets, Marina *Meinungsäußerungs- und Informationsfreiheit im Internet aus der Sicht des Völkerrechts* (Berlin Verlag Spitz Berlin 2002)

Ghorbani, Ali A., Lu, Wei and Tavallaee, Mahbod *Network Intrusion Detection and Prevention: Concepts and Techniques* (Springer New York 2010)

Goldsmith, Jack L. and Wu, Tim *Who Controls the Internet? Illusions of a Borderless World* (OUP Oxford 2006)

Gray, Christine D. *International Law and the Use of Force* (OUP Oxford 2008)

Greenberg, Lawrence T., Goodman, Seymour E. and Soo Hoo, Kevin J. *Information Warfare and International Law* (CCRP Washington 1997)
Grewlich, Klaus Werner *Governance in 'Cyberspace': Access and Public Interest in Global Communications* (Kluwer The Hague 1999)
Herdegen, Matthias *Völkerrecht* (Beck München 2009)
Herrmann, Christoph *Das Grundrecht auf Gewährleistung der Vertraulichkeit und Integrität informationstechnischer Systeme: Entstehung und Perspektiven* (Peter Lang Frankfurt am Main 2010)
Hettling, Jana Kristin *Satellite Imagery for Verification and Enforcement of Public International Law* (Heymanns Köln 2008)
Hobe, Stephan *Einführung in das Völkerrecht* (Francke Tübingen 2008)
Iburg, Holger *Abschreckung und Software: Computertechnologie als Instrument der amerikanischen Sicherheitspolitik* (Campus-Verlag Frankfurt 1991)
Jennings, Robert Y. and Watts, Arthur *Oppenheim's International Law* (Longman Harlow 1996)
Kamal, Ahmad *The Law of Cyberspace: An Invitation to the Table of Negotiations* (UN Institute of Training and Research Geneva 2005)
Kolb, Robert *Ius contra bellum: le droit international relatif au maintien de la paix* (Helbing & Lichtenhahn Bâle 2009)
Lehnardt, Chia *Private Militärfirmen und völkerrechtliche Verantwortlichkeit: Eine Untersuchung aus humanitär-völkerrechtlicher und menschenrechtlicher Perspektive* (Mohr Siebeck Tübingen 2011)
Lehto, Marja *Indirect Responsibility for Terrorist Acts: Redefinition of the Concept of Terrorism Beyond Violent Acts* (Martinus Nijhoff Leiden 2009)
Lessig, Lawrence *Code and Other Laws of Cyberspace* (Basic Books New York 1999)
Libicki, Martin *What is Information Warfare?* (National Defense University Washington 1995)
Libicki, Martin *Conquest in Cyberspace: National Security and Information Warfare* (CUP Cambridge 2007)
Libicki, Martin *Cyberdeterrence and Cyberwar* (RAND Santa Monica 2009)
Lindsay, David *International Domain Name Law: ICANN and the UDRP* (Hart Oxford 2007)
Lipson, Howard F. *Tracking and Tracing Cyber-Attacks: Technical Challenges and Global Policy Issues* (Carnegie Mellon University, Software Engineering Institute Pittsburgh 2002)
Lubell, Noam *Extraterritorial Use of Force against Non-State Actors* (OUP Oxford 2010)
Mani, V.S. *Basic Principles of Modern International Law: A Study of the United Nations Debates on the Principles of International Law concerning Friendly Relations and Co-operation Among States* (Lancers Books New Delhi 1993)
Matheson, Michael J. *Council Unbound: The Growth of UN Decision Making on Conflict and Postconflict Issues after the Cold War* (United States Institute of Peace Washington 2006)
Mayer, Patrick G. *Das Internet im öffentlichen Recht: Unter Berücksichtigung europarechtlicher und völkerrechtlicher Vorgaben* (Duncker & Humblot Berlin 1999)
Melzer, Nils *Targeted Killing in International Law* (OUP Oxford 2008)

Melzer, Nils *Interpretive Guidance on the Notion of Direct Participation in Hostilities under International Humanitarian Law* (ICRC Geneva 2009)

Meyer-Ladewig, Jens *Europäische Menschenrechtskonvention* (Nomos Baden-Baden 2011)

Murray, Andrew D. *The Regulation of Cyberspace: Control in the Online Environment* (Routledge-Cavendish Abingdon 2007)

Nowak, Manfred *UN Covenant on Civil and Political Rights: CCPR Commentary* (Engel Kehl 2005)

Oeter, Stefan *Neutralität und Waffenhandel* (Springer Berlin 1992)

Oppenheim, L. and Lauterpacht, H. *International Law vol. 2: Disputes, War and Neutrality* (Longmans Green London 1952)

Röcker, Isabel *Die Pflicht zur rahmenbeschlusskonformen Auslegung nationalen Rechts* (Springer Heidelberg 2012)

Rogers, Anthony P.V. *Law on the Battlefield* (Manchester University Press Manchester 2004)

Sanger, David E. *Confront and Conceal: Obama's Secret Wars and Surprising Use of American Power* (Crown New York 2012)

Seitz, Nicolai *Strafverfolgungsmaßnahmen im Internet* (Heymanns Köln 2005)

Sharp, Walter Gary *Cyberspace and the Use of Force* (Ageis Research Corp Falls Church 1999)

Sieber, Ulrich *Verantwortlichkeit im Internet: technische Kontrollmöglichkeiten und multimediarechtliche Regelungen* (Beck München 1999)

Stein, Torsten and Buttlar, Christian von *Völkerrecht* (Heymann Köln 2009)

Stelter, Christian *Gewaltanwendung unter und neben der UN-Charta* (Duncker & Humblot Berlin 2007)

Tikk, Eneken, Kaska, Kadri and Vihul, Liis *International Cyber Incidents: Legal Considerations* (Cooperative Cyber Defence Centre of Excellence Tallinn 2010)

Tzu, Sun *The Art of War* (Clarendon Press Oxford 1963)

Verdross, Alfred *Völkerrecht* (J. Springer Berlin 1937)

Villiger, Mark Eugen *Commentary on the 1969 Vienna Convention on the Law of Treaties* (Nijhoff Leiden 2009)

Weber, Rolf H. and Weber, Romana *Internet of Things: Legal Perspectives* (Springer Heidelberg 2010)

West-Brown, Moira J., Stikvoort, Don, Kossakowski, Klaus-Peter, Killcrece, Georgia, Ruefle, Robin and Zajicek, Mark *Handbook for Computer Security Incident Response Teams (CSIRTs)* (2nd edn Carnegie Mellon University Software Engineering Institute 2003)

Willisch, Jan *State Responsibility for Technological Damage in International Law* (Duncker & Humblot Berlin 1987)

Wingfield, Thomas C. *The Law of Information Conflict: National Security Law in Cyberspace* (Aegis Falls Church 2000)

Wolf, Joachim *Die Haftung der Staaten für Privatpersonen nach Völkerrecht* (Duncker & Humblot Berlin 1997)

Wolf, Sarah *Unterseeische Rohrleitungen und Meeresumweltschutz: Eine völkerrechtliche Untersuchung am Beispiel der Ostsee* (Springer Heidelberg 2011)

Wolfrum, Rüdiger *Die Internationalisierung staatsfreier Räume: Die Entwicklung einer internationalen Verwaltung für Antarktis, Weltraum, Hohe See und Meeresboden* (Springer Berlin 1984)
Wright, Quincy *Essays on Espionage and International Law* (Ohio State University Press Ohio 1962)

EDITED COLLECTIONS

Alexander, Yonah and Swetnam, Michael S. (eds) *Cyber Terrorism and Information Warfare* (Oceana Dobbs Ferry 1999)
Council of Europe (ed) *Cyberterrorism – The Use of the Internet for Terrorist Purposes* (Council of Europe Publishing Strasbourg 2007)
Crawford, James, Pellet, Alain and Olleson, Simon (eds) *The Law of International Responsibility* (OUP Oxford 2010)
Doswald-Beck, Louise (ed) *San Remo Manual on International Law Applicable to Armed Conflicts at Sea* (CUP Cambridge 1995)
Henckaerts, Jean-Marie and Doswald-Beck, Louise (eds) *Customary International Humanitarian Law Volume I: Rules* (CUP Cambridge 2005)
Hoeren, Thomas and Sieber, Ulrich (eds) *Handbuch Multimedia-Recht: Rechtsfragen des elektronischen Geschäftsverkehrs* (Beck München 2008 (19. EL))
International Institute of Humanitarian Law (ed) *Rules of Engagement Handbook* (IIHL San Remo 2009)
National Research Council (ed) *Making the Nation Safer: The Role of Science and Technology in Countering Terrorism* (National Academies Press Washington 2002)
Nordquist, Myron H. (ed) *United Nations Convention on the Law of the Sea 1982: A Commentary: Vol 3* (Nijhoff The Hague 1995)
Pictet, Jean (ed) *The Geneva Conventions of 12. August 1949: Commentary* (ICRC Geneva 1952–1960)
Program on Humanitarian Policy and Conflict Research (ed) *Manual on International Law Applicable to Air and Missile Warfare* (HPCR Harvard University Cambridge 2009)
Program on Humanitarian Policy and Conflict Research (ed) *Commentary on the HPCR Manual on International Law Applicable to Air and Missile Warfare* (HPCR Harvard University Cambridge 2010)
Sandoz, Yves, Swinarski, Christophe and Zimmermann, Bruno (eds) *Commentary on the Additional Protocols of 8 June 1977 to the Geneva Conventions of 12 August 1949* (Martinus Nijhoff Publishers Geneva 1987)
Schmitt, Michael N. (ed) *Tallinn Manual on the International Law Applicable to Cyber Warfare* (CUP Cambridge 2013)

CHAPTERS IN EDITED COLLECTIONS

Bing, Jon 'Building Cyberspace: A Brief History of Internet' in Bygrave, Lee A. and Bing, Jon (eds) *Internet Governance: Infrastructure and Institutions* (OUP Oxford 2009) 8–47

Borelli, Silvia and Olleson, Simon 'Obligations Relating to Human Rights and Humanitarian Law' in Crawford, James, Pellet, Alain and Olleson, Simon (eds) *The Law of International Responsibility* (OUP Oxford 2010) 1177–1196

Bothe, Michael 'The Law of Neutrality' in Fleck, Dieter and Bothe, Michael (eds) *The Handbook of International Humanitarian Law* (OUP Oxford 2008) 571–604

Bothe, Michael 'Friedenssicherung und Kriegsrecht' in Vitzthum, Wolfgang (ed) *Völkerrecht* (de Gruyter Berlin 2010) 639–740

Boulanin, Vincent 'Major Arms Industry Acquisitions, 2010' in Institute, Stockholm International Peace Research (ed) *SIPRI Yearbook 2011: Armaments, Disarmament and International Security* (OUP Oxford 2011) 263–269

Cathcart, Blaise 'Legal Dimensions of Special Forces and Informations Operations' in Gill, Terry D. and Fleck, Dieter (eds) *The Handbook of the International Law of Military Operations* (OUP Oxford 2010) 395–414

Crawford, James and Olleson, Simon 'The Nature and Forms of International Responsibility' in Evans, Malcolm D. (ed) *International Law* (OUP Oxford 2010) 441–471

D'Amato, Anthony 'International Law, Cybernetics, and Cyberspace' in Schmitt, Michael N. and O'Donnell, Brian T. (eds) *Computer Network Attack and International Law* (Naval War College Newport 2002) 59–71

De Frouville, Olivier 'Attribution of Conduct to the State: Private Individuals' in Crawford, James, Pellet, Alain and Olleson, Simon (eds) *The Law of International Responsibility* (OUP Oxford 2010) 257–280

Dinstein, Yoram 'Computer Network Attacks and Self-Defense' in Schmitt, Michael N. and O'Donnell, Brian T. (eds) *Computer Network Attack and International Law* (Naval War College Newport 2002) 99–119

Dolzer, Rudolf 'Wirtschaft und Kultur' in Vitzthum, Wolfgang (ed) *Völkerrecht* (de Gruyter Berlin 2010) 491–578

Doswald-Beck, Louise 'Some Thoughts on Computer Network Attack and the International Law of Armed Conflict' in Schmitt, Michael N. and O'Donnell, Brian T. (eds) *Computer Network Attack and International Law* (Naval War College Newport 2002) 163–185

Doyle, James H. 'Computer Networks, Proportionality, and Military Operations' in Schmitt, Michael N. and O'Donnell, Brian T. (eds) *Computer Network Attack and International Law* (Naval War College Newport 2002) 147–161

Dübendorfer, Thomas, Wagner, Arno and Plattner, Bernhard 'An Economic Damage Model for Large-Scale Internet Attacks' *Proceedings of the 13th IEEE International Workshops on Enabling Technologies: Infrastructure for Collaborative Enterprises* (IEEE Computer Society Washington 2004) 223–228

Dupuy, Pierre-Marie and Hoss, Cristina 'Trail Smelter and Terrorism: International Mechanisms to Combat Transboundary Harm' in Bratspies, Rebecca M. and Miller, Russell A. (eds) *Transboundary Harm in International Law: Lessons from the Trail Smelter Arbitration* (CUP Cambridge 2006) 225–239

Fitzmaurice, Malgosia A. 'The Corfu Channel Case and the Development of International Law' in Ando, Nisuke, McWhinney, Edward and Wolfrum, Rüdiger (eds) *Liber Amicorum Judge Shigeru Oda vol 1* (Kluwer The Hague 2002) 119–146

Garnett, Richard and Clarke, Paul 'Cyberterrorism: A New Challenge for International Law' in Bianchi, Andrea (ed) *Enforcing International Law Norms against Terrorism* (Hart Oxford 2004) 465–488

Gercke, Björn 'Kommentierung zu §110 StPO' in Julius, Karl-Peter, et al. (eds) *Strafprozessordnung* (CF Müller Heidelberg 2009) 577–587

Greenwood, Christopher 'The Law of Weaponry at the Start of the New Millenium' in Schmitt, Michael N. and Green, Leslie C. (eds) *The Law of Armed Conflict: Into the Next Millennium* (Naval War College Newport 1998) 185–231

Grzebiela, Torsten 'Internet-Risiken: Versicherungsmöglichkeiten und Grenzen der Versicherbarkeit' in Ernst, Stefan (ed) *Hacker, Cracker & Computerviren* (Otto Schmidt Köln 2004) 354–378

Hartwig, Matthias 'ICANN – Governance by Technical Necessity' in von Bogdandy, Armin and Wolfrum, Rüdiger (eds) *The Exercise of Public Authority by International Institutions: Advancing International Institutional Law* (Springer Heidelberg 2010) 575–605

Heintschel von Heinegg, Wolff 'Informationskrieg und Völkerrecht' in Epping, Volker and Ipsen, Knut (eds) *Brücken bauen und begehen: Festschrift für Knut Ipsen zum 65. Geburtstag* (Beck München 2000) 129–155

Heintschel von Heinegg, Wolff 'Die weiteren Quellen des Völkerrechts' in Ipsen, Knut (ed) *Völkerrecht* (Beck München 2004) 210–256

Helmbrecht, Udo 'Die aktuelle Bedrohungslage durch Ausfall von IT-Infrastrukturen' in Kloepfer, Michael (ed) *Schutz kritischer Infrastrukturen: IT und Energie* (Nomos Baden-Baden 2010) 39–46

Henckaerts, Jean-Marie 'The Development of International Humanitarian Law and the Continued Relevance of Custom' in Hensel, Howard M. (ed) *The Legitimate Use of Military Force: The Just War Tradition and the Customary Law of Armed Conflict* (Ashgate Aldershot 2008) 117–134

Hestermayer, Holger P. 'Transboundary Harm: Internet Torts' in Bratspies, Rebecca M. and Miller, Russell A. (eds) *Transboundary Harm in International Law: Lessons from the Trail Smelter Arbitration* (CUP Cambridge 2006) 268–280

ILA Committee on Formation of Customary (General) International Law 'Statement of Principles Applicable to the Formation of General Customary International Law' in ILA (ed) *Report of the Sixty-Ninth Conference, London 2000* (ILA 2000)

Ipsen, Knut 'Bewaffneter Konflikt und Neutralität' in Ipsen, Knut (ed) *Völkerrecht* (Beck München 2004) 1195–1290

Ipsen, Knut 'Völkerrechtliche Verantwortlichkeit und Völkerstrafrecht' in Ipsen, Knut (ed) *Völkerrecht* (Beck München 2004) 615–673

Ipsen, Knut 'Combatants and Non-Combatants' in Fleck, Dieter and Bothe, Michael (eds) *The Handbook of International Humanitarian Law* (OUP Oxford 2008) 79–117

Jacobsson, Marie 'Modern Weaponry and Warfare: The Application of Article 36 of Additional Protocol I by Governments' in Helm, Anthony M. (ed) *The Law of War in the 21st Century: Weaponry and the Use of Force* (Naval War College Newport 2006) 183–191

Kalshoven, Frits 'Reprisals and the Protection of Civilians: Two Recent Decisions of the Yugoslavia Tribunal' in Vorah, Lal Chand (ed) *Man's Inhumanity to Man: Essays on International Law in Honour of Antonio Cassese* (Kluwer The Hague 2003) 481–509

Klein, Eckart and Schmahl, Stefanie 'Die internationalen und die supranationalen Organisationen' in Vitzthum, Wolfgang (ed) *Völkerrecht* (de Gruyter Berlin 2010) 263–387

Krisch, Nico 'Article 39' in Simma, Bruno (ed) *The Charter of the United Nations – A Commentary* (OUP Oxford 2012) 1272–1296

Krisch, Nico 'Article 42' in Simma, Bruno (ed) *The Charter of the United Nations – A Commentary* (OUP Oxford 2012) 1330–1350

Kube, Hanno 'Neue Medien – Internet' in Isensee, Josef and Kirchhof, Paul (eds) *Handbuch des Staatsrechts der Bundesrepublik Deutschland vol. 4: Aufgaben des Staates* (CF Müller Heidelberg 2006) 843–883

Leben, Charles 'Obligations Relating to the Use of Force and Arising from Peremptory Norms of International Law' in Crawford, James, Pellet, Alain and Olleson, Simon (eds) *The Law of International Responsibility* (OUP Oxford 2010) 1197–1204

O'Keefe, Roger 'Proportionality' in Crawford, James, Pellet, Alain and Olleson, Simon (eds) *The Law of International Responsibility* (OUP Oxford 2010) 1157–1168

Ottis, Rain 'From Pitchforks to Laptops: Volunteers in Cyber Conflicts' in Czosseck, C. and Podins, K. (eds) *Conference on Cyber Conflict Proceedings 2010* (CCD COE Tallinn 2010) 97–109

Parks, W. Hays 'Special Forces' Wear of Non-Standard Uniforms' in Jaques, Richard B. (ed) *Issues in International Law and Military Operations* (Naval War College Newport 2006) 69–119

Pellet, Alain 'The Definition of Responsibility in International Law' in Crawford, James, Pellet, Alain and Olleson, Simon (eds) *The Law of International Responsibility* (OUP Oxford 2010) 3–16

Pierrot, Olivier 'Hacker' in Ernst, Stefan (ed) *Hacker, Cracker & Computerviren* (Otto Schmidt Köln 2004) 1–28

Pierrot, Olivier 'Computerviren' in Ernst, Stefan (ed) *Hacker, Cracker & Computerviren* (Otto Schmidt Köln 2004) 29–47

Proelß, Alexander 'Raum und Umwelt im Völkerrecht' in Vitzthum, Wolfgang (ed) *Völkerrecht* (de Gruyter Berlin 2010) 389–489

Randelzhofer, Albrecht and Dörr, Oliver 'Article 2 (4)' in Simma, Bruno (ed) *The Charter of the United Nations – A Commentary* (OUP Oxford 2012) 200–234

Randelzhofer, Albrecht and Nolte, Georg 'Article 51' in Simma, Bruno (ed) *The Charter of the United Nations – A Commentary* (OUP Oxford 2012) 1397–1428

Richter, Dagmar 'Humanitarian Law and Human Rights: Intersecting Circles or Separate Spheres?' in Giegerich, Thomas (ed) *A Wiser Century? Judicial Dispute Settlement, Disarmament and the Laws of War 100 Years after the Second Hague Peace Conference* (Duncker & Humblot Berlin 2009) 257–322

Schäuble, Wolfgang 'Schutz kritischer Infrastrukturen als Aufgabe der Politik' in Kloepfer, Michael (ed) *Schutz kritischer Infrastrukturen: IT und Energie* (Nomos Baden-Baden 2010) 21–25

Scheinin, Martin 'Extraterritorial Effect of the International Covenant on Civil and Political Rights' in Coomans, Fons and Kamminga, Menno T. (eds) *Extraterritorial Application of Human Rights Treaties* (Intersentia Antwerp 2004) 73–81

Schmitt, Michael 'Targeting in Operational Law' in Gill, Terry D. and Fleck, Dieter (eds) *The Handbook of the International Law of Military Operations* (OUP Oxford 2010) 245–275

Schröder, Meinhard 'Verantwortlichkeit, Völkerstrafrecht, Streitbeilegung und Sanktionen' in Vitzthum, Wolfgang (ed) *Völkerrecht* (De Gruyter Berlin 2010) 579–638

Shackelford, Scott 'State Responsibility for Cyber Attacks: Competing Standards for a Growing Problem' in Czosseck, C. and Podins, K. (eds) *Conference on Cyber Conflict Proceedings 2010* (CCD COE Tallinn 2010) 197–208

Silver, Daniel B. 'Computer Network Attack as a Use of Force under Article 2 (4) of the United Nations Charter' in Schmitt, Michael N. and O'Donnell, Brian T. (eds) *Computer Network Attack and International Law* (Naval War College Newport 2002) 73–97

Szurek, Sandra 'Circumstances Precluding Wrongfulness in the ILC Articles on State Responsibility: Force Majeure' in Crawford, James, Pellet, Alain and Olleson, Simon (eds) *The Law of International Responsibility* (OUP Oxford 2010) 475–480

Uerpmann-Wittzack, Robert 'Der Schutz informationstechnischer Systeme nach der Europäischen Menschenrechtskonvention' in Uerpmann-Wittzack, Robert (ed) *Das neue Computergrundrecht* (Lit Berlin 2009) 99–110

Vitzthum, Wolfgang 'Begriff, Geschichte und Rechtsquellen des Völkerrechts' in Vitzthum, Wolfgang (ed) *Völkerrecht* (De Gruyter Berlin 2010) 1–72

Walker, George K. 'Neutrality and Information Warfare' in Schmitt, Michael N. and O'Donnell, Brian T. (eds) *Computer Network Attack and International Law* (Naval War College Newport 2002) 233–263

Wolfrum, Rüdiger 'State Responsibility for Private Actors: An Old Problem of Renewed Relevance' in Ragazzi, Maurizio (ed) *International Responsibility Today: Essays in Memory of Oscar Schachter* (Nijhoff Leiden 2005) 423–434

JOURNAL ARTICLES

Aldrich, Richard W. 'How Do You Know You Are at War in the Information Age' (2000) 22 Houston Journal of International Law 223–263

Antolin-Jenkins, VM 'Defining the Parameters of Cyberwar Operations: Looking for Law in All the Wrong Places?' (2005) 51 Naval Law Review 132–174

Ashmore, William C. 'Impact of Alleged Russian Cyber Attacks' (2009) 11 Baltic Security & Defence Review 4–40

Bär, Wolfgang 'EDV-Beweissicherung im Strafverfahren bei Computer, Handy, Internet: Ermittlungsmöglichkeiten bei Internetstraftaten' (2007) Deutsche Richterzeitung 218–221

Barkham, Jason 'Information Warfare and International Law on the Use of Force' (2001) 34(1) New York University Journal of International Law & Politics 57–113

Bayles, William 'The Ethics of Computer Network Attack' (2001) 31 Parameters – US Army War College Quarterly 44–58

Beard, Jack M. 'Law and War in the Virtual Era' (2009) 103 American Journal of International Law 409–445

Beckett, Jason 'New War, Old Law: Can the Geneva Paradigm Comprehend Computers?' (2000) 13(1) Leiden Journal of International Law 33–51

Bedner, Mark '"Deep Packet Inspection" – Technologie und rechtliche Initiativen' (2010) (5) Computer und Recht 339–345

Belt, Stuart Walters 'Missiles over Kosovo: Emergence, Lex Lata, of a Customary Norm Requiring the Use of Precision Munitions in Urban Areas' (2000) 47 Naval Law Review 115–175

Benatar, Marco 'The Use of Cyber Force: Need for Legal Justification?' (2009) 1 Göttingen Journal of International Law 375–396

von Bernstorff, Jochen 'Democratic Global Internet Regulation? Governance Networks, International Law and the Shadow of Hegemony' (2003) 9 European Law Journal 511–526

Bossardt, Matthias, Dübendorfer, Thomas and Plattner, Bernhard 'Enhanced Internet Security by a Distributed Traffic Control Service Based on Traffic Ownership' (2007) 30(3) Journal of Network and Computer Applications 841–857

Bothe, Michael, Ipsen, Knut and Partsch, Karl Josef 'Die Genfer Konferenz über humanitäres Völkerrecht: Verlauf und Ergebnisse' (1978) 38 Zeitschrift für ausländisches öffentliches Recht und Völkerrecht 1–159

Brown, Davis 'A Proposal for an International Convention to Regulate the Use of Information Systems in Armed Conflict' (2006) 47(1) Harvard International Law Journal 179–221

Brownlie, Ian 'International Law and the Use of Force by States Revisited' (2001) 21 The Australian Yearbook of International Law 21–37

Bruha, Thomas 'Gewaltverbot und humanitäres Völkerrecht nach dem 11. September 2001' (2002) 40(4) Archiv des Völkerrechts 383–421

Buchan, Russell 'Cyber Attacks: Unlawful Uses of Force or Prohibited Interventions?' (2012) 17 Journal of Conflict and Security Law 212–227

Cassese, Antonio 'The Nicaragua and Tadic Tests Revisited in Light of the ICJ Judgment on Genocide in Bosnia' (2007) 18 European Journal of International Law 649–668

Cavelty, Myriam Dunn 'Critical Information Infrastructure: Vulnerabilities, Threats and Responses' (2007) 3 Disarmament Forum 15–22

Church, William 'Information Warfare' (2000) 82 International Review of the Red Cross 205–216

Condron, Sean 'Getting it Right: Protecting American Critical Infrastructure in Cyberspace' (2007) 20 Harvard Journal of Law & Technology 403–422

Creekman, Daniel M. 'A Helpless America? An Examination of the Legal Options Available to the United States in Response to Varying Types of Cyber-attacks from China' (2002) 17(3) American University International Law Review 641–681

Daoust, Isabelle, Coupland, Robin and Ishoey, Rikke 'New Wars, New Weapons? The Obligation of States to Assess the Legality of Means and Methods of Warfare' (2002) 84 International Review of the Red Cross 345–363

Dederer, Hans-Georg 'ICANN und die Dominanz der USA: Internet Governance auf dem Weg in die Internationalisierung' (2009) 47 Archiv des Völkerrechts 367–398

Dinstein, Yoram 'Unlawful Combatancy' (2002) 32 Israel Yearbook on Human Rights 247–270

Döge, Jenny 'Cyber Warfare: Challenges for the Applicability of the Traditional Laws of War Regime' (2010) 48 Archiv des Völkerrechts 486–501

Dörmann, Knut 'The Legal Situation of "Unlawful/Unprivileged Combatants"' (2003) 85 International Review of the Red Cross 45–74

Doswald-Beck, L 'The Legality of the United States Intervention in Grenada' (1984) 31 Netherlands International Law Review 355–377

Fleck, Dieter 'Searching for International Rules Applicable to Cyber Warfare – A Critical First Assessment of the New Tallinn Manual' (2013) 18(2) Journal of Conflict and Security Law 331–351

Franzese, Patrick W. 'Sovereignty in Cyberspace: Can it Exist?' (2009) 64 Air Force Law Review 1–42

Froomkin, Michael 'Habermas@discourse.net: Toward a Critical Theory of Cyberspace' (2002) 116(3) Harvard Law Review 749–803

Frowein, Jochen Abr. 'Der Terrorismus als Herausforderung für das Völkerrecht' (2002) 62(4) Zeitschrift für ausländisches öffentliches Recht und Völkerrecht 879–905

Gaycken, Sandro 'The Necessity of (Some) Certainty – A Critical Remark concerning Matthew Sklerov's Concept of "Active Defense"' (2010) 12(2) Journal of Military and Strategic Studies 1–6

Gaycken, Sandro and Karger, Michael 'Entnetzung statt Vernetzung: Paradigmenwechsel in der IT-Sicherheit' (2011) 14 Multimedia und Recht 3–8

Geers, Kenneth 'Live Fire Exercise: Preparing for Cyber War' (2010) 7(1) Journal of Homeland Security and Emergency Management Article 74

Geiß, Robin and Lahmann, Henning 'Cyber Warfare: Applying the Principle of Distinction in an Interconnected Space' (2012) 45 Israel Law Review 381–399

Gill, Terry D. and Ducheine, Paul A.L. 'Anticipatory Self-Defense in the Cyber Context' (2013) 89 International Law Studies 438–471

Gjelten, Tom 'Shadow Wars: Debating Cyber ‚Disarmament'' (2010) November/December 2010 World Affairs 33–42

Goldsmith, Jack L. 'Against Cyberanarchy' (1998) 65(4) The University of Chicago Law Review 1199–1250

Goodman, Marc D. and Brenner, Susan W. 'The Emerging Consensus on Criminal Conduct in Cyberspace' (2002) 10(2) International Journal of Law and Information Technology 139–223

Gosnell Handler, Stephenie 'The New Cyber Face of Battle: Developing a Legal Approach to Accommodate Emerging Trends in Warfare' (2012) 48 Stanford Journal of International Law 209–237

Grunwald, Lukas 'Profi-Attacke – Die schleichende Gefahr: Advanced Persistent Threats' (2012)(7) iX – Magazin für professionelle Informationstechnik 42–53

Hanseman, Robert G. 'The Realities and Legalities of Information Warfare' (1997) 42 The Air Force Law Review 173–200

Heintze, Hans-Joachim 'Theorien zum Verhältnis von Menschenrechten und humanitärem Völkerrecht' (2011) 24 Humanitäres Völkerrecht 4–11

Hoeren, Thomas 'Zoning und Geolocation – Technische Ansätze zur Reterritorialisierung des Internet' (2007) Multimedia und Recht 3–6

Hoffman, Michael 'The Legal Status and Responsibilities of Private Internet Users under the Law of Armed Conflict: A Primer for the Unwary on the Shape of Law to Come' (2003) 2 Washington University Global Studies Law Review 415–426

Hoffmann, Ralf 'Information War: Tendenzen – Optionen – Perspektiven' (2002) 15(3) Humanitäres Völkerrecht 158–165

Hoisington, Matthew 'Cyberwarfare and the Use of Force Giving Rise to the Right of Self-Defense' (2009) 32 Boston College International and Comparative Law Review 439–454

Hollis, Duncan B. 'Why States Need an International Law for Information Operations' (2007) 11 Lewis & Clark Law Review 1023–1061

Hollis, Duncan B. 'An e-SOS for Cyberspace' (2011) 52 Harvard International Law Journal 373–432

Holznagel, Bernd 'Netzneutralität als Aufgabe der Vielfaltssicherung' (2010) Kommunikation und Recht 95–100

Hughes, Rex 'A Treaty for Cyberspace' (2010) 86(2) International Affairs 523–541

Hunter, Philip 'Distributed Denial of Service (DDOS) Mitigation Tools' (2003) (5) Network Security 12–14

Jamnejad, Maziar and Wood, Michael 'The Principle of Non-Intervention' (2009) 22 Leiden Journal of International Law 345–382

Janssen, Jan-Keno 'Ionenkanonen gegen Wikileaks-Gegner: DDoS-Attacken: Ziviler Ungehorsam oder Straftatbestand?' (2011)(1) C't Magazin für Computertechnik 50–51

Jenik, Aviram 'Cyberwar in Estonia and the Middle East' (2009) 4 Network Security 4–6

Jensen, Eric Talbot 'Computer Attacks on Critical National Infrastructure: A Use of Force Invoking the Right of Self-Defense' (2002) 38(2) Stanford Journal of International Law 207–240

Jensen, Eric Talbot 'Unexpected Consequences from Knock-on Effects: A Different Standard for Computer Network Operations?' (2003) 18(5) American University International Law Review 1145–1188

Jensen, Eric Talbot 'Cyber Warfare and Precautions against the Effects of Attacks' (2010) 88 Texas Law Review 1533–1569

Jensen, Eric Talbot 'Cyber Attacks: Proportionality and Precautions in Attack' (2013) 89 International Law Studies 198–217

Johnson, David R. and Post, David 'Law and Borders – The Rise of Law in Cyberspace' (1996) 48(5) Stanford Law Review 1367–1402

Joyner, Christopher C. and Lotrionte, Catherine 'Information Warfare as International Coercion: Elements of a Legal Framework' (2001) 12(5) European Journal of International Law 825–865

Jurich, Jon P. 'Cyberwar and Customary International Law: The Potential of a "Bottom-Up" Approach to an International Law of Information Operations' (2008) 9 Chicago Journal of International Law 275–295

Kanuck, Sean 'Sovereign Discourse on Cyber Conflict under International Law' (2010) 88 Texas Law Review 1571–1597

Kanuck, Sean P. 'Information Warfare: New Challenges for Public International Law' (1996) 37(1) Harvard International Law Journal 272–292

Kastenberg, Joshua E. 'Non-Intervention and Neutrality in Cyberspace: An Emerging Principle in the National Practice of International Law' (2009) 64 United States Air Force Law Review 43–64

Kastenberg, Joshua E. 'Changing the Paradigm of Internet Access from Government Information Systems: A Solution to the Need for the DOD to Take Time-Sensitive Action of the NIPRNET' (2009) 64 United States Air Force Law Review 175–210

Kelsey, Jeffrey 'Hacking into International Humanitarian Law: The Principles of Distinction and Neutrality in the Age of Cyber Warfare' (2008) 106 Michigan Law Review 1427–1451

Korns, Stephen and Kastenberg, Joshua 'Georgia's Cyber Left Hook' (2009) 38 Parameters – US Army War College Quarterly 60–76

Krajewski, Markus 'Selbstverteidigung gegen bewaffnete Angriffe nicht-staatlicher Organisationen: Der 11. September 2001 und seine Folgen' (2002) 40 Archiv des Völkerrechts 183–214

Kranz, Jerzy 'Die völkerrechtliche Verantwortlichkeit für die Anwendung militärischer Gewalt' (2010) 48 Archiv des Völkerrechts 281–337

Krieger, Heike 'Krieg gegen Anonymous: Völkerrechtliche Regelungsmöglichkeiten bei unsicherer Zurechnung im Cyberwar' (2012) 50 Archiv des Völkerrechts 1–20

Lesk, Michael 'The New Front Line: Estonia under Cyberassault' (2007) 5(4) IEEE Security and Privacy 76–79

Lessig, Lawrence 'Law Regulating Code Regulating Law' (2003) 35(1) Loyola University Chicago Law Journal 1–14

Lewinski, Kai von 'Recht auf Internet' (2011) 2(1) Rechtswissenschaft 70–94

Lewis, James Andrew 'Cyberwarfare and Its Impact on International Security' (2010) UNODA Occasional Papers No. 19

Lukasik, Stephen 'Protecting the Global Information Commons' (2000) 24 Telecommunications Policy 519–531

Lynn, William J. 'Defending a New Domain: The Pentagon's Cyberstrategy' (2010) September/October Foreign Affairs 97–108

Mayer, Franz 'Recht und Cyberspace' (1996) Neue Juristische Wochenschrift 1782–1791

Meron, Theodor 'The Martens Clause, Principles of Humanity, and Dictates of Public Conscience' (2000) 94(1) American Journal of International Law 78–89

Metzl, Jamie Frederic 'Rwandan Genocide and the International Law of Radio Jamming' (1997) 91(4) American Journal of International Law 628–651

Minkwitz, Olivier and Schöfbänker, Georg 'Information Warfare: Die neue Herausforderung für die Rüstungskontrolle' (2000) 18(2) Sicherheit und Frieden 150–157

Möckli, Daniel 'Cyberwar: Konzept, Stand und Grenzen' (2010) 71 CSS Analysen zur Sicherheitspolitik 1–3

Morth, Todd A. 'Considering Our Position: Viewing Information Warfare as a Use of Force Prohibited by Article 2(4) of the U.N. Charter' (1998) 30(2/3) Case Western Reserve Journal of International Law 567–600

Nagaraja, Shishir and Anderson, Ross 'The Snooping Dragon: Social-Malware Surveillance of the Tibetan Movement' (2009) 746 University of Cambridge Technical Report No. 12

Nazario, Jose 'DDoS Attack Evolution' (2008)(7) Network Security 7–10

Noorden, Wolf D. von 'INMARSAT Use by Armed Forces: A Question of Treaty Interpretation' (1995) 23(1) Journal of Space Law 1–18

O'Donnell, Brian T. and Kraska, James C. 'Humanitarian Law: Developing International Rules for the Digital Battlefield' (2003) 8(1) Journal of Conflict and Security Law 133–160

Oellers-Frahm, Karin 'Der IGH und die "Lücke" zwischen Gewaltverbot und Selbstverteidigungsrecht: Neues im Fall "Kongo gegen Uganda"?' (2007) Zeitschrift für europarechtliche Studien 71–92

Pfanner, Toni 'Military Uniforms and the Law of War' (2004) 86 International Review of the Red Cross 93–130

Proulx, Vincent-Jöel 'Babysitting Terrorists: Should States be Strictly Liable for Failing to Prevent Transborder Attacks?' (2005) 23(3) Berkeley Journal of International Law 615–668

Puckett, Christopher B. 'In this Era of "Smart Weapons", Is a State under an International Legal Obligation to Use Precision-Guided Technology in Armed Conflict?' (2004) 18(2) Emory International Law Review 645–723

Ralston, P.A.S., Graham, J.H. and Hieb, J.L. 'Cyber Security Risk Assessment for SCADA and DCS Networks' (2007) 46(4) ISA Transactions 583–594

Ries, Uli 'Das Geschäft mit den Bugs: Sicherheitslücken als Handelsware' (2011) (5) C't Magazin für Computertechnik 82–83

Roeder, Tina 'Zum Kriterium der "unmittelbaren Kampfteilnahme" bei der humanitärrechtlichen Einordnung privater Konfliktdienstleister im internationalen bewaffneten Konflikt' (2010)(4) Humanitäres Völkerrecht 173–180

Roscini, Marco 'World Wide Warfare: Jus ad Bellum and the Use of Cyber Force' (2010) 14 Max Planck Yearbook of United Nations Law 85–130

Sankol, Barry 'Verletzung fremdstaatlicher Souveränität durch ermittlungsbehördliche Zugriffe auf E-Mail-Postfächer' (2008) 11 Kommunikation und Recht 279–283

Schaap, Arie J. 'Cyber Warfare Operations: Development and Use Under International Law' (2009) 64 Air Force Law Review 121–173

Schmahl, Stefanie 'The United Nations Facing the Challenges of the "Information Society"' (2007) Max Planck Yearbook of United Nations Law 197–231

Schmahl, Stefanie 'Zwischenstaatliche Kompetenzabgrenzung im Cyberspace' (2009) 47 Archiv des Völkerrechts 284–327

Schmitt, Michael N. 'Angriffe im Computernetz und das ius ad bellum' (1999) 41(5) Neue Zeitschrift für Wehrrecht 177–195

Schmitt, Michael N. 'Computer Network Attack and the Use of Force in International Law: Thoughts on a Normative Framework' (1999) 37(3) Columbia Journal of Transnational Law 885–937

Schmitt, Michael N. 'Computer Network Attack: The Normative Software' (2001) 4 Yearbook of International Humanitarian Law 53–85

Schmitt, Michael N. 'Wired Warfare: Computer Network Attack and Jus in Bello' (2002) 84 International Review of the Red Cross 365–399

Schmitt, Michael N. 'Precision Attack and International Humanitarian Law' (2005) 87 International Review of the Red Cross 445–466

Schmitt, Michael N. 'Humanitarian Law and Direct Participation in Hostilities by Private Contractors or Civilian Employees' (2005) 5(2) Chicago Journal of International Law 511–546

Schmitt, Michael N. 'International Law in Cyberspace: The Koh Speech and Tallinn Manual Juxtaposed' (2012) 54 Harvard International Law Journal Online 13–37

Schweizer Bundesamt für Justiz und EDA 'Gutachten über Rechtsgrundlagen für Computernetzwerkoperationen durch Dienststellen des VBS' (2009) VPB 3/2009 Verwaltungspraxis der Bundesbehörden 141–177

Scott, Roger D. 'Legal Aspects of Information Warfare: Military Disruption of Telecommunications' (1998) 45 Naval Law Review 57–76

Segura-Serrano, Antonio 'Internet Regulation and the Role of International Law' (2006) 10 Max Planck Yearbook of United Nations Law 191–272

Shackelford, Scott 'From Nuclear War to Net War: Analogizing Cyber Attacks in International Law' (2009) 27 Berkeley Journal of International Law 192–251

Shulman, Mark R. 'Discrimination in the Laws of Information Warfare' (1999) 37(3) Columbia Journal of Transnational Law 939–968

Simma, Bruno and Pulkowski, Dirk 'Of Planets and the Universe: Self-Contained Regimes in International Law' (2006) 17(3) European Journal of International Law 483–529

Sklerov, Matthew 'Solving the Dilemma of State Response to Cyberattacks: A Justification for the Use of Active Defenses against States who Neglect Their Duty to Prevent' (2009) 201 Military Law Review 1–85

Smith, George 'An Electronic Pearl Harbor? Not Likely' (1998) 15 Issues on Science and Technology 68–73

Smith, G. Stevenson 'Recognizing and Preparing Loss Estimates from Cyber-Attacks' (2004) 12(6) Information Security Journal: A Global Perspective 46–57

Stein, Torsten and Marauhn, Thilo 'Völkerrechtliche Aspekte von Informationsoperationen' (2000) 60(1) Zeitschrift für ausländisches öffentliches Recht und Völkerrecht 1–40

Streltsov, A.A. 'International Information Security: Description and Legal Aspects' (2007) 3 Disarmament Forum 5–13

Swanson, Lesley 'The Era of Cyber Warfare: Applying International Humanitarian Law to the 2008 Russian-Georgian Cyber Conflict' (2010) 32 Loyola of Los Angeles International and Comparative Law Review 303–333

Tams, Christian J. 'The Use of Force Against Terrorists' (2009) 20 European Journal of International Law 359–397

Terry, James 'The Lawfulness of Attacking Computer Networks in Armed Conflict and in Self-Defense in Periods Short of Armed Conflict: What Are the Tareting Constraints' (2001) 169 Military Law Review 70–91

Thomas, Timothy L. 'Russian Views on Information-based Warfare' (1996) Special Edition 1996 Airpower Journal 25–35

Todd, Graham H. 'Armed Attack in Cyberspace: Deterring Asymmetric Warfare with an Asymmetric Definition' (2009) 64 Air Force Law Review 65–102

Tomuschat, Christian 'Human Rights and International Humanitarian Law' (2010) 21(1) European Journal of International Law 15–23

Uerpmann-Wittzack, Robert 'Internetvölkerrecht' (2009) 47 Archiv des Völkerrechts 261–283

US Department of Defense 'Directive on Protection of DOD Information Systems' (2009) 64 Air Force Law Review 202–207

Walden, Ian 'Crime and Security in Cyberspace' (2005) 18(1) Cambridge Review of International Affairs 51–68

Wallace, David and Reeves, Shane R. 'The Law of Armed Conflict's "Wicked" Problem: Levée en Masse in Cyber Warfare' (2013) 89 International Law Studies 646–668

Watts, Sean 'Combatant Status and Computer Network Attack' (2010) 50 Virginia Journal of International Law 391–447

Wegener, Henning 'Harnessing the Perils in Cyberspace: Who is in Charge?' (2007) 3 Disarmament Forum 45–52

Wegener, Henning 'Der unsichtbare Feind: Die neuen Gefahrenlagen im digitalen Raum' (2009) 09–10 Internationale Politik 48–57

Westby, Jody 'Stabilität statt Cyberkrieg' (2009) 09–10 Internationale Politik 64–69

Wilmshurst, Elizabeth 'The Chatham House Principles of International Law on the Use of Force in Self-Defence' (2006) 55(4) International and Comparative Law Quarterly 963–972

Wilske, Stephan and Schiller, Teresa 'International Jurisdiction in Cyberspace: Which States May Regulate the Internet?' (1997–1998) 50 Federal Communications Law Journal 117–178

Wolfrum, Rüdiger 'Restricting the Use of the Sea to Peaceful Purposes: Demilitarization in Being?' (1981) 24 German Yearbook of International Law 201–241

Wolfrum, Rüdiger 'The Attack of September 11, 2001, the Wars against the Taliban and Iraq: Is there a Need to Reconsider International Law on the Recourse to Force and the Rules in Armed Conflict?' (2003) 7 Max Planck Yearbook of United Nations Law 1–78

Wolfrum, Rüdiger and Philipp, Christiane E. 'The Status of the Taliban: Their Obligations and Rights under International Law' (2002) 6 Max Planck Yearbook of United Nations Law 559–601

Ziolkowski, Katharina 'Computernetzwerkoperationen und die Zusatzprotokolle zu den Genfer Abkommen - Zum "virtuellen Raum" des Internet und dem Schutzstandard der vor 30 Jahren in Kraft getretenen Protokolle' (2008) 21 Humanitäres Völkerrecht 202–213

Ziolkowski, Katharina 'Stuxnet - Legal Considerations' (2012) 25(3) Humanitäres Völkerrecht 139–147

Zittrain, Jonathan 'The Generative Internet' (2006) 119 Harvard Law Review 1974–2040

ELECTRONIC ARTICLES

Dörmann, Knut 'Applicability of the Additional Protocols to Computer Network Attacks' (2004) at <www.icrc.org/eng/assets/files/other/applicabilityofihltocna.pdf> (date accessed 23 March 2011)

Fornefeld, Martin, Delaunay, Gilles and Elixmann, Dieter 'The Impact of Broadband on Growth and Productivity (Study on behalf of the European Commission)' (2008) at

<http://ec.europa.eu/information_society/eeurope/i2010/docs/benchmarking/broadband_impact_2008.pdf> (date accessed 22 February 2012)

Fox, Dirk 'Stellungnahme zur "Online-Durchsuchung": Verfassungsbeschwerden 1 BvR 370/07 und 1 BvR 595/07' (2007) at <www.secorvo.de/publikationen/stellungnahme-secorvo-bverfg-online-durchsuchung.pdf> (date accessed 23 April 2010)

Gaycken, Sandro 'Die Zukunft des Krieges – Strategische Konzepte und strukturelle Probleme des Cyberwarfare' (2009) at <http://events.ccc.de/sigint/2009/Fahrplan/attachments/1285_Die%20Zukunft%20des%20Krieges.pdf> (date accessed 2 March 2012)

Koh, Harold Hongju 'International Law in Cyberspace' (2012) at <www.state.gov/s/l/releases/remarks/197924.htm> (date accessed 18 December 2013)

Leder, Felix and Werner, Tillmann 'Proactive Botnet Countermeasures an Offensive Approach' at <www.ccdcoe.org/publications/virtualbattlefield/15_LEDER_Proactive_Coutnermeasures.pdf> (date accessed 22 June 2011)

Lewis, James A. 'Assessing the Risks of Cyber Terrorism, Cyber War and Other Cyber Threats' (December 2002) at <http://csis.org/files/media/csis/pubs/021101_risks_of_cyberterror.pdf> (date accessed 23 July 2010)

Minkwitz, Olivier 'Ohne Hemmungen in den Krieg? Cyberwar und die Folgen' (2003) at <www.hsfk.de/fileadmin/downloads/report1003.pdf> (date accessed 25 May 2012)

Ophardt, Jonathan 'Cyber Warfare and the Crime of Aggression: The Need for Individual Accountability on Tomorrow's Battlefield' (2010) at <www.law.duke.edu/journals/dltr/articles/pdf/2010dltr003.pdf> (date accessed 20 April 2010)

Schmitt, Michael, Harrison, Heather and Wingfield, Thomas 'Computers and War: The Legal Battlespace' (2004) at <http://ihl.ihlresearch.org/_data/n_0002/resources/live/schmittetal.pdf> (date accessed 4 June 2012)

Sofaer, Abraham D. and Goodman, Seymour E. 'Proposal for an International Convention on Cyber Crime and Terrorism' (2000) at <http://iis-db.stanford.edu/pubs/11912/sofaergoodman.pdf> (date accessed 27 April 2011)

Tikk, Eneken, Kaska, Kadri, Rünnimeri, Kristel, Kert, Mari, Talihärm, Anna-Maria and Vihul, Liis 'Cyber Attacks Against Georgia: Legal Lessons Identified' (2008) at <www.carlisle.army.mil/DIME/documents/Georgia%201%200.pdf> (date accessed 11 May 2011)

Wheeler, David and Larsen, Gregory 'Techniques for Cyber Attack Attribution' (2003) at <www.dtic.mil/cgi-bin/GetTRDoc?AD=ADA468859&Location=U2&doc=GetTRDoc.pdf> (date accessed 23 March 2010)

Woltag, Johann-Christoph 'Computer Network Operations Below the Level of Armed Force' in Krisch, Nico, Mälksoo, Lauri and Prost, Mario (eds) *ESIL 4th Research Forum Tallinn* 1 ESIL Conference Paper Series No 1 at <http://ssrn.com/abstract=1967593> (date accessed 19 June 2012)

ENCYCLOPEDIA ENTRIES

Benedek, Wolfgang 'Drago-Porter Convention (1907)' in Wolfrum, Rüdiger (ed) *MPEPIL* (OUP Oxford Update 2007)

Benvenisti, Eyal 'Occupation, Belligerent' in Wolfrum, Rüdiger (ed) *MPEPIL* (OUP Oxford Update 2009)

von Bernstorff, Jochen 'Martens Clause' in Wolfrum, Rüdiger (ed) *MPEPIL* (OUP Oxford Update 2009)

Besson, Samantha 'Sovereignty' in Wolfrum, Rüdiger (ed) *MPEPIL* (OUP Oxford Update 2011)

von Bogdandy, Armin and Rau, Markus 'Lotus, The' in Wolfrum, Rüdiger (ed) *MPEPIL* (OUP Oxford Update 2006)

Bingham, Tom 'Alabama Arbitration' in Wolfrum, Rüdiger (ed) *MPEPIL* (OUP Oxford Update 2006)

Blay, Samuel KN 'Territorial Integrity and Political Independence' in Wolfrum, Rüdiger (ed) *MPEPIL* (OUP Oxford Update 2010)

Blum, Gabriella 'Remnants of War' in Wolfrum, Rüdiger (ed) *MPEPIL* (OUP Oxford Update 2010)

Boothby, William H. 'Weapons, Prohibited' in Wolfrum, Rüdiger (ed) *MPEPIL* (OUP Oxford Update 2010)

Bothe, Michael 'Neutrality, Concept and General Rules' in Wolfrum, Rüdiger (ed) *MPEPIL* (OUP Oxford Update 2011)

Brabandere, Eric de 'Propaganda' in Wolfrum, Rüdiger (ed) *MPEPIL* (OUP Oxford Update 2010)

Breslin, Julia 'Region of War' in Wolfrum, Rüdiger (ed) *MPEPIL* (OUP Oxford Update 2010)

Brunnée, Jutta 'Sic utere tuo ut alienum non laedas' in Wolfrum, Rüdiger (ed) *MPEPIL* (OUP Oxford Update 2010)

Caminos, Hugo 'Hot Pursuit' in Wolfrum, Rüdiger (ed) *MPEPIL* (OUP Oxford Update 2009)

Carazo, María Pía 'Velásquez Rodríguez v Honduras Case' in Wolfrum, Rüdiger (ed) *MPEPIL* (OUP Oxford Update 2008)

Carter, Barry 'Economic Coercion' in Wolfrum, Rüdiger (ed) *MPEPIL* (OUP Oxford Update 2009)

Cassimatis, Anthony and Greenwood, Kate 'Arms, Traffic in' in Wolfrum, Rüdiger (ed) *MPEPIL* (OUP Oxford Update 2009)

Chazournes, Laurence Boisson de and Campanelli, Danio 'Neighbour States' in Wolfrum, Rüdiger (ed) *MPEPIL* (OUP Oxford Update 2006)

Chesney, Robert M. 'Prisoners of War' in Wolfrum, Rüdiger (ed) *MPEPIL* (OUP Oxford Update 2009)

Chesterman, Simon 'Secret Intelligence' in Wolfrum, Rüdiger (ed) *MPEPIL* (OUP Oxford Update 2009)

Conderman, Paul J. 'Status of Armed Forces on Foreign Territory Agreements (SOFA)' in Wolfrum, Rüdiger (ed) *MPEPIL* (OUP Oxford Update 2010)

Crawford, Emily 'Armed Conflict, International' in Wolfrum, Rüdiger (ed) *MPEPIL* (OUP Oxford Update 2011)

Crawford, Emily 'Proportionality' in Wolfrum, Rüdiger (ed) *MPEPIL* (OUP Oxford Update 2011)

Crawford, James 'State Responsibility' in Wolfrum, Rüdiger (ed) *MPEPIL* (OUP Oxford Update 2006)

Crawford, James 'Military and Paramilitary Activities in and against Nicaragua Case (Nicaragua v United States of America)' in Wolfrum, Rüdiger (ed) *MPEPIL* (OUP Oxford Update 2006)

Crawford, James 'State' in Wolfrum, Rüdiger (ed) *MPEPIL* (OUP Oxford Update 2011)

Dinstein, Yoram 'Aggression' in Wolfrum, Rüdiger (ed) *MPEPIL* (OUP Oxford Update 2009)

Dinstein, Yoram 'Command Responsibility' in Wolfrum, Rüdiger (ed) *MPEPIL* (OUP Oxford Update 2009)

Dinstein, Yoram 'Military Necessity' in Wolfrum, Rüdiger (ed) *MPEPIL* (OUP Oxford Update 2009)

Dinstein, Yoram 'Warfare, Methods and Means' in Wolfrum, Rüdiger (ed) *MPEPIL* (OUP Oxford Update 2009)

Dinstein, Yoram 'Air Warfare' in Wolfrum, Rüdiger (ed) *MPEPIL* (OUP Oxford Update 2010)

Dörmann, Knut 'Land Mines' in Wolfrum, Rüdiger (ed) *MPEPIL* (OUP Oxford Update 2011)

Dörmann, Knut 'Combatants, Unlawful' in Wolfrum, Rüdiger (ed) *MPEPIL* (OUP Oxford Update 2011)

Dörr, Oliver 'Use of Force, Prohibition of' in Wolfrum, Rüdiger (ed) *MPEPIL* (OUP Oxford Update 2011)

Douhan, Alena 'Liability for Environmental Damage' in Wolfrum, Rüdiger (ed) *MPEPIL* (OUP Oxford Update 2011)

Epiney, Astrid 'Lac Lanoux Arbitration' in Wolfrum, Rüdiger (ed) *MPEPIL* (OUP Oxford Update 2006)

Geiß, Robin 'Land Warfare' in Wolfrum, Rüdiger (ed) *MPEPIL* (OUP Oxford Update 2009)

Greenwood, Christopher 'Caroline, The' in Wolfrum, Rüdiger (ed) *MPEPIL* (OUP Oxford Update 2009)

Greenwood, Christopher 'Self-Defence' in Wolfrum, Rüdiger (ed) *MPEPIL* (OUP Oxford Update 2011)

Hailbronner, Kay and Heilmann, Daniel 'Aerial Incident Cases before International Courts and Tribunals' in Wolfrum, Rüdiger (ed) *MPEPIL* (OUP Oxford Update 2009)

Hakapää, Kari 'Innocent Passage' in Wolfrum, Rüdiger (ed) *MPEPIL* (OUP Oxford Update 2008)

Heintschel von Heinegg, Wolff 'Blockade' in Wolfrum, Rüdiger (ed) *MPEPIL* (OUP Oxford Update 2009)

Heintschel von Heinegg, Wolff 'Asymmetric Warfare' in Wolfrum, Rüdiger (ed) *MPEPIL* (OUP Oxford Update 2010)

Henckaerts, Jean-Marie 'Armed Forces' in Wolfrum, Rüdiger (ed) *MPEPIL* (OUP Oxford Update 2010)

Herdegen, Matthias 'International Economic Law' in Wolfrum, Rüdiger (ed) *MPEPIL* (OUP Oxford Update 2011)

Hestermayer, Holger P. 'Mercenaries' in Wolfrum, Rüdiger (ed) *MPEPIL* (OUP Oxford Update 2010)

Hey, Ellen 'Common but Differentiated Responsibilities' in Wolfrum, Rüdiger (ed) *MPEPIL* (OUP Oxford Update 2008)
Hofmann, Mahulena 'Remote Sensing' in Wolfrum, Rüdiger (ed) *MPEPIL* (OUP Oxford Update 2011)
Hostettler, Peter 'Neutrals, Disarming and Internment of Belligerents' in Wolfrum, Rüdiger (ed) *MPEPIL* (OUP Oxford Update 2009)
Ipsen, Knut 'Ruses of War' in Wolfrum, Rüdiger (ed) *MPEPIL* (OUP Oxford Update 2010)
Joyner, Christoph C. 'Coercion' in Wolfrum, Rüdiger (ed) *MPEPIL* (OUP Oxford Update 2006)
Kamminga, Menno T. 'Extraterritoriality' in Wolfrum, Rüdiger (ed) *MPEPIL* (OUP Oxford Update 2008)
Kearney, Michael G. 'Propaganda for War, Prohibition' in Wolfrum, Rüdiger (ed) *MPEPIL* (OUP Oxford Update 2009)
Kees, Alexander 'Responsibility of States for Private Actors' in Wolfrum, Rüdiger (ed) *MPEPIL* (OUP Oxford Update 2011)
Kingsbury, Benedict and Donaldson, Megan 'Global Administrative Law' in Wolfrum, Rüdiger (ed) *MPEPIL* (OUP Oxford Update 2011)
Klein, Eckart 'Self-Contained Regime' in Wolfrum, Rüdiger (ed) *MPEPIL* (OUP Oxford Update 2006)
Koivurova, Timo 'Due Diligence' in Wolfrum, Rüdiger (ed) *MPEPIL* (OUP Oxford Update 2007)
Kolb, Robert 'Human Rights and Humanitarian Law' in Wolfrum, Rüdiger (ed) *MPEPIL* (OUP Oxford Update 2006)
Kretzmer, David 'Emergency, State of' in Wolfrum, Rüdiger (ed) *MPEPIL* (OUP Oxford Update 2008)
Kriebaum, Ursula and Reinisch, August 'Property, Right to, International Protection' in Wolfrum, Rüdiger (ed) *MPEPIL* (OUP Oxford Update 2009)
Kunig, Philip 'Intervention, Prohibition of' in Wolfrum, Rüdiger (ed) *MPEPIL* (OUP Oxford Update 2008)
Lagoni, Rainer 'Pipelines' in Wolfrum, Rüdiger (ed) *MPEPIL* (OUP Oxford Update 2011)
Lamb, Susan 'Tadic Case' in Wolfrum, Rüdiger (ed) *MPEPIL* (OUP Oxford Update 2009)
Lehnardt, Chia 'Private Military Companies' in Wolfrum, Rüdiger (ed) *MPEPIL* (OUP Oxford Update 2011)
Lesaffer, Randall 'Kellogg-Briand Pact (1928)' in Wolfrum, Rüdiger (ed) *MPEPIL* (OUP Oxford Update 2010)
Lowe, Vaughan and Tzanakopoulos, Antonios 'Economic Warfare' in Wolfrum, Rüdiger (ed) *MPEPIL* (OUP Oxford Update 2011)
Lyall, Francis 'INMARSAT' in Wolfrum, Rüdiger (ed) *MPEPIL* (OUP Oxford Update 2006)
Lyall, Francis 'Broadcasting, International Regulation' in Wolfrum, Rüdiger (ed) *MPEPIL* (OUP Oxford Update 2007)
Lyall, Francis 'Satellite Broadcasting' in Wolfrum, Rüdiger (ed) *MPEPIL* (OUP Oxford Update 2007)
Mahmoudi, Said 'Transit Passage' in Wolfrum, Rüdiger (ed) *MPEPIL* (OUP Oxford Update 2008)

Malanczuk, Peter 'Data, Transboundary Flow, International Protection' in Wolfrum, Rüdiger (ed) *MPEPIL* (OUP Oxford Update 2009)
Malanczuk, Peter 'Information and Communication, Freedom of' in Wolfrum, Rüdiger (ed) *MPEPIL* (OUP Oxford Update 2011)
Marauhn, Thilo 'North Atlantic Treaty Organization' in Wolfrum, Rüdiger (ed) *MPEPIL* (OUP Oxford Update 2011)
Melzer, Nils 'Civilian Participation in Armed Conflict' in Wolfrum, Rüdiger (ed) *MPEPIL* (OUP Oxford Update 2010)
Orakhelashvili, Alexander 'Governmental Activity on Foreign Territory' in Wolfrum, Rüdiger (ed) *MPEPIL* (OUP Oxford Update 2010)
Oxman, Bernard H. 'Jurisdiction of States' in Wolfrum, Rüdiger (ed) *MPEPIL* (OUP Oxford Update 2007)
Palchetti, Paolo 'De Facto Organs of a State' in Wolfrum, Rüdiger (ed) *MPEPIL* (OUP Oxford Update 2006)
Palmisano, Giuseppe 'Fault' in Wolfrum, Rüdiger (ed) *MPEPIL* (OUP Oxford Update 2007)
Partington, Earle A. 'Manuals on the Law of Armed Conflict' in Wolfrum, Rüdiger (ed) *MPEPIL* (OUP Oxford Update 2011)
Pedrazzi, Marco 'Outer Space, Liability for Damage' in Wolfrum, Rüdiger (ed) *MPEPIL* (OUP Oxford Update 2008)
Pfeil, Julia 'Naulilaa Arbitration (Portugal v Germany)' in Wolfrum, Rüdiger (ed) *MPEPIL* (OUP Oxford Update 2007)
Proelß, Alexander 'Peaceful Purposes' in Wolfrum, Rüdiger (ed) *MPEPIL* (OUP Oxford Update 2009)
Roberts, Adam 'Occupation, Military, Termination of' in Wolfrum, Rüdiger (ed) *MPEPIL* (OUP Oxford Update 2009)
Röcker, Isabel 'European Organization for Nuclear Research (CERN)' in Wolfrum, Rüdiger (ed) *MPEPIL* (OUP Oxford Update 2009)
Rusinova, Vera 'Perfidy' in Wolfrum, Rüdiger (ed) *MPEPIL* (OUP Oxford Update 2011)
Sander, Gerald G. 'International Organization for Standardization (ISO)' in Wolfrum, Rüdiger (ed) *MPEPIL* (OUP Oxford Update 2006)
Sassòli, Marco 'Combatants' in Wolfrum, Rüdiger (ed) *MPEPIL* (OUP Oxford Update 2007)
Sassòli, Marco 'Military Objectives' in Wolfrum, Rüdiger (ed) *MPEPIL* (OUP Oxford Update 2007)
Schabas, William A. 'Application of the Convention on the Prevention and Punishment of the Crime of Genocide Case (Bosnia and Herzegovina v Serbia and Montenegro)' in Wolfrum, Rüdiger (ed) *MPEPIL* (OUP Oxford Update 2008)
Schaller, Christian 'Spies' in Wolfrum, Rüdiger (ed) *MPEPIL* (OUP Oxford Update 2009)
Scheinin, Martin 'Security, Right to, International Protection' in Wolfrum, Rüdiger (ed) *MPEPIL* (OUP Oxford Update 2007)
von Schorlemer, Sabine 'Telecommunications, International Regulation' in Wolfrum, Rüdiger (ed) *MPEPIL* (OUP Oxford Update 2009)
Steiger, Dominik 'Civilian Objects' in Wolfrum, Rüdiger (ed) *MPEPIL* (OUP Oxford Update 2011)
Steinorth, Charlotte 'Bankovic Case' in Wolfrum, Rüdiger (ed) *MPEPIL* (OUP Oxford Update 2010)

Stephens, Dale and Skousgaard, Tristan 'Flags and Uniforms in War' in Wolfrum, Rüdiger (ed) *MPEPIL* (OUP Oxford Update 2009)

Stephens, Dale and Skousgaard, Tristan 'Military Reconnaissance' in Wolfrum, Rüdiger (ed) *MPEPIL* (OUP Oxford Update 2009)

Stephens, Dale and Skousgaard, Tristan 'Naval Demonstrations and Manoeuvres' in Wolfrum, Rüdiger (ed) *MPEPIL* (OUP Oxford Update 2009)

Tams, Christian J. 'League of Nations' in Wolfrum, Rüdiger (ed) *MPEPIL* (OUP Oxford Update 2006)

Treves, Tullio 'Customary International Law' in Wolfrum, Rüdiger (ed) *MPEPIL* (OUP Oxford Update 2006)

Vöneky, Silja 'Analogy in International Law' in Wolfrum, Rüdiger (ed) *MPEPIL* (OUP Oxford Update 2008)

Waibel, Michael 'Corfu Channel Case' in Wolfrum, Rüdiger (ed) *MPEPIL* (OUP Oxford Update 2009)

Walter, Christian 'Terrorism' in Wolfrum, Rüdiger (ed) *MPEPIL* (OUP Oxford Update 2011)

Watts, Arthur 'Israeli Wall Advisory Opinion (Legal Consequences of the Construction of a Wall in the Occupied Palestinian Territory)' in Wolfrum, Rüdiger (ed) *MPEPIL* (OUP Oxford Update 2007)

Wenzel, Nicola 'Human Rights, Treaties, Extraterritorial Application and Effects' in Wolfrum, Rüdiger (ed) *MPEPIL* (OUP Oxford Update 2008)

de Wet, Erika and Wood, Michael 'Collective Security' in Wolfrum, Rüdiger (ed) *MPEPIL* (OUP Oxford Update 2010)

de Wet, Erika and Wood, Michael 'Peace, Threat to' in Wolfrum, Rüdiger (ed) *MPEPIL* (OUP Oxford Update 2009)

Wilske, Stephan 'Abduction, Transboundary' in Wolfrum, Rüdiger (ed) *MPEPIL* (OUP Oxford Update 2009)

Wolfrum, Rüdiger 'Common Heritage of Mankind' in Wolfrum, Rüdiger (ed) *MPEPIL* (OUP Oxford Update 2009)

Wolfrum, Rüdiger 'International Courts and Tribunals, Evidence' in Wolfrum, Rüdiger (ed) *MPEPIL* (OUP Oxford Update 2006)

Woltag, Johann-Christoph 'Coded Communications (Encryption)' in Wolfrum, Rüdiger (ed) *MPEPIL* (OUP Oxford Update 2009)

Woltag, Johann-Christoph 'Cyber Warfare' in Wolfrum, Rüdiger (ed) *MPEPIL* (OUP Oxford Update 2010)

Woltag, Johann-Christoph 'Internet' in Wolfrum, Rüdiger (ed) *MPEPIL* (OUP Oxford Update 2010)

Wood, Michael 'State Practice' in Wolfrum, Rüdiger (ed) *MPEPIL* (OUP Oxford Update 2010)

Wood, Michael 'United Nations Charter, Enemy States Clauses' in Wolfrum, Rüdiger (ed) *MPEPIL* (OUP Oxford Update 2006)

Zemanek, Karl 'Armed Attack' in Wolfrum, Rüdiger (ed) *MPEPIL* (OUP Oxford Update 2009)

Ziegler, Katja S. 'Domain Réservé' in Wolfrum, Rüdiger (ed) *MPEPIL* (OUP Oxford Update 2008)

Ziemele, Ineta 'Privacy, Right to, International Protection' in Wolfrum, Rüdiger (ed) *MPEPIL* (OUP Oxford Update 2009)

CASES

Affaire des biens britanniques au Maroc espagnol (1925) 2 RIAA 615
Affaire du Lac Lanoux (1957) 12 RIAA 281
Alabama Arbitration in JB Moore (ed) *History and Digest of the International Arbitrations to which the United States Has Been a Party* vol 1 Chapter XIV (Government Printing Office Washington 1898)
Amann v Switzerland (ECtHR) Reports 2000-II 245
Application of the Convention on the Prevention and Punishment of the Crime of Genocide (Bosnia and Herzegovina v Serbia and Montenegro) (Judgment) [2007] ICJ Rep 43
Armed Activities on the Territory of the Congo (Democratic Republic of the Congo v Uganda) [2005] ICJ Rep 168
Autronic AG v Switzerland (ECtHR) Series A No 178
Avena and Other Mexican Nationals (Mexico v United States of America) [2004] ICJ Rep 12
Banković v Belgium (ECtHR) Reports 2001-XII 333
Chassagnou and Others v France (ECtHR) Apps 25088/94, 28331/95 and 28443/95
Copland v United Kingdom (ECtHR) App 62617/00
Corfu Channel (United Kingdom of Great Britain and Northern Ireland v Albania) (Merits) [1949] ICJ Rep 4
Difference relating to Immunity from Legal Process of a Special Rapporteur of the Commission on Human Rights (Advisory Opinion) [1999] ICJ Rep 62
Factory at Chorzów (Germany v Poland) (Claim for Indemnity) (Merits) PCIJ Series A No 17
Gabčíkovo-Nagymaros Project (Hungary/Slovakia) [1997] ICJ Rep 7
Güleç v Turkey (Judgment of 27 July 1998) (ECtHR) Reports 1998-IV 1698
Isayeva v Russia (24 February 2005) (ECtHR) App 57950/00
Island of Palmas (Netherlands v United States of America) (1928) 2 RIAA 829
Issa v Turkey (ECtHR) Reports 2004-XI 629
La Ligue Contre Le Racisme et L'Antisemitisme v Yahoo!, Inc. ([20 November 2000] Tribunal de Grande Instance Paris)
Legal Consequences of the Construction of a Wall in the Occupied Palestinian Territory (Advisory Opinion) [2004] ICJ Rep 136
Legality of the Threat or Use of Nuclear Weapons (Advisory Opinion) [1996] ICJ Rep 226
Loizidou v Turkey (Merits) (ECtHR) Reports 1996-VI 2216
López Burgos v Uruguay UN HRC Communication No R 12/52 (29 July 1981) GAOR 36th Session Supp 40, 176
M/V 'SAIGA' (No 2) (Saint Vincent and the Grenadines v Guinea) (Merits) (Judgment) ITLOS Case No 2 (1 July 1999) 1999 ITLOS Reports 10
Medvedyev v France (Grand Chamber) (ECtHR) App No 3394/03
Military and Paramilitary Activities in and against Nicaragua (Nicaragua v United States of America) (Dissenting Opinion of Judge Jennings) [1986] ICJ Rep 528
Military and Paramilitary Activities in and against Nicaragua (Nicaragua v United States of America) (Merits) [1986] ICJ Rep 14
Nationality Decrees Issued in Tunis and Morocco (French Zone) (Advisory Opinion) PCIJ Series B No 4
Neer (USA) v United Mexican States (1926) 4 RIAA 60

North Sea Continental Shelf Cases (Federal Republic of Germany/Denmark; Federal Republic of Germany/Netherlands) [1969] ICJ Rep 3
Oil Platforms (Islamic Republic of Iran v United States of America) [2003] ICJ Rep 161
Oil Platforms (Islamic Republic of Iran v United States of America) (Separate Opinion of Judge Simma) [2003] ICJ Rep 324
Osman v United Kingdom (ECtHR) Reports 1998-VIII 3124
Partial Award: Western Front, Aerial Bombardment and Related Claims Eritrea's Claims 1, 3, 5, 9–13, 14, 21, 25 & 26 between the State of Eritrea and the Federal Democratic Republic of Ethiopia Eritrea-Ethiopia Claims Commission (19 December 2005) (2006) 45 ILM 396
Peck v United Kingdom (ECtHR) Reports 2003-I 123
Peter Pammer v Reederei Karl Schlüter GmbH & Co KG and Hotel Alpenhof GesmbH v Oliver Heller (ECJ) Joined Cases C-585/08 and C-144/09 (7 December 2010)
Prosecutor v Dusko Tadić (Judgment) (Separate Opinion of Judge Shahabuddeen) ICTY-94-1-A (15 July 1999)
Prosecutor v Galić (Judgment and Opinion) IT-98-29-T (5 December 2003)
Prosecutor v Nahimana (Judgment) ICTR-99-52-T (3 December 2003)
Prosecutor v Orić (Judgment) IT-03-68-T (30 June 2006)
Prosecutor v Strugar (Judgment) IT-01-42-A (17 July 2008)
Prosecutor v Tadić (Decision on the Defence Motion for Interlocutory Appeal on Jurisdiction) IT-94-1 (2 October 1995)
Prosecutor v Tadić (Judgment) IT-94-1-A (15 July 1999)
Rainbow Warrior (Ruling by the UN Secretary-General) (6 July 1986) (New Zealand v France) (1986) 19 RIAA 207
Responsabilité de l'Allemagne à raison des dommages causés dans les colonies portugaises du sud de l'Afrique (sentence sur le principe de la responsabilité) (Portugal contre Allemagne) (Naulilaa Case) (1928) 2 RIAA 1011
Rotaru v Romania (ECtHR) Reports 2000-V 109
The 'Lotus' (France v Turkey) (Dissenting Opinion of Mr Moore) PCIJ Series A No 10
The 'Lotus' (France v Turkey) PCIJ Series A No 10
Trail Smelter (United States of America v Canada) (1938/41) 3 RIAA 1905
Tzemel Adv v Minister of Defence and Commander of the Antzar Camp Israel Supreme Court (1983) 13 Israel Yearbook on Human Rights 360
United States Diplomatic and Consular Staff in Tehran (United States of America v Iran) [1980] ICJ Rep 3
Velásquez Rodríguez v Honduras (Judgment) IACtHR Series C No 4 (29 July 1988)
Venable (USA) v United Mexican States (1926) 4 RIAA 219
Weber and Saravia v Germany (ECtHR) App 54934/00
Wieser and Bicos Beteiligungen GmbH v Austria (ECtHR) App 74336/01
Zippo Mfg Co v Zippo Dot Com, Inc (US District Court WD Pennsylvania [16 January 1997] 952 F.Supp. 1119)

DOCUMENTS

UNITED NATIONS DOCUMENTS

Alston, Philip 'Report of the Special Rapporteur on Extrajudicial, Summary or Arbitrary Executions: Study on Targeted Killings (UN Doc A/HRC/14/24/Add.6)' (28 May 2010)

Greenwood, Christopher 'Legal Issues Regarding Explosive Remnants of War (UN Doc CCW/GGE/I/WP.10)' (23 May 2002)

UN Conference on the Human Environment 'Stockholm Declaration of the United Nations Conference on the Human Environment' (16 June 1972) UN Doc A/CONF.48/14/Rev 1, 3

UN High-Level Panel on Threats, Challenges and Change 'A More Secure World: Our Shared Responsibility' (2 December 2004) UN Doc A/59/565, 8

UN Human Rights Committee 'Government of Israel: Second Periodic Report (UN Doc CCPR/C/ISR/2001/2)' (4 December 2001)

UN ILC 'Draft Articles on Responsibility of States for Internationally Wrongful Acts' (2001) GAOR 56th Session Supp 10, 43

UN ILC 'Draft Articles on the Law of Treaties with Commentaries' (1966) vol II UNYBILC

UN ILC 'Text of the Draft Articles with Commentaries Thereto: Responsibility of States for Internationally Wrongful Acts' (2001) GAOR 56th Session Supp 10, 59

UN Secretary-General "Pay More Attention to Cyberwarfare, Verification, Secretary-General Advises in Remarks to Advisory Board on Disarmament Affairs' UN Doc SG/SM/12108' (18 February 2009) at <www.un.org/News/Press/docs//2009/sgsm12108.doc.htm> (date accessed 22 June 2011)

UN Secretary-General 'In Larger Freedom: Towards Development, Security and Human Rights for All: Report of the Secretary General' (21 March 2005) UN Doc A/59/2005

UN WSIS 'Declaration of Principles: Building the Information Society: A Global Challenge in the New Millennium (WSIS 03/GENEVA/DOC/4-E)' (12 December 2003) at <www.itu.int/wsis/docs/geneva/official/dop.html> (date accessed 17 December 2009)

UN WSIS 'Plan of Action' (12 December 2003) at <www.itu.int/wsis/docs/geneva/official/poa.html> (date accessed 30 August 2011)

UN WSIS 'Report from the Working Group on Internet Governance (Doc WSIS-II/PC-3/DOC/5-E)' (3 August 2005) at <www.itu.int/wsis/docs2/pc3/off5.pdf> (date accessed 17 December 2009)

UN WSIS 'Tunis Agenda for the Information Society (18 November 2005)' (2005) at <www.itu.int/wsis/docs2/tunis/off/6rev1.pdf> (date accessed 27 April 2010)

UN WSIS Thematic Meeting on Cybersecurity 'A Comparative Analysis of Cybersecurity Initiatives Worldwide' (2005) at <www.itu.int/osg/spu/cybersecurity/docs/Background_Paper_Comparative_Analysis_Cybersecurity_Initiatives_Worldwide.pdf> (date accessed 4 November 2009)

UNCTAD 'Information Economy Report 2005' UN Doc UNCTAD/SDTE/ECB/2005/1

UNGA 'Compilation of Decisions of International Courts, Tribunals and other Bodies: Report of the Secretary-General' (1 February 2007) UN Doc A/62/62

UNGA 'Developments in the Field of Information and Telecommunications in the Context of International Security: Russian Federation: Draft Resolution' Letter Dated 23 September 1998 from the Permanent Representative of the Russian Federation to the United Nations Addressed to the Secretary-General (UN Doc A/C.1/53/3 Appendix)

UNGA 'Developments in the Field of Information and Telecommunications in the Context of International Security: Report of the Secretary-General' (3 July 2001) UN Doc A/56/164

UNGA 'Developments in the Field of Information and Telecommunications in the Context of International Security: Report of the Secretary-General' (2 July 2007) UN Doc A/62/98

UNGA 'Developments in the Field of Information and Telecommunications in the Context of International Security: Report of the Secretary-General' (18 July 2006) UN Doc A/61/161

UNGA 'Developments in the Field of Information and Telecommunications in the Context of International Security: Report of the Secretary-General' (18 July 2008) UN Doc A/63/139

UNGA 'Report of the Group of Governmental Experts on Developments in the Field of Information and Telecommunications in the Context of International Security' (30 July 2010) UN Doc A/65/201

UNGA 'Report of the Special Rapporteur on the Promotion and Protection of the Right to Freedom of Opinion and Expression, Frank La Rue' (16 May 2011) UN Doc A/HRC/17/27

UNGA 'Report of the Special Rapporteur on the Promotion and Protection of the Right to Freedom of Opinion and Expression, Frank La Rue: Addendum: Summary of Cases Transmitted to Governments and Replies Received' (27 May 2011) UN Doc A/HRC/17/27/Add.1

UNGA Res 2131 (XX) 'Declaration on the Inadmissibility of Intervention in the Domestic Affairs of States and the Protection of Their Independence and Sovereignty' (21 December 1965) GAOR 20th Session Supp 14, 11

UNGA Res 217 A (III) 'Universal Declaration of Human Rights' (10 December 1948) GAOR 3rd Session Part I Resolutions 71

UNGA Res 2625 (XXV) 'Declaration on Principles of International Law concerning Friendly Relations and Co-operation among States in Accordance with the Charter of the United Nations' (24 October 1970) GAOR 25th Session Supp 28, 121

UNGA Res 3281 (XXIX) 'Charter of Economic Rights and Duties of States' (12 December 1974) GAOR 29th Session Supp 31 vol 1, 50

UNGA Res 3314 (XXIX) 'Definition of Aggression' (14 December 1974) GAOR 29th Session Supp 31 vol 1, 142

UNGA Res 41/53 'Principles Relating to Remote Sensing of the Earth from Space' (3 December 1986) GAOR 41st Session Supp 53, 115

UNGA Res 42/173 'Economic Measures as a Means of Political and Economic Coercion against Developing Countries' (21 December 1987) GAOR 42nd Session Supp 49 vol 1, 130

UNGA Res 55/63 'Combating the Criminal Misuse of Information Technologies' (4 December 2000)

UNGA Res 56/121 'Combating the Criminal Misuse of Information Technologies' (19 December 2001)

UNGA Res 58/199 'Creation of a Global Culture of Cybersecurity and the Protection of Critical Information Infrastructures' (23 December 2004)

UNSC 'Letter Dated 7 October 2001 from the Permanent Representative of the United States of American to the United Nations Adressed to the President of the Security Council' (7 October 2001) (2001) 40 ILM 1281

UNSC 'Note by the President of the Security Council' (31 January 1992) UN Doc S/23500

UNSC Res 568 'Botswana-South Africa' (21 June 1985)

UNSC Res 1172 'International Peace and Security' (6 June 1998) SCOR 53rd Year 104

UNSC Res 1333 'Afghanistan' (19 December 2000) SCOR 55th Year 32

UNSC Res 1373 'Threats to International Peace and Security Caused by Terrorist Acts' (28 September 2001) SCOR [1 January 2001–31 July 2002] 291

DOCUMENTS OF INTERNATIONAL ORGANISATIONS

Barroso, David 'Botnets – The Silent Threat (ENISA Position Paper No. 3)' (2007) at <www.enisa.europa.eu/act/res/other-areas/botnets/botnets-2013-the-silent-threat/at_download/fullReport> (date accessed 24 February 2011)

COE Committee of Ministers 'Recommendation on Measures to Promote the Respect for Freedom of Expression and Information with Regard to Internet Filters' (26 March 2008) CM/Rec(2008)6

Commission of the European Communities 'Decision of 26 July 2000 Pursuant to Directive 95/46/EC of the European Parliament and of the Council on the Adequacy of the Protection Provided by the Safe Harbour Privacy Principles and Related Frequently Asked Questions Issued by the US Department of Commerce' [2000] OJ L215/7

Communication from the Commission to the European Parliament, the Council, the European Economic and Social Committee and the Committee of the Regions 'On Critical Information Infrastructure Protection: Protecting Europe from Large Scale Cyber-Attacks and Disruptions: Enhancing Preparedness, Security and Resilience' (30 March 2009) COM(2009) 149 final

Communication From the Commission to the European Parliament, the Council, the European Economic and Social Committee and the Committee of the Regions 'A Digital Agenda for Europe' COM(2010) 245 final/2

Council Directive 2008/114/EC of 8 December 2008 on the Identification and Designation of European Critical Infrastructures and the Assessment of the Need to Improve Their Protection [2008] OJ L 345/75

ENISA 'Botnets: Detection, Measurement, Disinfection & Defence' (2011) at <www.enisa.europa.eu/act/res/botnets/botnets-measurement-detection-disinfection-and-defence/at_download/fullReport> (date accessed 22 June 2011)

ENISA 'CERT Cooperation and Its Further Facilitation by Relevant Stakeholders' (2006) at <www.enisa.europa.eu> (date accessed 2 September 2011)

ENISA Press Release of 7 October 2010 'EU Agency Analysis of 'Stuxnet' Malware: A Paradigm Shift in Threats and Critical Information Infrastructure Protection' (2010) at <http://enisa.europa.eu> (date accessed 28 April 2011)

EU Council 'Framework Decision 2005/222/JHA of 24 February 2005 on Attacks against Information Systems' [2005] OJ L69/67

EU Council 'Recommendation of 25 June 2001 on Contact Points Maintaining a 24-Hour Service for Combating High-Tech Crime' [2001] OJ C 187/5

European Commission 'Cyber Security: EU Prepares to Set Up Computer Emergency Response Team for EU Institutions (10 June 2011)' Press Release IP/11/694

European Parliament 'Resolution on the Existence of a Global System for the Interception of Private and Commercial Communications (ECHELON Interception System)' [2002] OJ C 72 E/221

European Parliament and EU Council ,Directive 95/46/EC of 24 October 1995 on the Protection of Individuals with Regard to the Processing of Personal Data and on the Free Movement of such Data' [1995] OJ L128/31

Heads of State and Government Participating in the Meeting of the North Atlantic Council in Bucharest on 3 April 2008 'Bucharest Summit Declaration' (2008) at <www.nato.int/docu/pr/2008/p08-049e.html> (date accessed 30 June 2012)

ICRC 'Direct Participation in Hostilities under International Humanitarian Law: First Expert Meeting Summary Report' (2003) at <www.icrc.org/Web/eng/siteeng0.nsf/htmlall/direct-participation-report_res/$File/2003-03-report-dph-2003-icrc.pdf> (date accessed 3 November 2009)

ICRC 'Third Expert Meeting on the Notion of Direct Participation in Hostilities: Summary Report' (2005) at <www.icrc.org/eng/assets/files/other/2005-09-report-dph-2005-icrc.pdf> (date accessed 25 November 2010)

ICRC *A Guide to the Legal Review of New Weapons, Means and Methods of Warfare* at <www.icrc.org/eng/assets/files/other/icrc_002_0902.pdf> (date accessed 4 June 2012)

ILA Committee on the Use of Force 'Initial Report on the Meaning of Armed Conflict in International Law' (2008) at <www.ila-hq.org/download.cfm/docid/0C19D883-3312-4731-92C4A18A55147597> (date accessed 4 June 2012)

Institut de Droit International 'Resolution on Self-Defence' (27 October 2007) 10A Resolution

ITU *Measuring the Information Society 2011* at <www.itu.int/net/pressoffice/backgrounders/general/pdf/5.pdf> (date accessed 4 June 2012)

ITU 'Global Cybersecurity Agenda' at <www.itu.int/osg/csd/cybersecurity/gca/pillars-goals/index.html> (date accessed 9 April 2012)

ITU 'Understanding Cybercrime: A Guide for Developing Countries' (2009) at <www.itu.int/ITU-D/cyb/cybersecurity/docs/itu-understanding-cybercrime-guide.pdf> (date accessed 30 August 2011)

ITU *Global Cybersecurity Agenda: High-Level Experts Group: Global Strategic Report* at <www.itu.int/osg/csd/cybersecurity/gca/global_strategic_report/global_strategic_report.pdf> (date accessed 30 August 2011)

ITU International Telecommunication Convention (signed 6 November 1982, entered into force 1 January 1984) 1531 UNTS 320

ITU Secretary-General Touré, Hamadoun 'Cyber Conflict and Cyber Defence in the Framework of the Global Cybersecurity Agenda' (17 December 2008) at <www.itu.int/osg/sg/speeches/2008/dec17.html> (date accessed 12 August 2010)

ITU-T Resolution 58 (2008) 'Encourage the Creation of National Computer Incident Response Teams, Particularly for Developing Countries'

NATO 'Allied Joint Doctrine for Information Operations AJP-3.10' (November 2009) at <http://cyberwar.nl/d/AJP-3.10%20nov%202009.pdf> (date accessed 26 February 2012)

NATO 'NATO Glossary of Terms and Definitions of Military Significance for Use in NATO' (2011) at <http://nsa.nato.int/nsa/zPublic/ap/aap6/AAP-6.pdf> (date accessed 26 February 2012)

NATO 'Statement by the North Atlantic Council' (12 September 2001) (2001) 40 ILM 1267

NATO Parliamentary Assembly 'NATO and Cyber Defence' (2009) at <www.nato-pa.int/default.asp?SHORTCUT=1782> (date accessed 24 June 2010)

NATO Research & Technology Organisation 'Overview of InfoOps Documents Doc. RTO-TR-SAS-057-WP1' (2006) at <http://ftp.rta.nato.int/public//PubFullText/RTO/TR/RTO-TR-SAS-057///TR-SAS-057-WP-1.pdf> (date accessed 19 November 2009)

OAS 'Conclusions and Recommendations of REMJA-VII' at <www.oas.org/juridico/english/cybVII_CR.pdf> (date accessed 9 April 2012)

OAS 'Resolution on Terrorist Threat to the Americas' (21 September 2001) (2001) 40 ILM 1273

OAS General Assembly Resolution 2004 (XXXIV-O/04) 'A Comprehensive Inter-American Cybersecurity Strategy: A Multidimensional and Multidisciplinary Approach to Creating a Culture of Cybersecurity' (8 June 2004)

OECD 'Guidelines for the Security of Information Systems and Networks: Towards a Culture of Security' (25 July 2002) at <www.oecd.org/dataoecd/16/22/15582260.pdf> (date accessed 31 August 2011)

OECD and ITU *M-Government: Mobile Technologies for Responsive Governments and Connected Societies* (OECD Publishing 2011)

OECD *E-Government for Better Government* (OECD Publishing 2005)

OECD *Information Technology Outlook 2010* (OECD Publishing 2010)

Sommer, Peter and Brown, Ian *Reducing Systemic Cybersecurity Risk, OECD/IFP Profect on Future Global Shocks Doc IFP/WKP/FGS(2011)3* at <www.oecd.org/dataoecd/57/44/46889922.pdf> (date accessed 4 June 2012)

GOVERNMENTAL DOCUMENTS

5th Ministerial eGovernment Conference 'Ministerial Declaration on eGovernment' (18 November 2009) at <www.egov2009.se/wp-content/uploads/Ministerial-Declaration-on-eGovernment.pdf> (date accessed 22 February 2012)

Australian Government 'Cyber Security Strategy' (2009) at <www.ag.gov.au/www/agd/agd.nsf/Page/CyberSecurity_CyberSecurity> (date accessed 19 August 2010)

Australian Government Department of Defence *Defending Australia in the Asia Pacific Century: Force 2030 (Defence White Paper 2009)* at <www.defence.gov.au/whitepaper/docs/defence_white_paper_2009.pdf> (date accessed 19 August 2010)

British Foreign Secretary William Hague 'Security and Freedom in the Cyber Age – Seeking the Rules of the Road (Speech to the Munich Security Conference)' (4 February 2011) at <www.fco.gov.uk/en/news/latest-news/?view=Speech&id=545383882> (date accessed 1 April 2011)

Bundesamt für Sicherheit in der Informationstechnik 'Analysis of Critical Infrastructures – The ACIS Methodology' (2004) at <https://www.bsi.bund.de/SharedDocs/Downloads/EN/BSI/Kritis/acis_paper_en_pdf.pdf?__blob=publicationFile> (date accessed 27 April 2011)

Bundesministerium der Verteidigung *Humanitäres Völkerrecht in bewaffneten Konflikten: Handbuch* (Bundesministerium der Verteidigung 1992)

Bundesministerium des Inneren 'Cyber-Sicherheitsstrategie für Deutschland' (2011) at <www.bmi.bund.de/SharedDocs/Downloads/DE/Themen/OED_Verwaltung/Informationsgesellschaft/cyber.pdf?__blob=publicationFile> (date accessed 7 April 2011)

Bundesministerium des Inneren *Verfassungsschutzbericht 2008* (BMI Berlin 2009)

Bundesministerium des Inneren *Verfassungsschutzbericht 2009* (BMI Berlin 2010)

Bundesministerium des Inneren *Verfassungsschutzbericht 2010* (BMI Berlin 2011)

Cashell, Brian, Jackson, William, Jickling, Mark and Webel, Baird 'The Economic Impact of Cyber-Attacks' in US Congressional Research Service (ed) *CRS Report for Congress* (2004)

Conférence Diplomatique sur la Réaffirmation et le Développement du Droit International Humanitaire Applicable dans les Conflits Armés (1974–1977 Genève) *Official Records of the Diplomatic Conference of the Reaffirmation and Development of International Humanitarian Law Applicable in Armed Conflicts: Geneva, 1974–1977* (Federal Political Department Bern).

Cyber Security Strategy of the Czech Republic for the 2011 – 2015 Period (2011) at <www.enisa.europa.eu/media/news-items/CZ_Cyber_Security_Strategy_20112015.PDF> (date accessed 8 April 2012)

Delegation of the Russian Federation 'Statement by Mr S Shestakov, Representative of the Russian Federation, at the Joint Meeting of the OSCE Forum for Security Co-operation and the OSCE Permanent Council' (10 June 2010) Doc FSC-PC.DEL/31/10

Estonian Ministry of Defence 'Cyber Security Strategy' (2008) at <www.mod.gov.ee/files/kmin/img/files/Kuberjulgeoleku_strateegia_2008-2013_ENG.pdf> (date accessed 23 July 2010)

Executive Office of the US President 'The Comprehensive National Cybersecurity Initiative' (2009) at <www.whitehouse.gov/cybersecurity/comprehensive-national-cybersecurity-initiative> (date accessed 10 March 2010)

French Government *Défense et Sécurité Nationale: Le Livre Blanc* at <http://lesrapports.ladocumentationfrancaise.fr/BRP/084000341/0000.pdf> (date accessed 31 March 2010)

General Keith Alexander (Commander US Cyber Command) 'US Cybersecurity Policy and the Role of US Cybercom' (2010) at <www.nsa.gov/public_info/_files/speeches_testimonies/100603_alexander_transcript.pdf> (date accessed 3 June 2010)

Georgian Government 'Russian Cyberwar on Georgia' (10 November 2008) at <http://georgiaupdate.gov.ge> (date accessed 18 August 2011)

Hildreth, Steven A. 'Cyberwarfare' in US Congressional Research Service (ed) *CRS Report for Congress* (2001)

Krekel, Bryan 'Capability of the People's Republic of China to Conduct Cyber Warfare and Computer Network Exploitation' Prepared for the US-China Economic and Security Review Commission (2009)

The President of the Republic of Estonia 'Address by Toomas Hendrik Ilves President of the Republic of Estonia to the 62nd Session of the United Nations General Assembly (25 September 2007)' (2007) at <www.un.org/webcast/ga/62/2007/pdfs/estonia-eng.pdf> (date accessed 6 May 2011)

The President of the United States of America 'International Strategy for Cyberspace' (May 2011) at <www.whitehouse.gov/sites/default/files/rss_viewer/international-strategy_cyberspace.pdf> (date accessed 1 June 2011)

The President of the United States of America 'Remarks by the President on Securing our Nation's Cyber Infrastructure' (2009) at <www.whitehouse.gov/the-press-office/remarks-president-securing-our-nations-cyber-infrastructure> (date accessed 11 March 2011)

The President of the United States of America 'The National Security Strategy of the United States of America' (September 2002) at <www.au.af.mil/au/awc/awcgate/nss/nss_sep2002.pdf> (date accessed 7 April 2011)

Russian Federation 'Information Security Doctrine of the Russian Federation (approved by President Putin on 9 September 2000)' (2000) at <www.mid.ru/ns-osndoc.nsf/1e5f0de28fe77fdcc32575d900298676/2deaa9ee15ddd24bc32575d9002c442b?OpenDocument> (date accessed 24 June 2010)

Russian Federation 'Военная доктрина Российской Федерации (Military Doctrine of the Russian Federation; no official translation available)' (5 February 2010) at <http://news.kremlin.ru/ref_notes/461> (date accessed 24 June 2010)

United Kingdom Cabinet Office 'Cyber Security Strategy of the United Kingdom: Safety, Security and Resilience in Cyber Space (Command Papers 7642 [2009])' (June 2009) at <www.cabinetoffice.gov.uk/media/216620/css0906.pdf> (date accessed 10 August 2010)

United Kingdom Ministry of Defence 'Information Operations: Joint Warfare Publication 3-80' (2002) at <http://ics-www.leeds.ac.uk/papers/pmt/exhibits/2270/jwp3_80.pdf> (date accessed 26 February 2012)

United Kingdom Ministry of Defence *The Manual of the Law of Armed Conflict* (OUP Oxford 2004)

United States Air Force 'Air Force Doctrine Document 2-5: Information Operations' (1998)

United States Air Force 'Cyberspace Operations: Air Force Doctrine Document 3-12' (15 July 2010) at <www.e-publishing.af.mil/shared/media/epubs/AFDD3-12.pdf> (date accessed 27 October 2010)

United States Air Force 'Dominant Cyber Offensive Engagement and Supporting Technology: Solicitation Number BAA-08-04-RIKA' (2008) at <www.fbo.gov/index?tab=core&s=opportunity&mode=form&id=b34f1f48d3ed2ce781f85d28f700a870> (date accessed 1 April 2010)

United States Army *Operational Law Handbook* (The Judge Advocate General's Legal Center & School Charlottesville 2009)

United States Department of Commerce 'Management of Internet Names and Addresses' (10 June 1998) vol 63 No 111 Federal Register 31741

United States Department of Defense 'Department of Defense Strategy for Operating in Cyberspace' (July 2011) at <www.defense.gov/news/d20110714cyber.pdf> (date accessed 26 July 2011)

United States Department of Defense 'Information Operations Roadmap' (2003) at <www.gwu.edu/~nsarchiv/NSAEBB/NSAEBB177/info_ops_roadmap.pdf> (date accessed 5 June 2012)

United States Department of Defense 'Joint Publication 1-02: DOD Dictionary of Military and Associated Terms (as amended through 31 October 2009)' at <www.dtic.mil/doctrine/new_pubs/jp1_02.pdf> (date accessed 8 March 2010)

United States Department of Defense 'Military Commission Instruction No. 2' (30 April 2003) at <www.fas.org/irp/doddir/dod/milcominstno2.pdf> (date accessed 7 January 2012)

United States Department of Defense Office of General Counsel 'An Assessment of International Legal Issues in Information Operations' (1999) at <www.au.af.mil/au/awc/awcgate/dod-io-legal/dod-io-legal.pdf> (date accessed 27 April 2011)

United States Department of Homeland Security 'The National Strategy to Secure Cyberspace 2003' (2003) at <www.dhs.gov/xlibrary/assets/National_Cyberspace_Strategy.pdf> (date accessed 25 March 2011)

United States Department of the Army *Field Manual No. 100-6: Information Operations* (Department of the Army Washington DC 1996)

United States Department of the Navy *The Commander's Handbook on the Law of Naval Operations (July 2007 Edition NWP 1-14M)* (Navy Warfare Library 2007)

United States General Accounting Office *Information Security: Computer Attacks at Department of Defense Pose Increasing Risks* (US GAO Washington DC 1996)

United States Joint Chiefs of Staff 'Joint Publication 3-13: Information Operations (13 February 2006)' (2006) at <www.dtic.mil/doctrine/new_pubs/jp3_13.pdf> (date accessed 21 April 2010)

United States Joint Chiefs of Staff 'The National Military Strategy of the United States of America' (2004) at <www.defense.gov/news/mar2005/d20050318nms.pdf> (date accessed 11 March 2011)

United States National Security Council *Cyberspace Policy Review: Assuring a Trusted and Resilient Information and Communications Infrastructure* at <www.whitehouse.gov/assets/documents/Cyberspace_Policy_Review_final.pdf> (date accessed 17 March 2010)

United States Presidential Decision Directive 63 of 22 May 1998 'The Clinton Administration's Policy on Critical Infrastructure Protection' (1998) at <www.justice.gov/criminal/cybercrime/white_pr.htm> (date accessed 27 April 2011)

United States-Canada Power System Outage Task Force 'Final Report on the August 14, 2003 Blackout in the United States and Canada: Causes and Recommendations' (April 2004) at <https://reports.energy.gov/BlackoutFinal-Web.pdf> (date accessed 3 September 2009)

United States-China Economic and Security Review Commission (ed) *2009 Report to Congress* (US Government Printing Office Washington 2009)

MISCELLANEOUS DOCUMENTS AND REPORTS

Carnegie Mellon University *CERT Research Annual Report* at <www.cert.org/research/2008research-report.pdf> (date accessed 17 March 2010)

Center for Strategic and International Studies *Securing Cyberspace for the 44th Presidency* (CSIS Washington DC 2008)

Falliere, Nicolas, Murchu, Liam O. and Chien, Eric *W32.Stuxnet Dossier Version 1.4* at <www.symantec.com/content/en/us/enterprise/media/security_response/whitepapers/w32_stuxnet_dossier.pdf> (date accessed 23 March 2011)

ICANN 'Plan for Enhancing Internet Security, Stability, and Resiliency' (16 May 2009) at <www.icann.org/en/topics/ssr/ssr-draft-plan-16may09-en.pdf> (date accessed 23 July 2010)

ICANN 'Bylaws for Internet Corporation for Assigned Names and Numbers' (effective as of 6 November 1998, as amended 24 June 2011) www.icann.org/en/general/bylaws.htm (date accessed 10 August 2011)

ICANN Governmental Advisory Committee 'Principles and Guidelines for the Delegation and Administration of Country Code Top Level Domains' (done 5 April 2005) <http://gac.icann.org/system/files/ccTLD_Principles_0.pdf> (Date accessed 19 July 2010)

ICANN Governmental Advisory Committee 'Principles and Guidelines for the Delegation and Administration of Country Code Top Level Domains' (done 5 April 2005) <http://gac.icann.org/system/files/ccTLD_Principles_0.pdf> (Date accessed 19 July 2010)

McAfee *Virtual Criminology Report 2009* at <www.mcafee.com/uk/local_content/reports/virtual_criminology_report/uk_virtual_criminology_09_report.pdf> (date accessed 15 October 2010)

Siemens 'SIMATIC WinCC / SIMATIC PCS 7: Information bezüglich Malware / Virus / Trojaner' (2011) at <http://support.automation.siemens.com/WW/view/de/43876783> (date accessed 28 February 2012)

Symantec *W32.Duqu: The Precursor to the Next Stuxnet* at <www.symantec.com/content/en/us/enterprise/media/security_response/whitepapers/w32_duqu_the_precursor_to_the_next_stuxnet_research.pdf> (date accessed 22 October 2011)

Thakur, Vikram 'W32.Stuxnet – Network Information' (23 July 2010) at <www.symantec.com/connect/blogs/w32stuxnet-network-information> (date accessed 28 February 2012)

The SecDev Group and Munk Centre for International Studies 'Tracking GhostNet: Investigating a Cyber Espionage Network' (2009) at <www.f-secure.com/weblog/archives/ghostnet.pdf> (date accessed 20 April 2011)

World Economic Forum *Global Risks 2008: A Global Risk Network Report* (World Economic Forum Geneva 2008)

World Economic Forum *Global Risks 2010: A Global Risk Network Report* (World Economic Forum Geneva 2010)

World Federation of Scientists Permanent Monitoring Panel on Information Security 'Top Cyber Security Problems that Need Resolution' (2009) at <www.unibw.de/infosecur/documents/published_documents/cyber_security_problems> (date accessed 5 June 2012)

NEWSPAPER AND MAGAZINE ARTICLES

— 'A Worm in the Centrifuge' in *The Economist* of 2–8 October 2010

— 'Berlin plant "Cyber-Abwehr-Zentrum"' in *Frankfurter Allgemeine Zeitung* of 27 December 2010

— 'Bushehr Plant Safe from Stuxnet Worm' in *Iran Daily* of 27 September 2010

— 'Cyberwar' in *The Economist* of 3rd-9th July 2010

— 'Hunderte Bundeswehr-Rechner von Conficker befallen' in *Heise Security* of 14.02.2009 at <www.heise.de/security/meldung/Hunderte-Bundeswehr-Rechner-von-Conficker-befallen-195953.html> (date accessed 3 January 2012)

— 'Marching Off to Cyberwar' in *The Economist* – Technology Quarterly of 6 December 2008

— 'Stuxnet-Wurm befällt Rechner in iranischem AKW' (26 September 2010) in *Spiegel Online* at <www.spiegel.de/netzwelt/netzpolitik/0,1518,719654,00.html> (date accessed 27 September 2010)

— 'The Consensus Machine' in *The Economist* of 8–14 June 2000

— 'War in the Fifth Domain' in *The Economist* of 3–9 July 2010

Broad, William J. and Sanger, David E. 'Iran Reports a Major Setback at a Nuclear Power Plant' in *The New York Times* of 25 February 2011

Broad, William J., Markoff, John and Sanger, David E. 'Israeli Test on Worm Called Crucial in Iran Nuclear Delay' in *The New York Times* of 15 January 2011

Dahlkamp, Jürgen, Rosenbach, Marcel, Schmitt, Jörg, Stark, Holger and Wagner, Wieland 'Prinzip Sandkorn' in *Der Spiegel* of 35/2007

Goetz, John, Rosenbach, Marcel and Szandar, Alexander 'Krieg der Zukunft' in *Der Spiegel* of 7/2009

Gross, Michael Joseph 'A Declaration of Cyber-War' in *Vanity Fair* of April 2011

Heintschel von Heinegg, Wolff 'Automatisierung des Krieges' in *Süddeutsche Zeitung* of 10 February 2011

Hersh, Seymour M. 'The Online Threat' in *The New Yorker* of 1 November 2010

Kittlitz, Alard von 'Stuxnet und der Krieg, der kommt' in *Frankfurter Allgemeine Zeitung* of 5 December 2010

Kurz, Constanze 'Kybernetische Krieger werden überschätzt' in *Frankfurter Allgemeine Zeitung* of 18 February 2011

Kurz, Constanze 'Sicherheit im Netz? Nur durch Vernetzung!' in *Frankfurter Allgemeine Zeitung* of 6 August 2010

Ladurner, Ulrich and Pham, Khue 'Iran im Krieg 2.0' in *Die Zeit* of 30 September 2010

Markoff, John 'A Silent Attack, but Not a Subtle One' in *The New York Times* of 26 September 2010

Markoff, John 'Before the Gunfire, Cyberattacks' in *The New York Times* of 12 August 2008

Markoff, John 'Halted '03 Iraq Plan Illustrates US Fear of Cyberwar Risk' in *The New York Times* of 2 August 2009

Markoff, John 'New Malicious Program by Creators of Stuxnet is Suspected' in *The New York Times* of 18 October 2011

Martin-Jung, Helmut and Krüger, Paul-Anton 'Gezielte Sabotage: Eine iranische Atomanlage könnte Ziel eines Trojaner-Angriffs gewesen sein' in *Süddeutsche Zeitung* of 23 September 2010

Petignat, Yves 'La cyber-impuissnace helvétique' in *Le Temps* of 13 April 2010

Rieger, Frank 'Angriff ist besser als Verteidigung' in *Frankfurter Allgemeine Zeitung* of 18 January 2011

Rieger, Frank 'Der digitale Erstschlag ist erfolgt' in *Frankfurter Allgemeine Zeitung* of 22 September 2010

Sanger, David E. 'Obama Order Sped Up Wave of Cyberattacks Against Iran' in *The New York Times* of 1 June 2012.

Schmitt, Eric and Shanker, Thom 'U.S. Debated Cyberwarfare in Attack Plan on Libya' in *The New York Times* of 17 October 2011

Singel, Ryan 'Egypt Shut Down Its Net With a Series of Phone Calls' (28 January 2011) at <www.wired.com/threatlevel/2011/01/egypt-isp-shutdown/> (date accessed 7 January 2012)

Traynor, Ian 'Russia Accused of Unleashing Cyberwar to Disable Estonia' in *The Guardian* of 17 May 2007

www.ingramcontent.com/pod-product-compliance
Ingram Content Group UK Ltd.
Pitfield, Milton Keynes, MK11 3LW, UK
UKHW051920100926
8556IPUK00021B/1287

9 781839 702358